COSMIC CANINES

COSMIC CANINES

The Complete Astrology Guide for You and Your Dog

MARILYN MACGRUDER BARNEWALL

BALLANTINE BOOKS · NEW YORK

A Ballantine Book
Published by The Ballantine Publishing Group

Copyright © 1998 by Marilyn MacGruder Barnewall

http://www.randomhouse.com/BB/

Library of Congress Cataloging-in-Publication Data
Barnewall, Marilyn MacGruder.
Cosmic canines : the complete astrology guide for you and your dog
Marilyn MacGruder Barnewall.
p.   cm.
ISBN 9780345424594
1. Astrology and pets.   2. Dogs—Miscellanea.   3. Dog breeds.
I. Title.
BF1728.3.B37   1998
133.5'86360887—dc21   98-34098
CIP

Cover design by Min Choi
Cover illustration by Jenny Tylden-Wright
Text design by Holly Johnson

Manufactured in the United States of America

146646482

Do I believe in astrology?

To those who ask this question, I answer with a question. Do golfers believe in their golf clubs? Golfers know that if they hold a certain club a certain way and swing it just right, they get a specific result. I believe the same is true of astrology. It is my golf club. If I use the knowledge gathered about astrology over several thousand years, it helps me stay out of sand traps. I *believe in* one thing: God.

I dedicate *Cosmic Canines* to Rusty, my Doberman Pinscher, the most wonderful, personable dog in the world. He proves everything I say about Sagittarius dogs is true. I'm glad our stars crossed, Rusty Man.

To my good friends in Grand Junction, Colorado, who were "there" for me. Your thoughtfulness was truly a unique experience.

When my computer's C drive took a hike while I was doing the final writing of *Cosmic Canines*, Gil Jungert was there to fix it (an every two weeks' occurrence, for a while).

When my creative juices went out for exercise, leaving me at home, Bill Fiegel was there with his gentle, caring sense of humor and encouragement. My next-door neighbor Virginia West did as much gardening in my yard as she did in her own so I could work on the book.

To Bob and Lea MacGruder, my brother and sister-in-law (who had the good sense to retire here in 1996). Thanks for understanding why I became a hermit for a while. And, to my mother, Hester, and stepfather,

Roy Brown, who, by calling from Denver every other day to ask how many chapters I had left to write, kept my nose to the grindstone.

Thanks also to Jennifers Engle and Steinbach and Muriel Nellis at Literary and Creative Artists Agency, my literary agents. They helped me redefine the book and improved it, greatly. I am in their debt.

CONTENTS

INTRODUCTION: THE PURPOSE OF DOGS

HOW ASTROLOGICAL INCOMPATIBILITY AND DOG BREED IGNORANCE CAUSE ONE MILLION DOG BITES A YEAR

Nothing can replace a good dog, purebred or otherwise. Dogs love their human companions despite the foolish things they do and for which they are often harshly judged—especially by people who claim, frequently, at great length, to be compassionate.

Dogs *are* compassionate. And they show their compassion in the nonjudgmental way they lovingly look at us even as we walk around our homes in the altogether with our flab showing and without makeup or other social disguises.

Dogs usually love us no matter what we do . . . sometimes (unfortunately) even *to* them. No human, in my opinion, can understand the merit of dogs as companions and not place a high value on that relationship. Dogs see into our very souls . . . and love us in spite of what they see. Yet too often we treat them like a convenience, put here to serve our needs, rather than as individuals, each with unique personal needs.

Cosmic Canines provides information about the potential of dogs as individual beings. It offers insights to help us give back to our canine friends some of the unearned, undisguised love and respect they have given us for so long. The purpose of this book, then, is to look at the personality possibilities of different dog breeds, but to do it using sun signs—to date (and somewhat selfishly, I believe) only applied to humans, never dogs.

Today, many experienced dog handlers serve as canine behavioral experts and try to help people deal with pet problems created either through poor breeding or inappropriate training techniques. It is a new science, "dog psychology," and individuals trained in it are being consulted more and more.

How much healthier would both dogs and their owners be if we could avoid the problems in the first place? That is the objective of this book: to utilize the centuries-old techniques of the science of astrology to help people adopt the pets with which they are most compatible. Dog breed information is provided to help readers find out in moments whether a specific breed is genetically engineered to perform the functions the human companion wants.

Hopefully, by achieving these objectives, there will be fewer problems between dogs and their human companions. It is far better to eliminate a problem than it is to try to solve it after it is discovered.

Of the 52 to 57 million dogs in the United States, over 8.5 million have problems with aggression, phobias, anxiety, or other serious psychological conditions. Too often, humans treat dogs with an "Oh, it's just a dog" attitude. We lump them into categories like we separate our laundry—whites in one pile, colors in another. But dogs are not lumps, nor should they be treated as a single, homogeneous group of lower animal life. Each breed is unique from the others; each dog is born under a specific sun sign, and has specific personality traits as a result.

We need to stop abusing our pets, and we need to learn how to train puppies so they do not become dogs that abuse people. In the United States, 4 million dogs are brought to shelters every year, and over half are euthanized. Some of that can be laid at the feet of irresponsible humans who run out and buy a "pet" for entertainment or protection but then find it's harder to teach the puppy not to relieve itself on the living room carpet than they thought. Or, after bringing the dog home and chaining it up in the backyard, offering the puppy no love or attention for six months, they wonder why it growls at a child who wanders into its territory. Who's at fault? The dog? Not likely!

Some abandonments are caused by poor breeding methods, which create dogs with unmanageable temperaments. Yet most of the problems are a result of people simply investing too little time learning the positives and negatives of dog breeds and how to train dogs in ways that prevent, rather than cause, problems.

Even more abandonments happen because people find out they just don't like the personality traits of the dog they bought.

A large number of people buy dogs for protection. Often, books about specific breeds describe only the positives. Pit Bulls, for example, make great pets and wonderful guard dogs when bred properly, trained properly, and placed in the hands of intelligent people who have some enlightened, positive experience with dogs. If you abuse them, however, they can be dangerous. Breed books are written to help explain and promote specific dog breeds, and they tell readers what the breeds are like in the hands of intelligent human companions. There is nothing wrong with that. The truth is, any genetically assertive dog who has been abused—rather than properly trained—is as likely to bite its owner or a neighbor's child as it is to bite an intruder. (Over 1 million dogs bite human beings each year, and from ten to fifteen people die as a result of those bites. Almost a million victims of dog bites require medical treatment.) The behavior has nothing to do with the dog breed, but with dull-witted dog owners.

Dog breeders do not usually tell the buyer that if he treats the dog like a child, it will likely become an unmanageable tyrant. They don't tell the buyer that if she allows her dog to become too possessive of her, it will become jealous of other humans with whom she associates and is likely to nip them. And since jealousy bites usually occur on the "offending" person's face, it can bring a quick end to a long-term friendship! Dogs are not human children, and it is unloving and disrespectful to treat them as such.

Which brings me to the reason I wrote this book. By combining, for the first time, research data from both breed and sun sign sources, I hope to bring people and dogs closer together. Maybe by helping people develop some of the same insights about canines that canines instinctively have for people, we can become even better friends. Certainly, we can become more informed friends.

PART ONE

The Purpose of Astrology for Dogs

1

GETTING STARTED

WHAT IS ASTROLOGY?

The science of astrology was born in Mesopotamia about five thousand years ago, and every year millions of people use it to answer such questions as "Who am I?" or "Why am I here?" Over the centuries, astrologers have correlated human activities and personality styles with star and planetary patterns and positions.

When any animal—including a dog—is born, the stars and planets in the sky are, at that particular moment, in very specific positions. Over the thousands of years since the science began, astrologers have used these astrological positions to devise and interpret human personalities. Until now, no one has translated these interpretations and applied them to canine traits.

For example, astrologers have determined that when people have numerous planets in the sign of Capricorn at the time of their birth, they will be very intolerant of inertia. If the sun is there, too, it increases the intolerance for a lack of forward movement. Such people are very practical. They make good research analysts. Louis Pasteur, for example, had six planets in Capricorn. No wonder he was a brilliant research scientist.

Did Lassie or Rin Tin Tin have Capricorn strongly aspected in their horoscopes? We don't know. No one bothered to note their exact time of birth, so a dog horoscope could not be created and interpreted for either of them.

After centuries of studying the personalities of people and noting the various star and planetary positions at the moment of birth, astrologers have gotten pretty good at their craft. They are capable of determining which personality traits will most likely be present under certain astrological aspects. Now we intend, using a little "dog sense," to apply the same principles (if not personality traits) to our four-legged friends.

For humans, astrologers can also predict likely future events by progressing an individual's natal chart forward to a future date, then comparing the progressed natal chart to the positionings of stars and planets on that future date.

But just because a person understands how to create a horoscope/natal chart does not guarantee that a good analysis of the data will be forthcoming. The amount of data that must be compiled and analyzed is substantial, and compiling data and analyzing it are two entirely different tasks. It takes quite a bit of intuitive skill as well as scientific knowledge to do a good job. The better the astrologer, the better the result.

WHAT IS THE PURPOSE OF ASTROLOGY?

Astrology, which paints an intimate portrait of people's personalities, is a science—a much maligned science, but a science nonetheless. And some of history's most famous people—Copernicus, Virgil, Horace, Cicero, Sir Isaac Newton, Carl Jung, Plato, Socrates, Nostradamus, Caesar, and Shakespeare, to name a few—subscribed to the theories that make up the science of astrology. In the New Testament, even Saint Luke tells us, "And there shall be signs in the sun and in the moon and in the stars."

Scientists have known for many years that the earth is affected by celestial bodies. Geologists, for example, have determined that earthquakes are related to certain aspects involving the planet Uranus, and that the Moon affects the tides of our mighty oceans. If the Moon controls bodies of water as vast as the oceans, it would seem to follow that it might also control far smaller bodies—the human body, for instance—which consist primarily of water. (Remember, the human body is 70 percent water.)

Even as we approach the millennium, our modern daily lives are affected by the astrological beliefs of the ancients. For example, did you know our modern calendars are the result of the work of ancient mathematicians who were the astrologers of Babylon? Did you know that our modern juries consist of twelve people because the ancient Greeks felt the best way to give someone a fair trial was to have one representative of each sun sign judge defendants?

The most powerful, and thus important, element in any horoscope relative to predicting personalities and behavioral modes is the Sun. If I know your sun sign, does that mean I can paint an intimate portrait of you? No. To gain insights into the very intricate personalities of humans (or dogs) requires a total horoscope (a natal/birth chart). Where was the Moon at birth? What planet is ascending at the moment of birth? These two—the Moon and Ascendency—are almost as important as the Sun in determining astrological personalities.

In addition to the positions of the Moon and Ascending signs, we need to know in what houses of your personal horoscope Jupiter, Mars, Venus, Uranus, Mercury, Neptune, and Saturn are located. Each star or planet, depending on which house of the zodiac it is in at birth, and depending on where it is located in relation to all other stars and planets, paints the intimate portrait. It takes a good astrologer to interpret all the astrological aspects contained within that portrait.

CAN THE SCIENCE OF ASTROLOGY BE APPLIED TO DOGS?

Are dogs' bodies comprised mostly of water, like the human body? Yes.

Do dogs weigh problems on the Scales of Justice like Librans? Do they dream like Sagittarians? To tell the absolute truth, no one is really sure. We cannot communicate with canines in their language. Can Scorpion stings be related to dog bites? Probably, just like a verbal insult can be related to that sting. Do dogs have good days and bad days like the Twins? Of course. Like humans, they have good sides and bad sides to their temperament.

During the years I trained dogs; raised and showed German Shepherds in the conformation and obedience rings; trained, prepared, and handled other people's dogs in the conformation ring at American Kennel Club dog shows; helped set up the Denver K-9 Corps; and raised and raced Greyhounds, I began applying my hobby of astrology to my then-career with dogs.

To say the words *dog psychologist* in the 1960s caused people to raise an eyebrow and look in the Yellow Pages for the name of the local funny farm. Today, though, pet psychologists are not uncommon. A lot of people work with dog or cat owners—horse owners, too—to help them better understand their pets' personalities. Astrology is merely a tool to be used as part of that process.

The sun sign is the most influential of all the stars and planets in determining the basic personality or approach to how animals—human or canine—view life and, thus, act or react to it. How we act or react to life's events and circumstances can be defined as "personality." For example, psychologists say people can be divided into two groups, fighters and runners. When a major problem occurs, do you fight? Or do you run? Dogs can be divided into those same two groups.

By knowing the sun sign, we can get a pretty good idea of what a basic personality is likely to yield.

DOGS AND ASTROLOGY: WHY IT WORKS

This book deals only with what the general dog personalities will be like when born under specific sun signs. Since the exact moment of birth must be known and a complex individual birth chart must be drawn to closely examine personality traits, it would be impossible to get more in-depth personality projections. Dog breeders do not yet record the moment of each puppy's birth, and so it is impossible to create an accurate horoscope for individual dogs.

But there are genetic traits inherent to specific dog groups and breeds. And as any dog lover knows, the temperament of the group of working dogs is very different from that of the Hound group.

We know that within the Hound group the Basset Hound is one of the most loving dogs. On the astrological side, we know spring and summer sun signs tend to exhibit more signs of warmth than fall and winter sun signs. Logic has told me for over thirty years that Basset Hounds born under the sign of Leo (a summer astrological sign that easily expresses love) will be the most loving of all Basset Hounds. In fact, such Basset Hounds might be too loving, too dependent, too clinging.

Terriers are bred to dig vermin from underground hideouts (to kill rats, moles, etc.), and their genes tell them that when something (like a rat) moves erratically in front of them, they should chase it. Terriers are very different than Herding dogs, who are far less likely to dig or chase the neighbor's cat because it runs erratically in front of them. Herding dogs were not bred to do those things. Terriers were. Herding dogs are larger, more powerful, and more protective than Terriers. They are more likely to be good guard dogs because for generations (sometimes for centuries) herding animals have been taught to protect other living beings.

Winter signs, being somewhat more aloof or independent than summer signs, offer good alternatives when selecting active dogs whose genetic qualities encourage them to react suddenly to outside stimuli (like unexpected, erratic movement). Adopting Terriers born under winter sun signs can make them calmer, more independent, and less reactive.

On the other hand, good guard dogs are not mean or aloof or too independent. Rather, they protect best when they protect out of love. If you are thinking of adopting a dog for security reasons, and are thinking of a Doberman Pinscher because this dog breed is purported to be good at guarding, read the breed personality profile. Does it say this breed is aloof or independent? If the dog you are reading about is a Chow Chow, it will say that. So you will do well to adopt a Chow Chow born under a summer sun sign. It will make him less aloof, less independent, and personally warmer.

On the other hand, if the breed personality data say the dog you are thinking of adopting is warm and loving, you would probably do better to adopt your future guard dog from a litter born under a winter sun sign. Otherwise, the dog may end up greeting a prowler with loving licks on the face regardless of the fact that its ancestors were bred to be good at guarding.

Some dog breeds have been bred to perform certain functions. This book identifies the key traits of the 110 most popular dog breeds. Each breed's traits have been evaluated, then analyzed to identify which human sun sign is most compatible with it.

Does this mean that if you, a Taurus, have a Manchester Terrier and I say the most compatible sun sign for that breed is Aquarius, you and your dog are not compatible? Of course not. What it means is you need to look at the listed personality traits of the Aquarian as things your dog most appreciates in human companions. By doing so, you can find hints about how to improve your relationship with your pet. *Cosmic Canines* can't tell you what dogs like and dislike about how their human guardians treat them, but the science of astrology can.

How many times have I heard dog owners say, "I love this dog dearly. If only he/she didn't. . . ." *Cosmic Canines* can help you do away with the last part of this thought. You were born under a specific sun sign. So was your dog. Each sun sign has innate personality traits that go with it. Other planets and stars may ameliorate those traits, but they are still there. If you are an Aries, you are probably competitive. If your dog is a Virgo, he or she is probably not. If you breed racing Greyhounds, the Aries drive to win won't overcome poor genetics, but it will light a fire that makes the dog *want* to win.

The mere process of understanding the innate differences between you and your pet can help you form a more compatible pet relationship— and that is the goal of this book. *Cosmic Canines* works because it offers insights and scientific knowledge that astrologers have for centuries applied and used to improve the human condition. Now that science is being applied to the condition of dogs so we can improve life for them, too. The same tried, tested, and proven principles are applied to dog personalities. By understanding how to use this book, each reader can determine for himself or herself not just what traits inherent to each dog breed are compatible with the reader, but under which sun signs it is more likely certain personality traits will be enhanced.

For example, if you don't want an independent dog, you should reject most herding and hunting dogs because their very jobs—those jobs for which they were genetically engineered—require them to be independent. You should also eliminate most Air and Fire sun signs because they, too, engender a sense of independence in those born under them.

Do you already have a herding or hunting dog or family pet born under Air or Fire sun signs? If you do, you've probably got an independent dog. As the human half in the relationship, you are the one who will have to understand what that means and learn to deal with it. Love your pets for who and what they are, not for who and what you wish they were. With this book to help you, when you adopt your next pet, it will be easier to find the one tailored to your compatible likes and needs.

HOW IS ASTROLOGY STRUCTURED?

Every month, the sun moves into a new astrological sign. The twelve sun signs and the from/to dates are listed below. The traits mentioned can be applied to all animal forms of life.

ARIES THE RAM, MARCH 22 TO APRIL 20: The Ram stands for courage and leadership. Aries is the first sun sign, and to be first at anything requires courage and leadership. Aries is ruled by Mars, the planet of fire and energy. Mars gives those born under its sun sign an active, positive view of life. Mars is also impulsive and does not tolerate constraints or delays very well. As the ruling planet, Mars adds energy and passion to the courage and leadership given by the sun sign's symbol, the Ram.

TAURUS THE BULL, APRIL 21 TO MAY 21: The Bull stands for vitality, tenacity, and practicality. Taurus is ruled by Venus, the planet of love and beauty. To the vitality of the Bull, this sun sign's symbol, is added Venusian social graces and warmhearted affection for all living things. Venus also brings a love of ease, comfort, neatness, and pleasure. Venus gives those born under the sun signs she rules (Taurus and Libra) the need to seek stability in life.

GEMINI THE TWINS, MAY 22 TO JUNE 21: The Twins stand for change and unpredictability—the unknown. Gemini is ruled by Mercury, who gives those ruled by it intelligence, adaptability, logic, and perception. The unpredictability of the Twins when combined with the perception and intelligence given by ruling planet Mercury may cause those born in Gemini difficulty with concentration and mental focus.

CANCER THE CRAB, JUNE 22 TO JULY 23: The Crab stands for loyalty, sensitivity, tenacity, and timidity. Cancer is ruled by the Moon, which gives a strong sense of domesticity and family and adds a fountain of imaginative wealth. The Moon also gives to those sun sign natives it rules a sense of moodiness combined with practicality, which, when combined with the Cancerian sensitivity of the Crab, can cause conflict.

LEO THE LION, JULY 24 TO AUGUST 23: The Lion stands for dominion, command, and pride. Leo is ruled by Earth's Sun, which gives the natives it rules vitality. Just as the Sun nourishes a young seed until it becomes a flower, it nourishes Leo life-forms by helping them grow beyond the temptation to be self-absorbed, directing their energies outward to become leaders. The Sun makes natives ruled by it organized, dignified, and gives them great strength of will and purpose.

VIRGO THE VIRGIN, AUGUST 24 TO SEPTEMBER 23: The Virgin stands for logic, analysis, and detail. Virgo is ruled by Mercury (which also rules Gemini). As the ruling planet of the Virgin, Mercury brings adaptability, subtlety, and an excellent memory. It also makes easier putting the logic and analytic and detail skills brought by this sun sign's symbol, the Virgin, to good use by giving these natives a ready ability to learn. Virgo natives may have difficulty concentrating when under pressure—such as when taking tests.

LIBRA THE SCALES, SEPTEMBER 24 TO OCTOBER 23: The Scales stand for justice, harmony, and beauty. Libra is the second sign ruled by the

Moon (Taurus is the other). The Moon adds a warm heart, so Libra can appreciate the beauty offered by the Scales, and a loving and peaceful attitude, which helps Librans find the harmony they are driven to seek. The Moon also gives Librans good luck, many friends, and an appreciation of life's finer things.

SCORPIO THE SCORPION, OCTOBER 24 TO NOVEMBER 22: The Scorpion stands for extremes in power, passion, and dominance. Scorpio is ruled by Mars, which dictates that success, if it is to be achieved, must be done utilizing positive, not negative, energy. Mars gives natives the determination and will to utilize their substantial powers for good rather than evil. It gives direction to Scorpion power in the form of ambition and gives stability to Scorpion passion, adding devotion to the equation.

SAGITTARIUS THE ARCHER, NOVEMBER 23 TO DECEMBER 22: The Archer stands for honesty, charm, independence, and freedom. Sagittarius is ruled by Jupiter, which gives those born here hope, popularity, social success, and benevolence (as well as luck). To Archer charm, Jupiter adds a reverence for beauty. To Archer independence and freedom, Jupiter adds faithfulness and enthusiasm as well as a respect for law and civil order. To Archer honesty, Jupiter adds the element of social graces (though Sagittarius can insult a lot of people without intending to, just by being honest).

CAPRICORN THE GOAT, DECEMBER 23 TO JANUARY 20: The Goat stands for practicality, patience, ambition, and overcoming inertia. Capricorn is ruled by the planet Saturn, the planet of restrictions and introspection. To the Goat's practicality, Saturn adds serenity and courage. To the Goat's patience, Saturn adds strength and will as well as caution, power, independence, and ambition. Without these things, you can be too patient.

AQUARIUS THE WATER BEARER, JANUARY 21 TO FEBRUARY 19: The Water Bearer pours knowledge, tolerance, intelligence, humaneness, and change from the urn on his shoulder (it is a masculine sun sign). Aquarius, ruled by the planet Uranus, is thought by astrologers to be involved with establishing the general principles on which the universe is built. It gives power to the Water Bearer's intellect, expanding the consciousness so it can direct change to more humanitarian matters than might otherwise be part of social progress. Uranus adds eccentricity, growth, and rebirth to the Water Bearer's gifts.

PISCES THE FISH, FEBRUARY 20 TO MARCH 21: The two Fish, swimming in opposite directions, reflect the constant battle humans have between their physical and spiritual selves. Jupiter rules this sun sign and gives a strong sense of right and wrong, provides goodwill, and stimulates the imagination. Those born under the Jupiter sun sign probably wrote the book on political correctness because this planet's natives like civility and wholeheartedly reject bad taste.

By identifying these twelve astrological houses, the ancients defined the twelve basic elements of human nature. Each of us weighs the right and wrong of things in our lives on an individual Scale of Justice, just like Libra. All human beings are capable of stinging like the Scorpion or aiming the arrows of our dreams at the Moon like the Archer or moving, one step at a time, up mountainous crags (or huge problems) like Capricorn Goats. All of us—human and canine—have dual personalities, like Gemini Twins. We have our good sides, and we have our bad sides.

By identifying the twelve basic principles of human nature and by giving each a place in the zodiac (horoscope), the ancient astrologers started the process of analysis. But astrology goes much further than that.

The Four Basic Elements of Life

All living things require four basic Elements for life—Earth, Fire (the Sun), Air, and Water—and each of them has identifiable traits. Earth signs, for example, are practical. Three sun signs are assigned to the Earth Element because they are, basically, as practical as the Earth. Three sun signs are also assigned to each of the other Elements—Fire, Air, and Water.

EARTH SIGNS: TAURUS, VIRGO, AND CAPRICORN

Earth signs offer solid physical strength, an easy acceptance of hard work, usually remember things easily (good and bad), and have very practical outlooks on life. Hunters looking for good water- and land-retrieving dogs will find that Earth signs tend to have the capacity to hunt when both wet and dry. Dog breed is, of course, important. Brittany Spaniels born under the sign of Capricorn excel at retrieving on water and land. German Shepherds born under this sun sign will not.

Earth sun sign dogs are born to serve and will be unhappy if they cannot benefit human guardians in some way. It doesn't matter if it's a Taurus Toy curling up on a companion's lap, or a Virgo guard dog, or a Capricorn sled dog competing in the Iditarod sled race in Alaska, Earth signs want to be part of the lives of their human companions in some meaningful way.

Earth sun signs encourage almost any kind of job involving obedience work and detail—such as drug search and police work. When well-bred and well-trained, if it's a breed that likes children, Earth signs make excellent pets for children. When improperly bred and/or left untrained, negative tendencies to be stubborn, lazy, jealous, and insecure increase.

FIRE SIGNS: ARIES, LEO, AND SAGITTARIUS

Fire signs represent enthusiasm, energy, resourcefulness, and intuition.

Those canine breeds that tend toward high energy levels will have this trait emphasized when born in Aries, Leo, or Sagittarius. They can be high-strung and hypersensitive.

When selecting dogs for work requiring physical energy, Fire signs fill the bill nicely. A day of marching in front of a security gate with a member of the military won't overly tire Fire sun sign guard dogs. Bloodhounds, sometimes required to scent trails for long days and nights, won't fall to pieces if they are born under Fire signs. Herding dogs born under this Element, often running after sheep or cattle during long, hot summer days, will be up to the task.

Because of their energy levels, Fire sign dogs need to be trained while puppies. They need to learn to discipline their energy levels, otherwise, as adult dogs, they can be tyrants—or they can be dangers to themselves. Natives of these sun signs can be impulsive (not a good trait around very small children), too forceful, in love with the sound of their own bark, and self-serving.

AIR SIGNS: GEMINI, LIBRA, AND AQUARIUS

Air sun signs are known for their intelligence. Depending on what breed of dog they are, these *Cosmic Canines* may be physically strong, too. They are, however, primarily known for their intelligence. No doubt about it, some dogs have innate intelligence, doing well those things they were bred to do—hunt, herd, track, or just be pleasing to human companions.

Some dogs, especially those born under Air signs, have intelligence that goes beyond the purpose for which they were bred. Canines function from a base of intuitive and instinctive intelligence (just as humans function from a base of logic and analysis skills). They learn more easily how to solve puzzles, like finding lost people or sniffing for drugs in airline baggage. They learn obedience work more easily—and enjoy it more.

Dogs born under Air sun signs generally do not display emotions often or well. Just because Gemini, Libra, and Aquarius dogs don't look offended when you raise your voice, don't think you haven't hurt their feelings. Any intelligent animal is a sensitive animal. People must be smart enough to see beyond the intelligence in the eyes of these dogs to uncover the hurt feelings residing there because you forgot to praise them. They won't tell you they're hurt. In their positive states, Air sun signs are usually cheerful, curious, and entertaining (funny). When negative, they tend to be aloof, forgetful, and stubbornly independent.

WATER SIGNS: CANCER, SCORPIO, AND PISCES

In water, everything changes. Our oceans, seas, and lakes are always there, but they are never the same each time someone dips his bucket for a drink or fishermen and -women their rods.

Water is associated with movement—the waves, the tides, the ripple effect of small stones being dropped into calm ponds. This should give human companions of dogs born under Water sun signs an idea of just how far-reaching their pet mistakes may go. An injustice to a Water sign pet lasts a lifetime. A punishment too harsh, a yell instead of a corrective tone of voice, won't be forgotten. If you are a believer in the old theory about using newspapers with which to slap/correct dogs, don't be surprised when your Water-born pet bites a newspaper carrier someday. Your dog remembers that newspaper and for what it was used.

These pets have great empathy for people. They have a lot of intuition and use it to overcome the inability most animals have communicating with humans.

These dogs will always be there to support their human companions. Natives born under Water signs are great pets to take to nursing homes or other places where lonely senior citizens dwell. Water sign dogs show immediate sensitivities to sick young people in hospitals because they truly connect with people. They sense the aloneness of those who suffer any form of debility and lovingly offer a head in the lap or a sympathetic glance to those who need to know they still matter.

Dogs born under Water signs are sensitive, intelligent, and changeable. They can have the most wonderful moods and the darkest. What determines these moods? Human companions.

USING THE ELEMENTS TO CHOOSE A PET

To adopt the pet to which you will be most compatible, you must know not only the pet's sun sign but whether it is an Earth, Fire, Air, or Water sign.

There are many other Elements involved in the science of astrology, but they are too many to mention in a book about dogs. It is difficult, in fact, to find a single book about astrology that explains all of the various Elements required to thoroughly interpret birth charts or project future planetary positions. It requires a library.

There is, however, one additional key element that has an application to understanding dog as well as human personalities and how they interrelate compatibly: Modalities.

Astrological Modalities

CARDINAL (LEADERSHIP OR DRIVE) SIGNS: ARIES, CANCER, LIBRA, AND CAPRICORN

The primary trait of Cardinal sun signs is activity. Dogs born under Cardinal signs reach out to human companions and help put them in touch with the outside world. They are active. They enjoy taking part in dog shows in both the conformation and obedience arenas.

Dogs born under Cardinal signs have the greatest need for discipline and obedience training, because of all the sun signs, they have the most difficult time learning proper household behavior. It is not an intelligence problem. It is a problem of concentration. These pets never achieve the potential of which they are capable without the loving attention of a human companion willing to spend the time teaching them what to do and how to do it.

Natives of Cardinal sun signs like activities requiring ingenuity. Cardinal sun sign dogs who are also of the compatible breeds for drug search work will excel at it. When obedience-training dogs born under Cardinal sun signs, use creativity. Place some of the learning burden on the pet. Do not just teach by rote or these dogs will be bored to death. Be playful and active.

Cardinal sun signs are known to be idealists, and idealists tend to be dreamers. If you have a dog born under a Cardinal sign, chances are his legs jerk a lot when he sleeps. He's probably dreaming about running through open fields on a sunny day.

FIXED (POWER) SIGNS: TAURUS, LEO, SCORPIO, AND AQUARIUS

Fixed sun signs are vital, self-willed, and quite the opposite of Cardinal signs; dogs born under Fixed signs have little difficulty concentrating. They are powerful. Mostly, Fixed signs are stable. They are also intense, stubborn, loyal, and very resourceful. If a puppy is born under a Fixed sign and his gums are aching during teething, this resourceful little animal will have no difficulty finding something to chew on to ease his discomfort.

Because dogs born under Fixed signs have such a high capacity for concentration and because they are so resourceful, they make wonderful scent dogs. Bloodhounds who track small children, dogs used as hunting companions, and K-9 corps members who work for police departments have an edge when born under Fixed signs. Certain dog breeds, of course, are more suitable to police work than others.

As you evaluate the pluses and minuses of the various dog breeds, pay attention to what dogs born under Fixed signs were bred to do. They have strong instinctive intelligence. Thus, Terriers born under Fixed sun signs will have more of a tendency to dig or chase small objects that move erratically in front of them than will dogs born under Cardinal or Mutable sun signs.

Fixed sun sign natives (human or canine) can be pretty resistant to change once an idea gets formed. Thus, it is important to begin obedience training at an early age—in fact, that's the best way to ensure that they resist urges to behave negatively. For example, it will be almost impossible to teach acceptable sanitary habits to dogs born under Fixed sun signs who were not housebroken as puppies. The only way to ensure they will "go potty" in the yard is to keep them in the yard.

MUTABLE (WISDOM) SIGNS: GEMINI, VIRGO, SAGITTARIUS, AND PISCES

Human companions of dogs born under Mutable sun signs will have no difficulty communicating with their pets. Because of their communications skills, Mutable sun sign dogs are very sensitive to nuances in your voice. Thus, the tone of voice you adopt when talking to or commanding them is of keen importance. Are you upset at the dog's behavior? Don't yell. It won't correct the dog. If you want to show approval, make the tone of your voice express it.

And these dogs love to learn. No matter what your lifestyle, dogs born under Mutable signs will adapt to it. City living, country living, apartment living, Mutable sun sign dogs are able to make any necessary adjustments. As a result, they make wonderful exercise companions and household pets. They are great for on-the-move families like diplomats or those in the military.

There is little stubbornness for the sake of being stubborn inherent to dogs born under Mutable signs. These pets have an innate sense of compromise. They want to listen, learn, and, most of all, be fair. These four sun signs can, if a dog has been properly bred for temperament and is a breed trustworthy with children, be the very best children's dogs.

USING MODALITIES TO CHOOSE A PET

Until you read through the Modalities of Mutable, Cardinal, and Fixed signs, you thought a German Shepherd Cancer or Capricorn would be quiet, loving, and the easiest of all sun signs to train. Now you find out that Cardinal signs—Cancer and Capricorn are Cardinal signs—have the most difficulty with concentration, a basic requirement for obedience or house-training.

HOW TO USE *COSMIC CANINES*
TO FIND YOUR IDEAL DOG

When you decide to adopt a pet, all three categories of astrological science need to be put to use—the sun sign, the Element under which each sun sign falls, and the Modality governing the sun sign.

On a yellow legal pad, make a list down the left margin of the dog personality traits most important to you. Leave several lines in between each trait.

To the right of this draw five columns.

Name the first column "Breed Traits." Read the information provided for each dog breed. Which possess the genetic traits most compatible to the personality you want your dog to have? Write those names in column one next to each personality trait.

Name the second column "Sun Sign Traits." Read the chapter that explains what Aries or Libra or Pisces puppies are like. Which sun sign adult dogs innately possess the personality traits you most want your pet to have? Put those names in your list under column two.

Name the third column "Element Traits." Read the above information about Earth, Fire, Air, and Water signs. Identify the personality trait most likely to result from a pet born under each Element. If you like competition and want your dog to enjoy afternoons chasing a Frisbee with you in the park, write "Fire" after the personality trait "competition." If you want an outdoor dog who thinks camping is great, write "Air" or "Fire" after the personality trait "outdoor dog." If you want a dog who loves his home and will be happy if his four little paws never see the other side of the mountains or the ocean, write "Earth" or "Water" after the personality trait "home-loving."

Name the fourth column "Modality Traits." Read the above information about Cardinal, Fixed, and Mutable signs. If having a dog who is sensitive to your needs is important, write "Mutable," after the word *sensitive*—if that is one of the words you have listed down the left margin of your yellow, lined legal pad.

Use the fifth column to tally your results. It should, through a process of elimination, tell you which dog breed born under which sun sign will be the very best pet for you. How accurate your results are will depend on how thoroughly—and honestly—you have listed the personality traits that are most important to you.

COMBINING THE GENETIC PURPOSES OF DOGS WITH ASTROLOGICAL PRINCIPLES

By combining the purposes for which the various breeds of dog were created with that part of astrological science that utilizes thousands of years of research to predict the personality traits of specific sun signs, it is possible to find your dream dog. And it will keep you from ruining the very temperament you desire in a pet.

It will help you know how to train that pet in the most effective way as well as help you to reinforce the positive aspects of your pet's personality rather than unintentionally bring out the negatives. For example, if you do not know that a Brittany Spaniel is very sensitive to your voice, and that all animals born under the sign of Cancer are very sensitive to sound, it can cause you to make mistakes. Say you adopt a Cancer-born Brittany (doubling up on breed and sun sign sensitivity to loud voices). Not knowing of this sensitivity, you may yell at the puppy when it does something wrong. That, by itself, can scar the dog's psyche for life. If the yell comes while you are housebreaking the dog, it may become a fear-wetter (a dog who, when it gets nervous or excited, leaks urine).

So, by understanding both the nature of the breed and the nature of the astrological sun sign—which you learn with this book—you will know that the only way to succeed when housebreaking Cancer-born Brittany Spaniels is to be alongside them and effusively praise them when they do the right thing. You have avoided a problem.

FINDING YOUR DOG'S SUN SIGN
WITHOUT A BIRTH DATE

The best dog I ever adopted I found at the Cincinnati Humane Society. He was so skinny and so big, I thought he was a cross between a Great Dane and a Doberman Pinscher. I took him home, had him treated for heartworm, and he blossomed into the biggest, most beautiful purebred Doberman I have ever seen. His name is Rusty.

The Humane Society did not know Rusty's birth date. I had to figure out for myself what his sun sign was and the method I used can be used by anyone. All the information you need is in this book.

I knew Rusty couldn't be a Cardinal sign because he had no difficulty concentrating. Though active, he didn't want to put me in touch with the world. We lived in the country and he loved it there. He didn't care if he saw other dogs or not. He was ingenious, though, and loved solving problems.

I thought he might be a Fixed sign—perhaps an Aquarian, like me, since we were so compatible—because he was very stable, loyal, and resourceful. He was not, however, intense. He could be a little stubborn, but it certainly wasn't a trait that dominated his personality.

After studying the Modalities, I realized he had to be a Mutable sign. What Modality traits did I identify that were compatible with Rusty's personality? He communicated so well, he might as well have talked. He picked up on my tone of voice, and he knew when I was unhappy with him. If I said "good dog" in a normal tone, he exhibited little excitement. But when I allowed my voice to become animated, he would drop down on his front legs, rear in the air, then jump and repeat the move several times.

Rusty loved to learn. When I moved from Cincinnati back to my permanent home in Colorado, he was equally as comfortable in my town home (I took him for a run every day at the Cherry Creek Reservoir) as he had been on our country acreage in Ohio.

I said he could be stubborn, but there was little stubbornness for the sake of being stubborn. And he did compromise with me. He loved—not liked, loved—traveling in the car. I was a bank consultant and owned my own company at the time, and Rusty just didn't fit into the bank boardroom, so I had to leave him home. He didn't pout or whine or try to make me feel guilty when I left him at home and drove off in the morning. He compromised. He did listen, he loved to learn, and he was very fair. When I was gone several days at a time, he let me know he felt a little hurt because, by my absence, I had ignored him.

Studying the Modalities and deciding Rusty was a Mutable sign narrowed the search. He was either a Virgo, Gemini, Sagittarius, or Pisces. Because he was so competitive, because he was such a clown, because he was so very expressive, I narrowed it down to a Sagittarius or Gemini.

When I studied Fire (Sagittarius) and Air (Gemini) sign personality traits, I had no doubt in my mind that Rusty was a Sagittarius. Never was there a more enthusiastic, energetic, resourceful dog than this Dobie. Fortunately for me, Rusty had been well trained as a puppy by his first owners. I noted, however, that I had to put him on a leash occasionally to keep him current on his lessons.

When I read the descriptions of Gemini and Sagittarius dogs, I had no doubt in my mind that my Rusty was a native of the Archer. He understood the concept "If you want to land on the moon, aim for the sun."

If you do not know your dog's birth date, I suggest you go through the same process I did. It was very helpful. We even created a Rusty birthday as a result of the process. A good friend of mine, a former bank client in Charlotte, North Carolina, was born on December 5. I decided that would be the date on which we would celebrate Rusty's birthday; it turned out to be a good way of remembering a good friend and business associate.

FINDING YOUR DOG'S GENETIC HERITAGE WITHOUT PAPERS

Most people have some idea of their dogs' genetic heritage. They are the color of German Shepherds but have long Collie hair. Or they are black and tan like Coonhounds and have wonderful scenting capabilities, but they are only ten inches high at the shoulder, have long hair and the head of a Spaniel (long ears, thick muzzle, etc.).

If you look at the dog breed chapters, you will find that Miniature Pinschers are black and tan and about ten inches at the shoulder. Maybe you have a mix. There are, in fact, about two or three dozen possibilities.

Only *you* know your dog. Read the compiled breed data, which has been arranged by dog size. In this example, you might want to start with the chapter on miniature and small breeds and work your way through medium-sized dogs. My bet is you'll get an idea of what your dog's genetic makeup is with very little research. Then you can continue on to determine his or her sun sign.

The only people who don't like mutts or mongrels (nonpurebred dogs) are those who have not owned them. Because they (obviously) haven't been inbred, mutts are often the brightest dogs on the block. If you have a mutt, try to determine by your best guess its background; you may then want to try breeding it to a purebred of the best-guess breed. The resulting puppies would tell you a lot—and they would represent the best of both worlds (even without registration papers).

PART TWO

DOG BREEDS

2

TOY BREEDS

AFFENPINSCHER

Positive Traits

Like the Texas flag said at one time, Affenpinschers ought to wear a sign saying "Don't Tread on Me." These fearless little dogs are energetic and proud. To members of their families, Affenpinschers are very affectionate; to others, they are not. These are extremely independent *Cosmic Canines* who will not tolerate abuse. Affens are intelligent and learn obedience lessons well (and quickly). They make wonderful companions and are plucky, attentive, and sturdy little dogs. They have conspicuous chins with tufts of hair and mustaches—thus the nickname Monkey Face or Monkey Dog. They have stiff, wiry coats and weigh eight pounds or less.

Negative Traits

These dogs are fiery, quick-tempered, and may be unfriendly to strangers. They are not the best children's pets. They are fine with adults who behave predictably and who understand that all God's children have rights, including canines. Though Toy in size, Affens are not likely to be lap dogs. They have moments where they both give and receive love and attention, but are not dependent on either to gain a sense of identity. When you correct Affenpinschers, don't play the bully. It won't work. In fact, it is likely to have the opposite effect. Businesslike attitudes for correction, happy enthusiasm for praise get the job done. Emphasize praise, correct when it is needed, but keep good behavior in the spotlight.

Job Opportunities for Affenpinschers

Affens are excellent watch-and-warn dogs. No stranger goes unnoticed. They enjoy taking exercise with human guardians and make pleasant travel companions. These pets enjoy obedience training and learning other lessons—tricks, for example. If human companions have always wanted to be part of circus life, maybe their Affenpinschers can make it possible for them. Affens are wonderful companions for seniors who have firm hands when it comes to teaching discipline to charming little puppies. Make no mistake about it, they do need discipline, but discipline applied intelligently, not abusively. When these dogs go to bed at night, be sure they remember praise for their good behavior, not corrections for bad behavior. This strategy will be sure to produce encore performances.

Most Compatible Sun Sign: Gemini

Gemini humans are logical and have the ability to analyze any situation. Combined with down-home sensibility, these traits make Affenpinschers think twice before trying to dominate their Gemini guardians. Affenpinschers require human companions who are assertive, forceful, and confident, yet refined and adaptable. And these traits describe Geminis perfectly. In addition, natives of this sun sign are charitable, functional, idealistic realists (perfect attitudes for guardians of Affens), and have diverse interests. Gemini humans are firm but loving, refined but tough (when needed). When natives of the sign of the Twins go through negative phases, Affenpinschers are more than sufficiently strong to handle their brief bouts with overconfidence, belligerence, moodiness, aloofness, and cantankerous inconsistencies. They periodically are tempted by the same moods. These two have a great deal in common!

AUSTRALIAN TERRIER

Positive Traits

These little Aussies—ten inches high at the shoulder and fourteen pounds or less—are clever, loving, and enjoy pleasing human companions. Like all Terriers, these dogs are courageous. Aussies are hardy, competitive, keen, alert, and are good watch-and-warn dogs. After giving warning, though, these affectionate *Cosmic Canines* may lick prowlers to death. Australian Terriers are loyal and devoted and utterly reliable with toddlers. They are excellent family companions and have a lot of speed for such small animals. They are excellent ratters (dispatchers of vermin). Their coats are weather resistant and make them adaptable to almost all climates. Australian Terriers are keen scenting dogs and have the skill and courage to hunt and attack food for themselves, should the need arise. That should tell people something about how independent they are!

Negative Traits

Aside from the usual things about which human companions need to be sensitive regarding Terriers, there are no noted drawbacks to these dogs. They need exercise and regular grooming, but present no particular problems beyond the norm in either area. Australian Terriers are better at figuring things out for themselves than they are at learning obedience lessons, but they are clever dogs nonetheless. The usual Terrier warnings: This group of dogs was created to dig prey from burrows—rabbits, rats, and such. If owners watch Terrier puppies carefully and strongly discourage any tendency to dig, their genetic inclinations are usually not a problem (unless a mole pops up from underground in your yard). Terriers instinctively respond to small "critters" that exhibit erratic, quick movements. To give Terriers their daily exercise, all that's needed is a dark room and a flashlight. Turn on the flashlight, point it toward the floor, and move it around erratically. They'll chase the light beam as it moves across the floor. Don't overdo it, though, or it will make them nervous.

Job Opportunities for Australian Terriers

These dogs are spirited companions with a lot of personality. Aussies are *Cosmic Canines* with strong inclinations to love and protect their families, especially young children. Their temperaments make them good exercise partners and their size, combined with their personalities, makes them excellent travel companions. Most of all, they are wonderful household pets. Aussies are good watch-and-warn dogs, but not good for guard work or personal protection (beyond warning of imminent danger). They are good company for singles.

Most Compatible Sun Sign: Sagittarius

Sagittarians have wonderful senses of humor. They are also devoted, confident, self-reliant, and, basically, just plain happy people. Positive Saggie personalities offer Australian Terriers just what they need to easily bond. Saggies are insightful and sense when these *Cosmic Canines* are honing in on the solution to a problem and will probably even try to help. Natives of the sign of the Archer are hopeful, purposeful, frank (to a fault, sometimes), honest, giving, and sincere. All these traits hold appeal to these bright, courageous, and intelligent dogs. Like these canines, Sagittarians are loyal and affectionate. These sun sign natives require freedom—and the size and independent temperament of Australian Terriers offer freedom in abundance. Individualistic Aussies won't try to tie Archers to backyards or family room couches. Instead, they gladly play the role of loyal companion that Sagittarians so much appreciate during their escapades.

BORDER TERRIER

Positive Traits

Border Terriers are strong, active dogs about eleven inches in height, weighing from eleven to fifteen pounds, and put together for maximum efficiency. They are fast, have historically kept pace with horses on fox hunts, and love digging or "nagging" foxes from their holes. They are very plucky dogs—brave (which is a trait of Terriers). These *Cosmic Canines* do not hesitate to face larger opponents when hunting. Border Terriers are good-natured, affectionate, amiable, and a handy size. They are hardy, reliable, and sporty Working dogs that haven't been overbred for the show ring. Thus, their hunting instincts have not been bred out of them because of too much emphasis on conformation. This is the smallest of the working Terriers with roots in England and Scotland. Border Terriers get along well with other animals. They are agile and alert. You can count on them. They have character.

Negative Traits

These dogs *need* exercise. They need to run, not walk. They need either very large yards or the country life. If their guardians are city dwellers, fast-paced runs keeping up with somewhat slow-moving bicycles (they are very small, remember) fill this need. If moles or other underground critters live on Border Terrier property, tell them to say their prayers and put this dog out on a cool summer evening. This dog breed still has very strong hunter instincts. Though they get along well with other animals, it's probably a good idea to make sure the "other animals" are larger than a rat or fox or other animal Border Terriers are used to hunting. If your neighbor has a Chihuahua that darts unexpectedly in front of one of these *Cosmic Canines*, you may have a problem. Terriers react to the erratic movement of small animals so quickly, it is sometimes impossible for human guardians to react fast enough to stop them.

Job Opportunities for Border Terriers

Border Terriers are excellent pets for families with post-toddler children. They make nontraditional but wonderful hunting companions—for fox, anyway. *Good pets for homes with multiple animals.* Good exercise partners (keep them leashed or walk them in the woods—let them run, if possible). Their size and temperaments make them excellent travel companions. Most of all, they are loving family pets with a charming independent streak.

Most Compatible Sun Sign: Aries

Aries natives, like these dogs, have character. They are agile and alert, original and energetic; they are explorers. Border Terriers are fast and sensible, strong and humorous. These are traits humans born under the highly competitive sign of the Ram understand and appreciate. Aries humans can be headstrong, impulsive, high-strung, and impatient—traits that won't bother independent Border Terriers. Aries natives are also good-natured, affectionate, reliable, and amiable—just like this dog breed. Natives of the Ram and Border Terriers are confident, intelligent, independent, and eminently sensible. Both communicate well. This is a good match.

CAIRN TERRIER

Positive Traits

The tousled Cairn Terrier looks like a black Scottish Terrier someone forgot to groom. These *Cosmic Canines* are less than a foot tall (like Scotties) and weigh less than sixteen pounds (Scotties weigh about twenty pounds). Cairn Terriers are happy animals. They are independent, smart, and adaptable. This is a hardy breed and these dogs have pleasing, affectionate dispositions. Cairns make wonderful family companions. Their roots are Scottish and, like all good Scotsmen, they are known for being able to find their way home. Though Cairns have rough, double coats, they are easy to groom. Their ancestors were used to find and retrieve vermin from stone grave markers (the word *cairn* means "heap of stones" in Scottish), but in the home they are quiet, well mannered, and considerate. Cairns enjoy traveling in the car. They have an alert kind of gaiety and are dedicated. They have an innate kind of sensitive intelligence and are very independent animals.

Negative Traits

Cairns like to dig and have been known to rearrange the family vegetable garden on occasion. If Cairn Terriers suddenly begin misbehaving (that isn't their usual style), it's probably because they aren't getting enough exercise. These *Cosmic Canines* are bundles of energy and need the opportunity to expend it. If that opportunity doesn't readily present itself, they find other ways to release their tension. They may bark or dig or do whatever energetic puppies do to release built-up energy caused by a lack of exercise. Cairns do not become friends with just anyone. They are pretty selective. Though too small to be grade-A guard dogs, they are good at giving warning. Cairns are not easy to quiet if intruders come around. They can be stubborn (but not often).

Job Opportunities for Cairn Terriers

These Terriers are expert ratters and hunters of small vermin. They are good family dogs and make excellent companions for seniors sufficiently active to make sure the dogs get all the exercise they need. Good farm dogs, good apartment dogs—they are adaptable. Cairns make good travel companions and watch-and-warn dogs. Mostly, they offer human companions the chance to love and be loved.

Most Compatible Sun Sign: Sagittarius

Humans born under this sun sign are devoted, confident, self-reliant, and bright, and they have happy dispositions. These Sagittarian personality traits sound a lot like the primary traits enjoyed by Cairn Terriers. Natives of the sign of the Archer are also joyful, hopeful, loyal, and affectionate again, traits very similar to the Cairn. This dog breed and the sun sign are both active, honest, giving, and sincere. Both are purposeful and require exercise and a certain amount of freedom. In their negative phases, Sagittarians can be restless, overactive, nervous, tense, and irritable. They can be domineering and lazy. So, too, can poorly raised or improperly bred Cairn Terriers. Cairns are too independent to be hurt by the negative moods of Sagittarians and are perky enough to help get these sun sign natives back on the positive track when they veer off it.

CHIHUAHUA

Positive Traits

Their convenient, small size makes Chihuahuas good traveling companions. They are ideal apartment dogs and very loyal and affectionate. They are also highly intelligent. They make great miniature guard dogs—though these *Cosmic Canines* sometimes appear to think of themselves as being as large as Great Danes. It is true that most Chihuahuas have more heart than common sense when it comes to protecting their loved ones. These are good pets for the elderly and/or disabled because Chihuahuas like but don't need much exercise. These dogs carefully observe owners and evaluate them to find out what they are like—figuring out who is going to be the boss in this house—before showing their true personalities. If the household boss isn't you, you're probably not the one with whom these somewhat political (and very selective) *Cosmic Canines* will bond. There's an old saying that suggests, "If you are loved by a Chihuahua, you must be very special."

Negative Traits

Chihuahuas are strong-willed little animals that are fearless beyond reason. They would just as soon fight a bear as the neighborhood cat. Owners must watch and help defend them against their little-dog attitude or their Chihuahuas will lose some nasty fights to very large opponents. They are defensive around nonfamily members. They don't particularly care for dogs of other breeds—very politically incorrect. Chihuahuas hate the cold and have a tendency toward joint diseases like arthritis and rheumatism. Other than these minor problems, Chihuahuas make charming pets!

Job Opportunities for Chihuahuas

Chihuahuas are wonderful companions who are great miniprotectors. Though they are too small to do more than warn human companions of danger, they have the heart to take on opponents of all sizes. They are definitely small dogs with big dog self-images. Though their size makes them ideal travel companions, some members of this breed can be made extremely nervous when moved from place to place. They are better homebodies than travelers and are too small to be exercise companions for human guardians—unless walking at a reasonable pace is your idea of exercise.

Most Compatible Sun Sign: Virgo

Virgo humans have the strengths needed to offset Chihuahua negatives. They are usually low key enough to motivate calm dog temperaments and their down-to-earth common sense will meticulously protect these dogs from themselves. It's been said Virgoans wrote the how-to manual on political correctness—sure to meet with Chihuahua approval. Virgoans understand the concept of being all you can be, but stop short of thinking their Chihuahua pets can successfully fight the neighborhood

Rottweiler who wanders into the yard by mistake. Still, the strengths of Virgo humans do not detract from the personality strengths of these *Cosmic Canines*—Virgoans won't put dampers on the charming, spirited natures of these dogs. Like Chihuahuas, Virgoans evaluate everything. This sun sign is very analytic, tactful, reasoned, and reasonable. Virgoans need warmth and loving attention while young and are an affectionate, curious sun sign. The values of Virgo personality—calm, wise, tactful—add to an already good compatibility package.

DACHSHUND (MINIATURE)

Positive Traits

Miniature Dachshunds can be either long- or short-coated, wiry or smooth. They weigh about ten pounds and are long-bodied—the famous "wiener dog." They are bold and confident, yet affectionate and great fun. They are intelligent and good obedience prospects. Dachshunds are relatively easy to look after and make loyal family pets. They will warn of prowlers and in this context are good watchdogs. Some are still bred as hunting dogs and will bravely tackle opponents larger than themselves— like badgers. Dachshunds have a lot of energy. They will defend what is theirs, including their human companions, to the death. These dogs love to dig rabbits from their holes and chase them out of gardens and agricultural fields. They still love to "go to ground" (a little hunting lingo, there). Dachsies make wonderful pets for teenagers, willingly bonding with them and making their loyalty and faithfulness known. In a world grown difficult for young adults, having a solid canine relationship with a Dachsie is often an invaluable anchor.

Negative Traits

Those long Dachshund backs are prone to disk trouble. They should not be allowed to jump on furniture—it's hard on their backs. And don't feed them too much—being overweight also stresses their backs. These energetic little dogs are self-willed and stubborn. They can be less than friendly with strangers and need strong correction from puppyhood to change this trait. It's a bit of a balancing act: teaching Dachsies not to be too assertive with strangers who happen to be family friends, but teaching them to be as assertive as they want with prowlers in the middle of the night. Be careful not to make them too friendly with strangers. In their past, these Cosmic Canines had a strong genetic instinct for digging bred into them. Though modern breeders have long ago done away with most of those genes and have produced wonderful family pets, genetic heritage still gives the occasional Dachsie the urge to get some dirt under its nails. They are good nonyard apartment dogs. They like children, but because they can be aggressive with strangers (including your tot's friends), they are better around preteens and teens.

Job Opportunities for Miniature Dachshunds

These dogs are wonderful, entertaining company for adults and older children, and good warning dogs whose bark makes them sound bigger than they really are. Size makes them good traveling companions. Dogs born under certain sun signs are more protective than others, and Miniature Dachshunds born under one of these signs will be very protective of family cars. Dachshunds have a lot of obedience-training potential. Don't let their stubbornness outfox you—they'll try!

Most Compatible Sun Sign: Capricorn

Capricorn human companions have great determination and persistence. It helps them understand and control Miniature Dachshund stubbornness. Natives of the Goat are balanced, fair, careful, diligent, self-reliant, determined, and patient. Both dog and sun sign natives are practical. Capricorn common sense and independence are very compatible with the Cosmic Canine attitudes Dachshunds have toward life. A Capricorn's calm will help settle these independent little cusses and each appreciates the loyalty of the other. Natives of this quiet, reflective sun sign help Miniature Dachshunds relate better with strangers—to be less aggressive with those friends who have been welcomed into the homes of their human companions. Miniature Dachshunds will understand and be there to support Capricorn natives when they become sad, negative, suspicious, gloomy, cold, distant, aloof, and despondent. These are very loyal, faithful dogs.

ENGLISH TOY SPANIEL

Positive Traits

Though it now weighs only about twelve pounds, these *Cosmic Canines* were originally bred to be gundogs. Authorities agree the history of English Toy Spaniels goes far beyond the time of England's King Charles II (seventeenth century), all the way back to ancient Japan and maybe even ancient China. Mary, Queen of Scots loved these little Spaniels—and they loved Queen Mary. One English Toy had a particularly close relationship with the Scottish monarch and accompanied Mary to the spot on the Tower grounds where she was beheaded. From the days of Mary, these dogs have been referred to as "gentle Spaniels." They are comfortable dogs (perhaps, as with Mary, Queen of Scots, comforting as well). English canine history is replete with stories about them. These are quietly contented dogs and are ideal companions who learn very quickly what people want them to do. They obey house rules once they are made aware of them. Their idea of a perfect day includes a quiet afternoon napping in a favorite corner. This is an affectionate, kind dog—words not often used to describe canine pals.

Negative Traits

There are no known negative traits regarding this dog breed.

Job Opportunities for English Toy Spaniels

These dogs have for centuries been bred to be companions for human beings. To enjoy people and belong to a family is this dog's whole purpose in life. As with all Toy-sized breeds, access to these pets by infants and toddlers should be limited and highly controlled. A small, probing, and curious human infant hand can do a lot of damage to very small Toy dogs. When subjected to threats, all animals defend themselves. English Toy Spaniels have great temperaments and are the perfect size to be the best travel companions possible. They may bark to warn of intruders, but much depends on how human guardians train them. They are very empathetic animals—even with prowlers, until taught differently.

Most Compatible Sun Signs: Pisces, Scorpio, Libra, Cancer, and Taurus

Natives of sun signs that make them the most quiet, peaceful, and giving—those to whom values like loyalty, faithfulness, and compassion are most important—are the human companions most compatible with English Toy Spaniels. Pisceans are known for their acceptance of others and for having calming, peaceful influences on animals. They are receptive to affection. Natives of the Fishes are sensitive, compassionate, tender, and warm. They have much in common with this dog breed. Scorpions are known to be tranquil, spiritually intuitive, friendly, and can have great strength of character (or a total lack of it). Libra's sense of balance and justice will strongly appeal to dogs of this breed. This sun sign is known for producing natives who are restful, calm, philosophic, and humane. English Toys will love them. Cancerians have a sense of empathy and understanding, calm, sympathy, and compassion. They also have great appeal to English Toy Spaniels. The enduring patience of Taureans, combined with their generous natures and soothing, peaceful gifts of healing, reaches out to English Toy Spaniels.

FRENCH POODLE, TOY

Positive Traits

Proud dogs. Elegant (as opposed to "cute"). Affectionate, gregarious, dainty, a great deal of fun. Toy poodles are long-lived, very intelligent, and good obedience-training dogs. Few pets have more appeal and beauty. Poodles are excellent Retrievers and enjoy retrieving in water (if permitted). If spoiled, Poodles can be temperamental with children (even though they like them). They usually bond with the household's adult female (if there is one) and are very protective of her. There is something magical about the love of life and people so apparent in the personalities of these *Cosmic Canines*. Any human being who can look into the eyes of these dogs and not see intelligence and caring . . . well, they simply aren't looking very hard!

Negative Traits

Control barking—Toy Poodles like the sound of their own voices. Before being obedience-trained and while young, they are too sensitive to be the best pets for children. Watch out for signs of ear trouble, nervousness, and joint malformations. Poodle cuts were designed to keep extra dog fur protection over joints because poodles are susceptible to rheumatism. Toy Poodles need to have the plaque scraped from their teeth periodically. They need consistent, extensive grooming. Mostly, they need attention from human companions who are not so besotted by their charm that they forget to correct and train these little charmers. Left untrained or undisciplined, Toy Poodles can become snippy tyrants who think the homes of their human guardians are "their" castles.

Job Opportunities for Toy French Poodles

These are fun dogs that provide comic relief. They are wonderful companions. If treated like children—that is, spoiled—these *Cosmic Canines* may be too temperamental to qualify for any job. Their intelligence makes them fun dogs to work with in obedience training. They are good bark-and-warn dogs but too small to protect. Human companions who train them to do tricks may be able to retire on the income earned when they appear in front of movie or television cameras, circus audiences, or wherever there are people who will applaud canine performances. They love attention! These are really fun dogs who love to travel and make good exercise companions if you don't go too fast. This is one of the most flexible of all toy breeds.

Most Compatible Sun Sign: Libra

Libra personalities do not intensify Toy French Poodle nervous energy. These human companions are just, balanced, kind, ordered, calm, harmonious, amiable, restful, perceptive, generous, agreeable, compassionate, humane, and pleasant. What else could Poodles ask for in a human guardian? Librans, though, can lack discipline, be restless, dream too much, and be combative, thoughtless, and indecisive when passing through negative cycles. Positive Libra traits strengthen Toy French Poodles; negative ones, however, do not add to breed negatives. These *Cosmic Canines* will be totally turned on by Libran charm and appreciation for the finer things of life—the refinement so much a part of Libran lifestyles. Equally, natives of the sign of the Scales will find Toy French Poodles worthy status symbols—Librans can be into staying ahead of the Joneses.

GERMAN SPITZ, SMALL

Positive Traits

These pets enjoy living in apartments, country homes, or mansions. They resemble Pomeranians, but are about two pounds heavier and two inches shorter. The size and temperaments of these *Cosmic Canines* make them ideal for families who move a lot. Small German Spitzes are beautiful dogs. While they are too small to walk the walk, they offer excellent bark-and-warn protection services. These pets make wonderfully loyal companions. They are very happy, very intelligent *Cosmic Canines*. Small German Spitzes do not need a lot of exercise but they do enjoy moments of togetherness with friends. They love their human companions and are not afraid to show it. The ancestry of these dogs is Nordic; genetics says they originated with larger sled dogs. Like all Toys, they can be monsters when treated like human children or otherwise spoiled.

Negative Traits

Small German Spitz dogs are naturally suspicious of strangers, which is a good trait and explains why these *Cosmic Canines* are such good watch-and-warn pets. Yet when it is equally applied to friends, it is most definitely a bad trait. If human companions allow Small German Spitz puppies to bark for the sake of barking, it will never be clear when they become adults if their bark is a warning or they just want to hear their own voices. Control the barking of these dogs from the day you bring them home. Otherwise, you'll be listening to it for a very long time. This breed requires vigorous, frequent brushing or a lot of dog hair will need to be cleaned off the carpets and furniture.

Job Opportunities for the Small German Spitz

These dogs make excellent companions. They are very intelligent, loving, and faithful pets. Small German Spitzes are good bark-and-warn dogs but are too small for guard dog work. They make excellent travel companions (actually, they enjoy change and moving about). All Spitz breeds, both large and small, are known for their loyalty, but they won't pester people for attention like other Toy breeds. They are, however, always there when human companions need a little tender, loving care.

Most Compatible Sun Sign: Capricorn

Like the Small German Spitz, humans born under the sign of the Goat are balanced, fair, careful, diligent, self-reliant, determined, and patient. Both are practical. The happy Spitz attitude can give positive support to Capricorn natives when they become sad, negative, suspicious, gloomy, cold, distant, aloof, and despondent. All humans (and canines) can be moody, and those are the symptoms of a Capricorn's negative cycle. Capricorns are calm, which can help settle the sometimes overenergetic Spitz. No sun sign native appreciates loyalty and faithfulness more than those born under the sign of the Goat, and German Spitzes have it to give in abundance. Human companions with roots from this quiet, reflective, and deep sun sign can help the Small German Spitz listen to voices other than its own.

GRIFFON (BRUSSELS GRIFFON)

Positive Traits

These Toys—of no more than eight inches in height and from six to twelve pounds—are lively, affectionate, and have great respect for their human guardians. They are independent, discriminating, and very hardy *Cosmic Canines.* Griffons are quite intelligent and usually live happy, long, full lives. They have strong personalities—called "monkey face," they did not become popular because of their looks. Rather, their appeal lies in their independent and forceful personalities. People who like animals with unique and independent personas are drawn to this breed. These happy-tempered dogs are obedient. Regarding coat, there are two types: one has a full, wiry coat, free from curl; the other type has a short, smooth coat. Griffons were originally bred to be watch-and-warn dogs and to catch vermin.

Negative Traits

The rough-coated variety need to have their undercoats removed twice a year. A good, strong wire brush can accomplish the task, but professional groomers can do a much better job of stripping this cottonlike fur. This undercoat is so close to the dog's tender skin, it can hurt to have it removed if the groomer has no experience. Smooth-coats need to be brushed and bathed regularly. Keep Griffon toenails clipped. Ratters (like Griffons) were genetically engineered to dig rats, rabbits, and moles from their holes. Not having long nails helps them forget their genetic heritage, though it is largely bred out of them today. Breeders now aim to produce canines of this breed who make the best possible pets. Discourage digging from day one, however.

Job Opportunities for Brussels Griffons

These dogs are wonderful, intelligent companions. They make great family pets and love to accompany human companions on walks. They will warn of prowlers but are too small to protect. No Toy breed is ideal for very young toddlers or infants and this one is no exception.* Dogs born to this particular breed have many of the independent personality traits of larger dogs. When they are raised from puppyhood with small humans, they are among the best dogs of this size group for children because they are so trustworthy, so happy.

Most Compatible Sun Sign: Gemini

Like these dogs, Gemini humans are adaptable, multifaceted, forceful, and sensible. Both are bold, assertive, confident, and progressive. Griffons, like Gemini natives, are sensitive, inquisitive, quick, and very intelligent. A good word to describe both is *functional*. In negative cycles, Geminis can be self-indulgent, cowardly, jittery, aloof, overconfident, belligerent, remote, and unreliable. These are normally not traits of even poorly bred Griffons. Thus, they are able to help Gemini humans going through negative cycles get back on a positive track. If Griffon human companions spoil them or they are poorly bred, both the sun sign and the

---

*Toy breeds are generally not the best companions for very young toddlers or infants, especially during puppyhood. Both toddlers and Toy pups are very vulnerable and can thus be somewhat defensive.

dog can be aloof, impetuous, worried, anxious, frivolous, somewhat unpredictable, and high-strung. Both can be moody, restless, cantankerous, and closed. These two understand each other (and the rest of us can be grateful neither Gemini humans nor Griffon *Cosmic Canines* pass through negative cycles often).

ITALIAN GREYHOUND

Positive Traits

They are lithe, weigh eight pounds, are about fourteen inches high, and are affectionate, intelligent, and easy to train. Italian Greyhounds may be the first Toy bred strictly as companions for humans and to provide guardian services. They are not shy, but, like Chihuahuas, take time to evaluate new owners and bond with them. These *Cosmic Canines* are discerning dogs, choosing for themselves where they want to sleep, what and when they want to eat, and who they want as friends. Loving and lovable, graceful, diminutive in appearance, odorless, and sensitive, they rarely shed. Italian Greyhounds have been called elegant, and mummies of them have been found in the tombs of pharaohs. This is an ancient breed whose members obviously gained the love and respect of ancient human companions in historic palaces.

Negative Traits

Italian Greyhounds, unlike other Toy breeds, *need* plenty of exercise. Human guardians of these pets should be up for daily walks. If they get too little exercise, they accrue too much energy, which results in a nervous animal. Italian Greyhounds are sensitive and can be deeply wounded by harsh words from those they love. So those who own them should be of moderate temperament. They are also hearing-sensitive dogs, and since under some sun signs dogs are more hearing-sensitive, that information should be taken into consideration before adopting Italian Greyhounds. If not, hearing sensitivity will be doubled. This also should be taken into constant consideration when obedience-training these dogs. Italian Greyhounds can be psychologically damaged when kenneled for any length of time. They truly attach their hearts to the humans with whom they bond.

Job Opportunities for Italian Greyhounds

These *Cosmic Canines* have served as companions for single adults, families, and children for thousands of years. They are good dogs for those wanting Toy-sized breeds who love obedience training. Though their personal sensitivities must be taken into consideration when training them, Italian Greyhounds are very intelligent and love learning their lessons. Time spent in companionable, thoughtful training sessions results in very meaningful pet-guardian relationships. They are excellent exercise partners and interesting, loving travel companions.

Most Compatible Sun Sign: Taurus

Taurus natives are solid, friendly, sincere, trustworthy, soothing, and peaceful. Taurus humans respect history and will respect these historic pets. All these traits make the Taurus-born compatible with such sensitive dogs. Italian Greyhounds are elegant, dignified, and historic in origin and appeal to the artistic streak that runs in the veins of all Taureans. Elegance and dignity are traits natives of the Bull most admire. Taureans are vital and strong—traits Italian Greyhounds respect. They feel protected by the powerful aura of these sun sign natives. Taureans are very practical, too, and will make sure Italian Greyhounds get the necessary exercise. Companionable Taureans will enjoy long walks with such pleasing company. Natives of the sign of the Bull are practical, patient, faithful, and determined. They do not like being yelled at and so are unlikely to hurt the feelings of Italian Greyhounds by yelling at them. Taurus natives soothe animals and are fearless, generous, persistent, tenacious, objective, and enduring. On the negative side, Taureans can be strong-willed, fearful, selfish, dishonest, opinionated, despondent, dogmatic, and indecisive. The loving and lovable Italian Greyhound will help Taurus work through "down" times.

JAPANESE CHIN

Positive Traits

Looking at Japanese Chin dogs, it is easy to see why some experts believe English Toy Spaniels have their roots in the East—the two breeds strongly resemble each other. Is the Chin the ancient ancestor responsible for this English arm of the family? Japanese Chins are fashionably earnest, though loving in a unique kind of way. And they have highly perceptive instincts. They seldom bark at friends and almost never lick the hands of enemies. With a total body weight of about seven pounds, Chins are fine watch-and-warn dogs who bark when strangers are around, although they are too small to physically protect. These are fancy, noble, and elegant dogs (after all, Pekingese roots can be traced to the Chin), with luxuriant coats of long, straight, silky hair.

Negative Traits

These are pretty independent little *Cosmic Canines* who develop their own likes and dislikes—and what human companions like may play only a small role in determining their preferences. Chins are suspicious of strangers. Though healthy and hardy while young, they may not be as long-lived as other Toy dog breeds. There is not a large number of them, and finding satisfactory breeding accommodations may be difficult. Grooming is required.

Job Opportunities for Japanese Chins

They are interesting and attentive companions to families with older children. Chins are lap dogs who give (and demand) a lot of attention. Their size and weight make them good travel companions. While they are not the best exercise partners, they do enjoy leisurely neighborhood walks in not very heavily populated areas. It's too easy for people not paying attention on downtown city streets to misstep and injure this Toy breed of dog. Chins are protective and make excellent watch-and-warn dogs who welcome friends but not prowlers. For human companions interested in the occult, intuitive Chins may provide good company when spirits start talking through mediums at local séances.

Most Compatible Sun Sign: Aries

Independent Ariens, with their prophetic, clairvoyant talents, are almost perfect matches for Chins. They are smart, decisive, idealistic, energetic, and amusing. So are these dogs. Competitive Aries enjoys being first and will probably enjoy the ancient roots of these dogs, who, through selective breeding, spawned so many other popular dog breeds. Talk about being first! Ariens are good communicators who understand that when Chins act as if they didn't hear a command, it is a means of avoiding things they do not want to do. And Aries natives will not be inclined to spoil these dogs. This is important because the Chin's regal attitude and noble background can make it pretty full of itself. Add "spoiled" to "regal" and you have a problem. In their negative states, Aries human companions are headstrong, impulsive, elitist, jealous, and aloof. None of these things bothers Japanese Chins. They, after all, have had centuries of experiencing royal elitism and aloofness, impulsiveness and egoism. It goes with the Chins' own regal attitude and historic lifestyle.

LHASA APSO

Positive Traits

Many people confuse Lhasa Apsos with Shih Tzus. The two resemble each other and both come from Tibet. Lhasa Apsos were around for centuries before being brought to Europe by early explorers and missionaries, and they look like the Holy Lion (symbol of the Buddha's dominance of animals). "Lhasa Apso" means "goatlike," and it is thought that this dog was bred to protect the wild goats of Tibet. Like Shih Tzus, Lhasa Apsos are beautiful and exotic. They stand about ten inches high and weigh thirteen to fifteen pounds. These dogs are referred to as "confident"—a word not often associated with dogs. Lhasa Apsos are affectionate, good with children, hardy and healthy, and enjoy either town or country. Some say their dark brown eyes reveal a new secret each time they look at human companions. These dogs are assertive (is that why some people define them as confident?).

Negative Traits

Lhasa Apsos are still in tune with their guard instincts, bred into them so many centuries ago. They are naturally suspicious of strangers and bark warnings when someone sets foot on their turf. They are assertive and appear to be the only ones who don't know they are Toy-sized dogs. Lhasa Apsos attempt to protect like large dogs. These Cosmic Canines need extensive grooming to care for their coats of long, dense, heavy, straight hair. Without almost daily attention to some part of their coats (e.g., face hair after eating), they can look a mess. Without daily brushings, knots form in their coats and can be painful when brushed out. Though they love all children, their suspicion of strangers may extend to friends of young tots. They are better with school-aged children than with toddlers.

Job Opportunities for Lhasa Apsos

Lhasa Apsos are excellent home watch-and-warn dogs, loving family pets, interesting canine companions, and energetic (though small) exercise partners on daily walking excursions. These are good dogs for families on the move. They enjoy travel and are not threatened by change. Lhasas are loving allies and loyal family friends, especially to children.

Most Compatible Sun Sign: Scorpio

The Scorpion is a spiritually intuitive mystic who, like Lhasa Apso dogs, is optimistic, talented, mysterious, tranquil, decisive, and inquisitive. Both the sun sign and the dog have great strength of character. Both are self-controlled and thrive on approval—and both are suspicious of strangers. Neither offers trust to just anyone, and both take their time in making the offer when it occurs. Scorpios and Lhasa Apsos are dignified, friendly, persistent, and very quick thinkers. Both can be affectionate once trust is earned. The sun sign and the dog breed are both determined and confident. Both are assertive. When in negative cycles, Scorpio humans can be willful, rigid, critical, and skeptical. So can poorly bred or untrained (or spoiled) Lhasa Apsos. Both have strong recuperative powers. Both can be boorish—or arrogant.

MALTESE TERRIER

Positive Traits

This is one of the best Toy-sized dogs for children; they are very good with little ones. These sweet-natured dogs are so admired that Goya and Rubens have done them in oils. Not many canines can claim portraits painted by such famous artists. Maltese Terriers are flexible with exercise—liking but not needing it—and are good traveling dogs. They make wonderful companions. Maltese usually have long, healthy lives and are devoted to the entire family (not just one or two members). They remain playful throughout life and adapt easily to many different climates. Their manners are gentle, yet they are vigorous and lively. Though they weigh only four to six pounds, they give human companions a bit of action without hyperactive nerves. Many Toys have eyes that bulge, but Maltese eyes are oval and always hold a look of interested curiosity.

Negative Traits

Aside from their profuse, long (almost always white) coats, which need fastidious (and frequent) grooming, there are no real negative comments that can be made about these dogs. The Maltese was originally bred to kill rats. It is known for having a strong dislike of cats and, like all Terriers, the Maltese may instinctively dart after any small animal that moves erratically in front of it. Digging should be discouraged.

Job Opportunities for Maltese Terriers

The sweet personalities of these dogs make them especially good for retirees who have time to provide the needed grooming. They are wonderful companions and will enjoy taking walks with their guardians. Maltese Terriers are only ten inches high and weigh six pounds. They do not bark at everything that moves and, unless trained to warn, may not tell people when strangers are around. All they want is to be loved and loving and to be interesting companions for human guardians. These personality kids enjoy being taught tricks and love making public performances. Maltese Terriers are good dogs to take on visits to hospitals and senior citizen residences. Their size makes it possible for them to be held and the sweetness of their personalities reaches out to the elderly and infirm to comfort them.

Most Compatible Sun Sign: Cancer

Like Maltese Terriers, sun sign natives of Cancer the Crab are sensitive, domestic, understanding, empathetic, resolute, diplomatic, self-possessed, self-reliant, logical, and rational. Cancer natives are calm, strong, purposeful, sympathetic, and compassionate. They are very loving. So, too, are Maltese Terriers. When in infrequent negative cycles, natives of the Crab can be fearful, defensive, frustrated by emotions, self-serving, and selfish. Calm but happy Maltese Terriers will help Cancer natives stay positive and keep them from the imbalance of negative Cancerian influences brought on by a lack of close, meaningful relationships. Sensitive, loving Cancerians find equality of caring in these pets who love and trust as much as they do.

MANCHESTER (OR ENGLISH) TOY TERRIER

Positive Traits

To describe this dog breed is a little like describing a sports car: sleek, cleanly built, elegant yet well balanced. These affectionate *Cosmic Canine* Toys are very good with children. They are good-looking, intelligent, and lively—and add to that attractive, intuitive, and loyal. How much more can pet guardians ask for in canine relationships? Well, there is more. Manchesters are usually healthy and easy to keep clean; they do not shed and require minimum grooming. Females birth easily. These are very alert, self-assured dogs. They love freedom and are very independent.

Negative Traits

Manchesters can be possessive—not just of the one person with whom they bond but of food and toys as well. Early training can cure toy or food possessiveness, but Toy Manchesters may be one-person dogs for life. Once they bond as puppies, they may stay possessive and be protective of that person for their entire life. Manchesters don't like outsiders. If you like Toy breeds because of their convenient size but find their insistent demands for attention a bit of a bother, the more aloof Manchester Terriers may offer a wonderful alternative. But when adopting an older dog, other breeds are safer bets. These *Cosmic Canines* bond so strongly with their first companions, and the tie may run so deep that they won't be able to bond with new guardians. Dogs who miss the human companion with whom they first bonded can brood themselves into ill health. Better to adopt these dogs as puppies!

Job Opportunities for Manchester Terriers

They are good bark-and-warn dogs who are too small to guard, but, like Chihuahuas and Dachshunds, they will try to protect their human companions, regardless of the size of the intruder. They have brave hearts. Dogs with heart almost always make great companions. For those who like Toy breeds with independent attitudes, Manchesters bring an added plus to the relationship table. They make entertaining, reliable, daily exercise walking companions who are curious and interested in everything and everyone. Properly trained, they are affectionate dogs who keep children company.

Most Compatible Sun Sign: Aquarius

Aquarius is usually not the most compatible sign for Toy breeds, which are not happy unless they get numerous outward displays of affection each day. Natives of the Water Bearer feel things very deeply but are more action oriented than affectionate in their expressions of love. Aquarians have a lot of mental energy. Water Bearer natives are also patient, quiet, unassuming, and loyal. Like Manchesters, they are dependable, logical, thoughtful, and principled. Sincere and kind, Aquarians are very intelligent and tend to be very selective when choosing friends. Manchesters share most of these personality traits with Water Bearers (who tend to be loners). Because of independent views, dog breed and human are thought to be cold and aloof. Both are honest, nonjudgmental, and steady. The negative traits of Water Bearer natives include possessiveness, selfishness, and a lack of focus. They can be wily, tricky, arrogant, and inflexible as well as undisciplined and distant. Aquarius humans and Manchester Terriers will totally understand one another.

NORFOLK AND NORWICH TERRIERS

Positive Traits

The Norfolk has dropped ears; the Norwich has prick ears. They are two different breeds but are very, very similar. Both are even-tempered, hardy dogs. They are adaptable to most lifestyles, are fearless, and make good watch-and-warn pets. Their size, of course, prevents them from being good guard dogs. They can be feisty, but it is unusual for either to be quarrelsome. They are good with children and very lovable. These are happy dogs. For such small animals (among the smallest of the Terrier group at about ten inches high, weighing twelve pounds), they are quite powerful. These are very bright *Cosmic Canines* who enjoy working on obedience-training lessons with human companions. Be sure training sessions are not done by rote. Make them interesting and fun.

Negative Traits

Aside from having coats that need to be plucked periodically, these active tykes have no known negatives. They do need exercise. If they live in apartments, Norfolk and/or Norwich Terriers should have daily walks. Otherwise, physical energy natural to the breed gets bottled up and turns into nervous energy. This, however, is not a breed negative. Rather, it is caused by environment.

Job Opportunities for Norfolk and Norwich Terriers

These Terriers are wonderful family dogs and make excellent companions for singles, especially senior citizens. They are good company—intelligent, curious, a little more independent than some Toys. Norfolks and Nor-wiches make good obedience-training prospects. With the power per pound of these pets—and because most Terriers need a sense of purpose—human companions should have an interest in some form of dog training or other hobby in which these pets can participate. They are a little too small for fetching things since most "things" are bigger than they are.

Most Compatible Sun Sign: Gemini

Adaptable, forceful Gemini natives have much in common with adaptable, forceful Norfolk and Norwich Terriers. Also like these dogs, Geminis are changeable and sensible. Both dog breed and sun sign are bold, assertive, and confident; sensitive, inquisitive, quick, and very intelligent. A good word that describes Gemini human companions, Norfolk Terriers, and Norwich Terriers is *functional*. When in negative cycles, Gemini humans can be self-indulgent, cowardly, jittery, aloof, overconfident, belligerent, remote, and unreliable. These are normally not traits of even poorly bred Norfolk or Norwich Terriers—well, maybe aloof and over-confident. When spoiled, or if these dogs have not been properly bred,the sun sign and the dog can be easily influenced, rash, worried, inconsistent, anxious, frivolous, and high-strung. Both can be moody, restless, cantankerous, and closed. No Gemini human guardian of Norfolks and Norwiches could go into negative cycles often or for long periods. Not with these cheerful pets around to remind them how good life is!

PAPILLON

Positive Traits

Affectionate and petite in size, strong and hardy Papillons make outstanding house pets. Papillons are Toy Spaniels whose name in French means "butterfly." The breed name is explained in the way the ears are set on the heads of these *Cosmic Canines*—like butterfly wings (though some members of this breed, called Phalenes, have floppy ears and are known as "moths"). Papillons are active, flexible, and they birth easily. For families on the move, they adapt quickly to different climates and don't have moody personalities that will pine away for their old house, old yard, old friends, and such. These Toy dogs are friendly. Genetics (along with positive attitudes when dogs are well bred) make Papillons good family pets.

Negative Traits

Papillons have a tendency to be possessive of owners and do not play the welcome wagon game very well when visitors arrive. They are a little suspicious of strangers anyway, and so they are not the best pets with children who have friends coming in and out of the family home. If a new baby arrives on the scene, there may be some jealousy. Human guardians who have empty nests or can't for some reason have children but want them should become foster parents, not dog companions. Don't treat Papillons like human children. Those who do will have spoiled brats on their hands. No one will be able to touch spoiled Papillons except their "mommies" and "daddies." Never, never, never spoil *Cosmic Canines*—especially these *Cosmic Canines*. Papillons tend to be possessive; jealousy results—and along with jealousy comes nipping or biting. These dogs are so cute, it's easy to spoil them. It would be a shame to ruin otherwise wonderful pets.

Job Opportunities for Papillons

These dogs make good companions—especially for seniors with no children or grandchildren. They enjoy walking (as do all Toys) and will help retired pet owners keep in shape. Papillons bark at strangers out of fear, possessiveness, or jealousy, but otherwise are not good protection dogs. They are catlike in cleanliness. Papillons have been used to hunt rabbits and rats, and they may chase any small animal that runs in front of them. Be careful.

Most Compatible Sun Sign: Gemini

Like these dogs, Gemini humans are adaptable, changeable, refined, and sensible. Both are bold, assertive, confident, and progressive. Papillons, like Geminis, are functional, sensitive, inquisitive, quick, and very intelligent. Both have Twin (or dual) personalities—Gemini's having to do with mood, the Papillon's having to do with its sometimes catlike behavior. Both the dog and the sun sign can be self-indulgent, cowardly, jittery, aloof, overconfident, belligerent, remote, and unreliable when in negative cycles. Gemini humans are normally nice, calm people with a strong sense of refinement. In negative cycles, though, they can be remote, aloof, worried, inconsistent, anxious, frivolous, and high-strung. Papillon dogs can lovingly help their Gemini guardians stay on the positive side of their natures. Both the dog and the sun sign can be moody, restless, and closed. They innately understand one another when these negatives occur.

PEKINGESE

Positive Traits

These dogs are beautiful, calm, and good-tempered. Pekingese *Cosmic Canines* are also courageous and bold—brave guard dogs even though they're six- to fourteen-pound balls of fur (they come in three size categories). Pekes are healthy and intelligent, regal and dignified but not delicate. They love having toys to play with and are fun and funny. Fearless attitudes in Toy-size Pekes place responsibility on owners. Don't let them try to bite off more than they can chew, so to speak. They are independent and confident. Some experts say this implies combativeness rather than delicacy. Well-bred Pekes may be good with children but are best as adult companions. They like having the run of the house—kings of all they survey. Pekes enjoy but do not require exercise. They are known as "Lion Dogs." At one time it was illegal for anyone other than the Chinese royal family to own a Pekingese (their theft was punishable by death—a slow, torturous death that could not be viewed by the dog). They were kept in the Buddhist sacred temple.

Negative Traits

Pekes expect to be petted and pampered. They have aloof, independent natures. Watch for eye trouble (and ask breeders about it at the time these dogs are adopted). They need daily grooming. Pekes don't like being challenged—a trait that makes obedience training a must. While spoiling other Toy breeds creates a brat rather than a companion, if you spoil a Peke you create a monster. These dogs are best for adults and they expect to be numero uno in their masters' eyes. They do better in cool climates. Human guardians must guard against vigorous exertion and overheating of Pekes in warm weather. These dogs require extensive and regular grooming.

Job Opportunities for Pekingese

They serve best as companions in adult households. Pekes are not walking/exercise buddies, especially in warm weather. They make excellent friends and hobbies for lonely singles. Though their size makes them good travel companions, be sure they never get left in cars. They are intelligent and enjoy the time spent with human companions, though obedience training is a must in order to deal with their regal attitudes.

Most Compatible Sun Sign: Aries

Ariens, like Pekes, are original, energetic, sensible, strong, and humorous. Both like to explore (and both enjoy winning)! Also like Pekes, Aries sun sign natives can be headstrong, impulsive, high-strung, and hypersensitive. Both have a tendency to appear aloof and distant, though neither is. Aries humans are confident, intelligent, independent, and sensible—very compatible traits with the Pekingese. Both the dog breed and the sun sign are sociable, amusing, and genial. Both communicate well. Aries natives, when in negative cycles, can be jealous, domineering, shallow, impatient, and disloyal. These traits are not unfamiliar to Pekes who have been poorly bred, left untrained, or treated like human children (spoiled). Ram natives are good for these *Cosmic Canines*, and they are good for their Aries human guardians. Who can stay in negative cycles with Pekingese canines as pets?

PINSCHER (MINIATURE)

Positive Traits

These dogs are not miniatures of Doberman Pinschers, as the name im plies. Miniature Pinscher, or MinPin, markings are, however, like the Doberman, in either black and tan, stag red, or chocolate and tan. In physical build, Miniature Pinschers resemble Chihuahuas. MinPins make wonderful house dogs and enjoy obedience training. They are easy to care for and rarely shed. They are fearless, bark, and make good warning dogs; they also have spirited personalities and are known as King of the Toys. MinPins have graceful, proud gaits. These *Cosmic Canines* are very intelligent. Though not categorized as Hunting dogs (they were bred to kill rats), MinPins do follow scents and are capable of tracking. Bloodhounds have no need to be worried about their jobs, but Toy trackers are a bit unusual. Ancient genes may motivate MinPins to chase small animals that dart in front of them.

Negative Traits

Note the lack of reference to MinPins as warm, loving pets. They are not cold or aloof, but they are a little more independent than most Toys—not always looking for laps to land on. If, when human companions bring MinPins home, they let them bark, these *Cosmic Canines* learn to enjoy their own voices. It becomes a sound their guardians get to listen to for . . . some would say an eternity. If such an alternative is not attractive to you, control puppy barking from day one. Do not overfeed MinPins. They need high-protein, low-fat diets (achieved by feeding low-fat cottage cheese and ground beef mixed with low-fat dried dog meal).

Job Opportunities for Miniature Pinschers

Too small to be guard dogs, MinPins will bark and warn of danger. They are good companions, especially for those who are obedience-training hobbyists. These *Cosmic Canines* scent and bark at small vermin—mice or rats. If a pet rabbit runs in front of this dog, look out. Keep MinPins close to home when the Easter bunny is hiding hard-boiled eggs in neighborhood backyards. When the local police department's scent-and-track dog retires, MinPins trained to track might want to apply.

Most Compatible Sun Sign: Leo

Just as the MinPins are Kings of the Toys, natives born under Leo the Lion's sun sign are Kings of the Sun Signs. These dogs and this sun sign have a great deal in common—if, indeed, there is anything common about royalty. Leo natives are vital, kind, warmhearted, and noble—all things admired by MinPins. Leo humans attract others to them, a valuable asset with what is perceived as aloof dogs (though they really aren't). Leo human guardians offer MinPins personality traits that help them mellow out—Lion natives are loving, ardent, sympathetic, self-conscious, and sincere; faithful, earnest, persevering, and generous. They are energetic and decisive, just like this breed of dog. In negative cycles, Leo the Lion is egotistical, impulsive, willful, arrogant, insecure, and very superficial, with no depth or character. Only poorly bred MinPins carry these character flaws.

POMERANIAN

Positive Traits

Versatile, faithful, and loving to owners, aloof to strangers (and sometimes friends), Pomeranians are a convenient size for travel and are good for apartment dwellers. These *Cosmic Canines* normally have docile temperaments. Poms are bouncy, active, and adapt cheerfully to life in most environments—big yard, small yard, no yard. They are made to be lap dogs and enjoy that status immensely. Poms enjoy daily walks with human companions. They are able to amuse themselves in most settings and are said to be vivacious. Poms are devoted companions with curious natures and facially intelligent expressions.

Negative Traits

Poms like to hear themselves bark—some would call it "yapping." Control this from day one or don't blame these dogs when all they do as adults is bark. At eleven inches in height and six pounds in weight, these *Cosmic Canines* are not big dogs. Don't let your little Pom anger big dogs by barking at them; you may end up being a referee at a dog fight. This breed of dog needs training to help develop a calm attitude. Though they are very curious, Poms won't roll out the welcome mat for visitors. Though docile, they may not be the best dogs for very young children or households with multiple pets. Poms are great for retirees. They require regular grooming.

Job Opportunities for Pomeranians

Poms are good exercise partners (provided that exercise consists of walking) and loving pets. They will warn of danger—fire or intruders. They are not terribly demanding but give a lot of attention to the important humans in their lives. Poms were originally bred to be sheep dogs and their ancestors once pulled sleds (they were a little bigger then). They find any lifestyle acceptable, provided it is comfortable. Good apartment dogs and travel companions.

Most Compatible Sun Sign: Pisces

Human natives of this sun sign have personality traits that are truly good for Pomeranians. They are receptive, peaceful, giving, accepting, warm, original, and imaginative. Much like Pomeranians, Pisces natives are loving, tender, controlled, endearing, and neighborly—all of which offset the few potential weaknesses of this dog breed. Negative Pisces traits—unsettled, uncommitted, melancholy, excitable, introspective, fearful, and dissatisfied—can be helped by Pomeranian stability. Pomeranian consistency and bouncy attitude support Pisces weaknesses. When Pisces is down, these *Cosmic Canines* can help them stabilize. Piscean magnetism attracts aloof Pomeranians and helps them keep their calm and loving attitudes.

PUG

Positive Traits

Pugs are really miniature Mastiffs and can trace their family tree back to the Orient. They are about ten or twelve inches in height and weigh about eighteen pounds. Their coats are short, fine, and soft—smooth. They have clearly defined wrinkles on their faces. Their manageable size makes them good apartment dogs and travel companions. They have very happy dispositions and are good with children. Pugs are affectionate and intelligent, but they can also be imps with charming personalities. They make good family pets, amusing everyone. These *Cosmic Canines* are devoted to their families.

Negative Traits

People who like having their pets share their bedrooms may find Pugs create problems for them. An old wives' tale has it that Pugs snore. True or not, they do have respiratory problems—their bronchial tubes and lungs are not the best they can be. Vigorous exercise is a no-no, especially in hot, humid weather. Be careful how much you let these dogs exert themselves and don't let Pugs get overheated. No dog should ever be left alone and locked in a car, regardless of open windows. With Pugs, it can be a life-and-death situation. If their guardians overfeed them, the dogs' lives are shortened. Why? Because of limited exercise capacity, Pugs gain weight easily. They do best on high-protein, low-fat diets. To achieve this, feed low-fat dog meal, nonfat cottage cheese, and low-fat ground beef simmered in water. Save the broth and use it to pour over the dried dog meal. It gives added flavor.

Job Opportunities for Pugs

Pugs do best what they do most often: serve as family pets and good company for human guardians. Pugs can be good watch-and-warn (but not guard) dogs and will bark a warning when strangers approach. They aren't good exercise companions and should never be exposed to vigorous exercise. Provided they are not left in parked cars for any length of time while their human companions take a break at freeway restaurants, Pugs are good travel companions. These happy *Cosmic Canines* make wonderful apartment dogs and are good company for shut-ins.

Most Compatible Sun Sign: Gemini

Just as Pugs have breathing problems, lung and respiratory problems are the health weaknesses associated with human Geminis. This is not the best sun sign for Pug birthdays (just for their guardians) because it doubles breed tendencies for respiratory problems (sun sign and breed). Human Gemini natives innately sympathize with Pugs when they have difficulty breathing. Gemini human companions are adaptable, sensible, logical, analytic, and forceful. So are Pugs. Diet and sleep are key to the health of Gemini humans, as they are to this dog breed. Like Pugs, Geminians are functional, intelligent, and charmingly amusing. The happy natures of Pug dogs reach out to Twin natives (who many astrologers call "cold"). The impish natures of Pug dogs charm Gemini humans.

SHIH TZU

Positive Traits

In Chinese, Shih Tzu means "Tibetan Lion Dog." These animals hold their proud heads high, befitting their noble ancestry. The faces of these *Cosmic Canines* have been said to resemble chrysanthemums. Shih Tzus have long, dense, and luxurious coats—at least they appear luxurious when well maintained. These dogs adore human company, responding to affection in very human ways. They are hardy, intelligent, love children and other animals, and live well in either town or country. Shih Tzus are said to be resilient and have carefree, big-dog attitudes. They are happy, attractive, and extremely intelligent. Some say they are arrogant. Others simply say their proud heritage is reflected in their attitudes. They look forward to *long, daily* grooming sessions. Shih Tzus are serene, outgoing, and have generous personalities, giving all they are capable of giving.

Negative Traits

For these dogs to look as they should—which is beautiful—requires a lot of grooming. A prospective human companion should look at those beautiful faces with the long hair falling from canine muzzles and noses over their mouths and try to picture how they will look after eating dinner. Imagine the face hair dripping with beef broth. It needs to be washed. Ask yourself if you're up to giving any dog the kind of consistent, daily care these dogs require. If you are, this is one of the best Toy pets there are. If you are not such a person, chances are you might be happier with another dog breed. Shih Tzus need attention. Face hair needs to be tied in a topknot or their eyes will disappear—and they won't be able to see much of anything. Eye trouble can result if face and head hair are allowed to grow too long. Shih Tzus can also be arrogant. These dogs hate to be neglected. Human guardians need to be sure to keep matted hair and other objects out of the dog's ears.

Job Opportunities for Shih Tzus

Adorable and adoring house pets who truly understand the word *companion*, these *Cosmic Canines* provide excellent company. Seniors who seek the company of man's best friend but who are a little unsure of whether they will understand canine needs find Shih Tzus communicate in ways that are quite easily understood. These Toys are excellent bark-and-warn family members. They are also good exercise partners (though they're too small to take jogging, walks take care of their exercise needs nicely). Their size and temperaments make them ideal travel companions. Human companions who become guardians to Shih Tzu dogs truly add another member to the family.

Most Compatible Sun Sign: Leo

Can any human sun sign other than Leo qualify as most compatible with these noble animals? Just as Shih Tzus need attention, so do Leos. Leo the Lion and the Tibetan Lion Dog go together like love and marriage. Leo natives are vital, kind, warmhearted, and noble—and many (except other Leos or Shih Tzus) read arrogance into their royal carriage. People born under the sun sign Leo attract others like magnets and Shih Tzus are charmed by them. No one can be aloof with Leo humans. Both the Lion native and the Lion dog are loving, ardent, sympathetic, self-conscious, and sincere. Leo natives are faithful, earnest, persevering, and generous—just what the vet ordered for these intelligent, resilient, carefree dogs. Both are energetic and decisive. When in negative cycles, both Lions are egotistical, impulsive, willful, arrogant, insecure, and very superficial, with no depth or character. How can Leo humans and Shih Tzu dogs help but understand one another?

SILKY TERRIER

Positive Traits

Silkies are dainty, alert, and affectionate dogs. Though small (nine inches in height, eight to ten pounds), these *Cosmic Canines* are hardy and make good pets. They are intelligent and sensitive and have well-developed Terrier instincts. Remember, Terriers were originally bred to dig up rabbits, rats, and other vermin destructive to agriculture. Breeders have pretty much gotten rid of all those old genes, begetting charmers in place of rat and rabbit killers. It's still a good idea, though, to watch them as puppies. Old instincts sometimes die hard. People who live in apartments and have Silkies for roommates might want to drive out in the countryside and let them run in open fields occasionally. Silkies love to run, but be forewarned: Their luxurious hair tends to get filled with briars and weeds. They'll need a good brushing afterward.

Negative Traits

Silkies need a lot of attention. For such small dogs, they have a great deal of hair. Their coats are five or six inches long—the dog is only about nine inches high—and require frequent grooming. They can be difficult to train, especially if born under the emotionally sensitive sun signs—Cancer, Scorpio, Pisces, Taurus, Virgo, and Capricorn. Humans who choose to be Silky guardians should first check sun sign data to see which ones produce emotionally sensitive life-forms. Breeds that already produce genetically sensitive canines double that trait when born under zodiacally sensitive sun signs.

Job Opportunities for Silky Terriers

As companions to the entire family, it's hard to beat Silkies. They need a little tender, loving care and special attention to puppyhood sensitivities, but once they get through the "teenage stage" of youth with emotions intact, they are very hardy little Toys. They make good exercise partners for those who walk city blocks (let Silkies run at their own speed). Humans are quite a bit larger than they, and it can be difficult for such small *Cosmic Canines* to keep up with joggers. Once they reach emotionally solid ground in adulthood, Silkies are loving pets who provide good watch-and-warn services for human guardians. If seasonal gardens in the yard get invaded by moles, humans are in good hands with Silkies on the job. Like all Terriers, Silkies are courageous and, regardless of size, big-hearted. It's a required part of the Terrier charter.

Most Compatible Sun Sign: Pisces

Pisces natives are receptive, endearing, peaceful, giving, loving, and tender; accepting, changeable, warm, original, neighborly, and imaginative. These are all traits Silky Terriers love. Pisces humans happily give Silky Terriers all the attention they need and on which they thrive. Humans born under the sign of Pisces have what can only be called emotional magnetism, sending out and receiving vibrations from other forms of life. As a result, Pisceans are among the best people to raise emotionally sensitive young canines. When in negative cycles, Pisces natives can be unsettled, uncommitted, melancholy, excitable, introspective, fearful, and dissatisfied. Silky Terriers are stable and affectionate and stand as solid friends, easing Pisces human guardians through their negative moods. Piscean magnetism not only attracts Silkies, it also receives this dog's positive energy (which Silkies send in abundance to those they love). These life-forms are good for each other.

TIBETAN SPANIEL

Positive Traits

These Toy dogs make themselves known in their households, asserting themselves with independent, somewhat aloof and distant attitudes—all the while checking out the digs to see if they are suitable. Tibetan Spaniels are lively and, like Toy Poodles, tend to love women and bond with them more easily than they do with men. They are also known as pets for the clergy, having reputations as being somewhat prophetic, mystically spiritual animals. Aside from their shyness and aloof attitudes toward strangers, Tibetan Spaniels are well balanced and quite happy animals. These dogs have higher than average intelligence.

Negative Traits

Tibetan Spaniels don't accept as friends everyone who comes to your front door. If a lot of people stop by to visit, you might find it helpful to put your Tibetan Spaniel in his room until the drop-ins leave. Or make sure friends know that they must wait to pet these dogs until they ask for human attention. It's not that Tibetan Spaniels don't like people, they're just a little shy—though they won't tell you so. Once they get used to people, the shyness disappears. There is a limited population of these Spaniels, which make them difficult to breed. Tibetan Spaniels require some grooming, but nothing beyond reasonable.

Job Opportunities for Tibetan Spaniels

One thing about Toys with somewhat withdrawn attitudes—the kind not always looking for human laps to jump on—is that they make good watch-and-warn dogs. If it takes them awhile to warm up to family friends, it's easy to imagine the welcome prowlers will get from these *Cosmic Canines*. At ten inches in height and an average weight of twelve pounds, they are of a perfect size and attitude to make excellent travel companions (but don't leave them alone in hotel/motel rooms for maids to discover—they may get the scare of their lives when Tibetans protect family valuables). These are good pets for families with older children and are among the best pets for seniors. These Spaniels are good exercise partners. Most of all, they are intelligent, loving pets.

Most Compatible Sun Sign: Scorpio

Mysterious Scorpio and inscrutable Tibetan Spaniels go together. Like this dog breed, natives of the Scorpion are somewhat suspicious of strangers and do not offer friendship to those that have not been analyzed and tested. Scorpio human guardians have been known to seek out as friends members of the clergy and have been called mystic and spiritually intuitive. This is a dignified human companion for a dignified dog and both have mystical, spiritual learnings. Both dog and sun sign are quick-thinking, persistent, tranquil, and inquisitive. They are self-controlled, determined, and they thrive on approval (keep that in mind while training these *Cosmic Canines*). In negative cycles, Scorpions can be willful, rigid, harsh, critical, skeptical, boorish, and brusque. Tibetan

Spaniels will become slightly aloof toward Scorpio human companions during these periods and wait patiently for them to swing back to their positive sides.

YORKSHIRE TERRIER

Positive Traits

Yorkshire Terriers are devoted, hearty, fearless (even though they weigh only seven pounds or less) and, like other Toys, are good watch-and-warn (but not guard) dogs. They are ideal for apartment dwellers—tireless companions who don't need a lot of exercise. They are healthy, hardy, and fearless and show deep affection and loyalty to owners. They like everyone and are said to have a big dog's heart in a small dog's body. For their size, they are courageous and brave. People with friends who prefer not to be around dogs will either have to meet human companions of Yorkies at restaurants, or the Yorkshire Terriers need to be kept away from such people when they visit. These *Cosmic Canines* love everyone (unless spoiled rotten by doting owners, in which case they will snap at visitors). Yorkies are intelligent and energetic.

Negative Traits

Yorkies do not make good guard dogs because they like everyone. They will warn of strangers, though. If human guardians do not control barking when these dogs are young, they will be stuck with it throughout the life of their canine. Yorkshire Terriers require frequent baths and regular grooming. They also need their teeth cleaned regularly (Toy breeds lose their teeth earlier than other dogs). They should see veterinarians regularly for scheduled cleanings.

Job Opportunities for Yorkshire Terriers

People who own Yorkies swear there is no better pet companion in the world. They don't require a lot of exercise but are plucky and won't mind taking daily walks with their human companions. They are "okay" watch-and-warn dogs (a lot depends on whether they were allowed to bark at everything when they were puppies). Senior citizens love these dogs and

Yorkies are very devoted to the stability offered them in the homes of older human guardians. These dogs make great travel companions and are one of the best apartment dogs you can own. Teach them as many parlor tricks as you can—they love it and have the canine intelligence for it.

Most Compatible Sun Sign: Taurus

Taurus natives are solid, vital, practical, patient, and reserved; fearless, generous, persistent, psychic, tenacious, objective, trustworthy, enduring, and calming. It is a peaceful, sincere, reliable, faithful, determined, and friendly sun sign. These traits tend to soothe other animals and, thus, tone down the nervous energy associated with Toy breeds, and they have an especially positive effect on Yorkshire Terriers. Natives of Taurus the Bull can be just as stubborn as Terriers, which is pretty stubborn. They are strong-willed but can be fearful people who appreciate the added safety Yorkie warnings offer when trouble appears.

3

SMALL AND
MINIATURE DOGS

BASENJI

Positive Traits

The wrinkles that fill Basenji foreheads make them appear worried. Known as "the barkless dog," Basenji history goes back to the pharaohs of ancient Egypt. When Egypt fell, the dog breed was maintained in its native land of central Africa. Males are about seventeen inches high at the shoulder; females are somewhat smaller. They are proud dogs who are also beautiful and graceful. Basenjis are adaptable to most climates, are loving and gentle with children, intelligent (though they may not be the best students), very clean, and odorless. Though barkless, they growl and whine and can express themselves feelingly with unique chortles or yodels. Basenjis are very curious, love to solve problems, and are mischievous. They bait owners into playing by rubbing a paw over their face. They are fastidious about cleanliness—very much like cats. They bathe with their front paws and require little formal grooming.

Negative Traits

It is said Basenjis may bite with little or no provocation. So while they may love children and be gentle with them, parents need to weigh rumors against possible dangers. Basenjis do not like rain and beg for entry into their homes when it starts. They can be very aloof with strangers and have reputations for being independent and not very obedient. They may be difficult to breed because bitches sometimes come into season only once a year.

Job Opportunities for Basenjis

The best job for these dogs is as companions to strong people capable of handling spirited, independent animals. Generally, the only time Basenjis have social behavioral problems is when their handlers or human companions are not up to the task of disciplining and training them. Households inexperienced with dogs and families who enjoy numerous visitors all day—friends of the family, perhaps, but strangers to these dogs— might find other breeds easier to manage. These active, independent *Cosmic Canines* make good exercise and travel companions.

Most Compatible Sun Sign: Gemini

Basenji behavior is a definite reminder of the sign of the Twins—bathing like a cat? Gemini humans, like Basenji dogs, are known to change personalities at the drop of a hat. Both are multifaceted. Geminis and Basenjis are capable, refined, sensible, bold, assertive, and love analyzing and solving puzzles and problems. Both the sun sign and the dog are confident, quick, inquisitive, and sensitive, and both can be stubborn (both are viewed as aloof). Gemini humans are definitely up to giving Basenjis the kind of tough and disciplined love they need. In their negative cycles, Gemini natives can be self-indulgent, overconfident, belligerent, impetuous, worried, moody, and closed. These are all personality traits Basenjis experience themselves and, thus, understand. Diet and sleep are important to both Gemini natives and these dogs for good health to be maintained.

BEAGLE

Positive Traits

Hounds can be the most affectionate of the various breed groups, and Beagles are among the most affectionate of the Hound group. They adore children and love adults and other pets. Families with multiple pets will find Beagles fitting in very nicely. These are intelligent animals with positive, happy attitudes. They are excellent family pets, and when properly bred and trained, they still love to hunt. Beagles watch and warn of prowlers but are not guard dogs; they just love people too much to be counted on to be sufficiently assertive with prowlers. They normally do not bark without reason. Beagles are long-lived dogs with wonderful dispositions. They are notoriously healthy and robust and can keep themselves fit, even in small yards. They are very gentle and are suitable pets even for toddlers (though if not raised with very small human children, it is best to supervise them to see how they handle the unpredictability of little people).

Negative Traits

You've probably heard of the wayward wind; well, Beagles wander, so keep the garden gate closed. They don't like to be alone. These dogs are about fifteen inches high and weigh less than thirty pounds, but exercise is no problem. Beagles can be stubborn; for example, when human companions tell their *Cosmic Canines* to sit, they usually mean now, not ten minutes from now. Beagles tend to think they can do it when *they* want as long as they do what is asked of them. Don't punish Beagles. It doesn't work. Be firm; watch for them to do something right (rather than wrong) and give lots and lots of praise. Don't ignore misbehavior, just correct it in a businesslike manner—downplay the bad, emphasize the good. That way, they'll remember how human companions want things done and not the attention they got for misbehaving. Whatever they get attention for is what Beagles remember—and unfortunately repeat.

Job Opportunities for Beagles

Hunting quail, rabbit, and pheasant and helping horsemen find and chase foxes are natural jobs for these dogs. They are wonderful family pets and companions for children of all ages. They will watch and warn (most of the time), but are too affectionate to make reliable guard dogs. They are not terribly assertive about protecting their families—it's almost as if they expect their families to protect them. If a prowler opens a window, Beagles will pause and think over whether they should use this new escape hatch and roam the neighborhood, or bark a warning.

Most Compatible Sun Sign: Taurus

Like Beagles, Taurus natives are solid, vital, patient, and enduring; friendly, faithful, companionable, reliable, and sincere—trustworthy, too (very like this breed of dog). They are generous, tenacious, objective, soothing, and, generally, peaceful. Both sun sign natives and this dog breed are affectionate and giving of themselves. In negative cycles, natives of Taurus the Bull can be lazy, stubborn, strong-willed, obstinate, fearful, and selfish, as can poorly bred Beagles in bad moods. There are several sun signs that can out-stubborn any member of the Hound group, and Taurus is at the top of the list. Can Taurus humans out-stubborn Beagles born under the sign of Taurus? A tough question. Like Taurus humans, Beagles may have to watch their diets as they age.

BEDLINGTON TERRIER

Positive Traits

Energetic Terriers were born to "go to ground"—that is, dig prey from burrows in the ground. As a group, they are very loyal dogs with a noble character. In addition, Bedlingtons adore children and are good family pets. These *Cosmic Canines* are well behaved and hardy (they look like lambs that have just been shorn). They are affectionate and protective of their families and especially committed to making sure children are protected. Bedlingtons are speedy, with very fast gallops for animals of their size (about sixteen inches at the withers). Like all Terriers, they are courageous. They have been known to hold wild animals three times their size at bay. Bedlingtons are muscular, solid, hardy dogs who seldom gain weight as they age. Their positive, enthusiastic attitudes make them easy to train. They have unique senses of canine humor and sometimes appear to be laughing at, rather than with, their human companions.

Negative Traits

Bedlingtons can be aggressive and are formidable fighters when provoked. European Gypsies once used them as pit fighters—they may look sheepish, but are more than able to take care of themselves. Bedlingtons can be jealous. While they are good protectors for children, they are not the best dog for youngsters under age ten. Their coats, which are a combination of hard and soft hair that usually curls, need consistent grooming. These dogs are fast. They need to be kept leashed in public places where a small animal might run in front of them. They can be gone before human companions can get the word *no* out of their mouths.

Job Opportunities for Bedlington Terriers

Bedlingtons are good household pets for families with older children. If raised with very small human children so they grow used to them from puppyhood, they will also be good around very little people. They make good protectors, particularly of children and property. When properly bred and trained, they are hunters of rats, otters, badgers (game that burrows underground), and small game. As long as they are properly leashed, they make fun, interesting exercise companions. These dogs have very positive attitudes toward life.

Most Compatible Sun Sign: Scorpio

Natives of the Scorpion, like Bedlington Terriers, are optimistic, decisive, and inquisitive. Both the sun sign and the dog breed have great strength of character and exhibit loyalty and faithfulness, but both have dominant personalities. Human Scorpios and Bedlingtons are self-controlled and thrive on approval. Both are suspicious of strangers and do not give their trust to just anyone. Scorpio humans and Bedlington dogs are friendly, persistent, and very quick thinkers. Both can be affectionate once trust is earned, and both are determined and assertive. In their negative cycles, Scorpions can be willful, rigid, critical, skeptical, and aggressive. So can poorly bred Bedlington Terriers. Both are practical and tend to see things as they are. Both can be overly protective and both adore children. These two have a great deal in common!

BICHON FRISE

Positive Traits

Looking a bit like foot-high, stocky French Poodles, their plumed tails holding a slight curl and carried over their hindquarters, these *Cosmic Canines* are active, cheerful, and devoted. Carefree should be the middle name of all Bichons. They've been around since before the 1300s and know tomorrow always comes, so why worry about it? They will never suffer from stress-induced high blood pressure. They are just too happy and stress-free. They have peppy gaits and look exactly like what they are: glad to be alive! This dog breed may not have IQs quite as high as those of Poodles, but their one-of-a-kind canine charm more than makes up for it. Though Bichons Frises have abundant, curly white outer coats with an undercoat of substance, they almost never shed. They are sweet natured pets who are forever busy doing something. They have a curious, entertaining nature and thrive with human companions who create simple mysteries for them to solve.

Negative Traits

Human companions who want their white balls of Bichon Frise fur to look their best will find they require regular grooming at home, with occasional trips to the beauty shop. They are not the best watch-and-warn dogs—they like everyone and have no particular suspicion of strangers. They may not be the easiest dogs to house-train and require more diligent attention to learn household manners than some other pets. Animals born under Cardinal Modalities have similar problems with concentration and learning. Doubling up on a learning difficulty trait (breed genetics plus astrological inclinations) should be avoided. Be sure and check sun sign information to see which ones are Cardinal. Bichons Frises are only slightly larger than most Toy breeds and should not be exposed to unsupervised playtime with children younger than school age without adult supervision.

Job Opportunities for Bichons Frises

These *Cosmic Canines* are devoted household companions, particularly for singles, seniors, and families with older children. Good daily-walk exercise companions. Both size and temperament make them good apartment dogs. It is, however, more difficult for those who live in apartments to potty-train canines and people should ask themselves if they are up to the task of gently but firmly making sure these dogs get sufficient exposure to the outdoors (or indoor accommodations). Bichons are clowns and entertainers who love to perform for audiences. Human companions can train these canines and try to get them jobs when Ringling Brothers raises circus tents locally or Hollywood cameras come to town looking for talent.

Most Compatible Sun Sign: Leo

These dogs make Leo humans laugh, and that laughter encourages Bichons Frises to rise to even greater heights of entertainment. Leo natives have forceful, magnetic personalities and hearts tempered with kindness and love. Human Lions charm these dogs right out of their socks. Since Bichons Frises have been entertaining human companions since the Dark Ages, these dogs may even be able to give natives of the Lion a lesson or two in the charm department—an art at which Lions excel. Leo's nobility makes Bichons Frises feel right at home and this sun sign's sense of sincerity and earnestness makes these dogs feel they are in the presence of God—all of which will be accepted by Leo natives as their due. Leo human companions can be impulsive, willful, and arrogant, but this negative side to the human Leo's nature won't bother a Bichon Frise at all. If anyone can be more egotistical then Leo humans going through negative cycles, it is this dog.

BOSTON TERRIER

Positive Traits

Boston Terriers are attractive, affectionate, and easy to look after. They are *excellent* watch-and-warn dogs (among the best), and they do it all with smiles on their faces. At least, it looks that way. Some people say the sole purpose of this dog breed is to give and receive attention. The same people say companionship is the primary function in life for Boston Terriers. These dogs are easy to live with and easy to love. They are good family pets, require little grooming, are odorless, and don't shed much. They love to play with children of all ages, but are primarily good with school-aged children. They are obedient and have a playful nature. Boston Terriers hold great appeal for apartment and city dwellers because they need minimum care and minimum outdoor exercise. They are not much bigger than some of the Toy breeds, and though they are not aggressive, they can defend themselves should the need arise. Perhaps the best word to describe Boston Terriers is charming. Or maybe the word is loving . . . perhaps, playful. Whatever words are used, they should be positive. Boston Terriers are.

Negative Traits

Boston Terriers have very big egos. They can be arrogant little things, especially when treated like children rather than canines. When spoiled, they can be jealousy nippers and act like little Bonaparte tyrants. They are not the hardiest of dogs—keep them out of drafts or they can catch cold. And Boston Terriers are not the easiest dogs to breed. Keep an eye out for eye trouble. These clever little dogs are living proof of the old axiom "Give them an inch, they'll take a mile." These *Cosmic Canines* have a bit of a stubborn streak, too. Their human companions should be of the patient variety, calm of nature, and capable of giving enthusiastic praise. Those three things will be required to complete any kind of training, especially obedience work.

Job Opportunities for Boston Terriers

These *Cosmic Canines* are good watch-and-warn dogs and wonderful, loving family pets. They make excellent companions, especially for seniors. To show how flexible and multifaceted they are, Boston Terriers also make equally good play pals for school-aged children. They are good canines for apartment dwellers and people confined indoors. They are quite intelligent, capable of learning whatever human companions are capable of teaching.

Most Compatible Sun Sign: Pisces

No one understands companionship better than receptive, peaceful, and accepting natives of the Fishes—except maybe Boston Terriers. Like these dogs, natives of this sun sign are easy to live with, easy to love. Also like the dog, Pisceans can be charming, loving, endearing, and compassionate. The sensitivities of humans born under the sign of the Fishes are very similar to those of these dogs—as are their egos and, sometimes, resulting arrogance. They see themselves as "one of a kind"—and they are. Pisces humans are very pro-individual. Both dog breed and human Pisceans are neighborly, warm, and sympathetic. Both have unique senses of humor and love to play—though Pisces natives can be a little too intense for real humor. Piscean magnetism both gives and gains peace in relationships with Boston Terriers. When Pisces humans get in one of their Fishy moods—obsessive or narcissistic or afraid or dissatisfied—Boston Terriers are good friends who can help bring Pisceans back to their positive sides. And these dogs are patient enough to outwait almost anyone about almost anything. One word accurately describes both of these life-forms: original. They fit like white on rice.

CAVALIER KING CHARLES

Positive Traits

These are loving, devoted *Cosmic Canines*, very similar in looks and nature to English Toy Spaniels (though slightly bigger and heavier). Like Toy Spaniels, the Cavalier King Charles (also Spaniels) have genuinely warm, sweet personalities. They are loyal but playful. They love children of all ages and, if properly bred (and if the child is properly trained to respect canine friends), can be trusted with very small children. These pets love to please their companions and are highly responsive to them. If you need cheering up, this is one of the best pets to do it. In addition to all of the "cute" things about Cavalier King Charles Spaniels, there is a certain elegance about them, too. They were, after all, bred to please the tastes of England's ruling monarch. Cavalier King Charles Spaniels are easily cared for, are good roommates, and are a little less fragile than English Toy Spaniels.

Negative Traits

Aside from being slightly more difficult to house-train than some other dog breeds, these dogs have no known negatives. Though Cavalier King

Charles Spaniels are very good even with toddlers, adults should supervise play sessions to ensure that no disrespectful behavior toward the dog
(motivated by normal toddler curiosity) occurs and that absolutely no
assertive moves by the dog are made toward little people. All dogs will defend themselves against pain, but should never be aggressive, especially
with little humans.

Job Opportunities for Cavalier King Charles Spaniels

They are, in the twenty-first century, what they were bred for hundreds of
years ago: loving and devoted home companions to human beings of all
ages. They were at one time bred to flush fowl and, properly trained,
could probably still flush woodcocks for interested hunters. Excellent
walking exercise and travel companions, they love and need exercise. For
humans who live in apartments and have the discipline to make sure dogs
get sufficient exercise, these *Cosmic Canines* are wonderful pets.

Most Compatible Sun Sign: Taurus

Not only do Taureans' loving natures and patient, attentive personalities
appeal to these dogs, but the sensitivity, loyalty, faithfulness, and cheeri-
ness of Cavalier King Charles personalities will captivate natives of the
Bull. Taurus-born humans have the gentle tenacity that gives added attention to the detail required to house-train these dogs. Both are gentle
yet vital, elegant yet down-to-earth, generous yet practical. These two
were made for each other. Both dogs and sun sign natives are faithful, reliable, sincere, and trustworthy. Who could ask for anything more? Well,
maybe these *Cosmic Canines* when Taurus natives go into negative cycles
and become obstinate, dogmatic, and excitable. This Spaniel will coax
them out of it rather quickly. Who can resist such charm? And any dog
that can handle a monarch can easily handle Taureans!

DACHSHUND (STANDARD)

Positive Traits

The name Dachshund translates to "badger dog." There is artwork as
early as the fifteenth century showing dogs with long bodies, short legs,

and long, Hound-type ears on the hunt looking for badgers. Strength, stamina, courage, and persistence were required to hunt opponents weighing upwards of forty pounds, especially for dogs weighing from sixteen to twenty-two pounds. Today's modern Dachshunds, bred to be house pets, are still vigorous and tireless when outside. Inside they are affectionate and responsive, funny, and good watch-and-warn dogs—they have loud barks for such small animals. Dachshunds are brave, easy to look after, and make wonderful, loyal family pets. These *Cosmic Canines* truly have a sense of fun about them and will entertain everyone, young and old. They are friendly, sleek, and easily kept. Yet they are hardy. They do like to dig. Some Hound lovers believe Dachshunds are more Terrier than Hound. They are clever, lively, courageous to the point of rashness— all Terrier traits.

Negative Traits

Though Dachshunds are one of the more intelligent breeds in the Hound group, they are also known for their self-willed disobedience. Dachshunds should not be allowed to jump on furniture. It strains their backs—and they are prone to disk trouble. Human companions need to be considerate of this potential problem when teaching these pets tricks that might harm their backs. In addition to good old-fashioned German stubbornness, Dachshunds can be slightly aggressive with strangers. They are suspicious of nonfamily members until they get to know them. They can be distant and aloof when unhappy; despondent when sad.

Job Opportunities for Dachshunds

These *Cosmic Canines* make good household and family pets and excellent companion dogs. Their loud barks make them exceptionally good watch-and-warn dogs. Prowlers will hear their big bark and think they are dealing with Dobermans rather than Dachshunds! These pets are good travel companions, but lift them into the car, don't let them jump. Dachsies also enjoy making the jogging or brisk walking rounds with human companions. With proper training, they are still good hunters of otter, badger, and fox. These are not the best pets for obedience training for seniors—Dachsies are built very close to the ground; if you have arthritis, their stubbornness may require numerous bends to get them to comply with your requests.

Most Compatible Sun Sign: Capricorn

Capricorn is a balanced, fair, persevering, and persistent sun sign. So, too, are Dachshunds. Capricorns are careful, have an independent sense of humor (very like these dogs), and are self-reliant, determined, and patient. These two were made for each other! Natives of the Goat, like Dachshunds, pay attention to detail. In their negative states, Capricorns can be obstinate, suspicious, sad, cold, distant, and aloof. Dog breed and sun sign need cheerful environments in order to thrive. Despondency and melancholy can make both ill. Both need and give affection, but pretty much on their own terms. Capricorn natives will not be deterred by Dachshund stubbornness. Neither will they compete with it (like natives of some other sun signs might).

DANDIE DINMONT TERRIER

Positive Traits

Dandies were bred to hunt otter and badgers. These quiet, brave *Cosmic Canines* were made famous—indeed, were given their breed name—by Sir Walter Scott (who owned several Dandie Dinmonts) in his book *Guy Mannering*. Scott referred to them as fearless little creatures. Indeed, they are courageous; many of them died during World War II. Though not famous outside the Netherlands, the "Hollandse Smoushond" (as the Dutch call them) are so filled with personality, they are capable of schmoozing people. They are also affectionate and make very good house pets. Dandies are longer than they are tall (about ten inches high), have short front legs, large heads, and, with their large, sensitive eyes, can be called nothing short of cute. Their looks and personalities won royal favor in the 1700s and 1800s, as can be seen in a Gainsborough painting from 1770. Dandie Dinmonts have keen senses of humor and are excellent watch-and-warn dogs. They are responsive but sufficiently self-willed to give handlers a "Why are you making me do this?" look when asked to do something they do not like. This dog breed is independent, determined, and reserved.

Negative Traits

Some trainers have questioned the adaptability of Dandies to obedience work. Perhaps these dogs are just too independent for it. They can be clowns and are industrious, but they can also be stubborn. When roused (usually in hunt settings), Dandie Dinmonts can be the fiercest of all Terriers. And that's pretty fierce. They tend to be one-person dogs whose friendship and respect must be earned. To prove how much the companions with whom they bond mean to them, they are downright rowdy and loud when playing, but quite standoffish and quiet when they are around strangers. They have deep barks (sure to deter prowlers) for such small animals and need yard space. Dandies definitely have their own ideas about the way things ought to be and won't hesitate to let people know when their ideas disagree with those of their human companions. They need firm hands to guide them. They can find some troublesome roads to go down when left to their own devices.

Job Opportunities for Dandie Dinmont Terriers

These *Cosmic Canines* are good companions for people with common sense and firm (yet gentle) pet hands. They need guidance from people, not abuse. They like to obey but are not the best (maybe not even good) obedience-training prospects. A lot depends on human companion training techniques. It's not so much attitude problems as it is independence statements. Dandies are excellent watch-and-warn dogs, and both size and temperament make them good travel companions. They are wonderful exercise partners. When properly bred and trained, Dandie Dinmonts can still excel at sport hunting or digging moles out of yards.

Most Compatible Sun Sign: Libra

The fair, balanced, and very independent Libra personality is just what these dogs need. This sun sign is well ordered, kind, amiable, courteous, and will brook no nonsense from stubborn household pets. Librans correct their pets intelligently, with gentle firmness, but they do correct them. No sun sign natives are kinder or more pleasant while making it very clear that though the pets are loved, the household does not revolve around them and their wishes. Like Libra native Dwight Eisenhower, command comes naturally to this sun sign. Librans are also very perceptive and intuitive—required talents with these clever, brave dogs. Dandies will love Librans for their generous, compassionate, and idealistic outlooks on life, and will find them restful, calming companions. The Libra sense of humanity bridges the negatives Dandie Dinmonts may exhibit (many of which are just part of their charm). Just like Dandies, if Libra natives get pushed into corners, they tend to come out fighting. That's a personality Dandie Dinmonts can understand and appreciate!

FOX TERRIER (WIREHAIR AND SMOOTH)

Positive Traits

Remember Nick and Nora Charles's dog, Asta, in the now-classic *Thin Man* movies—the dog's name used so often in crossword puzzles? That personality kid was a Fox Terrier, and they were originally bred to run with Foxhound packs. Males are only about fifteen inches at the shoulder (females are somewhat smaller), and so larger dogs in the pack ran the fox to ground. At that point, Fox Terriers took over and burrowed (dug) into the fox's tunnel for the kill. This history should give you some insights into the personalities of these *Cosmic Canines*. They are jaunty, impulsive, flamboyant, and vogue. Fox Terriers are first-rate companions and are very good with children older than school age—they may try to dominate younger children. They are a little too exuberant for toddlers and infants. They are intelligent and look it. Fox terriers are cheerful and, as it relates to their hunting functions, when properly bred for it, are easily trained. These are very alert dogs, full of (as the old saying goes) piss and vinegar. They may be scrappy, but like Poodles, they enjoy learning tricks and performing for audiences.

Negative Traits

Fox Terriers need a lot of exercise. Older children who can toss Frisbees for them will gain the loyal appreciation of these dogs. They need human companions who are steady and firm. Consistent, disciplined training of Fox Terriers needs to begin no later than six months of age. If they are not trained while puppies, they can be very stubborn. If spoiled—treated like a child—Fox Terriers can become dominating tyrants. Wirehaired Fox

Terriers need regular home grooming plus visits to a professional. The smooth-haired variety need only occasional brushings. These dogs are not really suited for apartment living.

Job Opportunities for Fox Terriers

Whatever their job, these clever dogs need handlers who can outthink them. They are good exercise companions—though they need more than daily walks—and are good household pets for families with older children. They make good bark-to-warn dogs but are not good for guard work. Their energy levels and exercise needs do not make them the best travel companions other than for very well-organized humans who will make sure these dogs have time to exercise. These canines need yards (or at least daily jogging exercise). A run in the country every so often will be a hit with Fox Terriers.

Most Compatible Sun Sign: Sagittarius

Sons and daughters of the Archer share with this dog breed bright, lively, happy dispositions. Fox Terriers and Sagittarius natives are enterprising, purposeful, loyal, affectionate, and both require freedom (and exercise). Sagittarians are insightful, active, honest, giving, and sincere—and so are Fox Terriers. This sun sign is devoted, intuitive, and not stubborn by nature; they are very capable of providing the firm, steady, and consistent direction required. It is unlikely that natives of the Archer will allow Fox Terriers to either outthink or dominate them. Negative Sagittarian traits include a tendency to be domineering, lazy, restless, and irritable. Like these dogs, Sagittarians need exercise, but they also need to guard against overexertion. These two share very similar personalities, though Sagittarians may be a little less flamboyant.

IRISH TERRIER

Positive Traits

Said to have been in Ireland before Saint Patrick got there, these very animated, daredevil *Cosmic Canines* are alert and very loyal protectors. Irish Terriers can be very assertive—not to be confused with aggressive (except with other animals)—but they love people. They have been called versatile and spirited by some and are known to be unrelenting in courage and individuality. Terriers have reputations for being snappy, but Irish Terriers have managed to avoid this tag. They are good with children over ten but may be a little too energetic and plucky for very small youngsters. These dogs are very faithful and have been known to track their owners over long distances. Their solid wheat or red coat even makes these people-loving, good-tempered dogs *look* Irish.

Negative Traits

These may not be the best canines for multiple-pet homes. Human companions who are guardians of more than one pet might do better with another choice. Irish Terriers don't care for other animals and have been known to pick fights with them. If you own an Irish Terrier and are thinking of buying your kids a pet rabbit or hamster, don't. Irish Terriers were bred as ratters and may have some lingering genetic view of small animals as fair game—and a genetic propensity to dig. It largely depends on whether they get sufficient exercise. Puppyhood training is the key (it can help if you keep Terrier toenails trimmed).

Job Opportunities for Irish Terriers

These are courageous protectors of hearth and home, family pets, and faithful companions. When properly bred and trained, they are versatile gun- and fox-hunting dogs. These *Cosmic Canines* were used to deliver messages during World War I. Obedience-training Irish Terriers makes for a good hobby. They are enthusiastic exercise companions and good travelers. Teach these dogs to fetch the paper, slippers, or whatever is of a size these eighteen-inch-tall canines can handle. They are intelligent and enthusiastic and enjoy learning whatever human companions are capable of teaching them.

Most Compatible Sun Sign: Aries

Humans born under the sun sign of Aries are, like Irish Terriers, assertive, versatile, spirited, original, and energetic. Ariens are one of the zodiac's primary risk-takers and they are also sensible, strong, and humorous. Also like Irish Terriers, natives of the Ram can be headstrong, impulsive, a little too competitive, and hypersensitive about winning. Both appear to be aloof and distant. Aries natives are confident, intelligent, independent, and sensible—very compatible traits with these *Cosmic Canines*. The dog breed and the sun sign are sociable, amusing, and genial. In their negative cycles, natives of the Ram can be jealous, domineering, egocentric, deceptive, and disloyal. These words are not unfamiliar to Irish Terriers who have been poorly bred or improperly raised.

LAKELAND TERRIER

Positive Traits

These dogs, from the Lake District (Cumberland) of England, are one of the oldest working Terriers. As hunters of fox, badger, and otter, Lakeland Terriers are known for their persistence, dedication, and courage. These *Cosmic Canines* are very solidly built animals. In home settings, Lakelands are attractive dogs with nice, quiet dispositions. They are excellent with children and are fine watch-and-warn dogs. They have a strong warning bark. Though they are among the best hunting Terriers, Lakelands adapt nicely to life as home-dwelling pets, make good family dogs, and are known for their faithfulness to human companions. They are a convenient medium size (about fourteen inches at the shoulder), and humans who have served as their guardians know them to be hard workers.

Negative Traits

Though Lakeland Terriers have quiet dispositions, they are very lively—perhaps too lively to be the best dogs for very young children. A lot depends on the parents of little people, on their ability to discipline both dog and child for inappropriate behavior. Parents who have difficulty controlling their children may not be able to control these dogs. Lakelands need regular exercise. Their coats are dense and weather-resistant, requiring regular (though not frequent) grooming. All Terriers have a tendency to dig—that's what they were bred for—and, depending on their genetic makeup, may find irresistible the urge to chase small animals who run in front of them. So keep them leashed when in public.

Job Opportunities for Lakeland Terriers

Their primary love and occupation is hunting fox, otter, badger, rats, and all underground vermin. Since few vermin of this kind are found in suburban backyards, jobs are a little scarce these days. However, Lakelands can get jobs with commerce and industry, finding underground vermin in storage compartments and warehouses, then digging them from their underground hideouts. And they can get paid (probably the minimum wage). Lakelands are wonderful companions for seniors and make excellent family pets in homes with school-aged children. They are good exercise and travel companions, watch-and-warn dogs, and loving additions to any household with human adults capable of working with spirited animals.

Most Compatible Sun Sign: Taurus

Like Lakeland Terriers, Taureans are practical, solid, enduring, persistent, determined, and faithful. One story about these dogs from English history (1871) exemplifies the applicability of these traits to the dog breed as well. While hunting fox, a Lakeland Terrier followed an otter twenty-four feet underground. For three days, the Lakeland's owners had to blast the earth away to get the dog. Taurus humans understand such persistence and commitment. Lakeland Terriers are lively and respond positively to the soothing, peaceful aura of Taurus humans. In their negative cycles, both the dog and the sun sign humans can be obstinate, stubborn, strong-willed, excitable, and selfish. What's the old saying? It takes one to know one.

MANCHESTER TERRIER

Positive Traits

These *Cosmic Canines* are clean, friendly, lively pets who love their families. Manchesters are great sporting companions, long-lived, and they enjoy homes in either town or country. They are hardy dogs who are seldom ill. Fix them a bed by the family room fireplace, and Manchester Terriers think they are in dog heaven. That's where they are happiest—around their families (and feeling just a little pampered). Manchesters were originally bred to hunt and kill rats and need no lessons in fulfilling that function. Obedience training is a different matter. They have been called "wise"—a rather unusual human description for canines—because they have shown what appears to be judgment. Manchesters, like Arabian horses, are sleek and streamlined. They are individualistic, eager, and good-natured. They are congenial pets of a convenient size for travel and require minimum grooming. They do need exercise—more than a daily leisurely walk around the block. Those who love them say no breed is superior to Manchesters. They have innately clean habits, are easy to care for, and, in the olden days, were known as the "gentleman's Terrier" (in England, of course).

Negative Traits

Like all Terriers, Manchesters can be stubborn. They aren't trying to be difficult; they just sometimes get a stubborn bee in their bonnets and have a difficult time shaking it loose. Praise and patience work better than voices raised in recrimination. Remember, dogs that tend to be stubborn can be led, but seldom pushed or dragged. Manchesters tend to be one-person dogs. And like most Terriers, they react almost instantly to small objects darting erratically in front of them. Keep them leashed when they are in public places because unexpected movement can cause them to leave your side like a shot—too fast for people to stop them. These Terriers are known to be great individualists with good-natured temperaments and nice personalities.

Job Opportunities for Manchester Terriers

The more excitable the dog, the easier it is for them to bark at strangers. Manchesters are as high-strung as some Terriers and so are not the best watch-and-warn dogs. Though not the greatest dogs with small children, they are wonderful family pets, travel and exercise companions, and the best for single seniors. Though no longer bred to do so, most Manchesters can still find and take care of burrowing animals or rats. These are very convenient, easy-care animals.

Most Compatible Sun Sign: Aquarius

Natives of the Water Bearer are patient, quiet, unassuming, and loyal—just like Manchester Terriers. Aquarians will easily lead these pets through their stubborn streaks, using the logic skills for which they are famous. There are many things about Water Bearers these *Cosmic Canines* like and respect. They motivate trust, are dependable, are very intelligent, and have a tendency to be loners—neither the sun sign humans nor the dog breed thrives on crowds. Nor do either of these two make a lot of friends, but the ones they have are very close and loyal. Natives of this sun sign are honest, steady, principled, and sincere. They, too, can be pretty fixed about bees that land in their bonnets. In their negative cycles, Aquarians can be disorganized, scattered, arrogant, inflexible, unfocused, and undisciplined. Having loyal, quiet pets like Manchester Terriers around—pets requiring disciplined schedules and care—helps Aquarians stay on the positive side of their personalities.

POODLE (MINIATURE)

Positive Traits

These dogs are easy to enjoy (if not easy to keep groomed). They are affectionate, dainty, and hold much appeal for dog lovers. Miniature Poodles are extremely intelligent and make wonderful obedience-training students. These *Cosmic Canines* are solidly built and elegant, graceful, and full of fun. They love pleasing those they love, and enjoy even more being pleased by them. They are sensitive to companions' needs and expect the same. They love to learn tricks and perform stunts. In fact, they love to perform. Period. They can learn just about anything it's possible to teach canines. Miniature Poodles generally enjoy long, healthy lives. As much as the author loves German Shepherds and Dobermans (and admires their intelligence), she must admit that Poodles tend to learn things in about one-third less time than these other, highly intelligent breeds of dog.

Negative Traits

Control unnecessary barking from the day you welcome Miniature Poodles home. They can be pretty noisy adults if barking is left unchecked in their youth. Miniature Poodles can be very sensitive and may not be the best dogs for young children. Professional grooming is required. Their coats are luxuriantly thick and closely curled and must receive consistent grooming because, like humans, their fur grows.

Because Miniature Poodles are so popular, it is necessary to do more investigative work into parental temperament and background than with other dogs. Whenever a breed becomes as overwhelmingly popular as this one, all puppies are easy to sell. Unscrupulous people, more interested in manufacturing puppies in puppy mills than in careful dog breeding, take advantage of breed popularity. They inbreed and inbreed until severe temperament problems result. Such is the case with many Miniature Poodles (and German Shepherds and Doberman Pinschers . . . with all popular dog breeds).

Properly bred, there are few animals with more pleasing personalities or who can make greater contributions to happy family life. Improperly bred, they are insufferable and, sometimes, dangerous. Because of their intelligence, Miniature Poodles are preferred by older people looking for pets to replace children who have left home. Aside from poor breeding, the other way to spoil Miniature Poodles is to treat them like human children rather than the wonderful canine friends they are. When treated as children rather than dogs, they have a tendency to become jealous and nip at anyone they perceive to be a threat to their relationships with their owners—like grandchildren.

Job Opportunities for Miniature Poodles

Poodles are excellent retrievers who enjoy swimming into the lake or pond to bring ducks back to happy hunters. They are good Gundogs. People who need clowns to perform at birthday parties can teach their Miniature Poodles some tricks and turn them loose. Excellent for obedience-training hobbyists and wonderful family companions. Properly bred, raised, and trained, Poodles actually add a new dimension to family life with their intelligence and humor.

Most Compatible Sun Sign: Leo

Who but Leo the Lion could compatibly understand what it's like to be born to live life on center stage? Leo humans are just as magnetic as Miniature Poodles and just as warmhearted, too. Leo natives are vital, kind, and noble. They are very generous and sympathetic. And like Miniature Poodles, Leo human companions are very sensitive. They have egos that bruise with the slightest unintended insult. Both dog and sun sign are faithful and protective, intelligent and forceful. Leo humans enjoy Miniature Poodle personalities tremendously, laughing at the comic antics of these *Cosmic Canines.* Humans born under the sign of the Lion enjoy teaching these pets both obedience and tricks. And no one enjoys performing in the conformation ring with champion-quality canines more than natives of the Lion (remember, Leo, it's the dog that's on stage).

SCHIPPERKE

Positive Traits

The original name for these dogs was Scheperke, which means "shepherd." Later, it was changed to Schipperke, which means "little skipper." These *Cosmic Canines* have foxy faces and abundant black coats (some are tan or a fawn color, but the official AKC color for this breed is black) and were originally bred to guard canal barges, tied up for the night along riverfronts. These are active, lively dogs who are also faithful to human companions. They love the outdoors and are hardy little animals (weighing up to eighteen pounds). These days, Schipperkes are more at home in front of family room fireplaces than they are guarding barges, but they are still excellent watch-and-warn dogs. If they were bigger, they would also guard and protect. Schipperkes are particularly good with school-aged children and their handy size (maximum twenty pounds) makes them good city or country dogs, good apartment or house dogs. They are very affectionate and, with the right families, tend to live long, happy lives.

Negative Traits

Canines of this dog breed can be unfriendly to strangers—remember Schipperke roots. These dogs need affection (and return it in abundance). Schipperkes don't take to strangers, even family friends. They need individual attention and like to be treated as members of the family (and may have hurt feelings when they are left out of people-only functions). The small size of Schipperkes and their quick reactions to erratic movements are the only things that prevent them from being recommended as good for very small children. Schipperkes can be loners and may not be the best dogs for families with multiple pets.

Job Opportunities for Schipperkes

If you are into boating and want a watch-and-warn dog onboard, Schipperkes were bred for the task. These lively animals can be quite noisy. They are good exercise and travel companions and make good family pets with school-aged, or older, children.

Most Compatible Sun Sign: Capricorn

Independent humans born under the sign of Capricorn understand and are understood by Schipperkes. Both are faithful companions who understand the significance of loyalty and commitment—and neither gives either indiscriminately. Like these *Cosmic Canines*, Capricorn natives are balanced and fair. Both are self-reliant, calm, determined, and patient. Though friendly, Schipperkes are suspicious of strangers—and so are Capricorns. Both need individual attention and affection. Like all independent creatures (human or canine), Capricorns and Schipperkes are thought to be aloof or distant, even cold, by those more dependent for happiness on the approval of others. Nothing could be farther from the truth. Sun sign natives of the Goat, along with this dog breed, simply need out of love; they do not love because of need. Careful, persistent, practical Capricorn humans are ready-made companions for careful, persistent, and practical Schipperkes. When Capricorns go into negative cycles—sad, despondent, suspicious, gloomy, impatient—these dogs, with their lively, affectionate personalities, pull them back to the positive side of the tracks.

SCHNAUZER (MINIATURE)

Positive Traits

Identifiable by their elegant, mixed gray and salt-and-pepper wiry coat, abundant wiry whiskers, and stocky, stable build, Miniature Schnauzers are intelligent, obedient dogs, lively and very good-natured. They can be personality kids, too. Miniature Schnauzers adore children—and owners are frequently tempted to treat them like children (resist the urge). Their affectionate natures make them highly appealing. Schnauzers are Terriers, though their larger size prevents them from burrowing underground.

They have largely lost their genetic instinct for digging. These *Cosmic Canines* are, nonetheless, among the best watch-and-warn dogs. Miniature Schnauzers are perfect examples of the difference between "assertive" and "aggressive." They are usually not at all "overly assertive"—meaning they are not at all aggressive. Yet they are certainly capable of asserting their own unique and lovable personalities within their homes. They usually enjoy long, happy lives. Properly raised as puppies, Miniature Schnauzers are known for their good, balanced temperaments. They are most happy sharing homes with their families—they are definitely not outside dogs. Their high intelligence makes them easy to obedience-train.

Negative Traits

There are no negative traits associated with this dog breed. If Schnauzers are spoiled (which everyone is tempted to do because they are *so* sweet), they can exhibit aggressive behavior motivated by jealousy when visitors arrive or another family member spends too much time away from the dog—for example, helping kids with their homework, you know, parental nonsense (from the dog's point of view). They do require grooming and, usually, annual clips, but nothing of substance. They may need to be dipped annually as treatment for possible skin problems.

Job Opportunities for Miniature Schnauzers

Primarily, these *Cosmic Canines* are bred to be family pets and companions to humans of all ages. They are good exercise partners (at a slow jogging speed); they are perfectly sized and have ideal temperaments to be travel companions. Protective Schnauzers are also excellent watch-and-warn dogs (not guard duty, though). Mostly, these dogs were created to love and be loved.

Most Compatible Sun Signs: Taurus, Gemini, Cancer, Leo, Virgo, Libra, Scorpio

Those sun signs known for their ability to express warmth outwardly are precisely what these *Cosmic Canines* need. Miniature Schnauzers tolerate Taurean stubbornness and love and respond very positively to the calm, peaceful nature exhibited by natives of the Bull and the vitality for life they exude. Gemini Twin human companions offer these dogs playful, charitable, ever-changing, and refined environments—and Miniature

Schnauzers easily overlook occasional Gemini bouts with moody, self-indulgent, cantankerous, and aloof behavior (who can be cantankerous for long with these pets around?). Cancerians so love their homes—they are calm, compassionate, and have a gently giving nature—all of which enchants Miniature Schnauzers. They will ignore the darker side of the Crab (fearful, limited, brooding, and timid). Leonine showmanship, kindness, and warmhearted exhibitions of love of pets captivate these playful animals. They can overlook the willful arrogance, the egotistical behavior, and the lack of depth that sometimes plagues natives of the Lion. Virgoan tact and innocence bring out the best in Miniature Schnauzers. They love Virgo's calm, wise, reasoned, and precise approach to life, but won't much care for the Virgin's tendency to criticize or be overly sensitive, dull, boring, or greedy. Libra natives are affectionate, balanced, kind, and amiable (humorous and refined, too)—attitudes that appeal to most animals. They are restful and pleasant, though this dog will more than anything appreciate their courtesy and harmony. Miniature Schnauzers will overlook a Libra human's sometimes combative, insensitive, unfocused, thoughtless, and indecisive ways. As for Scorpio human companions, Miniature Schnauzers are curious and enjoy solving puzzles as much as any *Cosmic Canine.* Mysterious by nature, Scorpio humans are happy to give Schnauzers new puzzles to solve each day. And Scorpions show these pets all the love and affection they can handle. These dogs work hard to earn the trust of their Scorpio human companions and willingly overlook those days when natives of this sun sign are willful, rigid, harsh, skeptical, and fault-finding—well, maybe they won't overlook the fault-finding part.

SCOTTISH TERRIER

Positive Traits

Scotties are strong, solid dogs, well muscled and hardy. They are vigorous and lively—and they look it. Scotty facial expressions mirror their thoughts. And what you see is what you get. These dogs are straightforward and honest. They are among the best watch-and-warn dogs, partly because they are utterly loyal and home-loving. While their Scottish West Highland counterparts are known as a "gentleman's dog," Scotties are known as "ladies" and "gentlemen." Scotties can withstand almost any climate and are equally adaptable when it comes to living in either town or country. Their size of less than twenty-five pounds makes them good travel companions. These *Cosmic Canines* do not look for trouble, but when it finds them, they always fight fair. They love to play—to carry sticks or balls in their mouths—and are devoted companions to their owners. This breed tends to produce very independent dogs.

Negative Traits

Scotties can be one-person dogs. They have little time for strangers and are not the best pets to have around children. They still carry their ratter genes, and if a burrowing animal appears in your garden, you may find your tulips in China. Left to their own devices and lacking training while puppies, Scotties will find all kinds of interesting things to do. They may, for example, find creative ways to help you redesign your ornaments while you decorate your Christmas tree. Without training as puppies, Scotties can be stubborn throughout their adult lives. Properly trained, they are a delight! It takes some creativity and handler discipline to obedience-train these dogs—plus maybe a little humorous human stubbornness.

Job Opportunities for Scottish Terriers

Do you own a warehouse where perishables are stored and vermin control is important? Perhaps you own a self-storage rental business? Put Scottish Terriers to work. They do to vermin what Doberman Pinschers and German Shepherds do for crime prevention at lumber yards and car dealerships: they eliminate the problem. Scotties are good travel, exercise, and adult family companions. They are among the best of pets for singles. Teach them to bring the morning paper—they love being of service!

Most Compatible Sun Sign: Aquarius

Aquarians, like Scottish Terriers, are not into public displays of affection. Some people think them cold and distant when actually they are merely nonexhibitionistic about their feelings. Scotties are a little like that. Note the lack of words like "affectionate and loving" in the description of these dogs. Rather, hardy, strong, vigorous, lively, straightforward, and honest are the words used (sounds like a description of Abe Lincoln, a well-known Aquarian). Those same words describe natives of the sign of the

Water Bearer. Like Scotties, Aquarians are independent, loyal, and determined. They are unassuming and faithful, too, and are known for their sense of the humane and love of those with whom they share life—human and canine. They may express love through sacrifice, time, commitment, and thoughtfulness (like Scotties) rather than with hugs and kisses, but their love of humanity runs deep. This sun sign motivates trust, and Scotties appreciate it when trust is a two-way street. In negative cycles, Aquarians can be disorganized and scattered, unfocused and forgetful, as well as undisciplined. Fortunately, most of these sun sign natives move quickly through negative personality cycles so only a few Scotty training sessions will be forgotten in the temporary state of human companion disorganization.

SEALYHAM TERRIER

Positive Traits

Strong-willed and assertive, these agile representatives of the Terrier group are also beautiful in appearance. Even though they have hard, wiry outercoats and soft, weatherproof undercoats, Sealyhams do not shed much. Like Scotties, Sealyhams (originally bred in Wales) need a firm training hand as puppies to get off on the right foot. Lacking such firm guidance when young, these Cosmic Canines lose much of their personality appeal and potential. They can be tyrants if spoiled. Sealyhams are very good watch-and-warn dogs. They are filled with joie de vivre and, when properly trained, very lovable. They are devoted to human companions and reliable with school-aged children. They are just too quick in their reactions to stimuli to be totally reliable with very young children. Though just slightly larger than Toy breeds (a foot high and about twenty-five pounds), Sealyhams are not Toys and should not be treated as if they are. They are field (Hunting), not lap, dogs.

Negative Traits

Sealyhams enjoy a scrap too much to always be good with other pets. Though they do not shed much, they do need a lot of grooming. Stubborn can be this dog's middle name—or obstinate. Sealyhams can be snappy if not firmly but kindly disciplined while puppies. And that's a shame, because they can make wonderful adult pets. Firmly discourage any digging, from day one. These are not dogs whose temperaments can withstand being spoiled. It ruins them and makes them selfish little tyrants who may resort to jealousy biting or bullying other neighborhood dogs—even those bigger than they are.

Job Opportunities for Sealyham Terriers

These *Cosmic Canines* make wonderful companions for seniors, singles, or families with older children. They are also good watch-and-warn dogs. Their size and temperament make them good travel companions and their energy level makes them great exercise companions—these dogs have a lot of endurance. Hire them out to local warehouses because they are still very good finders and destroyers of vermin. If you have burrowing animals in your yard (or a warehouse that attracts rats), they won't last long with Sealyhams on the job.

Most Compatible Sun Sign: Cancer

Natives of the Crab are notably tenacious. Crabs will literally allow their claws to be cut off rather than give up that which they hold in them. Sealyhams understand this personality trait and grudgingly pay homage to it, giving up their position of obstinacy to more formidable opponents. And Cancer human companions innately understand the sensitive, lively natures of these *Cosmic Canines*. Natives of the Crab are also domestic, retentive, determined, understanding, empathetic, and diplomatic. Once Cancer pet guardians understand the need their Sealyham pets have for firm but gentle guidance in healthy social behavior, they give it with precise regularity. Cancerians are calm people who are also sympathetic and compassionate. If they can avoid the temptation to spoil these pets, they have all of the personal qualities required to help Sealyhams achieve their substantial potential. In their negative cycles, however, Cancerians can be reticent, fearful, brooding, and self-serving. They can be downright selfish. Sealyham Terriers are strong and independent enough to keep reminding natives of the Crab that they need to get back in touch with their positive selves—or their pets may do some brooding of their own.

SHETLAND SHEEPDOG

Positive Traits

These beautiful miniature Collie look-alikes are sound, sturdy, and, above all, faithful. Shelties are highly intelligent and ideal dogs for competitive obedience hobbyists. When you combine their intelligence with their responsiveness, it is easy to see why they make training sessions an enjoyable hobby rather than a job. They are unceasingly loyal to their families and are very good warning dogs. Gentle Shelties make wonderful family dogs and are very intuitive. If any dog can be described as sweet and genuine—truly themselves and comfortable with that identity—it is the Shetland Sheepdog. Their roots go back to the Shetland Islands (which seem to specialize in producing adorable animals).

Negative Traits

If, in this day and age, it is negative to be wary of strangers, then Shelties must admit to this trait. They do not take kindly to being petted by non-family members. Poorly bred Shelties can be shy, timid, nervous, and stubborn. Aside from being too sensitive and reacting negatively to harsh treatment or punishment, well-bred Shelties have practically no personality defects. Training, however, will not compensate for poor breeding. Because Shelties are so popular as a breed, you can find many who haven't been well bred (unless you are careful). They need to be brushed weekly, thoroughly groomed occasionally, and they shed regularly throughout the year.

Job Opportunities for Shetland Sheepdogs

Good but not great bark-and-warn dogs, Shelties are definitely not good guard dogs. They make very good companions for older children and seniors and are good exercise companions. Shelties are excellent obedience hobbyist pets. Sheepherding instincts are very strong in these dogs. Lacking a herd of four-legged critters to move from one spot to another, Shelties will try to herd your friends—for example, as they walk to their car, which is parked in your driveway.

Most Compatible Sun Sign: Aquarius

Like Shelties, natives of the Water Bearer are very intelligent, sincere, dependable, and, above all, faithful. Both are unassuming, patient, quiet, and just a little unconventional. Aquarians respect knowledge no matter what life-form package it comes in and will be immediately drawn to Shelties because of their smarts. Like these *Cosmic Canines*, Aquarians are honest to a fault. Natives of the Water Bearer do not roll out the red carpet for strangers either. They, like Shelties, give their friendship only when they know well those to whom they are giving it because, once given, it will not be withdrawn. Both Shelties and people born under this sun sign are highly intuitive, sometimes appearing to gain insights right out of thin air. Aquarians motivate trust, a needed element in helping what can be aloof animals bond with human beings. No living being can be more aloof than Aquarius.

SKYE TERRIER

Positive Traits

These dogs are beautiful, even under their flowing outer- and soft under-coats (for which they are known). Skyes have pleasant dispositions and can be very patient animals with the one human to whom they bond. To this one person, Skye Terriers offer their undying devotion and loyalty, and have for the four-hundred-plus years of their existence. Bred in Scotland to hunt foxes, skunks, otters, and badgers, they are hardy animals. These *Cosmic Canines* have wonderful senses of humor and sometimes you would swear they are laughing at you—or at themselves. They are less than a foot high and weigh around twenty-five pounds. Skyes are smart and faithful and have in abundance the two basic requirements to be really good Terriers: coat and courage.

Negative Traits

It's hard to look at these little dogs and realize what relentless fighters they can be when aroused. Today's house pets aren't likely to fight unless they see rats or moles or other small, burrowing animals—or perhaps a neighbor's Chihuahua. Then, instinct takes over. Skyes are not vicious, but they do tend to give their total trust and devotion to one person or one family. They have little time or use for strangers and really don't warm up to friends of the family as much as human companions might want. Considerable grooming is required.

Job Opportunities for Skye Terriers

Skyes are very good watch-and-warn dogs. They make wonderful companions for seniors who live in low-traffic environments or for families with older children. They are a convenient size for travel and have the kind of attitudes that make them good exercise companions. Teach them tricks (so you can laugh back at them when they laugh at you) and give them an audience. They love being assigned duties, like retrieving newspapers and slippers for human companions. These are intelligent dogs and are easily trained. They make excellent neighborhood clowns. Rent them out for kids' birthday parties.

Most Compatible Sun Sign: Libra

Skye Terriers have an innate understanding of Libra humans (and vice versa), especially when it comes to appreciating family and things of beauty. Libra Cosmic Canine guardians are generous, balanced, perceptive, and courteous. Natives of this sun sign are very droll and will love the sense of humor with which Skye Terriers are blessed. Libran calm sends out restful vibes that help take some of the edge off Skye Terrier suspicions of strangers and tendencies to become irately aroused by other animals. Both sun sign and dog breed are a bit reserved and very intuitive. Both are orderly and kind. Skyes find that Libra humans have sympathetic and compassionate natures that act like magnets, drawing and calming them. These Cosmic Canines gently urge Libra human companions to be a little more decisive. When, in negative cycles, Libra humans become thoughtless, combative, and insensitive, Skye Terriers are quite strong enough as individuals to withstand it and encourage these sun sign natives to mellow out and get back to normal once again.

WELSH CORGI (CARDIGAN)

Positive Traits

There are two types of Welsh Corgis: Cardigan and Pembroke. They have the same origins but slightly different temperaments and appearances. Both are devoted companions and have foxlike faces. Cardigan Welsh Corgis may be any color except white and have short- to medium-length harsh coats and foxlike tails (Pembroke tails are docked, very short). Corgis are hardy, tireless pets and make good watch-and-warn dogs. Because the primary purpose for which Corgis (both types) were bred was to nip at the heels of cattle, some say they possess natural guard instincts. They are fond of children (though their tendency to nip makes them less than ideal for young children). They are gentle and cordial with family and friends but don't roll out the red carpet for strangers. Cardigan Welsh Corgis have calm temperaments and hold themselves in very high esteem. They are very bright dogs and easily learn obedience lessons. Cardigans are a bit more aloof and reserved than Pembrokes.

Negative Traits

In the past, Cardigan Welsh Corgis have had eye defects. Corgis need to be trained while young; they have dominant personalities that need early direction and discipline. Without direction as puppies, their aloofness can turn into downright frigidity and their instincts to guard may become a little too aggressive.

Job Opportunities for Cardigan Welsh Corgis

Historically (in the twelfth century), the Celts assigned Cardigan Welsh Corgis responsibility for guarding their children. They were used to find game (though they are not hunting dogs). And they nipped at the heels of cattle when a farmer's herd wandered off his land to graze on the land of his neighbor. These are adaptable dogs who have a long history of service where needed. They are good family pets but do better with older rather than younger children. They are good home companions and exercise partners for seniors and are very good watch-and-warn dogs. They can be excellent travel companions.

Most Compatible Sun Sign: Virgo

Like these *Cosmic Canines*, Virgo natives are self-contained, reasoned, and precise. Though Virgo human guardians may be a little more tactful than Cardigan Corgis (Cardies always let you know where they stand and, unless they know you well, may not be too tactful), both enjoy learning and are discriminating, detailed, and usually maintain their calm. Cardigan Welsh Corgis appear to evaluate just about everything, and so, too, do Virgo natives (many are stockbrokers and bankers). Virgoans show a lot of ingenuity, and the history of this dog breed certainly proves Cardigans are ingenious, adaptable dogs. Both Cardie dogs and Virgo humans can be prideful, oversensitive, defensive, and a bit arrogant. Like these dogs, when under the negative influences of this sun sign, Virgoans can overvalue themselves and bore everyone who will listen to their high opinions of themselves.

WELSH CORGIS (PEMBROKE)

Positive Traits

The British press has certainly not kept secret the nipping incidents involving Queen Elizabeth's Pembroke Welsh Corgis. Nor has the queen kept secret her high opinion of this ancient dog breed and her love for them. Pembrokes are a bit taller and shorter of body than Cardigans and their legs are straighter; the coat is finer and longer and Pembrokes are somewhat daintier. Pembrokes have pointed ears; Cardigan ears are rounded. And Pembrokes have very short, docked tails. Pembrokes are more lively, bolder, and have more assertive personalities than Cardigans—maybe that's why the queen's Corgis nip people. Pembrokes are thought to be one of the most good-natured of smaller house pets. These *Cosmic Canines* are affectionate, but they don't fawn over people or beg for their attention. They make excellent watch-and-warn dogs and Corgi intelligence makes them fun to obedience-train. These are very alert, lively, and bold dogs with strong personalities. They need training when young to discourage the tendency to nip.

Negative Traits

For most pet owners, nipping is a pretty serious negative. Is there an unwritten law that Corgis will undoubtedly nip small hands that reach out to them while they are eating? No, but left untrained, there is a possibility it will occur. Must Corgis intimidate nonintimate friends of the family who drop by for a chat and reach out to pet them without being solicited by the dog to do so? Of course not! These are really very good-natured pets, but they need to be trained while young. Nipping is a serious offense and requires a strong disciplinary response using the choke chain and leash—never human hands (which are for praise, alone). People who enjoy spoiling dogs (or, more specifically, treating dogs like children rather than dogs) may find these are not the right pets for them. Spoiling Corgis turns them into temperamentally unreliable little tyrants who demand "their space." Corgis are independent animals who simply won't curl up and die if they do not get human approval. To some, that is a negative. To others, it is a refreshing sign of self-reliance. For canine guardians who spend time teaching puppies appropriate behavior rather than just petting and grooming and talking to them, Corgis are excellent pets.

Job Opportunities for Pembroke Welsh Corgis

These independent little souls make excellent watch-and-warn dogs and are wonderful companions for families that train and discipline their pets (better for older rather than younger children). They are good exercise and travel companions, too. Obedience-training enthusiasts will find willing and capable partners to work with them at their hobbies. The best possible companions for people with discriminating tastes and disciplined personalities.

Most Compatible Sun Sign: Capricorn

Pembroke Welsh Corgis and sun sign natives of the Goat can enjoy their independence together. Neither will insult the other's personal space and both will accept as normal that all individuals, regardless of life-form, are entitled to it. Capricorns have balanced, fair, accurate, and persistent approaches to life. This sun sign provides human companions who will discipline and train these little Welshmen while remaining calm and exacting—just what the Corgi doctor ordered. Like these dogs, Capricorns are independent, self-reliant (not relying on the approval of others for their own sense of identity), and patient. When Capricorn humans get moody or sad, obstinate or aloof, Pembroke Welsh Corgis happily stay out of the way. These smart little dogs know Capricorn guardians will get back on the positive side of the Goat's street pretty quickly. When natives of the Goat become impatient or obstinate, these dogs are perfectly capable of dealing with it.

WELSH TERRIER

Positive Traits

A very old breed, Welsh Terriers are clever and happy. These *Cosmic Canines* are generally pretty quiet. Welshies are affectionate yet bold. They have good temperaments (are not shy or timid) but can be volatile. Overall, they are great fun as pets. They are a handy size—about fifteen inches at the shoulder—and obedient. Welsh Terriers make good household pets for families with children past the toddler stage. They are curious, energetic, and love having children around. Welsh Terriers are not mean or vicious dogs, but they are fearless and energetic. They are assertive and make good watch-and-warn dogs.

Negative Traits

For people who have dominant personalities, there are no negatives about this dog breed. Welsh Terriers are energetic and they can be volatile. Quiet people who may have a basic fear of dogs might find other dog breeds more suitable; though once trained, Welshies are very loving and obedient—they just require people who are comfortable with dogs to get them trained. Welsh Terriers, quite simply, are not lap dogs. They have wonderful temperaments and make fine family pets, but given an opportunity, they will dominate the pet-owner relationship. Also, their genetic backgrounds make them instinctive diggers (like all Terriers). Keep their nails trimmed and discourage digging from day one. They have such quick reactions and are so energetic that they do not deal well with unpredictable or erratic human behavior. Toddlers are not predictable. Thus, these *Cosmic Canines* are not the best pets for families with very young children.

Job Opportunities for Welsh Terriers

Hunting in dog packs for otters, badgers, and other animals who live underground is the primary occupation of these canines. They make good guard dogs, are great companions for older children and seniors. Welsh Terriers are good family pets but have genetic digging tendencies. Don't let it get started. They are very smart, and people with an inclination to enjoy training pets will find willing students in these dogs. Teach them tricks.

Most Compatible Sun Sign: Scorpio

Weak people have no appeal to natives of the Scorpion, and these dogs are happiest with strong human companions. Like Welshies, Scorpio humans can be volatile—or they can be the calmest people alive. This is a sun sign of extremes, good and bad. They are optimistic, talented, mysterious, persistent, friendly, and very curious—like Welsh Terriers. The sun sign and the dog are strong of character. Curiosity is as much a part of Scorpio's love of mystery as it is a part of typical Welsh Terrier personalities. What you see is what you get with dog and sun sign, but you may not see it all. Remember, both are clever, both love puzzles, and both are a bit mysterious.

WEST HIGHLAND WHITE TERRIER

Positive Traits

These pure white dogs are cuteness come to life. They are happy, active Highlanders and easy to train. They get along well with other dogs; in fact, Westies get along well with practically everyone. These *Cosmic Canines* are self-reliant and adaptable to a variety of lifestyles; in a word, they are sociable. They are happiest when loved (and they make that easy to do). Westies are energetic and pleasing, game, hardy little dogs that are very attractive. These wee Scottish pets are curious animals who like to find their own answers as they identify problems. They are too small to be effective guard dogs and they tend to like company too much to be the best watchdogs. They are good at digging up burrowing animals—say good-bye to your tomato patch if a mole suddenly appears. Like all good

Terriers, like all good Scotsmen, Westies are courageous. They are the best possible of canine companions for school-aged children.

Negative Traits

Westies can be impatient—too impatient for toddlers. They require regular but relatively easy grooming. In fact, it is recommended that too much bathing be avoided. Instead, a dry shampoo and regular brushing can keep this dog's beautiful coat in pure white mint condition. Westies do not shed much, but the soft undercoat needs to be brushed out when it loosens at shedding time. These dogs have few negatives. They are even easy to house-train. You take the high road, and I'll take . . . a Westie!

Job Opportunities for West Highland White Terriers

Their handy size of less than twenty pounds makes them very suitable travel companions. They not only fit into bureau drawers, they are also top-drawer family pets. For people who seek pets for their entertainment value, Westies are good choices. They are good game-playing entertainers. For people who have taken up the challenge of regular exercise, these pets make good companions. They are active while in the home or apartment and don't need constant walks, but love sharing the time and experience with loving owners. Sociable animals who are both curious and intelligent, these *Cosmic Canines* enjoy learning tricks and performing—they even give encores.

Most Compatible Sun Sign: Leo

Who but the sun sign most capable of expressing love could be most compatible with these loving little dogs? Westies are drawn to Leo's magnetism and Leo natives are drawn to this dog breed for its many positive personality traits. Natives of the Lion are vital, kind, warmhearted, loving, and generous. People born under the sign of Leo the Lion have nobility and individualistic senses of self and are well served by West Highland White Terriers, known for their ability to make others feel loved. Westies enjoy the energy of Leo humans as well as this sun sign native's perseverance, generosity, and ambition. These *Cosmic Canines* enjoy the Lion's sense of forward momentum. In their negative cycles, of course, Lion natives can be as unloving as they can be loving. They can be impulsive, willful, arrogant, egotistical, authoritarian, and very manipulative. They will, in fact, use love to manipulate the outcome of circumstances important to them. Leo human guardians who try to manipulate Westies may find they have tigers by the tail. Westies may be sociable, but they're not stupid.

4

MEDIUM-SIZED
DOGS

ALASKAN MALAMUTE

Positive Traits

These great sled dogs are fast, strong, and affectionate. To wrap the package in the best possible gift paper, Malamutes also love children and are very sociable. Though not to be confused with Greyhound speed, they are fast, and they have a great deal of endurance. These *Cosmic Canines* wear an expression on their faces that says "kind." It's for real. They are kind, gentle, sweet, loving, and devoted to their owners. Alaskan Malamutes won't drive their guardians crazy, begging them to play, but when invited to play, they are fun and amusing. As they age, Malamutes become more dignified (they are great clowns as puppies) and even achieve a certain degree of nobility. These are fun-loving, sociable animals who are positive additions to any family.

Negative Traits

This dog breed's history is replete with stories about sled-pulling skills. When training them to do almost anything else, however, intelligence is average. These dogs can be very slow to respond to verbal obedience commands. I will always hold in my mind the picture of a Malamute at one of my eight-week dog training classes. After "heeling" around the top of a large barn, the "halt" command was given. When "halt" is called after walking at the "heel," dogs are supposed to immediately sit. The Malamute took its time sitting, moving from one back leg to the other as he lowered himself to the floor (looking unconcernedly straight ahead the entire time). Usually, a small slap on a dog's rump at the instant the trainer stops is sufficient to wake the dog up and let him know he should sit. *Now!* Not this dog. Throughout the eight weeks, nothing could get the Malamute to sit quickly! He was, however, much loved by his human companion for the rest of his charms. Malamutes can be stubborn and, in all but pulling sleds and charming their human guardians, may be a little slow on the uptake.

Job Opportunities for Alaskan Malamutes

Whether in the wilds of Alaska or on a snowy neighborhood street, these are reliable animals to harness to children's sleds or wagons (or for Roller Blading in warmer climates). Kids love the action, and so do these dogs. Roller skaters and bladers can leave the driving to their Malamutes, lean back and enjoy the ride. And it's a great way to give these dogs the exercise they need. These are loving companions and loyal pets who are faithful to their families. Not good guard or watch-and-warn dogs. They are just too friendly to everyone.

Most Compatible Sun Sign: Virgo

Tactful, constructive, and ingenious Virgo humans are perfect with affectionate, friendly Alaskan Malamutes. Instead of yelling at these dogs to do something, Virgoan companions are sure to offer constructive criticism—the only kind to which Malamutes pay attention. Another Virgoan quality these dogs respect is this sun sign native's love of knowledge. Virgo humans enjoy studying things like the ancient working history of the breed and its positive impact in helping settle the far north regions. Virgo human companions will easily adapt to the loving yet independent nature of these dogs. Hunting and sledding dogs are the most independent of the canine world. The jobs for which they were bred create that need. It is a good influence on Virgo natives who can sometimes be a little passive. When these sun sign natives enter negative phases and become prideful, defensive, or arrogant, it won't phase Alaskan Malamutes. They understand those three traits very well.

BASSET HOUND

Positive Traits

There are several varieties of Bassets. Among them are the Artesian Normand, Bleu de Gascogne, Fauve de Bretagne, and the Griffon Vendeen (long-tailed and short-tailed). All Basset Hounds are gentle and affectionate with their own families. Generally, they are standoffish with strangers, are usually not fighters, and are all stubborn. It is said Artesian Normand Bassets are more faithful than Bleu de Gascogne Bassets, and that Bleu de Gascogne Bassets are more stubborn than Fauve de Bretagne Bassets (which are more enterprising than the short- or long-tailed Griffon Vendeen Bassets). Vendeens are the most animated of the Basset Hound group. Perhaps it's their self-confident sense of humor that makes them so jaunty, or their self-willed, independent, yet faithful personalities.

Then there's the good old Basset Hound with which most dog lovers are familiar. These dogs are equally loved in America and Great Britain for their even-tempered, warmhearted, cheerful, and loving ways. They are good with children and make ideal family pets. Though friendly, agreeable family pets, Bassets still retain strong scent-and-find Hound instincts. They tend to be very slow workers, but they are highly effective. In short, Bassets are lazy. These *Cosmic Canines* do not sit by doors awaiting the return of kids from school in order to run and play in the yard. People who want something from Basset Hounds need to learn to flatter and cajole, not yell. They are stubborn, and loud voices only make them more so. Bassets are cooperative within family settings and need attention and love. They are wonderful children's dogs, even for toddlers. If they gave blue ribbons for Most Loving Dog, Basset Hounds would win their share.

Negative Traits

Gates need to be kept closed or Basset Hounds may be found in the next county—or state. Left to their own devices, they wander for miles. These dogs have minds of their own and can be just plain stubborn. Part of that stubbornness exhibits itself when you tell the dog to do one thing and the dog quite clearly chooses not to obey. Bassets are lazy, but they need a lot of exercise to stay healthy. Pay attention to Basset ears and toenails—keep the ears clean and the nails clipped (not the other way around). Of all Basset breeds, Vendeens are the only ones who tend to be one-person dogs. The rest are very much family animals. All are self-willed and disobedient and can be just downright hardheaded. These are not the smartest dogs in the world, but when God handed out hearts, they were at the head of the line. Bassets are too easygoing for guard work. If they hear a prowler and wake up, they *may* warn, but they seldom play the role of watchdog. Basset Hounds born under Air and Fire astrological signs can be counted on to bark when they hear unfamiliar noises or see strangers prowling around the house. Often, Basset Hounds do not like thunder and lightning and can be destructive to dog runs as they seek ways to get out of them and into the house so they can be with human companions.

Job Opportunities for Basset Hounds

If people owe you money and they skip town, put Basset Hounds on their trail. They may take more time than you'd like, but you can be sure of the result. They are good newspaper and slippers dogs. Absolutely the best family pets and very good with small children when properly bred and properly trained, of course. Great exercise partners (though at times unwilling ones). Though slightly inconvenient travel companions on public transportation because of size, they make good company in the car.

Most Compatible Sun Sign: Capricorn

Natives of the sign of the Goat and Basset Hounds have a great deal in common. Both are practical, self-conscious, independent, calm, persistent, and careful. Capricorns will understand the stubbornness that is so much a part of the temperaments of these dogs and deal with it more effectively than most other sun signs (Virgo and Cancer handle stubbornness well, too). Both are even-tempered, warmhearted, cheerful, and loving. These *Cosmic Canines* respond positively to Capricorn's balanced, fair approach to decision making, and Capricorns respond positively to the open show of affection Bassets give those they love. Natives of the Goat sometimes have difficulty showing affection but wilt a bit when those they love don't show it. Bassets innately understand this need and happily fill it. Capricorns, like Bassets, are laid-back and reflective. This sun sign's attention to detail helps these dogs get on exercise schedules and stay there. Capricorns are patient—the best personal trait to outlast a bout of Basset stubbornness. When natives of this sun sign get sad, gloomy, cold, and distant because of negative cycles, Bassets help provide the cheerful environment Capricorn guardians need to get back on the positive side of the street. These *Cosmic Canines* will, in fact, soothe the nervous natures that cause the sense of aloneness that sometimes overwhelms those born under the winter sun sign of Capricorn.

BORDER COLLIE

Positive Traits

When people first see Border Collies, strains of the song "Born Free" should be playing in the background. In spirit, these dogs *are* born free. Border Collies have a strong sense of loyalty to their human companions, are extremely intelligent, and make great dogs for obedience training, but they never lose their sense of independence. They are equally good as family and Working dogs. These *Cosmic Canines* easily learn the hand signals of utility obedience work and are thought by many to be the smartest, most easily trained dog in the universe. People who have shared their homes with these canines say they are the closest thing to human companionship that can be found in the world of canines. They *do*, however, need a job. These are not the sit around, look beautiful, and let someone spoil them kind of dog. They are first-class, everyday Working dogs who are not only eminently sensible but also good with children. They are trustworthy. These dogs have a unique kind of independence, which, from their perspective, doesn't hamper one iota their ability to love human companions. Quite simply, they are not possessive and do not want to be possessed. Border Collies can be rugged, they can be soft and loving. They are the sharpest of sharp dogs, but they *need* a purpose, and the purpose should involve exercise and this breed's natural herding instincts. Nothing, including human beings, can stare down a herd of goats or sheep quite as well as Border Collies.

Negative Traits

Whenever more than two of anything that moves is in the presence of Border Collies, they automatically think themselves in charge of the group. Their herding instincts are so strong, they will herd anything, people included, if sheep and cattle are not available. If you don't want to be involved with your dog, doing something meaningful that requires the dog to learn and the human companion to teach, this is not the dog for you. Teach the word *fetch* when they are puppies, and apply it to everything you can think of—the newspaper, your slippers, a ball, a Frisbee, the watering hose in the garden, whatever. Give them jobs. Give them several jobs. If you are a personality type who considers these kinds of activities negatives or distractions from other priorities, another dog breed will better serve your needs. Aside from job needs and medium-length coats that need weekly brushing, there are no negatives about these dogs.

Job Opportunities for Border Collies

These dogs can be trained to do just about anything. If you want the best possible dog to train for the movies so you can sit back and earn a fortune from the sweat of your dog's brow, get a Border Collie. They make excellent obedience-training dogs, home companions, protectors of children, loving family members, working dogs, travel companions—and they will love having you put their intelligence to practical use around the house and yard. They retrieve anything you teach them to fetch and are good multiple-pet family dogs—though if the household has more than two pets, expect Border Collies to herd them around.

Most Compatible Sun Sign: Aquarius

Aquarians love in very much the same way Border Collies do. They do not want to be possessed, nor are they possessive. Aquarius is one of the most independent signs in the zodiac and this dog breed is certainly one of the most independent canines. Aquarians may feel their love to the very depths of their soul, but they are not given to numerous outward displays of affection. They would not hesitate to put their lives on the line for those they love—just like Border Collies. Aquarius humans motivate trust and these *Cosmic Canines* are trustworthy. Both are extremely bright (there are more geniuses born under the sign of Aquarius than any other). Both have strong needs for life purposes, usually in the service of others. And both enjoy a wide range of interests. Neither is limited in scope. Aquarius is loyal, dependable, a clear reasoner, honest, sincere, and nonjudgmental. Border Collies appreciate all of the Water Bearer's positive traits and understand when negative pulls cause their human friends to become disorganized, unfocused, distant, arrogant, and undisciplined. Count on Border Collies to herd Aquarians back to the positive side, quickly!

BRITTANY SPANIEL

Positive Traits

Of French heritage, Brits, though more assertive than other Spaniels, have sensitive feelings and do not respond well to loud-voiced recriminations. They need teachers, not tyrants, as human companions. They are affectionate, gentle, outgoing, and loyal. They are excellent Pointers with good noses, gentle mouths, and in the field can be tireless. In some ways, their temperaments are reminiscent of Setters—trustworthy and calm. Brits are agile, versatile, hardy, and (except for their feelings) rugged. They can cope with difficult terrain in the field (if not the home). Brittany Spaniels are very intelligent, easily groomed, and are very loving to children of all ages who treat them lovingly. They are too energetically active to be the best pet for children of less than school age.

Negative Traits

Brits can be one-person dogs if not encouraged to bond more with a single family member. They are sensitive and need kind but firm handling combined with outdoor exercise. They expect and deserve every consideration from their masters, but it is a narrow path between being considerate of and spoiling these dogs. Though they are a little more assertive than most Spaniels, they are not suited to guard work—they *may* bark and warn of intruders.

Job Opportunities for Brittany Spaniels

All-around Hunters, Pointers, and Retrievers on land or water. Brittany Spaniels are wonderful family pets and companions (though they need regular exercise). Too energetically enthusiastic to serve as companions to toddlers. They are not good guard dogs and are not reliable watch-and-warn dogs. These *Cosmic Canines* are just too friendly. They make good newspaper and house-slipper retrievers. Provided obedience training is begun by six months of age, these sessions make good jobs for Brits. Make training fun for them. It helps them become more confident and independent.

Most Compatible Sun Sign: Aries

Like Brittany Spaniels, Aries natives are intelligent, assertive, energetic, sensible, amusing, and adaptable to new and different surroundings. Natives of the Ram are known for their good communications skills. When made aware of Brittany Spaniels' sensitive feelings, they speak carefully to these pets in the most gentle, effective ways possible. Yet human guardians born under this sun sign can be firm. Like Aries, these Spaniels will go and go and go until they drop, will sleep deeply, and be ready to get up and go and go again. Both are a little independent by nature. From day one, Brits will understand the competitive natures of Aries natives. Both have an innate need to excel at whatever they do. When Aries humans go into negative cycles and become aloof, distant, unfeeling, and domineering, Brittany Spaniels will gently urge them to get over it. When Ariens become argumentative, the Brit's hurt silence will remove anything about which to argue.

BULLDOG (ENGLISH)

Positive Traits

Bulldogs are usually calm of temperament, a bit lazy, easygoing, and they love children. These *Cosmic Canines* are courageous and, in their younger years, enjoy playing games with children. Their short coats make them easy to groom. Bulldogs make loyal watch-and-guard animals and, when properly bred and trained, lovable family pets. Their ancestry boasts of fighting dogs who were so savage the breed became almost insensitive to pain. For over a hundred years, Bulldog breeders have worked to take the ferocity out of these dogs. Just looking at them gives viewers an inner sense of tremendous power. These dogs have large jowls and they sometimes slobber. They can be very determined animals but, in very subtle ways, have made meekness part of their charm. Bulldogs are intelligent, obedience trainable, and enjoy working with their human companions. They are very loyal to their families and will protect hearth and home against intruders. Bulldogs are affectionate, but whether or not they will be good with toddlers or even preschool children depends largely on breeding, training, and whether or not the dogs have been raised from puppyhood with young children in the home.

Negative Traits

If Bulldogs had not been ferocious, they would not have survived. The breed was created to bait bulls in the "sporting" arenas, beginning during the rule of the Roman Empire and continuing until the mid-nineteenth century. These dogs were not bred for beauty but for courage and heart, and they are not glamorous animals. Typical Bulldog lives are shorter than those of other breeds. Their "smashed-in" noses just don't equip them to breathe rapidly and care must be taken not to give this very solid, powerful dog too much exercise too fast. Running, for example, is not permitted, especially in hot weather. Bulldogs should never be placed in confined spaces without plenty of cool air circulating. For that reason, Bulldogs are not the most flexible travel companions.

Job Opportunities for English Bulldogs

Loved and loving family pets, advertising symbols of power and determination for businesses and governments, excellent companions for seniors and other adults who are physically strong enough to contain and train them. Fun dogs to train. Bulldogs are good watch-and-warn dogs (possibly guard dogs, depending on breeding and training).

Most Compatible Sun Sign: Sagittarius

Like Bulldogs, Sagittarius humans are survivors. Sons and daughters of this sun sign have happy dispositions and a strong sense of purpose—a needed requirement for controlling and training these *Cosmic Canines*. Bulldogs appreciate the frank, honest, giving, and sincere personality that goes with being a Sagittarius human who serves as a dog guardian. Like Sagittarians, with Bulldogs what you see is what you get. Both sun sign and dog are loyal and affectionate. Sagittarius natives are on-the-go people, but these dogs are limited in physical activity. This bothers Sagittarians less than other sun signs. They enjoy freedom and personal independence and will happily adjust their schedules to do their going thing while Bulldogs take naps (and as they age, Bulldogs take a lot of naps). These confident, devoted people easily gain this dog's trust and loyalty (both qualities Sagittarians greatly admire). Both dog breed and sun sign are courageous, intelligent, and self-reliant.

BULLDOG (FRENCH)

Positive Traits

French Bulldogs are about half the size of the English breed, weighing from twenty-two to twenty-eight pounds. Their legs are slightly more bowed, their muzzles better formed (which reduces the breathing problems English Bulldogs have). These *Cosmic Canines* are clean-looking and very muscular. French Bulldogs are famous for their commitment to a purpose. It's part of their charm—and they *are* charming. They can be very determined, which, left uncontrolled, results in stubbornness of substance. French Bulldogs have a great deal of drive and energy. Because of improved health resulting from better-developed muzzles, these dogs are far more active and energetic than their English counterparts. The French say these dogs love to please and are very obedient. This is a physically well-balanced dog that is also compact and very muscular. They have typical smooth Bulldog coats and are powerful, heavy-boned little dogs. And they do not have the unhappy, irascible look of the English Bulldog. Rather, French Bulldogs appear alert and ready to play.

Negative Traits

Of the Bulldog group, the French variety is ranked in the medium intelligence category. When compared to working breeds like Shepherds, Collies, and Poodles, their "medium intelligence" slips a little farther down. They are not the smartest dogs in the world, but they have a charm all their own. These are determined, stubborn dogs who require good obedience training as puppies in order to make them stubborn about the right things. French Bulldogs are not the most affectionate but have an independent kind of substance to them. They are not good watch-and-warn or guard dogs. Not the best pet for children of less than preschool age. It helps if these dogs are raised with children from puppyhood.

Job Opportunities for French Bulldogs

Interesting and enjoyable family pets with a unique kind of independent charm. This breed's size and temperament make them good travel companions. Good walking exercise partners.

Most Compatible Sun Sign: Scorpio

Power and determination are the two dominant personality traits of natives of the Scorpion. The same two traits dominate French Bulldog personalities. Whether or not they are invincible, both dog and sun sign think they are. And just like their Scorpio human guardians, French Bulldogs seldom leave neutral impressions. Others either like Scorpio humans and French Bulldogs, or they do not. Most people and canines are ruled by either their heads or their hearts. Scorpio humans and French Bulldogs utilize both equally. It is said that when Scorpio natives are in their positive mode, they represent the epitomes of courage (few things in life frighten Scorpio) and magnetism. The same is true of these *Cosmic Canines*. And both dog and sun sign are quite unconcerned with what others think of them. Just like this sun sign, these dogs do not offer friendship to everyone and anyone. They discriminate when choosing their friends, and once friendships are formed, they remain loyal to them. Natives of Scorpio are self-controlled, thrive on approval (though are not dependent on it), and have great strength of character. French Bulldogs have very similar personality traits. When Scorpio people become negative—willful, rigid, critical, and harsh—these dogs determinedly and patiently wait for the return of a positive attitude.

BULL TERRIER

Positive Traits

What do Spartacus and Bull Terriers have in common? Both are famed, historic gladiators. Bull Terriers were originally bred from old fighting dogs to be the very best at it. The breed was begun during an era that considered it entertainment to watch dogs fight one another—often to the death. Though fans of today's Bull Terriers strongly defend them as gentle dogs that are utterly reliable with children, there are still a lot of doubting Thomases among canine lovers. Those arguments, however, are best left to breeders to determine. Aside from the pro and con arguments about the suitability of the temperament of these *Cosmic Canines* as household family pets, they are very strong, agile, and devoted dogs. No one questions this breed's courage. These dogs have it in abundance. And they are Grade A guard dogs that are also healthy, hardy animals. Those who love these dogs say they have class and style and that they are refined and well mannered. Bull Terriers have a carefree bearing and some who have owned them swear they are witty. Others (who have also owned them) say they are pugnacious. Well-bred and raised in gentle but disciplined environments, there is little doubt these dogs can be intelligent, lively, and obedient family pets. They are, however, always ready for a fight with other dogs. In single-pet home environments, they can be very friendly dogs who thrive on affection.

Negative Traits

Bull Terriers are best suited to country life. They need humane training and loving discipline as puppies to be good home pets. Without the advantages of a loving family life and being raised in an environment of affection, there is some question as to whether Bull Terriers should be viewed as pets. They need plenty of exercise and human companions must remember at all times what powerful dogs they are. Leash training must occur by no later than four months of age. Even with good training and a loving environment, if provoked by other dogs these Terriers will fight to the death. When Bull Terriers bite, it is very difficult to get them to let go. They are rather insensitive to pain (which is, perhaps, why they made such good gladiators in the olden days). There is little doubt the Bull Terrier, pound for pound, is one of the most powerful dogs on earth.

Job Opportunities for Bull Terriers

For the right human companions, these dogs can be great exercise company (though only when properly leash-trained and when the exercise route is one that avoids other dogs). If unleashed animals approach, it is at their own risk. These are not good guard dogs when raised on chains in backyards. Quite simply, such treatment may turn Bull Terriers into unsafe, mean animals. They can be good adult companions if the adults know how to train and control them. They will retrieve objects, if taught.

Most Compatible Sun Sign: Taurus

These, the most physically vital human sun sign and the most powerful dog, seem made for each other—but for a lot of reasons that do not involve vim and vigor. Taurus human guardians have practical natures that inherently understand Bull Terriers. Add to that the dog's objective, soothing, and peaceful spirit and fearless attitude, and you have a good match. Also, Taurus is patient, persistent, companionable, and—the thing most likely to please these *Cosmic Canines*—reliable. Just as Bull Terriers are known for not letting go once they get something in their mouths, Taurus humans are known for their determination and persistence. Natives of this sun sign are objective, sincere, and trustworthy. So are these dogs. Taureans are fearless, powerful, and friendly. So are Bull Terriers. This is a match made in heaven, except for those times Taurus goes into a negative cycle and becomes weak, indecisive, authoritarian, fearful, and temperamental. One nice thing about having dominant pets like Bull Terriers around is that people won't want to stay on the negative side for long because their dogs will assertively let them know they prefer their positive personalities.

BULL TERRIER (STAFFORDSHIRE)

Positive Traits

Like Bull Terriers, Staffordshires were bred to bait bulls. They were also used to bait bears. The primary requirement of the breed was courage and a sense of fearlessness. All Bulldogs are rugged and tough. One look at Staffordshires is enough to tell all interested observers that these are muscular, powerful, and confident *Cosmic Canines*. They are in the medium range of intelligence within the Bulldog group. Today's breeders say it has been many years since Bull Terriers were bred to be fighters and modern Staffordshires are tame and friendly. When properly bred and trained, they are obedient. They are very devoted and faithful to their human companions but still love a good fight. Staffordshires are not friendly to strangers but generally show good judgment toward family friends after being introduced to them. They are excellent guard dogs. These are good dogs to adopt at an older age, not having the tendency to brood for the human with whom they first bonded, as some dogs do.

Negative Traits

Train Staffordshires while they are young. It should be done with kindness but firmness, with discipline for bad behavior and praise for good. Inhumane training methods can make most dogs mean. It is, however, dangerous to treat members of Bulldog and Terrier groups in-humanely. Staffordshires are relatively calm dogs—until a strange dog enters their territory or approaches them aggressively. Like Bull Terriers, this breed spent time in England's dog-fighting pits when the "sport" was legal. All members of the Bull group require human handlers strong enough (physically, mentally, and emotionally) to handle them. When properly raised, they are wonderfully affectionate, obedient animals with fun personalities. When improperly bred or left undisciplined (or abused), they are not pets. They are powerful tyrants. Bull Terriers make better adult's than children's pets (though that is somewhat dependent on how well the adult human companion controls and trains the dog). Not the best choice for families with multiple pets.

Job Opportunities for Staffordshire Bull Terriers

Excellent pets for seniors who have had prior experience with strong dog personalities. In the proper environment and with appropriate train-ing, they make excellent guard dogs. Human companions need to re-member that mean dogs are not good guard dogs. Mean dogs are as likely to bite the hands that feed them as they are to bite prowlers. Dogs who protect out of a sense of love and controlled discipline make good guard dogs. These dogs are not good exercise companions unless their human companions can control whether other dogs along the exercise route will be leashed.

Most Compatible Sun Sign: Leo

Forceful Leos charm Staffies and are charmed by them. This vital, kind sun sign will reach out to Staffordshires with Lion magnetism and offer them warmhearted, loving human companions with whom to share life. Human Leos have physical and mental energy that is more than a match for these brave and dominant dogs. If there is a problem, it will result from Leo companions' tendency to direct emotional energy inward. Like these dogs, Leo natives can be faithful and sincere, sympathetic and gen-erous. This sun sign's decisiveness and vital, forceful personality is just what the veterinarian ordered for Staffordshires. Natives born under the sign of the Lion will make meaningful demands for discipline in such a lighthearted way, it will leave Staffordshire Bull Terriers well trained without realizing how they got that way. Leo natives will be kind but de-manding, loving but disciplined. This is precisely what is required to help these *Cosmic Canines* reach their full potential and turn on their own fun-loving personalities as members of a family. When Leo becomes willful, arrogant, egotistical, and insecure, it won't bother Staffordshires in the least. They get that way themselves, every now and then.

CLUMBER SPANIEL

Positive Traits

Fine Gundogs, Clumbers are built low to the ground and are rather slow workers, but they are sure to find their prey (and make wonderful Retrievers when they do). These Spaniels do not have "typical" Spaniel builds. They are short-legged, have long bodies, are heavily boned, and have very large heads with heavy muzzles. These *Cosmic Canines* are about twenty inches at the shoulder and weigh an average of seventy pounds (compared to the American Cocker's fourteen-inch height and twenty-five pounds). Clumbers are better known and more popular in England than America, probably because they are seen as "dignified" dogs. In addition to flushing birds and retrieving, Clumber Spaniels are also good tracking dogs. They are very loyal, affectionate pets of average intelligence. They are easily trained for fieldwork, for which their instincts are strong, but require a little more work for obedience training.

Negative Traits

Clumbers are a bit sluggish. They do not have a lot of get-up-and-go, but from their perspective that leaves them more time to spend with human companions. These are not good watch-and-warn or guard dogs. There are no other known negatives about this dog breed.

Job Opportunities for Clumber Spaniels

Clumbers are affectionate, loyal family pets and make good (if somewhat slow-moving) exercise companions. These Spaniels are good dogs for multiple-pet families. Their laid-back personalities set good examples for other pets in the households. Outstanding Retrievers, they are slow but very purposeful when flushing birds. They make great dogs for seniors because of their settled temperaments. Clumber Spaniels are good visitors to those who are confined—again because of their settled temperaments (but also because of their loving, sympathetic attitudes).

Most Compatible Sun Sign: Libra

Libra human guardian temperaments have a great deal in common with Clumbers. Both are ordered, kind, amiable, restful, calm, and pleasant. Librans do not like to move fast any more than these dogs do. Natives of this sun sign take whatever time they need to make decisions and to move on them. And both have a great deal of instinctive intelligence. Librans have compassionate, balanced, and courteous demeanors that attract Clumber Spaniels like magnets. These *Cosmic Canines* are not known to be stubborn and will not cross wires with Libra natives when, in negative phases, they become combative, judgmental, and insensitive. Rather, Clumbers are likely to take an "Oh, well" attitude and wait for their Libra companions to return to normal.

COCKER SPANIEL (AMERICAN)

Positive Traits

Cocker Spaniels got their name from woodcocks, a game bird these *Cosmic Canines* find, flush from hiding, then retrieve so well. High-energy, playful Cocker Spaniels are adaptable to city or country living, to apartments or houses. They are beautiful dogs who make excellent family pets. Many seniors and preseniors will recall the years during which Cocker Spaniels were so popular they became victims of indiscriminate breeding practices—from inbreeding to any trick breeders could use to mass produce them. Their usually happy-go-lucky, affectionate personalities were destroyed. Whenever a dog breed becomes popular, this problem proliferates. Good breeding, though, has brought American Cockers back to the forefront of desirable home pets. They are intelligent and enjoy obedience training and performing in obedience rings (they love competing in conformation, too). Cockers are gentle, easy to get along with, and they are just plain cheerful. When well-bred, they are bright, adaptable, and trustworthy.

Negative Traits

These are high-energy dogs with a lot of endurance—not necessarily negatives unless people live in apartments and for some reason can't give dogs the exercise they need. If human companions have large yards and can throw sticks, balls, or Frisbees, Cocker energy will be properly directed. Cockers also need a lot of grooming—not difficult grooming, but consistent brushing and cleaning. If you show them in conformation competitions, professional grooming is required. A progressive retinal atrophy exists in this breed, so before adopting Cockers people should be sure appropriate breeder warranties exist (and medical assistance is sought should symptoms appear). It is very handy for those wanting to adopt Cocker Spaniels to spend a little time with at least one (and, if possible, both) parents. All puppies take on the personality traits of their parents at early ages. Cocker Spaniels may be too easily excitable for very young children—it depends on individual dogs. Normally, however, they are very gentle and loving with children. If you can meet the sire and dam, it tells you a lot about the suitability of a particular puppy for children.

Job Opportunities for Cocker Spaniels

Properly bred and trained, Cocker Spaniels are excellent bird dogs. They are also gentle, loving, and devoted family pets who are particularly excellent companions for singles. Whether human companions walk or run, Cockers are good exercise partners. Excellent for obedience-training hobbyists—these *Cosmic Canines* enjoy learning.

Most Compatible Sun Sign: Pisces

This calm water sun sign is receptive as well as giving. These human companions are of the kind who appreciate what Cocker Spaniels have to offer, and these dogs can sense it. Like Cocker Spaniels, Pisceans are easy to get along with. Sun sign natives of the Fishes are original and imaginative, thus interesting. They are sensitively sympathetic, thus compassionate. Pisces natives have a unique magnetism that both absorbs energy vibrations from other living beings and sends out energy vibrations when a sixth sense tells them another needs help or understanding. Cocker Spaniels can expect to receive Piscean vibrations filled with endearing warmth and the sense of peace unique to these natives. And they can expect Pisces to absorb doggie vibrations when they are sent. Some of Pisceans' bad vibes are likely to include selfish love, shyness, melancholy, and dissatisfaction. Pisceans are meticulous and technical by nature, and will bounce back to the positive side quickly. Their obsession to keep commitments will help keep on track the obedience-training lessons Cocker Spaniels so enjoy.

COCKER SPANIEL (ENGLISH)

Positive Traits

To be altogether proper—that is, English—Cockers must have ability and agility. English Cocker Spaniels are about five pounds heavier and an inch or two taller than their American cousins, and their muzzles are somewhat thicker. These *Cosmic Canines* are happy, on-the-go dogs who make wonderful family pets. They are excellent with children. English Cockers are so friendly that they do not make good guard dogs. They are more likely to greet prowlers than protest. If, however, prowlers make noise while breaking and entering—or knock on doors or ring doorbells—they may bark (but don't count on it). English Cockers enjoy learning new things, particularly the part that lets them share uninterrupted time with human companions. They just beam when they get a "good dog" (in America) or a "well done" (in England). Praise is definitely the way to this dog's heart. Equally, they require firm hands and an unchanging agenda. Set a training time and stick with it. If you have several children, English Cockers will keep them all busy and entertained. They like the city as well as the country but need room to exercise. And they are sufficiently active when in the house to require early obedience training. These are dogs for members of all age groups, but are not dogs for couch potatoes or the infirm. They need to get up and move around.

Negative Traits

Like all Spaniels, English Cockers shed and need regular brushing. An occasional trim by a professional is nice but not absolutely required. Training must start early and a little patience with house-training may be required. Keep to reliable schedules. Put them out to "do their business" (as they say) at the same, predictable times every day. These dogs need to know what you expect of them and when. Cockers are not good guard dogs nor reliable watch-and-warn dogs. The only real Cocker negatives are that they may lack concentration and need brushing and a little room to run.

Job Opportunities for English Cocker Spaniels

When properly bred and trained, English Cocker Spaniels flush game and retrieve very well. They are one of the best dogs for children—gentle, loving, and devoted family pets—and excellent companions for singles. Good exercise partners. Excellent for obedience-training hobbyists—all Cockers enjoy learning. Teach them to fetch your paper and slippers.

Most Compatible Sun Sign: Cancer

Cancer natives have a calming effect on these energetic dogs. Natives born under the sign of the Crab have many traits with strong appeal to English Cocker Spaniels. They are strong, purposeful, notably tenacious, and diplomatic. These are things English Cockers need. Cancer human guardians will not yell and will happily and sensitively praise pets for each good deed—and when reinforcement is in the form of praise, there will be many. Cancer natives are also sympathetic and compassionate and so are these dogs. When English Cockers decide to watch butterflies rather than learn their obedience or hunting lessons, Cancer natives will resolutely but with great empathy urge them back onto more focused tracks.

ENGLISH SPRINGER SPANIEL

Positive Traits

Probably one of the most famous dogs in America was Millie, the English Springer Spaniel belonging to George and Barbara Bush and about whom Mrs. Bush wrote a best-selling book (Millie died May 20, 1997). These beautiful *Cosmic Canines* are friendly, happy, and easy to please, learn lessons quickly and easily, and are willing workers who eagerly obey commands. They are very strong dogs and, combined with their exuberance for life, can be very entertaining. They are not passive animals who sit and wait for life to come to them; they look for good experiences and good friends. With the exception of toddlers, who, if they get in the dog's way, may be too small for so much energy, Springers are excellent with children. They excel at "springing" game—not coincidental to the breed's name—and are good, hard (and fast) workers in the field. Springer Spaniels are showmen at heart. They like just about everyone and do not make good guard dogs, but will usually watch and warn. They rank very high in intelligence, are loyal, and make wonderful home companions and house pets.

Negative Traits

Springer Spaniels may need doggie dips, special diets, or veterinary assistance with skin problems. It's nothing serious or dramatic; they just have sensitive skin. And as they age, Springers (sharing problems with humans) gain weight if they do not get enough exercise. They need low-fat, high-protein meals that are best achieved by feeding them small amounts of low-fat ground beef cooked in water served over a low-fat dry dog meal. A little low-fat cottage cheese can be added. Springers need regular grooming and bathing and they shed twice a year. Other than these minor irritants, there are no negatives about this dog breed.

Job Opportunities for English Springer Spaniels

First Dog at the White House and wonderful pets for children (even toddlers, if you're home with your children and can keep their enthusiasm under control). Great additions to families, they not only add love to the existing mix but are entertainers to boot. Springers retrieve whatever people teach them to fetch. They are good exercise and travel companions. When properly bred and trained, English Springer Spaniels still excel at fieldwork. Because Springers are so bright, they are wonderful dogs for obedience training.

Most Compatible Sun Sign: Aquarius

It's only logical (a talent at which Aquarians excel) for the breed that produced the dog memorialized in print by First Lady Barbara Bush to be most compatible with the sun sign during which President's Day is celebrated. English Springer Spaniels draw Water Bearers out. These sun sign natives are not known for outward displays of affection. Like these dogs, Aquarian humans are known for their patient determination, loyalty, honesty (Honest Abe Lincoln, remember?), and sincerity. Like Springers, natives of this sun sign are dependable, very intelligent, unassuming, kind, humane, and faithful. These two have a great deal in common. Unlike these *Cosmic Canines*, however, Aquarians are quiet and studious. Natives of the sign of the Water Bearer are good, quieting influences on these pets and make good teachers for dogs who love to learn. When in negative phases, Aquarian humans become disorganized, inflexible, unfocused, and undisciplined, but English Springer Spaniels will not be intimidated. These negatives are not unfamiliar to them (which is why the normally organized, flexible, focused, and disciplined Aquarius will be good with these dogs).

FIELD SPANIEL

Positive Traits

Field Spaniels are about as long as they are tall, are strong and built close to the ground. They possess great endurance, have average speed, and are moderately agile. In fact, those with liver-colored coats look a little like Irish Setters in Cocker Spaniel bodies. It is a pleasing result. Field Spaniels are attractive dogs and are known to be levelheaded. These *Cosmic Canines* can also be stubborn (though their fans call it "perseverance"). They are docile and obedient, moderately intelligent, patient, and quite affectionate. They make excellent home pets. They are good at flushing birds, excellent Gundogs, and successful Retrievers. Like all Spaniels, they love to learn.

Negative Traits

Field Spaniels need special attention paid to ear cleanliness and toenail trimming. Their coats are of medium length and they are feathered with longer hair on the chest, underbody, and legs. They require periodic brushings and baths, and they shed. Other than these relatively insignificant inconveniences, there are no known negatives about this breed.

Job Opportunities for Field Spaniels

When properly bred, Field Spaniels are good game and Gundogs. Few dogs can beat these *Cosmic Canines* in their roles as home companions. They are good dogs for the infirm or handicapped—besides their patience and levelheadedness, they are sympathetic and empathetic. Human companions can teach Field Spaniels to fetch just about anything they want brought to them. Excellent exercise and travel companions.

Most Compatible Sun Sign: Gemini

Adaptable, sensible, logical Gemini humans share many personality traits with Field Spaniels. Both are levelheaded, charitable, confident, and inquisitive. Field Spaniels love to learn, and Geminians love to teach (and learn). People born under sun sign Gemini have a tendency to display dual personalities but change won't shake up these easygoing, patient dogs. The happy one day, sad the next, charming one day, cynical the next style of the Gemini human guardian won't upset these dogs at all. In fact, Field Spaniels will likely consider getting acquainted with multiple-personality Gemini humans to be an interesting learning experience. Like this Spaniel, Geminians absorb all knowledge that comes their way throughout life. These sun sign natives have a lot of energy and like to be on the go—and Field Spaniels have the energy to keep up with them. People born under the sign of the Twins prefer to let their minds rule their hearts, disallowing emotional displays of affection. It will, however, be difficult for Gemini human companions to live with these charming dogs without getting their hearts entwined in the relationship. When these sun sign natives go into their negative cycles and become moody, high-strung worriers, Field Spaniel patience, levelheadedness, and affection will wait them out and help bring them back to the positive side. Gemini natives see nobility in the demeanor of these dogs.

GRIFFON (WIREHAIRED POINTING)

Positive Traits

When someone named these dogs "Wirehaired," they knew what they were doing. The breed standard refers to Griffon coats as somewhat like "the bristles on a wild boar." Translated, that means the coat is rough and coarse, a little harsh to the touch. And it serves an all-weather purpose. Wirehaired Pointing Griffons are strong dogs with protective temperaments. They are very good guard dogs and they are good with children. Add to that their affectionate, polite personalities and Wirehaired Pointing Griffons make wonderful pets. These *Cosmic Canines* are excellent hunting dogs, show independence and have confidence in their own abilities. And they have the determination to complete whatever field tasks they undertake. No quitters here! Griffons swim strongly (thus, excellent water Retrievers), point, and hunt small game. These flexible dogs will join you for a morning of duck hunting, chase foxes in the afternoon, and destroy rats and other vermin at night. Their unkempt appearance is part of this breed's charm. They are very intelligent, versatile working dogs.

Negative Traits

One of the best, most versatile of hunting breeds, these dogs are happiest in the outdoors, not in your kitchen or at your fireside. They enjoy time with their families, but the function of household pet comes second on their list of priorities. Their wirehaired coat requires stripping and that requires a stripping knife (which grabs and pulls loosening hair out without cutting it).

Job Opportunities for Wirehaired Pointing Griffons

First and foremost, they are sporting animals who love hunting and fieldwork. Griffons are polite members of the household and are gentle with children. Teach them to fetch and retrieve any reasonable object. These dogs fit right into the lifestyles of their human companions if they are into boating. Griffons love the water! Good exercise companions and, when properly trained, wonderful protectors (especially of children).

Most Compatible Sun Sign: Aries

People born under the sign of the Ram bring to this relationship the very independent style of individualists—almost a mirror reflection of Wirehaired Pointing Griffon traits. Along with Aries independence comes decisiveness, self-confidence, intelligence, and humorous energy. All are highly compatible with these *Cosmic Canines*. Sociable Ariens enjoy polite Griffon attitudes, especially when they are exhibited toward children.

It brings smiles to all idealistic Arien faces. Without human companions who communicate well—those who are outspoken and sensible—independent dogs can become too aloof and distant. Aries humans are outspoken, sensible, and have a great deal of determination. Natives of the Ram are energetic, strong, resolute, and prepared. So are these dogs. Wirehaired Pointing Griffons find Aries companions entertaining, original, and ready to explore new fields with them. The dogs may be more adaptable and flexible than the sun sign, but Ram natives are always ready to learn new things. When, because of negative cycles, Aries humans become headstrong, distant, and impatient, Wirehaired Pointing Griffons maintain their own sense of individuality and self-confidence. They patiently wait for their positive pals to rejoin them.

KEESHOND

Positive Traits

The wolf-gray Keeshond is recognized by the Netherlands as its national dog. Once guard dogs for barges, these *Cosmic Canines* are good, loyal watchdogs who bring mild temperaments to family settings. They are very loyal pets but may bond more with one person than with all family members. They attach themselves firmly to the member of the household they perceive as boss. Keeshonds have never been used for hunting or sled-pulling, which is somewhat unusual because of this dog's strength, heritage, and intelligence. They have performed limited Terrier functions—digging rabbits and rats from their underground tunnels. They are excellent family pets (preferring people to any other activity) who are as happy on Fifth Avenue as in the country. Keeshonds are alert and do not require a lot of exercise (another good reason for a Fifth Avenue address). Their ancestors include the Samoyed, Chow Chow, Norwegian Elkhound, and the Finnish Spitz. One big difference between a Keeshond and these now-distant relatives is that while the ancestors need substantial grooming, the Keeshond does not. According to owners of these affectionate pets, the less they're brushed, the more well groomed they look (but there are arguments about whether this is really true). Keeshonds became popular in Holland because of their charm not their utility. These easy-to-love dogs get along very well with children of all ages and their mild temperaments help them enjoy long lives.

Negative Traits

Loving Keeshond owners, breeders, and other dog personages argue about whether these dogs need regular grooming. All dogs with long hair and thick undercoats need to be brushed regularly and bathed periodically. And they shed. The only other negative about these dogs is a minor one. They are very loyal to a single member of the family. This problem can be reduced somewhat by making sure each family member spends meaningful time with the puppies when they first enter the family home. And with single-person-bonding pets, it is very important to have a Doggie Bill of Rights to which all family members adhere when correcting pets. That way, everyone appears to be "boss," not just one person. Other than these two minor negatives, these dogs are total positives.

Job Opportunities for Keeshonds

These beautiful dogs have the potential to be the supermodels of the dog world. Their expressive faces are intelligent and kindly (and very photogenic). Keeshonds are wonderful family pets, good children's dogs, and good exercise companions; they are good for households with multiple pets, can be taught to fetch newspapers and other useful articles, and won't hesitate to join you on family yachts whether traveling on rivers, lakes, or oceans. Good camping and travel companions (though their nineteen-inch height at the shoulder makes them a little large). And for those who want hunting companions, these versatile dogs respond positively to field training. These are wonderful dogs to take to nursing homes on visits to the elderly and infirm and to children's hospitals, where they can help cheer young patients.

Most Compatible Sun Sign: Libra

Who but sun sign natives whose ruling planet, Venus, gives them such a deeply felt appreciation for beauty and harmony could be most compatible with Keeshonds? Libra humans, like Keeshonds, have pleasant, amiable, and charming personalities. They are also naturally kind. Libra natives will, in fact, be the first to volunteer their time to take their loving Keeshond on visits to nursing homes and hospitals. Librans can charm the white off rice—and be sincere doing it! Like Keeshonds, Libra humans have an invisible kind of empathy, and both seem to naturally live their lives by the Golden Rule, instinctively treating others as they wish to be treated. Both dog and sun sign have good, balanced senses of justice and fair play. (Some say Solomon, with all his wisdom, was born under the sign of Libra.) Both these *Cosmic Canines* and sun sign natives are social animals who enjoy giving and receiving friendship (though, if allowed to do so, Keeshonds bond so strongly with the family member they perceive to be master/mistress, it will limit their friendships). Librans can be pretty materialistic, and sometimes need to be reminded that virtue is its own reward and charity is something one gives with one's heart, not one's head or pocketbook. Having Keeshond dogs helps Libra natives keep their priorities in order. And when Libran idealistic and humane natures turn negatively combative, judgmental, impractical, and thoughtless, having these dogs around as reminders of what positive Librans can be like helps bury the negativity quickly.

KERRY BLUE TERRIER

Positive Traits

These Irishmen gained their names from their mountainous homeland in County Kerry. Kerry Blues are gentle, lovable, and intelligent dogs. These *Cosmic Canines* were bred to hunt small game and birds, to retrieve on land and in water. In the early days, they were mostly known for being good farm dogs. But like all entrepreneurs, Kerry Blues adapted their professional skills to include hunting. None surpass their trailing and retrieving instincts. Then Kerries decided to expand their value to humans and became top-of-the-line watchdogs and companions. They got so good at it, they were used by Irish constables for police work. This dog's name might well be Kerry Blue Flexible Terrier because he has also been used to herd sheep and cattle. Like any good Irishman, Kerry Blues do not walk away from fights. They can be pugnacious with other dogs, but with their human companions are always affectionate. They are responsive to training (and are too spunky to go beyond puppyhood without it). These are well-rounded family pets who are normally good-humored and easy to get along with. In all of their jobs—farming, hunting, herding, police work, guard dogs—Kerries have shown themselves to be competent and courageous. In addition to all that, Kerry Blue Terriers are, when properly bred and trained, excellent with children.

Negative Traits

They have Irish tempers when aroused and their love of a good scrap with fellow canines doesn't make them the best multiple-pet family dog. When these good-natured animals go out in public, make sure they are leashed—Kerries are not averse to being the ones to start fights with other dogs (seldom, if ever, with human companions unless abused and misused). Like all happy, spirited animals, Kerry puppies need firm but gentle training during puppyhood to curb assertiveness (which may turn aggressive without training or when training is done with club in hand rather than brain in head).

Job Opportunities for Kerry Blue Terriers

What do you need done? Can it be done by a dog? If so, take the ad out of the Help Wanted section of the paper and give the job to Kerry Blues. There is really no limit to the talents these dogs bring to the canine work world. They are wonderful family pets, good watchdogs and companions, and will help on the farm or go hunting with you. They can be taught to fetch, play with the children, and jog a few miles every evening; they love to go anyplace in the car and protect people at their campsites—these dogs are highly versatile.

Most Compatible Sun Sign: Leo

Leo's appreciation for the dramatic and need for occasional impulsiveness will tickle the fancy of Kerry Blues. They share these same traits. Both dog and sun sign are forceful and vital yet kind and warmhearted. Both are loving individualists, decisive, energetic, faithful, and sincere. With all these things in common, these two have to be compatible! The dog breed may be occupationally more versatile than the sun sign humans, but Leos are wonderful actors and can play whatever roles are required. Kerries will never guess that their Leo companions didn't know how to do something when they first set out to achieve it. Like Kerry Blues, Leo natives are not famous for walking away from fights, even when it's the intelligent thing to do. Those born under the sign of the Lion are, like the dog, courageous, generous, and persevering. When someone tries to flatter Leo humans into doing something (Leos may follow you anywhere if you flatter them enough), sensible Kerry Blues will plant themselves firmly in front of the wandering Lion and, with a single look, tell him or her to "get real." Leo's sometimes loud arrogance and pushy attitudes won't upset these strong dogs. Kerries will likely raise an eyebrow, smirk, and think sarcastic thoughts over such pretentious behavior. Both of these animals (human and canine) are vibrant, authoritative, and assertive. There will be clashes of will, but in the end these *Cosmic Canines* and their Leo companions will be declared winners. When these two are together, they *are* winners.

PINSCHER (MEDIUM GERMAN)

Positive Traits

Built very much like Doberman Pinschers but much smaller (about eighteen inches at the shoulder and weighing thirty pounds or so), these *Cosmic Canines* are elegant medium-sized dogs. They are not, however, the best family pets. They are alert, distrust strangers (even if they are your friends), and make excellent guard dogs. German Pinschers are energetic and high-spirited. Plus, they are very quick. They are very loyal to their human companions. Color their temperament red, however—they can be fiery creatures. Because they are a little too energetic and playful (and independent) to be trusted with youngsters not yet teens, they are not a good mix with children. This is a very old breed that has protected European farms for many years. When properly bred and trained, they are well behaved, happy, active, attentive, and trustworthy in the home. Only human companions with dog-training experience—people used to independent, free-spirited, assertive animals and who know how to handle and train them—should adopt these dogs as pets.

Negative Traits

German Pinschers are aggressive to strangers, have quick tempers, and are not good with children. It can make a difference when they are raised with small humans from puppyhood, but parents need to be aware that they are not natural companions for little ones. They can be well behaved, happy, affectionate, and trustworthy once trained. They need attention (not bullying). German Pinschers need firm but humane discipline given with a lot of love. And they need praise given with exuberant enthusiasm when they do the right thing. It helps guarantee encores.

Job Opportunities for Medium German Pinschers

These are good guard dogs, protectors, good pets for adults comfortable around assertive animals who need training. They also serve as police, drug enforcement, military, and search-and-rescue dogs. Teach them to fetch, take them jogging (keep them leashed in public places), and, above all, obedience-train them. They are very intelligent and if they receive good training, make wonderful pets. There is no problem with these dogs or their temperaments. If problems exist, it is with people who are too passive to be companions for assertive, intelligent dogs like German Pinschers.

Most Compatible Sun Sign: Capricorn

Capricorns, like this dog breed, are similar to steel. Both are deemed by fate to work for life's happiness and satisfaction, to forge a purpose, friends, love, career. Dog breed and sun sign find it difficult to form lasting relationships because both tend to be intense, taking life very seriously. Those friends they make are very close and trusted allies. A great many people have tremendous respect and admiration for Capricorn and German Pinschers, but the independent attitudes of both (along with the intensity that goes with individualism) keep admirers at arm's length. On the outside, natives of the Goat appear very confident. On the inside, they question their own abilities. The same is true of these Pinschers. This personal insecurity is part of the reason they don't trust strangers. Capricorns are precise, exacting, persevering, persistent, and very self-reliant; so are German Pinschers. These two are a great deal alike—right down to their growls (usually worse than their bites). Capricorns are fair and balanced. Their approach to life is sure to please German Pinschers and go a long way toward earning their loyalty and trust. German Pinschers won't get their muzzles out of joint when Capricorn humans go through the cold, distant, aloof, and despondent personality cycles associated with this sun sign. These *Cosmic Canines* are intelligently independent and rely on their own resources during Capricorns' negative times.

SAMOYED

Positive Traits

They call these beautiful animals "smiling" or "reindeer" dogs. Sammies are devoted to their owners, are mostly obedient (if sometimes a little slow or stubborn), are possessive of their families, and are excellent watchdogs. These dogs are intelligent and adaptable. Sammies truly like people and feel affection for humankind. They are happiest in open country fields with new snowfall in which they can romp and play, but they won't complain about being restricted to household yards. Their personalities are quite complex. On the one hand, they are dignified; on the other, they love fun and have carefree attitudes. They are agile, dignified, gentle, and loyal. For their size, they are very graceful dogs, and their physical assets include higher-than-average energy and endurance. Sammies are as white as the snow they love so well and their coats are thick and long. At one time they herded reindeer. They have also served as guard dogs and have lived in close proximity to humans for many years. Samoyeds have lived in the same ice huts with people since the time of settlement of the Northwest Territories and have formed strong bonds with humans. Contrary to what many people think, Sammies have not been used much as sled dogs. The smile on the face of these dogs isn't phony. These are truly kind, caring, and friendly animals. Sammies are pure dog. Breeders say no mix of wolf or fox runs in their veins. Perhaps that's why they are so gentle and calm. Also, this dog (unlike others) has never been cast in the role of "killer." Maybe that's why they've been able to maintain their almost childlike demeanor. It is as natural for Samoyeds to guard as it is for them to be gentle and kind. They are seldom troublemakers. With their generous, giving personalities, white winter coats, and love of winter weather, Samoyeds have been dubbed the dog that best represents "the Spirit of Christmas."

Negative Traits

Human companions to Samoyeds need to devote daily time to brushing their luxurious coats. And Sammies shed twice a year. These dogs are a bit independent and can exhibit stubbornness. They need gentle but firm training with a lot of praise for what they do right. Emphasize the positive, eliminate the negative. Aside from these minor distractions, there are no negatives regarding this breed of dog.

Job Opportunities for Samoyeds

These dogs are not distrustful—just the opposite: They are quite friendly. Neither are they shy or overassertive. Yet they make wonderful guard dogs. Though not bred for sledding, they love the snow so much their human companions can harness them to children's sleds for days of winter fun. They can be easily trained for this function. Sammies make exceptional family pets and are very good with children (of whom they are protective). They are loving companions and protectors, good exercise pals, and they love accompanying you on trips in the car (though they're a little big for cross-country jaunts).

Most Compatible Sun Sign: Sagittarius

This imaginative but practical sun sign will truly appreciate the countless positives this dog brings to canine-human relationships. Like these *Cosmic Canines*, Saggie is independent and requires a certain amount of freedom. Both are friendly, and because they are social animals, they are successful in gaining many friends. Just as there is something basically honest about Samoyeds (there are no hidden agendas with these dogs), Sagittarians are also honest and forthright (sometimes too honest—or blunt—for their own good). Like Samoyeds, Sagittarians like people and have very high standards of behavior. They are very direct and honest—no Walter Mittys live here. What you see is what you get. Both dog breed and sun sign love the outdoors, and Samoyeds enjoy time camping under the stars or cavorting in the sun or snow with their Sagittarius human companions. Saggies are devoted, happy, confident, self-reliant, bright, hopeful, purposeful, honest, giving, and sincere. Samoyeds share all of these qualities. When natives of the Archer hit negative cycles and become sad, negative, gloomy, cold and distant, impatient and compulsive, Samoyeds patiently wait it out, quietly but stubbornly encouraging Sagittarians back to their normal, happy states of mind.

SCHNAUZER (STANDARD)

Positive Traits

Bred in Germany in the fifteenth century, Standard Schnauzers once were cattle drovers, protected sheep from coyotes, and served as effective watchdogs. Schnauzers have guarded market carts filled with German farm produce since the 1400s. These ruggedly built, likable pets seldom fight. Devoted and brave, Schnauzers were once used (in Germany) as police dogs by the army and as messenger dogs by the Red Cross. Like Miniature Schnauzers, Standards have faces with personality: arched eyebrows poised over deliberate eyes, and lots of whiskers. It is all part of a very distinctive Schnauzer aura—reliable, personable, curious, and alert. These *Cosmic Canines* are excellent guard dogs with a sixth sense about impending danger. They have moderate temperaments, are good Retrievers, and usually don't pick fights with other dogs. They are one of the top dogs for children, though their size and weight (about twenty inches and thirty pounds) when combined with Schnauzer enthusiasm can be dangerous for toddlers until after the dog has been reliably obedience-trained—until owners can physically contain them using verbal commands. Though Schnauzers do not require a great deal of exercise, it helps keep their energy under control when they get plenty of it. Standard Schnauzers are affectionate, intelligent, good-natured, lively, full of fun, and they love children and games. They are very little trouble and handy to have around the house.

Negative Traits

Their salt-and-pepper Schnauzer-gray coats are thick and harsh and require grooming. They need periodic clips, especially seasonally. Standard Schnauzers mistrust strangers and need careful introductions to family visitors. Depending on the visitor and until these dogs are trained, it may sometimes be smart to put Standard Schnauzers in private rooms when guests arrive. They were once used as ratters (which means they have a genetic heritage of digging). Watch them carefully as puppies and put an instant halt to little paws curious about Mother Earth. Keep their nails trimmed, too. Until well trained, Standard Schnauzers are not the best dogs for toddlers. Their temperaments are not the problem. Their energy and get-up-and-go personalities are the problems. There are no real negatives about the temperament of this dog breed.

Job Opportunities for Standard Schnauzers

These dogs make excellent house pets and family members. When human companions adopt Standard Schnauzers, they truly add a family member to their households. They make great exercise companions and can be taught to fetch. These *Cosmic Canines* are very good protectors and guard dogs. They are especially protective of children with whom they bond. Schnauzers are one of the best breeds to serve as travel companions, regardless of size. When traveling by car, special accommodations may need to be made at motels. These are personality kids who enliven any home. Standard Schnauzers are good for multiple-pet households if they are introduced to other pets while still puppies.

Most Compatible Sun Sign: Gemini

Natives born under the sign of the Twins (dual personalities) have a great deal in common with Standard Schnauzers. Both are adaptable, flexible, refined, sensible, charitable, bold, assertive, and confident. Geminis are known for their get-up-and-go personalities and for being charming, witty, and just plain happy. So are Standard Schnauzers. Gemini natives, along with Librans, are the two most charming sun signs in the zodiac. These people have few predetermined prejudices and are known for maintaining open minds and being open to new ideas. Geminis become bored and restless when faced with too much routine (and so do Standard Schnauzers) or get too close to ruts. Natives of this sun sign are alert, intelligent, great communicators—Schnauzers can't talk, but they sure do communicate—and are just a bit of an enigma. This sun sign and these *Cosmic Canines* are a great deal alike. Less evolved Gemini natives are self-indulgent, belligerent, unreliable, impetuous, inconsistent, aloof, high-strung, and moody. Having these charming pets around does much to motivate positive Gemini behavior.

SHAR-PEI

Positive traits

Once thought to be the rarest dogs in the world, Shar-Peis, known for their bravery, are excellent watchdogs, loyal to human companions, and, unless provoked, amiable. These *Cosmic Canines* were once known as the Fighting Dogs of China and were used to hunt wild boar and herd flocks. Though highly intelligent, and though breed books say they enjoy human companionship and are good with children, care must be taken with these aloof, independent animals. Pay attention to the words *unless provoked*. What is fun and play for one dog may be provocation to another. If your ninety-year-old mother or father feels bad about the wrinkles that go with aging, make sure they get the chance to see Chinese Shar-Pei puppies—they are born with wrinkles and keep them throughout life. These dogs are alert and there is an aura of dignity about them. They enjoy people with whom they have bonded, but are not the safest pets to have in the same room with exploring toddler hands. Even adult hands belonging to friends who are strangers to the dog may provoke it. Some people are nervous around dogs and these particular dogs can sense that fear. It may make them a little assertive.

Negative Traits

Chinese gladiators, Shar-Peis have short, porcine prickly coats and, like Chow Chows, blue tongues. They may be more susceptible to skin diseases than other dog breeds. Shar-Pei dogs need room to burn up their substantial energy. The somewhat unpredictable temperaments of these dogs don't make them good companions. They tend to bond very strongly with one person and are sometimes a little standoffish (at best) or hostile (at worst) to others. They were pit fighters in China when dog fighting (and ownership) was legal. This is not a good first pet, but experienced dog people who are used to handling spirited, powerful animals will be comfortable with Shar-Pei dogs. They are not recommended as pets for children.

Job Opportunities for Shar-Peis

Their unique physical appearance makes Shar-Peis great dogs for modeling and advertising purposes. Good guard and protection dogs. Good companions for dog fanciers who have experience handling and training powerful, dominant animals. First-time Shar-Pei companions should take these canines to professional trainers, but be sure you're not so shy around them as to be unable to implement ongoing training once the professionals have completed their jobs. When properly bred and trained, they are still good herding animals. They are good exercise partners (but only in areas where there are no unleashed dogs running around—and always keep Shar-Peis leashed when in public).

Most Compatible Sun Sign: Scorpio

Powerful, determined Scorpio humans command respect from Shar-Pei dogs, which is a big first step in controlling their energetic, somewhat unpredictable personalities. Scorpio natives are a little unpredictable, too, and are said to be invincible. Like this dog breed, those born under this sun sign are dominant, forceful, and have great strength of character. Shar-Pei dogs will find that they, like Scorpio humans, thrive on approval and are decisive, quick thinkers. Both are persistent, dignified, and inquisitive. They can be friendly but are suspicious of strangers and trust only a few very close friends. There is an aura of mystery around both the Scorpio sun sign and this dog breed, so these two will spend many happy hours trying to solve the puzzle presented by the other. Scorpio humans weren't hiding when they handed out brains and neither were Shar-Peis. Scorpios, too, have tempers and have been known to wound those who "provoke" them. Neither canine nor human is frightened of much in life and neither worries much about what others think of them. They set their own unique standards and are laws unto themselves. Scorpio human companions are known for their courage and resourcefulness. They are also known for willful, rigid, harsh, faultfinding, and ignorant behavior. Other negative Scorpio traits: They are critical, skeptical, uncontrollable, and boorish. Negative Scorpio behavior won't impact Shar-Pei dogs one tiny bit. They, too, are resourceful.

SIBERIAN HUSKY

Positive Traits

These very reliable dogs are the most friendly of the Arctic Spitz breeds and are very good with children. Their history comes from far northeastern Asia and originated with the Chukchis tribe. Faithful Huskies are gentle with all people, big and small. An added bonus is that they carry no doggie odors. They are versatile, attentive, graceful, submissive, affectionate, and kind. Siberians are not just sled dogs, these *Cosmic Canines* are *eager* sled dogs. Huskies *love* sledding! These are at the top of the list as sled team members, but otherwise—when taking part in dog functions requiring non-sled-oriented training—are only of average intelligence. And they can be stubborn, stubborn, stubborn. As puppies, few dogs can outplay them, but they become more reserved with age. Huskies need exercise—need to run—and need to be around people, especially children. They have happy temperaments and *need* these things to stay that way. They have very high energy levels and are almost always moving. Huskies are powerful animals and have great endurance.

Negative Traits

Siberian Huskies need a lot of exercise and grooming, shed twice a year, and are stubborn animals. Huskies don't bark; rather, they howl. To make them howl is to leave them alone. They hate being alone. They are not good guard or watch-and-warn dogs. They like people too much, including prowlers. It can be difficult to contain Huskies and they may be too energetic for small children (it depends on individual dogs and owners' abilities to train and control them).

Job Opportunities for Siberian Huskies

If you're putting a dogsled team together, don't leave home without your Siberian Husky. Hitch these stars to your children's wagons or sleds, turn them loose in the yard, and let both be entertained for hours. They are wonderful, loving companions for families with school-aged children and especially for seniors who want loving canine companions but do not need watch-and-warn or guard dogs. Huskies are good company for the lonely but are not the best dogs for the infirm. They are too active and need too much exercise. Regardless of size, they are great exercise partners and travel companions (though accommodations for size may need careful planning when traveling cross-country by car). Not the best obedience-training dogs for hobbyists. Their stubbornness shows itself during training sessions.

Most Compatible Sun Sign: Pisces

Those born under the sign of the Fishes are sympathetic and understanding. They motivate trust, have peaceful natures (which is good for these overly energetic dogs), and have the patience to deal effectively with Husky stubbornness. So, too, will the control that is so much a part of the Piscean personality be good for the personal development of these dogs. In addition to having personality traits that compensate for Husky weaknesses, Pisces humans are compassionate, sensitive, warm, and sympathetic—just what Siberian Huskies need to be happy. Natives of the Fishes earn the loyalty of these dogs, and a good thing, too. Pisceans are hurt when others are disloyal (so are these dogs). Huskies need love and Pisces humans have a lot of it to give. Pisces canine companions also need love and Huskies have a lot of it to give. These two are really good together! Those born under this sun sign are moodier than natives born under the other eleven signs, and Huskies will patiently and lovingly offer support to help them through these periods. Pisces humans are very sensitive and get hurt easily, something loving Huskies would never intentionally do. When in their negative cycles, Pisceans are unsettled, contradictory, and excitable; they can also be melancholy. None of these negatives are foreign feelings to Siberian Huskies, who can relate to how their human companions feel when negative phases occur. They will patiently wait for the moods to pass and will be there to welcome their positive companions home!

SPITZ (FINNISH, NORBOTTEN, AND JAPANESE)

Positive Traits

The brilliant reddish-coated Finnish Spitz (which cleans itself with its paws like a cat) is Finland's national dog. The pure white Japanese Spitz is the smallest of the three at fifteen inches high and thirteen pounds (the Finnish averages seventeen inches and thirty pounds; Norbotten, sixteen inches and twenty-eight pounds). The Norbotten (or, Nordic) Spitz has limited cream, red, or brown spots on its mostly white and much shorter coat. Each of these three Spitz breeds has a unique beauty all its own. Each is brave (though the Finnish is a little more cautious than the Nordic or Japanese). All three *Cosmic Canines* make excellent guard dogs, are faithful, home-loving, and sociable. Spitzes are independent dogs with the Japanese characterized as very clean, vigorous, and daring; the Norbotten is adored by the Swedish for being quiet and affectionate; and the Finnish makes headlines as sensitive, sometimes stubborn, and requiring less affection and attention from human companions than the other two breed representatives. All are of medium intelligence. In addition to being excellent family pets, they are mostly small-game hunters and farm dogs.

Negative Traits

All have thick, heavy coats and require several brushings each week; they shed twice a year. The Finnish Spitz is a little less likely to make good pets for small children because they are too independent. The Japanese Spitz tends to be a one-person dog who distrusts strangers. There are, however, no known negatives of substance about any of these three Spitz breeds.

Job Opportunities for Finnish, Norbotten, and Japanese Spitz Dogs

Most Spitz breeds have heritages anchored in Viking lore. Properly bred and trained, they still serve as hunting and sporting dogs. The Finnish Spitz has a wonderful Alpine yodel and can sing with the best of them. All three of these Spitz breeds make excellent family pets: with the Japanese you get all the advantages of the Toy breeds in a somewhat larger package, Norbottens are quiet and loving pets with positive outlooks on life, and the Finnish give human companions independent animals who are excellent protectors. All are good guard or watch-and-warn dogs. The Norbotten and Japanese Spitz make good travel companions. The suspicious nature of the Finnish variety might make travel, a function in which many strangers are encountered, difficult.

Most Compatible Sun Sign: Cancer

One of the most loving of sun signs, Cancerians do not express their emotions outwardly very often. This suits the independent natures of these Spitz dogs—especially the Finnish Spitz, who just doesn't go for public displays of affection and prefers to be the one to determine when love will be dispensed and received. Natives of the sign of the Crab are friendly (and are usually there when you need them most), reserved, a little shy, and very gentle. They are also very determined people and pretty self-possessed and independent. All of these zodiacal personality traits are compatible with these dogs. Just as the Spitz is home-loving, Cancer natives are among the most home-loving of all sun signs. Also like Spitz breeds, Cancerians are very sensitive, kind, and warm. There is nothing superficial or phony about these Spitz dogs, or Cancerians. There is a kind of honest openness about both. Cancer humans also have the patience to deal with occasional Spitz stubbornness and independence and are notably tenacious (yet diplomatic). This is a very rational, logical, calm, strong, and purposeful sun sign—just what dogs of these breeds need! And all three of these dog breeds are quite emotionally strong enough to deal with Cancer humans when they become fearful, brooding, self-serving, and worried. These *Cosmic Canines* even handle negative Cancerian selfishness pretty well. These are independent dogs who can prove to Cancer natives that they are not the only ones who understand "a friend in need is a friend indeed." These dogs buy into that philosophy one hundred percent.

WELSH SPRINGER SPANIEL

Positive Traits

Welsh Springer Spaniels are high spirited yet very good natured. They are very polite (the most politically correct of the Spaniel set), and they expect their companions to be the same. They are loyal, willing, and fine Gundogs with excellent scenting capabilities. When properly handled, they can be tireless. They are good water dogs with a lot of endurance. They make very good family pets provided they get proper exercise. They are lively, enthusiastic dogs with adaptable natures. Unlike their counterparts in the Spaniel group, Welshies have worked at trades other than hunting—like herding cattle. When properly bred and raised, they can be flexible and adaptable pets. They are active, obedient, and friendly. These dogs seldom forget lessons learned in their youth, so teach them young and teach them right. You will enjoy your training for the dog's entire life. They are faithful, real pals, and gentle with children.

Negative Traits

Welsh Springer Spaniels need training or they can become lone, destructive hunters. Without good training, they may use their excellent scenting capabilities independently of human companions. They are better country than city dogs, but if you don't mind driving them to country fields a few times a month so they can have good runs, Welsh Springer Spaniels can adapt nicely to life with families in city settings.

Job Opportunities for Welsh Springer Spaniels

Springers can be trained to herd cattle (as in the past). They are not the best watch-and-warn dogs, but are better than other Spaniels at the task. Excellent waterfowl hunters with superior scenting abilities, they make good Gundogs. On the home front, Welsh Springers are faithful and loyal pets. For those who get their morning newspapers delivered, you can send your Welsh Springer out to the curb to bring it in. They will also happily retrieve slippers and other "totables." These are wonderful family pets provided they receive sufficient exercise. They are also good companions for children. Good exercise partners and travel companions (by car or boat).

Most Compatible Sun Sign: Cancer

Cancer loves anything to do with the water, and Welshies love the water. Cancer natives tend to be polite—they are known for their diplomacy—and Welsh Springer Spaniels expect to be treated politely (because that is how they treat others). Loyal, adaptable, and enduring are words used to describe both natives of this sun sign and these dogs. Natives of Cancer the Crab are sensitive, determined, understanding, self-reliant, and rational. They are also strong, purposeful, sympathetic, and compassionate. All are traits appreciated by dogs of this breed. Cancer human companions stay calm when Welshies become excited and that helps settle these dogs down. These two have a great deal in common. Cancer human companion negatives include emotional frustrations, brooding natures, and the inability to bring balance to their lives. Natives of the Crab can be worried, selfish, and cowardly. The positive nature of Welsh Springer Spaniels helps keep Cancer humans on positive, productive roads.

WHIPPET

Positive Traits

These miniature English Greyhounds are sporting dogs. Whippets are trim, graceful, dignified, gentle, and faithful. If school-aged children have been sufficiently trained to deal with high-energy (sometimes nervous—usually resulting from too little exercise rather than temperament) pets, Whippets can be good companions for them. Quiet of temperament most of the time, Whippets may be nervous when placed in strange surroundings—or when familiar surroundings suddenly involve the unknown (like when visitors unknown to the dog drop in). Like the Greyhounds they so resemble in everything but size, these Cosmic Canines are built to run. They are lean and muscular and make healthy, hardy pets. Whippets have short coats, making grooming and bathing tasks minimal and easily accomplished. Bred to be rabbit hunters and racing dogs, they are beautiful animals and have also been used as ratters. Sight (rather than scent) Hounds tend to chase things that move in rapid, irregular patterns in front of them. Children who have hamsters will need to keep them in their cages. Whippets are affectionate, willing to please, and beautiful. They can be a bit possessive, but when properly trained to be watch-and-warn dogs on grounds other than possessiveness (which results in jealous, not protective, dogs), they serve well in this role. Whippets have a subtle kind of dignity about them and, if good breeding techniques have been observed, are usually quiet, calm animals.

Negative Traits

Some Whippets still have strong hunting instincts and, like Basset Hounds, are known to be wanderers. Keep backyard gates closed. Knowing the sire and dam is important because unless carefully bred, Whippets can be high-strung and nervous. Whippets need a lot of exercise. If they are forced to be too sedentary, they can become hypertensive. Bottled-up energy can easily be reduced by taking this dog for long runs or fast walks. Whippets are great sight hunting dogs, which, for hunters, is great. The tendency of these animals is to see everything going on around them. And this adds a difficult dimension to obedience training. Begin basic obedience training by six months of age.

Job Opportunities for Whippets

Depending on the level of physical fitness, Whippets are wonderful companions for seniors. People who are able to hop on bicycles for daily rides can train their Whippets to trot alongside their bikes. For sedentary, city-dwelling seniors, these are not the best pets. Whippets are excellent rabbit hunters, are good pets for families with older children who are familiar with high-energy pets, and make excellent watch-and-warn dogs. If calm of nature (properly bred, they will be), Whippets are great travel companions. Teach them to fetch papers, slippers—whatever. They're good at it. Whippets are wonderful farm dogs, especially if the farm has a lot of fields in which these dogs can run!

Most Compatible Sun Sign: Libra

Graceful, gentle, and faithful—that's Libra humans. And it's Whippets, too. Also like this dog breed, balanced Librans are courteous, enjoy pleasing others, work to create harmonious surroundings, and, under most circumstances, are noted for their calm demeanor. And the Libran trait of having a calming effect on others when they become nervous or tense offers a positive plus to Whippet temperaments. In fact, natives of this sun sign are known for their perceptive insights and will probably be able to tell when these dogs are about to become upset. Libra humans are not possessive and will not encourage their Whippet pets to be either. This generous, compassionate, and humane sun sign also sends out restful vibes to those around them. When Librans become thoughtless and restless, unfocused or impractical, Whippet charm brings charm-loving Librans back to positive reality.

5

LARGE DOGS

AFGHAN HOUND

Positive Traits

Were Afghan Hounds Noah's choice for the dog family when he filled the ark two by two? There are those who say so. The ancient Jebel Musa (the Mountain of Moses) is on the peninsula of Sinai, and Afghans, an ancient breed, come from that part of the world. Others say Noah had too much common sense to take on this journey dogs who needed so much grooming to maintain their proud beauty. Afghans have much to recommend them as pets, though. They are loyal, trustworthy, and affectionate. These *Cosmic Canines* are good with school-aged children who are well behaved and experienced around dogs, but they don't handle childish teasing very well (whether it comes from children within the family or their friends). These dogs are dignified and aloof. They love their creature comforts and won't sit by the car, tails wagging, begging to go spend the night in the great outdoors when human companions start to load their camping equipment. Though they tend to be reserved, it is impossible to show Afghans too much affection and attention. They do not respond well to loud-voiced bullying. Their dignity, intelligence, and independence are insulted by such treatment and their normally happy temperaments may turn sullen when human companions try to dominate through brute force rather than brain matter. They have been used as hunters, herders, and watchdogs. Once trained, Afghan Hounds appear to have a sixth-sense kind of wisdom in home protection. Some mystic force seems to tell them who is a friend and who is a foe.

Negative Traits

Afghans require daily exercise and, as large dogs, quite a bit of it. At the very least, they need large yards and are not suitable for apartments. They need daily grooming. Unless very well trained, Afghans should be adopted by no later than three months of age. If they are not taught who the boss is while they are small, there is a chance they won't learn it at all. Afghans have a lot of character, but most of it is very independence-based. They can be charming and affectionate in the hands of human companions who have the right dog stuff. With the wrong ones, they can be demanding, aggressive tyrants. As puppies, they can have overly as-sertive temperaments and, because they grow to be such large animals by six months of age, very basic obedience and control training must occur at a young age. If the human guardians of these dogs don't teach Afghans who is boss while they are puppies, upon reaching maturity they will gladly dominate relationships. People who aren't capable of giving firm discipline without becoming bullies in the process should get smaller dogs with lighter temperaments.

Job Opportunities for Afghan Hounds

These *Cosmic Canines* are big- and small-game hunters. They herd and guard sheep and cattle and, when properly trained, are excellent home-protection guard dogs. Afghans can be the very best of companions for humans not afraid of leadership (as opposed to command) and capable of implementing it. They are wonderful country and/or exercise compan-ions where room to run is available (whether on leash, trotting alongside bicycles, or running freely in country fields). Teach them to fetch, but do it carefully and in a way not likely to demean their sense of dignity. Afghans are good family pets only when older children have been taught canine manners and don't think it great fun to tease dogs. Inhumane treatment of any kind can be dangerous when you're playing with Afghans. They just don't tolerate it very well.

Most Compatible Sun Sign: Gemini

Many people think Gemini natives are cold and distant. In reality, they feel things deeply, but simply display their reactions to life in more action-oriented ways than others. Just as Aries natives are idealistic from the heart (and often leap into things without thinking them through), Geminians are idealistic from the head, and they withhold their heart until they think everything through. Like Afghan Hounds, then, Geminis are a bit of an enigma. Both sun sign and dog breed are loyal, trustworthy, and affectionate to a select few. To those for whom they do not feel close enough to show affection, both appear aloof and distant. Both are dignified and love creature comforts—as a percentage of total zodiac personalities, fewer Gemini natives want to spend weekends camping. Also like Afghans, it is impossible to show Gemini humans too much affection and attention. They usually don't give a lot of it themselves, but they thrive when it is given to them. And though Gemini humans are capable of being one of the biggest bullies in the zodiac, they do not respond well to loud-voiced bullying themselves—just like these dogs. In fact, the best way to make Gemini humans or Afghan dogs behave like bullies is to treat them in a bullyish way. This dog breed and these sun sign natives have the ability to make friends quickly, but neither forms many close, long-lasting personal relationships. Both are too critical of others and find too many motes in other people's eyes. When Gemini companions take the negative road and begin bullying—and they are often not aware that they are doing it—the sullen, bully-boy attitudes of their Afghans will make them aware of their behavior.

AIREDALE

Positive Traits

Airedales are the largest of the Terrier group and are attractive—dapper, if you will. These dogs are very energetic (like most Terriers), and they have sound temperaments. These *Cosmic Canines* are intelligent, faithful, loyal to human companions, and are usually very good with children. Airedales are not just energetic, they have lasting stamina and need exercise to let off some of the nervous energy that naturally occurs when energetic dogs are forced to be too sedentary. They make excellent family pets and, when properly trained, very good guard and protection dogs. Airedales have worked as patrol dogs on the docks and with the railroads. During World War II, they served in both the Russian and British armies and also worked for the Red Cross, locating the wounded and carrying messages. During their combat experience, it was determined that Airedales would execute commands even when wounded. Such is their tenacity. Like most Terriers, they are very courageous and show wonderful patience with children. In the field, they are indefatigable hunters and can be trusted to use good judgment. Because of their high energy levels and somewhat excitable natures, Airedales are better around older children than tots (though this somewhat depends on human abilities to train and discipline both dog and child). These dogs will defend their families and their homes fearlessly. Airedales are okay with city life despite their high energy levels, but need exercise. They have the intelligence for obedience training and, once the job is done, usually display perfect manners in all social situations.

Negative Traits

Airedales have hard, wiry coats that shed periodically and require regular brushing. They need to be hand-stripped (which requires a special stripping knife that any pet store can demonstrate how to use), but otherwise need very little care. Airedales can be overprotective, especially of children, and they are territorial. These *Cosmic Canines* have been known to start fights with strange dogs who enter "their territory" and, as a result, require early obedience training. They like to run and play, indoors and out. They are aloof to strangers, distant. They are usually polite to outsiders (people and dogs) unless attacked. When provoked into fights, Airdales are fearless and unstoppable.

Job Opportunities for Airedales

Want a Retriever—both land and water? A dog to flush birds? A Gundog? A dog to hunt otters or badgers or rabbits? Need a hunting machine to kill rats and other vermin? Adopt an Airedale. Or perhaps you want a polite family friend with whom to share your home and to protect it? Again, Airedales fill the bill. These dogs also make wonderful companions for school-aged children and good exercise partners, and they travel well. Don't leave these dogs in your motel or hotel room while you go have breakfast, or you may have to rescue a maid who chances into the room to clean. Teach Airedales to retrieve and to play games. Their temperaments make them highly versatile.

Most Compatible Sun Sign: Virgo

Like Airedales, Virgo human companions are self-contained and polite, reasoned and tactful. Also like this dog breed, no sun sign is more dependable. When they say they'll do something, take it to the bank: they *will* do it! And just as Airedales pounce on rats in the blink of an eye, Virgoans have been known to pounce as quickly on faults they see in people—or dogs. They will find little in these pets to criticize. Virgo natives are as down-to-earth as Airedales and will appreciate the rather unusual canine common sense these pets display. Both dog and sun sign are intelligent, faithful, and loyal, and they love children. There is one particular trait these two share, and it is unique between canines and sun sign natives: both need to be of service to others. Both are into learning and self-improvement. Those born under sun sign Virgo are useful people, Airedales are useful dogs. Like these *Cosmic Canines*, natives of this sun sign are active, discriminating, and constructive. Both are calm even though they are energetic and both need good diets to achieve and maintain maximum health. When natives of the Virgin become defensive, domineering, filled with self-pride, or critical, Airedales are quite strong enough to wait out the negative spell. They are likely to ignore Virgo companions, which does a lot to motivate a Virgo to return to the positive side of life.

AKITA (JAPANESE)

Positive Traits

Unfortunately, these proud and bearlike dogs came to the public eye when Nicole Brown Simpson's pet Akita was heard barking and howling after she was brutally murdered. Much attention was paid in court to the dog's behavior the night of the tragedy. According to Stanley Coren, in his book *The Intelligence of Dogs*, Akitas are ranked fairly low in the working and obedience categories of intelligence. Though the American public has only recently become aware of this breed, their Japanese roots are ancient. These *Cosmic Canines* were originally bred to be hunters of wild boar, deer, and black bear. To that task, they are adaptable and easily trained. They are also known to be excellent guard dogs with amenable, even temperaments. Akitas are members of the Spitz family. If not raised with children in the family, they may not be good with them. When raised from puppyhood with children, they are generally very good and trustworthy. Until children are school-aged, however, dog-children activities should be supervised. When raised with children, they are usually very protective of them. Generally, Akitas are said to be loyal and have a great deal of integrity.

Negative Traits

When set upon by other animals or abused by humans, Akitas can respond with ferocity. They were bred to be fighting dogs and gained their reputation in Japanese dog pits. They are sometimes perceived as a bit aloof and withdrawn. Though their air of detachment makes them appear less than affectionate as pets, they have an independent nature and rely less on human beings for their sense of identity than some other breeds. They are very loyal dogs who simply don't fawn over people to prove their loyalty. They have very heavy coats that require regular brushing but little professional grooming. If not properly exercised, Akitas can become lazy, do-nothing animals. And they can be prideful and stubborn.

Job Opportunities for Japanese Akitas

Good dogs for mountainous areas where bears are present. Having Akitas around will likely keep them from trying to get into your kitchen or trash. This happens with periodic regularity in overpopulated bear areas, where people are spilling over from large cities into suburban mountain communities. Akitas are excellent guard dogs, good companions for families with older children or who adopt these puppies while the children are very young. Not the best travel companions, but very good exercise partners.

Most Compatible Sun Sign: Scorpio

Like Akitas, human Scorpios are filled with power and determination. Both are strong and seldom make neutral impressions on others. People either like them or do not. Both natives of Scorpio and Akitas have a passion for life within their spirits. It is not dependent upon any outside force, it just simply is. The sun sign of the Scorpion is associated with the mysteries of life, and Akitas will forever live as the canine representative most closely associated with one of America's greatest mysteries. Like these *Cosmic Canines*, natives of Scorpio are careful about whom they associate with. Neither wants to become too close to anyone; to do so causes Scorpions to reveal too much about themselves and, thus, lose their auras of mystery. There is little that frightens either the dog or natives of this sun sign. Courage, both moral and physical, is the byword of Scorpio humans and Akitas. Neither cares much about the opinions of others when it comes to themselves. Both dog and sun sign have firm views of who they are and that is more important to them than what others think. When angered, the Scorpion can strike out in a way that causes lifelong wounds. The same is true of Akitas. In their negative cycles, Scorpio humans have a tendency to be cruel—a trait intelligent people (and Scorpions are intelligent) would not visit on such physically strong and dominant opponents as these dogs. Thus, the very powerful nature of Akitas helps Scorpio natives keep a potential negative trait at bay. These two peas are from the same pod.

AMERICAN WATER SPANIEL

Positive Traits

Animated, friendly, and loving, the American Water Spaniel appears to have evolved primarily in the Midwest and, as Retrievers, are outstanding performers. These *Cosmic Canines* will retrieve numerous fallen birds and are equally as good with rabbits and chickens as with quail, pheasant, or ducks. People who live on farms should keep chicken coops closed. American Spaniels have typical Spaniel personalities—energetic, affectionate, intelligent—and are excellent scent-and-find dogs. They are enthusiastic and thorough. American Water Spaniels are good family dogs and serve as efficient watchdogs. Unlike more harshly coated Irish Water Spaniels, American Water Spaniels work thickets and rough ground easily. They don't need massive grooming in the aftermath because briars and burrs don't stick so readily to their fine coats. These are intelligent dogs who like to please their human companions. In the field, which is where they prefer to be, they have speed and endurance. In the home, they are agreeable and energetically happy pets.

Negative Traits

American Water Spaniels have fine, dense, curly coats that need brushing periodically. Other than grooming responsibilities, there are no known negatives about this dog

Job Opportunities for American Water Spaniels

Hunting companions, family companions, protector guard dogs, they also add positive, happy attitudes to any household. Good dogs for obedience training and wonderful exercise partners and travel companions Teach these dogs to retrieve just about anything; their gentle mouths will bring it undamaged. These pleasing dogs love doing just that: pleasing others. Another plus, these Spaniels are wonderful boating and yachting companions. They guard boats and everything on them. They even enjoy swimming with human companions on boating holidays. These are excellent employees for barge captains and/or owners. American Water Spaniels provide the kind of protection to barges that Doberman Pinschers and German Shepherds provide for police departments.

Most Compatible Sun Sign: Pisces

Water sun sign Pisces, like Scorpio, is a bit of a mystery and, like Gemini, this sun sign has a dual nature. The same is true of American Water Spaniels. This dog breed is a mystery to a lot of people who have not heard of it, and these *Cosmic Canines* certainly are dual in purpose—as sporting and family dogs. They do very well at both. And Pisces natives, like these dogs, are ruled by Water Both have sympathetic natures, are perceptive, and have a kind of kinship for humanity Pisces natives, like these dogs, are receptive and loving and can be easily hurt by disloyalty. Both perform at their peak when encouragement is given and confidence is placed in them (criticism is seldom viewed by either as constructive). Also like American Water Spaniels, Pisces humans are happiest at home. Natives of this sun sign offer many personality traits required by this dog breed to be truly happy: excitement, a sense of peace and calm, compassion, sympathy, and warmth. When Pisces humans become melancholy

and sad, or irresolute and unsettled, American Water Spaniel temperaments urge them back to their normally happy, peaceful states of mind.

BELGIAN SHEEPDOG (GROENENDAEL)

Positive Traits

If you're driving west on I-70 in Colorado, about fifteen minutes beyond
the small town of Rifle is an even smaller town called Parachute. Along
the north side of the highway is a Native American curio shop owned
by the ex-mayor of the town—and his Belgian Sheepdog. If you want to
see a perfect example of this dog breed, stop and meet Dave's dog, Radar.
He's alert and curious, very well behaved, quite intelligent (and well
trained), and amiably protective of the store. He lies quietly but alertly
behind a small gate, but when given permission to cross into the cus-
tomer area of the store, he walks behind the counter and looks curiously
at customers who express an interest in him. He is friendly yet guarded.
Belgian Sheepdogs are very protective—especially of children—and make
excellent guard dogs. They are hale and hardy. Historically, Belgian Sheepdogs have been used for hunting and herding. They also served as Red
Cross messengers in wartime. In fact, they were the first dogs trained
for war duty, and according to the record books, many lost their lives.
Belgian Sheepdogs are beautiful, with coal-black, medium-length, somewhat harsh coats. The Belgians have bred two additional sheepdogs: the
Laekenois and the Malinois. The Laekenois has a temperament not suited
for children, is quite dominant, and wary of people. The Malinois can be
nervous and has been known to pick fights with other dogs, though it is a
better family pet than the Laekenois Belgian Sheepdog. Black Groenendael Belgian Sheepdogs are devoted to their families and are very protective of them (sometimes to a fault—don't let them get too possessive).
Guarding is almost as inherent to this breed as curiosity. They show no
fear of or timidity with strangers. These are very courageous dogs, too.

Negative Traits

Their medium-length and feathered black (sometimes with small white
patches) coat does require care. Belgian Sheepdogs do best in open
spaces. At the very least they need large yards and are not good apartment

dogs. They need firm but kind handling as they are firm but gentle and kind dogs. Belgians are very possessive and, if spoiled, they can become jealous. A jealous Shepherd is a dangerous Shepherd (or Sheepdog). They compete for the attention of their primary human companions. These dogs need obedience training to blossom into the superior human companions they are capable of being. If you have no desire to train a dog, this is not the best dog breed for you to adopt as your pet.

Job Opportunities for Groenendael Belgian Sheepdogs

Once trained, there are few dogs who can live up to the companionship, protection, and hunting and herding skills offered by Groenendael Belgian Sheepdogs. They guard families and property, are seldom timid or shy, are great exercise (or business) partners, travel well, and happily fetch whatever human companions teach them to retrieve. They are very curious dogs (which makes them excellent drug search and police dogs) and are able to serve in a variety of military dog capacities. About the only things these dogs are not are cuddly lap dogs (although they sometimes try to be). Hire them to quietly guard merchandise in retail outlets where detached friendliness with customers must be maintained. Like Dave's Radar, Belgian Sheepdogs thrive on such challenges.

Most Compatible Sun Sign: Sagittarius

If humans born under the sign of the Archer had a twin personality, it would have most of the traits inherent in Belgian Sheepdogs. These two are very much alike. Both are curious souls with very positive attitudes who show high degrees of loyalty, sincerity, and honesty. Both need to learn discipline to achieve maximum potential, are giving, sincere, loyal, affectionate, and require freedom. Sagittarians are well liked, active, devoted, confident, self-reliant, and have a great joy for life, and Belgian Sheepdogs share these traits. The outstanding personality trait these two share is independence—the kind that brings a cheerful, optimistic, good-humored personality (until freedom is threatened). Both dog breed and sun sign are well balanced in their physical, mental, and emotional energies. Freedom-loving Sagittarius will properly discourage any tendency by these *Cosmic Canines* toward possessiveness. Natives of this sun sign often get themselves into trouble because they are just too painfully honest (blunt), but since the words never come out in an angry or cynical tone of voice, Belgian Sheepdogs will be totally unaware when arrows from the Archer's bow border on insult. Sagittarians don't mean their bluntness as insults, really! Belgian Sheepdogs answer with a lighthearted "None intended, none taken."

BERNESE MOUNTAIN DOG

Positive Traits

Looking a bit like double-sized Border Collies (with a little less white on their chests and thicker muzzles), Bernese Mountain Dogs are beautiful, easily trained, and excellent watch-and-guard dogs. Strong, faithful, and loyal, these healthy, hardworking dogs once pulled small wagons loaded with retail goods to Swiss markets for their human companions. Bernese *Cosmic Canines* are good with other animals and fit well into multiple-pet families. They truly like people and show a lot of affection. Their attitude is obedient and temperate. Bernese gentleness combined with their size motivates trust. Though gentle, loving dogs, they need obedience training while still puppies. After six months of age, it can be difficult to push ninety-pound dogs into "sit" or "down" positions. And it can be impossible to make effective corrections when teaching dogs to walk by people's sides on leashes (rather than letting them drag you down the street). Bernese canines are intelligent, willing, and capable of handling all dog-sized tasks. These dogs are totally domesticated and live to please their families. Once they give their love, they are extremely faithful. The Bernese will not try to establish friendships with strangers once they have bonded with someone. This is a good reason to adopt these puppies at less than three months of age, so they bond with their lifelong human companions, not breeders. As an added plus, these dogs are also courageous.

Negative Traits

There are no known negatives about Bernese Mountain Dogs, but they are large animals. Their long, silky coats require regular brushing. They tend to be one-person animals. If raised around little ones (and if properly bred), Bernese canines are good with all children, but because of their size, they should be supervised when with toddlers.

Job Opportunities for Bernese Mountain Dogs

Corporate executives who are looking for a marketing strategy designed to attract new customers should hitch Bernese Mountain Dogs to wagons filled with the product and walk them up and down streets of small towns. These dogs make great models for corporate logos, representing kindness and strength. Teach these dogs to fetch the paper (or whatever) and count on them to be responsible about doing it each day. Above all, they are excellent family pets, good exercise partners, and wonderful protectors. Their size makes them less than ideal travel companions.

Most Compatible Sun Sign: Libra

All of the adjectives used to describe Libra natives are compatible with the Bernese: just, balanced, calm, restful, harmonious, kind, amiable, courteous, agreeable, pleasant—to name just a few. Libra natives love beauty and these are beautiful dogs, so the appeal goes in both directions. Librans are sweet, generous people who, like these obedient *Cosmic Canines*, are always tactful and polite. The phrase "a touch of class" was written to describe people born under this sun sign. Librans seldom lose arguments or make enemies (and the same can be said of the Bernese). Both are, quite simply, likable.

BLACK-AND-TAN COONHOUND

Positive Traits

Though not the fastest of the Hound group, Black-and-Tan Coonhounds are excellent scenting dogs, have good temperaments, and are strong, hardy animals. Their life's passion is to hunt possum and raccoon. They are keen and very determined hunters—like Bloodhounds, once on the trail, they do not give up easily. Also like Bloodhounds, they do not kill their prey. Black-and-Tans are powerful dogs yet maintain a high degree of agility. They are very good-natured, alert, friendly, and eager. Black-and-Tans are not shrinking violets. They have assertive personalities but, when properly trained, are very obedient pets. They are intelligent, loyal, lively, energetic animals, and their tenacity makes them particularly good watch-and-warn guard dogs. These *Cosmic Canines* are equally as good in the homes of human companions as they are in the field hunting (and they enjoy both equally).

Negative Traits

Dogs with assertive personalities always need obedience training begun by no later than six months of age. Like all dogs with long flaps over their ears, Black-and-Tans need their ears kept clean and free of infection. They have short, jet black coats, but still require regular grooming. These dogs need a lot of exercise and are not the best pets for the sedentary. Nor are they the best choice as companions for very young children. It's not a problem of temperament, just energy.

Job Opportunities for Black-and-Tan Coonhounds

The only want ads these dogs are likely to respond to are those asking for hunting companions. Though they make great pets and greatly enjoy that role, pet status comes second on this dog's list of priorities—though not by much. Black-and-Tans are somewhat slow, but very steady in the field. Good household protectors, exercise partners, and good-humored companions.

Most Compatible Sun Sign: Taurus

Black-and-Tan dogs and Taurus humans can be as down-to-earth as mud. Charming mud, but mud nonetheless. Both are tenacious, steady animals who quietly achieve their objectives. Both are careful, reliable workers. Just as the Black-and-Tan is not the fastest of the Hound group, Taurus humans are not the fastest of the zodiac group. Both, however, seldom fail to finish what they start. Natives of the sign of the Bull are good-natured, alert, friendly, and eager. So are Black-and-Tan Coonhounds. Both make good companions, both have assertive personalities and strength of purpose (once a purpose is determined—for example, Taurean Paul Revere's strength of purpose helped him keep his horse galloping during his famous midnight ride). Taurus humans are achievers. This is one of the most vital of all sun signs. Both dog and sun sign natives are loyal and exhibit strong self-control. Taurus natives are known for keeping their cool in emergencies and, like Black-and-Tans, are more comfortable exhibiting physical rather than mental or emotional skills. When Taurus tenacity becomes stubbornness (as it does in all animals strongly committed to a purpose), Black-and-Tans have sufficient tenacity of their own to not be terribly intimidated.

BLOODHOUND

Positive Traits

The largest and most powerful of the Hound group, these gentle army tanks have been used to track and hunt wolves, deer, bear, and other large game. No one argues that other dogs lack the scent capabilities of Bloodhounds. Drooping eyelids and drooping lips aside (and the slobbering that accompanies the latter), these *Cosmic Canines* can follow even the slightest scent. Once on the trail, it is a matter of pride for these dogs to find what they seek. Though they may be very slow, they are also very deliberate. They are strong dogs with the persistence of a mule. Charming to look at, Bloodhounds are one of the friendliest breeds around. They are extremely affectionate and good with children, great trackers and trailers, and, if you have room, they make ideal family pets. At the very least, Bloodhounds require large yards. These are shy, dignified dogs who have very sensitive feelings. If insulted, Bloodhounds actually become arrogant, acting as if their human companions really don't matter to them. It's a defense mechanism for hurt feelings. They are greatly loved by children and are not quarrelsome with either family members or other household dogs. Tolerant, affectionate, and independent when scenting, Bloodhounds are balanced. They are not clowns, though sometimes their very solemnity makes them pretty funny.

Negative Traits

Bloodhounds have been known to slobber—when they shake their heads, get out of the way. They are not good guard dogs and, like Newfoundlands, are more likely to greet prowlers with smiles and kisses than barks or growls. These dogs simply do not have a mean bone in their bodies. Like Black-and-Tan Coonhounds, their very large, long, floppy ears need special attention and cleaning to prevent infections. When using instinctive intelligence—that is, when doing what they were bred to do—Bloodhounds are extremely intelligent. Regarding nongenetic training exercises (e.g., obedience work), they are not the easiest to train nor are they the smartest dogs around. For search work, however, they are the best!

Job Opportunities for Bloodhounds

These are scent, search, and find dogs—let them seek out lost people, illegal drugs, and explosives. If you need to find something or someone, put Bloodhounds to work. Very loving family pets and good with children, their calm temperaments make them perfect for multiple-pet households. Excellent hunting companions and exercise partners. They have served as expert witnesses in courtrooms (if a Bloodhound finds evidence, it is accepted by American courts). These are people dogs who happen to love scent-based hunting.

Most Compatible Sun Sign: Capricorn

Typical Capricorns have a great deal in common with this breed of dog (starting with their slow but sure one-step-at-a-time need for forward momentum). They can take themselves pretty seriously sometimes, but when trying to be most serious, they are at their funniest. Words used to describe natives of the Goat are very similar to words used to describe Bloodhounds: strong, dignified, honest, reliable, serious, hardworking, and, as you would expect of a truly compatible sun sign for these dogs, balanced. No sun sign natives are more fair than Capricorns (though Librans are equal in this regard). And natives of the Goat are persevering, persistent, careful, independent, determined, and patient. The adjectives normally used to describe sun sign Capricorn make them sound as if they should be out there in the field with Bloodhounds, looking for escaped criminals. Truly, these two have innate insights into one another from the very beginning of what will be long-lasting, meaningful pet/guardian relationships. Neither Capricorn humans nor Bloodhounds would have it any other way. Both pay a lot of attention to detail, and both can be difficult. When Capricorns go through negative phases wherein sadness and suspicious thoughts make them moody and despondent, all they have to do is look at what appears to be the sad face of their Bloodhounds and their practical, positive selves will reappear.

BORZOI (RUSSIAN WOLFHOUND)

Positive Traits

Borzois are beautiful dogs who exude style and grace. In two words, they are elegant and classy. They were bred to run—and they do. Fast They were designed to chase wolves (as a matter of "sport"), a dangerous, hard-nosed form of animal gaming. Borzois aren't for everyone; they are aloof and need space and a lot of exercise And they are not the most affectionate members of the canine world; as a result, they are not the best large dog for small children They are very intelligent hunters, but they may have difficulty learning nonhunting obedience exercises. They are faithful, dignified, good-natured, keenly alert, and though somewhat standoffish, have sweet dispositions. When properly bred, Borzoi *Cosmic Canines* are almost always even-tempered.

Negative Traits

Bred to course wolves (at one time the national sport of Russia), Borzois are not ideal family pets. They look like longhaired Greyhounds and their coats require regular and rather extensive grooming. They are sensitive and carry aristocratic airs as casually as some people carry umbrellas Perhaps that's why the Russian royal family took such a shine to them. They are not likely to enjoy playing games with children, but when raised with little ones tend to be gentle Remember, "gentle" for large dogs—thirty-one inches at the shoulder and around a hundred pounds—is different from "gentle" for small dogs. Prospective human companions need to keep this in mind when making decisions about how well certain pets fit their lifestyles.

Job Opportunities for Borzois

These dogs make super models for upscale products and lifestyles—they are definitely status symbols. Borzois make good hunting and exercise companions. They are good pets for seniors looking for dogs around whom they can build hobbies—training, exercising, protection, and so on. These dogs make amiable, even-tempered family pets who stand somewhat aloof from some family activities. These dogs are great attention getters for singles trying to meet other singles—one walk through the park with a couple of Borzois should result in numerous comments from other people—interested in the dogs, of course.

Most Compatible Sun Sign: Virgo

Self-contained Virgoans are sensitive, discriminating, and reasoned. And they are impressed by these beautiful, elegant dogs (and the attention they attract). Borzoi attitudes appeal to Virgo natives who have highly artistic and literary tastes. Natives of Virgo are the epitome of tact and innately respect Borzoi needs for personal privacy. Few sun signs understand as well and accept as naturally the aloofness and dignity so much a part of the personalities of these *Cosmic Canines*. Like Virgo human companions, Borzois are faithful, dignified, good-natured, alert, and both have sweet dispositions. Virgoans are a little standoffish and can be aloof themselves. Natives of this sun sign sometimes don't make a whopping first impression, but these dogs do, and Virgo humans will enjoy the recognition that goes to human companions of such classy pets. Like these dogs, Virgo humans are sensitive, dependable, and tend to be perfectionists (though Borzois won't admit it, they are, too). Also like these dogs, Virgo humans are a little shy with strangers. They want to be sure of their audience before performing. Virgo human companions seek perfection, which may bore these dogs, but they'll just give a royal yawn and go on with their lives. Or they may tell Virgoans to take care of the motes in their own eyes before expecting perfection from others. As stated above, Borzois are pretty open and honest.

BOUVIER DES FLANDRES

Positive Traits

Looking a little like rugged, giant Scottish Terriers, these powerfully built, courageous dogs are alert and very intelligent. Bred to herd cattle, Bouviers des Flandres (Cow Dogs of Flanders) can be kept as pets and are easily trained. They are impressive in size, squarely built, and make good guard dogs. Bouviers are very loyal and affectionate toward their families. These *Cosmic Canines* can be trusted to protect their homes and all who live in them. They have long, rough outercoats and thick undercoats that guarantee they can thrive in all kinds of weather. Bouviers are lively, personable, and very powerful animals.

Negative Traits

These loving and very big animals can be one-person dogs. When adopted into families, they need equal exposure to all individuals who make up the family unit. They are not suited for city living or apartments. These are large dogs that need room to run—large yards at a minimum. They have substantial coats (the outercoat is harsh to the touch) that need regular brushing and occasional professional grooming. They are not the best dogs for toddlers (from a size aspect rather than temperament), but when properly bred and trained, make excellent family pets. If they are going to be exposed to very young children, they should be raised from puppyhood with them.

Job Opportunities for Bouviers des Flandres

Doing what comes naturally, Bouviers are good herding animals for sheep or cattle, as well as excellent choices for guard and protection duties. They are good exercise partners, but need more than a casual walk around the block a few times a week—a mile of jogging or trotting alongside bikes is best. Bouviers are good at fetching. With a little training, they can be hitched to sleds or wagons, giving children safe rides around their yards. It's good exercise for the dogs and great fun for the kids. Though large, Bouviers are not horses and should not be expected to give pony rides to little humans. It will hurt their backs.

Most Compatible Sun Sign: Taurus

Powerful and vital are the two dominant words best used to explain both this dog breed and this sun sign. Loyal and dependable are also applicable. Both are down-to-earth, practical, solid, patient, and reliable. Taurus natives are known for their persistent determination—a personality trait required of all herding animals who want to move other four-legged critters from one point to another Both sun sign and dog are fearless and protective, companionable and sincere. Neither takes life or their place in it too seriously. Bouviers love Taurean kindness and gentle, loving ways and respect the tower of physical strength humans born under this sun sign exude. Everyone looks up to true Taurus natives, just as they look up to well-bred, trained Bouviers des Flandres. Both accept others for what they are (though neither will get involved in the harebrained ideas of their creative friends). These two are good together not just because they are so much alike, but because both are calm and bring a sense of soothing peace to serious, long-term relationships.

BOXER

Positive Traits

These brave clowns with their Mastiff and Bulldog backgrounds are good guard dogs who love children and are very loyal to their families. They are highly energetic, very personable *Cosmic Canines* and, in a word, cocky. They are also delightful animals who are forever childlike. They seem to take forever to mature. Boxers have served humanity as military and guide dogs. People tend to either love or hate them. Maybe it's because they fear Boxers' energetic unpredictability—and they are unpredictable. Boxers are filled with a zest for life, which, because they are powerful animals, intimidates some people—at least all intelligent ones. They need reasonably sized homes and yards, and if a gate is left open, they will wander anywhere and everywhere, including into the middle of heavy traffic if something raises their curiosity (of which they have an abundance). They like to entertain and be entertained. My fondest memory from my youth regarding these dogs was watching my sister-in-law cry as she picked up her laundry from the mud. Her Boxer got bored after being alone all day and decided to run, jump, and swing on the laundry as it waved in the wind on the clothesline (which will tell you how long ago this was). Boxers have a unique kind of substance; it sometimes seems the people best able to describe them are science fiction writers with a great sense of humor.

Negative Traits

Charge-ahead dogs: prior to maturity and obedience training, Boxers charge ahead regardless of who or what is in their path. These dogs do not like to be ignored, and if left alone too long, they can find all kinds of trouble. Of all dogs, Boxers need obedience training as puppies more than most. Their own sense of élan is destructive to them without it. Untrained, they simply have no sense about reckless behavior—from running out into the street in front of oncoming cars to not knowing where their homes are once they wander away. If they were human, psychologists would probably deem them sociopaths. They really have no conscience about their charge-ahead attitude. It requires discipline and a firm hand to train Boxer puppies. These dogs do not accept abuse willingly. At some point in time, some person, somewhere, pays for the abusive treatment that has been heaped on these intelligent heads. Boxers can be belligerent, especially with strangers. Though they are kind to children, they cannot really be trusted with them even after they are trained, until the children are at least of school age. They just have too much roughhouse energy in them to be safe with toddlers.

Job Opportunities for Boxers

When properly bred and trained, Boxers make excellent guard dogs. Lively companions, they are good exercise partners provided their human companions are into a lot of exercise. They do well in service as military and police dogs, guide dogs for the blind, and drug enforcement agents. For on-the-go people, Boxers make good family pets (though not the best for children of less than school age). Their muscular bodies and strength of character shining from intelligent eyes make them wonderful corporate symbols. What a strong message goes with this logo!

Most Compatible Sun Sign: Aries

Ariens, like Boxers, never get lost in a crowd. Just as Boxers are the great individualists of the dog world, Aries natives are the great individualists of the zodiac. Both are strong-willed and forceful, intelligent and energetic, quick and alert. These two aren't just compatible, they are maternal twins! Aries humans, however, have one strength Boxers definitely lack but need, very much: common sense. These sun sign natives communicate very effectively, which will be helpful when obedience-training Boxer puppies—a necessity. And Aries humor helps get them through some of the concentration problems these energetic (sometimes nervous) *Cosmic Canines* are likely to have when the dog training school bell rings. Like these dogs, Ariens are very smart, and they can be highly original, which keeps Boxer dogs amused and interested. Aries natives, like this dog breed, are sociable, amusing, independent explorers. These are strong dogs and when natives of the Ram become headstrong, impulsive, high-strung, and hypersensitive, Boxers easily understand—and sympathize. They suffer the same negatives, and so Ariens understand when Boxers go through negative cycles.

BRIARD

Positive Traits

These French hunting and guard dogs (Berger de Brie) have histories that date to the twelfth century. Initially utilized to guard their masters, they evolved into Herding dogs, guiding flocks, and guarding farm property. Well mannered around the house, they bark only when necessary and are homebodies who do not like to wander. Though Briard *Cosmic Canines* do not bark a lot, they do give warning of strangers on the premises. Briards are lively, are tone-of-voice sensitive to harsh criticism, and like to please human companions. In general, they are happy, intelligent dogs. They are vigorous, appealing, strong, intelligent, and enjoy performing daily, dutiful routines. Thoughtful human companions will be sure to provide such routines for these tasteful pets. Uniquely French in personality, these dogs have perfect Hollywood star potential. Their large ears stand up in a "vee" from their heads and are heavily coated with long black, gray, or tawny hair falling over both ears and eyes. Though it's impossible to see the eyes of these dogs (because of their hair), they maintain intelligent, curious looks on adorable faces, and that is a good word for them: adorable. Briards are independent and intelligent, as all herding animals must be to do their jobs. They have both quiet and rowdy sides. Briard personalities can be pretentious yet arrogant, organized yet scattered, and finicky yet practical as dirt—very French. These very intelligent dogs are easily trained and every Hollywood producer should have one under contract.

Negative Traits

These dogs are animated, high-energy pets. They need exercise, firm but gentle discipline, and human companions who won't underrate their intelligence because they somewhat resemble clowns. Though Briards have wonderful instinctive intelligence when it comes to doing what they were bred for—herding—they tend to learn obedience (from housebreaking to just having someone say no) slowly. Once they learn something, however, it won't be forgotten. They are longhaired dogs with coarse, dry coats. They shed and need to be brushed. Special attention needs to be paid to moving long hair over the ears out of the way and keeping the ears clean. They can be rowdy and because of their size can knock little ones over. With school-aged children, they are, when properly bred, just fine. Other than these minor inconveniences or warnings, there are no known negatives about Briards.

Job Opportunities for Briards

Movie stars, models for dog food ads, an added photo opportunity that brings interesting dimension to family albums—Briards are good for all of these purposes. They still herd sheep and cattle well. They are wonderful, loving, and dutiful family pets who take family responsibilities seriously. They watch and-warn human companions. Teach Briards to fetch. They have a lot of energy and make excellent exercise partners. Even though they are large dogs, they make good travel companions.

Most Compatible Sun Sign: Aquarius

Not Leo (who is too much of an actor and too competitive to be compatible with such high-performance, charming animals), but Aquarius is most compatible with Briards. Patient, quiet, unassuming natives of the Water Bearer will appeal to these dogs; this sun sign's loyalty, thoughtfulness, humanity, honesty, and sincerity are important to Briards. Aquarians don't take anything too seriously, including Briard arrogance, pickiness, or disorganization They will, in fact, find it humorous. These sun sign natives motivate trust in others and, though unconventional at times, are very dependable and faithful. Rather than compete with these charming *Cosmic Canines* to see who can captivate more hearts (like Leo humans might), Water Bearer natives take more interest in managing Briard careers. Unassuming Aquarius humans don't mind one bit giving the spotlight to dogs and are logical enough to understand Briards are in the spotlight because that's where they want to be and they have the personalities to earn them their place in the sun. Both dog and sun sign natives are very independent, intelligent, and kind. Briards are more physical, Aquarius more mental; each is good for the other, bringing strengths to the table the other can gain through sharing Aquarian loyalty sits very well with dogs of this breed. They, too, are loyal.

BULLMASTIFF

Positive Traits

Gamekeepers in jolly old England led difficult lives in the late 1800s. Poachers were known to attack gamekeepers and Bullmastiffs were bred to protect them (Robin Hood was on the other side of this issue). Bulldogs were, at that point in history, too ferocious and Mastiffs too slow. So the two were crossbred. Bullmastiffs are affectionate, loyal, first-class guard dogs, good with older children when properly trained and temperamentally sound—and when raised from puppyhood around small humans. They are extremely strong *Cosmic Canines*. They tend to be lovable, happy, watchful, and trustworthy. They are no-nonsense dogs who are quick and agile. Adopt Bullmastiffs from reputable breeders. It's important with dogs born to this breed. Find out as much as you can about the dog's sire and dam; meet them if possible. Puppies learn aggressive behavior from their parents at very young ages. Bullmastiffs are a little like John Wayne: strong, silent types. There are probably few peers in the canine world when it comes to protection and guard duties. These dogs weigh up to 130 pounds, so the need for early obedience training is obvious. People who are not experienced dog handlers need the services of one. Getting well-bred Bullmastiffs is half the battle. Getting them well trained by six months of age is the other half. If these two things are in place, these are wonderful dogs for families with older children, large yards, or country estates and who enjoy lively lifestyles in which Bullmastiffs can take part.

Negative Traits

These dogs have ferocious biographies. Remember, the only contests in which Bullmastiffs competed were against humans. They are wonderful guard dogs and will protect the homes and possessions of human companions, but if improperly bred or left untrained (or trained with a baseball bat rather than a human brain), they can be dangerous—and no intelligent human wants to be their adversary. They must be trained while puppies because of their large size. If you are not the kind of person who can give rigorous, disciplined obedience training that relies on brains not brawn, you should probably get another pet. These are not the best pets for children younger than school age who have no experience with large dogs. Bullmastiffs need plenty of exercise Be careful when introducing these dogs into your social life: an arm raised by a friend in a playful gesture at a party might be in danger if these canines perceive it as a threat to you.

Job Opportunities for Bullmastiffs

Protection and guard services are the occupations over which these dogs are the supreme commanders. Just looking at Bullmastiffs dissuades most criminals from risking an encounter with them. They are excellent exercise partners provided their human companions are in controlled environments where no other dogs are running loose. They can be trained for search-and-rescue or for drug enforcement activities The size of these dogs prevents them from a lot of travel.

Most Compatible Sun Sign: Scorpio

Like this breed of dog, natives of the Scorpion can be very, very good—or very, very terrible. These sun sign natives are capable of more behavioral extremes than any other sign in the zodiac, but they are so strong they can be almost anything they choose in life. It all depends on heritage and training—for both Bullmastiffs and sun sign natives. One thing is certain: Scorpions are dominant (which these dogs need), and they are leaders. More U.S presidents were born under the sign of Scorpio than any other. Scorpio natives are decisive, determined, controlled, persistent, and very intelligent And nothing frightens either these *Cosmic Canines* or natives of this sun sign. When Scorpions accept something as a life purpose, they (like Scorpio Teddy Roosevelt) have tremendous strength of character to dedicate to that purpose. These strong dogs have great potential to be outstanding family members if properly bred and trained, but it takes people born under a very strong sun sign like Scorpio to understand the mysteries of the Bullmastiff Like Scorpio natives, Bullmastiffs thrive on approval, and harsh treatment is never forgotten or forgiven Scorpio is one of the strongest sun signs in the zodiac; Bullmastiffs are one of the strongest canines in dogdom When Scorpions go through negative cycles and become cynical, sarcastic, and resentful, it won't intimidate these strong dogs.

CHESAPEAKE BAY RETRIEVER

Positive Traits

Some people think the term *Big Red* relates to the University of Nebraska football team. Those who own Chesapeake Bay Retrievers know it refers to their dogs (though a haylike color is equally acceptable). Chessies are first-class Retrievers who learned to ply their retrieving trade in the icy waters of the Chesapeake Bay. These dogs are sportsmen's favorites. They are noted for their intelligence, courage, loyalty, and willingness. Chessies are powerful animals who love children and they are ideal playmates for preteens and older. They can be too headstrong and assertive for toddlers, but most Chesapeakes are not terribly sensitive to curious hands and are not likely to snarl or growl the first time a little one pulls an ear. When with children of less than ten years of age, however, they should be supervised by adults. These yellow-eyed canines love their families and, truly equal opportunity employees, they work equally well for men and women. They have positive, alert, happy dispositions and are very strong-willed animals. Improperly trained, their strong wills can turn into stubbornness.

Negative Traits

These dogs need General Patton, not General MacArthur—more a commander, less a leader. Chessies can be very headstrong, sometimes aggressive and difficult to train. They are good jumpers, so don't let a fence-jumping habit get started by allowing puppies to stand on their haunches with front feet on the fence. When they get bigger, if they see something on the other side of the fence, they may say "adios" to their yards. Chesapeake Bay Retrievers are hard, powerful dogs with stubbornness as strong as Superman. And they can be as belligerent, too. Keep the ear flaps and inner ears clean to stave off infections. The short, thick, and coarse coat requires regular brushing.

Job Opportunities for Chesapeake Bay Retrievers

The best when it comes to a duck-hunting helper and companion, relentless and tireless in the field. They are good exercise companions, and they *need* a lot of exercise. These dogs are such good Retrievers, teach them to fetch anything and everything. Shoot tennis balls out of mechanical shooters and let them retrieve the balls—it's good exercise. They make excellent boating companions and boat watch-and-warn dogs. They love the water and swim as naturally as the ducks they are so good at retrieving. They can be good family pets provided obedience training occurs by six months of age. Without obedience work, these dogs have too much unrestrained energy to make good household pets.

Most Compatible Sun Sign: Cancer

Who but calm, strong, purposeful, and determined Water sun sign natives could be most compatible with this dog breed? It is hard even for Chessies to out-stubborn Cancer natives. Those born under the sign of the Crab aren't just tenacious, they are determinedly tenacious. They are also sensitive, domestic, understanding, empathetic, self-possessed, and self-reliant. Cancer humans can rationalize anything and use their highly logical minds to find ways to contain the strong wills of these rather independent dogs. Cancerians can be very diplomatic and sympathetic, but once they set their sights on an objective, they won't give up on it. Like General Patton pushing his tanks through Europe, they have the tenacity to mold the Chesapeake character into the wonderful family pets they are capable of being. Chessies love the kind, thoughtful attention Cancer natives show them, but innately understand and relate to the quiet strength of this sun sign. These *Cosmic Canines* will likely show a great deal of respect for Cancer human companions. Like these dogs, Cancerians are known to be intelligent, courageous, and loyal. In short, natives of this sun sign have the personal characteristics to help these dogs be all they can be.

CHOW CHOW

Positive Traits

Chow Chows were in China as early as the Han dynasty, around 150 B.C. They are a bit standoffish and have been called "regal of nature." These dogs are beautiful, have good endurance, and are incredibly loyal to the human companions with whom they first bond. They are not good dogs to take to another family for baby-sitting—their loyalty to primary human companions does not extend to that person's friends and family. As an added bonus, they are odorless. Like the Akita, Chow Chows are descendants of the Spitz family. They look a bit like lions, proud, tawny manes and all They are best known for their blue-black tongues. Chow Chows have been utilized for scenting and pointing, and are known to be sly, shrewd hunting dogs with great speed and stamina. These are very stubborn, aloof, assertive, and independent dogs whose history reveals great courage. Chow Chows are usually quiet dogs who can be trained as exceptionally reliable guard dogs. Unfortunately, in China the Chow Chow is still regarded as a dietary delicacy for human holiday menus.

Negative Traits

Chows have a tendency to devote themselves exclusively to one family member. They can be strong-willed—even aggressive—toward anyone else who tries to correct them. They need quiet but firm handling. They are aloof with an almost arrogant standoffish attitude toward all but the human companion with whom they bond. Even for that person, obedience-training a Chow Chow can be difficult. To be around Chow Chows, children should have at least reached their teenage years. These dogs do not like strangers and should not be exposed to friends or expected to "adjust" to them. Chow Chows can be fearsome fighters and very strong opponents. Their long coats require a lot of brushing and grooming. These dogs have either good temperaments or bad ones, and this breed of dog is among the five most likely to bite humans.

Job Opportunities for Chow Chows

Chows have been used to guard caravans, to watch boats, and to pull sleds. They are difficult dogs to train and, thus, their job opportunities are limited. Because of their tendency to bond with a single human companion in a family and be aloof to everyone else, these are not the best dogs to adopt for home-protection purposes. They are good, protective companions for singles experienced in handling strong, assertive dogs.

Most Compatible Sun Signs: Scorpio, Leo, Aries, and Sagittarius

These four sun signs—Scorpio, Leo, Aries, and Sagittarius—are among the most dominant in the zodiac. It takes dominant human companions to raise and train Chow Chows. Scorpio natives have the potential to be the most powerful, persistent members of the zodiac; Leo humans have the potential to be the most forceful, persevering, and energetic; Ariens, the most decisive, independent, and physically strong. As for Sagittarians, they are independent, confident, and self-reliant. Chow Chows are very strong dogs who may require the talented personalities of all four sun signs rolled up in one human being. They are unique *Cosmic Canines* and their potential to be either totally good or totally bad very much resembles this same trait so dominant in natives of Scorpio. Both have very strong character, but that strength can reside at either end of the hate/love spectrum. Chow Chows have the confidence and self-reliance of Sagittarius natives—the same need for personal freedom, the same purposeful attitude. Chow Chows as a breed are one of a kind. That's what they require in sun sign human companions: people who are one of a kind.

COLLIE

Positive Traits

Collies make devoted pets who are not just good with children, they love them. They aren't quite all what Lassie would make you believe they are, but these *Cosmic Canines* are intelligent, playful, loyal, easily trained, affectionate, and lovable. Supple, strong, sensitive, and active are words that describe these dogs well. With their graceful warmth and dignified beauty, Collies are pictures of true balance. They are loyal dogs and take family responsibilities seriously. Given enough outdoor exercise, they are not overly active in the home, but like all herding animals, they do require exercise. If they are well bred, Collies are good around children of all ages; if poorly bred or of unknown heritage, they are only for preteens and up. For dogs, sheepherding is the oldest occupation. Collie ancestry goes far back into early dog history. These dogs originated in northern Scotland, and while visiting Balmoral, Queen Victoria fell in love with them. They are never timid or pouty and, along with their glorious coats, wear looks of intelligence on their faces. They have about them an air of security alertness. Combined with their intelligent, curious countenance, it makes them appear dignified. They are.

Negative Traits

Those Collie coats are gorgeous, but they need a lot of grooming. There's a lot of hair on these dogs. They shed most of the year (but particularly in spring and fall—even the shorter-haired Smooth Collie), but professional groomers are not needed except for conformation shows. Very loving and affectionate with family members, Collies are not keen about welcoming strangers. Avoid punishing these dogs; concentrate on motivating and rewarding good behavior rather than correcting for bad because Collies are very sensitive and do not respond well to correction. When these *Cosmic Canines* do something wrong, correct them but place more emphasis on praise. Never hit Collies. Human companions should never hit any dog, and it can make Collies aggressive. Human companions must be smarter than their dogs. Left untrained beyond six months of age, Collies may become stubborn (though true of most dogs, it is especially true with this dog breed). It would be a shame to ruin dogs with so much potential as loving family pets through an irresponsible lack of training.

Job Opportunities for Collies

These dogs are natural herding animals. If there's more than two of you in the family, Collies are likely to try to herd your group as you walk through the backyard to look at the flowers or check your tomato plants to see what's ripe. Collies are wonderful, loving family pets and among the best home-protection devices. They are very protective and suspicious of strangers. You can train them either to guard or to watch and warn. Super exercise partners, they won't cause trouble with other animals on your exercise route, but other dogs may approach you. Be prepared. When properly bred and trained, these are among the best dogs for children of all ages. Improperly bred or left untrained, they are only for children of school age. Train them to be movie stars, or rent them out as models.

Most Compatible Sun Sign: Libra

I surprised myself by choosing Libra as the most compatible sun sign for this breed. I thought I'd choose Cancer. After all, Lassie's personality was patterned after the traits associated with sun sign Cancer. But Lassie was only an act, not a real dog (it's a little like hearing Santa Claus isn't real, isn't it?). Libra human characteristics are most compatible with Collies—

the key word here is balance Other words are: graceful warmth and dignified beauty. Ruled by Venus, Libra, more than any sun sign, has been given the gift of appreciating beauty. These natives exhibit warmth and are almost always dignified. Natives of the Scales bring harmony, calm, intuition, and courtesy to the lives of all who are close to them—traits shared by these dogs. Libra human companions are restful and calming, always a plus to high-energy pets. Both dog and sun sign are agreeable, friendly, loving, and generous. Air sign Libra loves ideas, which is compatible with that look of canine intelligence on the faces of Collie dogs. Just like Lassie, Librans can charm fleas into bees. Collies and Librans both appreciate people and both have sensitive souls that respond better to praise than criticism.

CURLY-COATED RETRIEVER

Positive Traits

Curly-Coated Retrievers, a breed that originated in the early 1800s, look a little like Chesapeake Bay Retrievers with slightly longer hair, more refined muzzles, and a good beauty shop perm. Even the hock-long tail has short, tight curls. Curlies have moderate temperaments and are said to be "kind" dogs, yet maintain enthusiastic attitudes about almost everything. Like all good Retrievers, Curlies have independent natures and are fine swimmers with good scenting skills. They are beautiful *Cosmic Canines* and make excellent guard dogs. Curly-Coated Retrievers have great stamina and are very hardy animals, totally committed to the singular purpose of hunting while in the field They are intelligent hunters, faithful and loyal. Though they are usually friendly to visitors, they are discerning dogs who perceive when unwanted strangers should be encouraged to leave. Most of all, they are reliable.

Negative Traits

These are large dogs, built like Sherman tanks, and care needs to be taken when they are around toddlers. Though their enthusiasm is usually reserved for hunting, just one energetic bump can knock a toddler down with some force. Aside from their faces, these Retrievers are covered with curly hair but they don't present much of a grooming problem beyond regular brushing. The flaps over their ears and the inner ear need regular cleaning with a cotton pad and alcohol to prevent infection. As to temperament negatives, none are known.

Job Opportunities for Curly-Coated Retrievers

Curlies are intelligent, friendly hunting companions who won't get upset because their human companions in the field wear out before they do. When properly bred and trained, they are good watch-and-warn (or even guard) dogs. Tireless exercise partners, Curlies are dogs people can train to fetch almost anything. Hunting-related tasks (like fetching) will be easier to teach than obedience, but Curlies are willing in their efforts to learn. Great boating companions, they respond positively to the opportunity to leap into the water and save someone. Curlies will enjoy sleeping on deck, guarding family yachts or corporate barges.

Most Compatible Sun Sign: Pisces

Intelligent, compassionate, warm, and giving, Pisces natives are perfect matches for Curly-Coated Retrievers. A Water sun sign for water-loving dogs. Natives of the sign of the Fishes are naturally sensitive to the kindness of these *Cosmic Canines* and offer it back in abundance. No sun sign natives are more compassionate that Pisceans. These people are down-home neighborly if, sometimes, a bit controlled when showing emotion. Curlies, with their friendly and enthusiastic attitudes, can help Pisces humans lighten up a bit. Natives of this sun sign are very sensitive and get hurt easily, which is why they withhold emotional displays from those about whom they care. These loyal, straightforward dogs will never be a source of disappointment to their human companions Pisceans usually love boating and that gives Curlies opportunities to take to the water—to be sure, more exposure to wet stuff than non-Water sun signs offer by simply letting dogs run through the garden hose. Like this dog breed, the Pisces personality has many subtleties—some positive, some negative Because Pisceans give so much, they tend to be pretty demanding and need pets who are up to that challenge. Curly-Coated Retrievers can handle Piscean demands. And Curlies are positive enough for both themselves and their human companions—sure to help those born under the sign of the Fishes recoup from negative-cycle bouts of moodiness.

DALMATIAN

Positive Traits

When properly bred, dogs born to this centuries-old breed have amenable, even temperaments. Dalmatians are loyal and reliable with school-aged children and are protective of them. These are happy-natured dogs, devoted to their owners. They rarely fight. Dalmatians have served with militaries around the world, have worked as sheepherders, and, of course, are known for their daring deeds as fire wagon (later truck) mascots because of their winning ways with horses. In addition to all these things, Dalmatians have been good bird dogs, trail Hounds, and Retrievers, and have been used to hunt deer and boar They have hauled wagons and sleds and have been circus performers for years. Talk about flexible! Dalmatians have wonderful memories and willing attitudes along with speed and endurance. Combine their endurance with power and it may be too much for some people. These *Cosmic Canines* love to work; they especially love to work with their primary human companions. They are a bit aristocratic, quiet and reserved when called for. At other times, they can be absolute clowns. Aside from human attention, Dalmatians require minimum care. For the right companions, these dogs are loyal pets who take great pleasure in making people happy.

Negative Traits

The words *properly bred* are significant regarding this dog breed. Because of all the Disney movie hype about Dalmatians, unscrupulous breeding practices—in the attempt to provide large numbers of them to fulfill people's whims—a problem has been created. This dog breed is one of the five most likely to bite humans. Of course, there are more Dalmatians as pets than most other breeds, and so the odds are pretty good that there will be more bites because of this (the same is true of Cocker Spaniels and German Shepherds, also among the "fearsome five" breeds that bite). But poor breeding techniques to produce large numbers of dogs negatively impact the normally positive temperaments of all animals. Get to know the dog's parents and examine the bloodlines before adopting one. Dalmatians also need a lot of exercise. Otherwise, their high, rather intense energy level turns to tension and that results in overstressed, nervous dogs. Dalmatians are too big and enthusiastic for small children (this is an energy, not a temperament, problem). They love to run and romp with older children Have Dalmatians tested for deafness and ear problems before adopting them (basic white dogs tend to inherit ear problems). These are powerful, energetic animals whose enthusiasm for life needs kind but firm discipline in the form of obedience training.

Job Opportunities for Dalmatians

Mascots, movie stars, models for corporate logos, horse riding partners, bird dog hunters, trail Hounds, Retrievers, and big-game hunters—they pull wagons and sleds or, when properly trained, perform at circuses. Or Dalmatians can just be one of the best, most loving pets around. When properly bred and trained, they are happy, enthusiastic members of your household. Excellent exercise partners; in fact, to maintain stable temperaments, Dalmatians need exercise as an outlet for all their energy. To qualify for any job, these happy white dogs with black spots *must* be obedience-trained by about six months of age.

Most Compatible Sun Sign: Leo

If anyone is more self-conscious than Dalmatians it is natives of Leo the Lion. Both are always aware of themselves and the impact they are having on audiences. Like these dogs, Leo humans are forceful and magnetic, vital and kind, warmhearted and loving. Both are great individualists with tremendous personal power. When Dalmatians try to exercise their independence and direct these human companions in scheduling events, Leo humans are decisive and take leash firmly in hand and say, "No, we're doing it my way." These dogs love Leonine generosity and sympathy. They share Leo's nobility and thus understand it. Like these dogs, Leo human companions are energetic, faithful, and dominant, and Dalmatians need dominant human companions or their own sense of dominance gets them in trouble Sun sign Leo's ruler is Earth's Sun, which gives all of its natives strength, positive attitudes, and confidence. The Sun governs public life, and Dalmatians have so much public exposure, the Sun *must* be an integral part of this dog breed.

DEERHOUND (SCOTTISH)

Positive Traits

Their name tells us what they were bred to do, but it doesn't explain how royalty helped them do it. This is one of the oldest breeds of the British Isles. To own Deerhounds in the Age of Chivalry, men had to be earls, at the very least. Deerhounds have been among royalty for centuries (and are known as the Royal Dog of Scotland). These *Cosmic Canines* are beautiful and have sound temperaments. Any day on which they can please their families is a good day for them. They have their own kind of canine dignity; they are gentle, obedient, courageous, faithful, and intelligent. They would never use their size to intimidate (they can be 32 inches at the withers and weigh up to 110 pounds), at least not intentionally. They are too gentlemanly or ladylike; they are even polite when expressing affection. Deerhounds are the politically correct canine of the dog world. These are healthy animals, very strong, who ask no more than to be close to their human companions. Keen scenting dogs on the hunt, they are strong, fast, and powerful. Because of their agreeable natures, they make ideal pets for those families with enough space to house them. These dogs are, above all, dependable.

Negative Traits

None known—but you do need sufficient space (a very large yard at a minimum). Deerhound coats are coarse and harsh, about four inches in length. They need brushing and they shed seasonally. Deerhounds can be pretty persistent when they make their minds up to something. Be sure your kitchen is big enough so both of you can turn around at the same time, otherwise feeding time might present problems. Not good for guard-dog work (though their very size will deter most prowlers). Too big to be good companions for small children, regardless of how gentle the nature of these dogs.

Job Opportunities for Scottish Deerhounds

They are deer-hunting companions supreme! While too friendly and politically correct to be good guard dogs, they may watch and warn (if trained to do so). Excellent exercise partners but not good travel companions. They are, however, good company on camping trips. Wonderful pets for families with country estates. Deerhounds make good logos for sporting goods companies that offer deer-hunting products. Deerhounds and deer hunting are synonymous.

Most Compatible Sun Sign: Pisces

These dogs have dual personalities: assertive, competitive hunters who excel in the field when hunting large game, and totally giving, pleasing personalities in the home after hunts are over. There are two sun signs with dual personalities: Pisces and Gemini. With Gemini humans there is little acceptance of political correctness. Pisceans are loaded with it. And Gemini is too mental, changeable, diverse, logical, and analytic to be truly compatible with Deerhounds. Pisces natives, on the other hand, are very much like Scottish Deerhounds. They can be very competitive and assertive in the workplace, but totally giving and peaceful in their home environment. Pisceans are honest and methodical, but melancholy and impressionable, too. Natives of the sign of the Fishes are receptive, accepting, sympathetic, sensitive, and compassionate. They have even been called "tender" by astrologers (and Pisces is a magnetic sun sign that draws others to it—like Deerhounds). Like these dogs, Pisceans are neighborly, warm, endearing, and very polite. Though loving and affectionate, Pisces human companions are, like these dogs, pretty polite about expressing their feelings. Like Scorpion humans, Pisceans are a bit of a mystery (which Deerhounds quietly enjoy analyzing). The sign of Pisces rules the unknown, and Deerhounds represent a bit of the unknown. Both Pisces natives and Deerhounds have subtle personalities that can be difficult to understand. These two are perfect together and have much in common.

DOBERMAN PINSCHER

Positive Traits

After breeding German Shepherds for years to show in American Kennel Club conformation rings, I never thought I would love another breed of dog quite as much—and I still love Shepherds. But the dog I adopted from the Cincinnati Humane Society in 1989 to serve as a guard dog at my residence in the country (there were only five families on several hundred acres)—who I thought at the time was a Doberman/Great Dane mix (but turned out to be purebred Dobie)—won my heart. This was the best companion in the world! To be truthful, I was a little reticent about getting too close to all that Doberman power and muscle But as I got to know Rusty, I found no breed of dog is more alert, brave, loyal, intelligent, or loving than well-bred Dobermans. They are skilled at tracking and have done well working as police dogs or with the military during wartime. My Doberman had more personality than any dog I've owned, boarded, or bred. He was a superb animal physically—muscular, powerful, noble, energetic, and he had endurance as well as speed. No dog could have done a better job of watching my property than Rusty did He was determined and fearless, yet loyal and obedient. This *Cosmic Canine* was an elegant clown with great courage, as I found out one day when Rusty placed himself between me and a snake that had crawled into my garage. Even when he was clowning, he had the stamp of nobility. Dobermans were originally bred by a tax collector to protect him from irate citizens and their aggressive dogs. Dobermans are wonderful companions, intelligent workers, and are delightful animals to show in the conformation ring.

Negative Traits

It would be nice to say, "No negatives are known about this breed," but that's not true. Dobies have somewhat aloof attitudes toward those outside family circles. Even within their families, they have a tendency to be one-person dogs. If another dog starts a fight, Dobies are the odds-on favorites to win. Left untrained, these dogs aren't above starting fights themselves. And improperly bred, they can have fiery tempers. Even when properly bred, they need training at a young age to reduce potential aggression. Don't ever show fear to Doberman Pinschers. They are very intelligent and use the fear of what they perceive to be opponents against them. It's how they command situations. They need to know who's boss Human companions who don't have temperaments required to control very large, powerful dogs who, when left untrained and if spoiled, can do a lot of damage, should adopt another pet. Dobies are wonderful with children of an age to be predictable—preteens and up. If raised with children from puppyhood, Dobies are wonderful protectors and guard dogs of the entire family. Do not physically abuse these puppies during training, mistaking firmness and a demand for proper behavior for harsh treatment. Doberman Pinschers do not forget abuse. They need plenty of exercise.

Job Opportunities for Doberman Pinschers

First and foremost, Dobies are loving family pets and home protectors but only if properly bred and trained by six months of age. They are great animals for long-term careers in military and police work. Excellent drug enforcement dogs, too (and, like all canines, above bribery and politics). They are excellent exercise companions provided their companions exercise at a pace faster than a walk—bicycling, jogging, and such. Big dogs have big exercise appetites. Though they are big travel companions, they are also calm ones. I took Rusty cross-country three times and he behaved wonderfully—and I felt very safe (of course, he barked at every footstep that sounded outside my motel room door). These dogs are added safety factors when driving and parking in cities, but don't take dogs with you and leave them in cars parked in the sun, even on cold winter days.

Most Compatible Sun Sign: Sagittarius

Like Dobermans, Sagittarius humans are independent, freedom-loving, and filled with enthusiasm for life. Both like people and are liked by them. And there's that Sagittarius honesty. Don't ever ask natives of the Archer questions to which you do not want direct, honest answers. Doberman Pinschers are a little like that. Other common grounds for these two: an innate need to keep learning, true devotion to only a few people while liking many, single-mindedness, purposefulness, loyalty, and an affectionate nature. Both sun sign and dog breed are giving and sincere, both require a certain amount of personal freedom. Sagittarians are impressionable and Dobies don't forget wrongs done to them. Both are active, honest, enterprising, and have happy dispositions. No sun sign has quite the joy for life that is exhibited by Sagittarians and, like Dobies, they *need* exercise. They can be overactive, nervous, defiant, disinterested, and lazy in their negative cycles, but a good exercise workout with man's best friends gets them back on the positive side of the fence. Both sun sign natives and this dog breed are high-energy, high-impact individuals. Both need discipline and training to achieve their potential in life. And Sagittarius humans are strong enough to train and direct Doberman energy while maintaining totally happy, positive attitudes.

FLAT-COATED RETRIEVER

Positive Traits

These solid black or liver-colored dogs, who somewhat resemble longer-haired, lighter-built Labrador Retrievers, are hardy, healthy animals that are easy to train. Part Newfoundland, part Setter, they are natural, versatile (dry and wet) Retrievers and very little training is required before taking them hunting. Flat-Coats are intelligent, and they look it. They have lively, outgoing personalities but, with only a small amount of training, are obedient and enjoy pleasing their human companions. Very strong and built of the right stuff, they can easily be trained as good watchdogs. They are very dynamic *Cosmic Canines.* Flat-Coated Retrievers are outgoing and affectionate and make excellent family pets. They are friendly, yet watchful; cheerful, yet independent; versatile and adaptable, yet stable.

Negative Traits

These dogs have dense, medium-length, somewhat feathered coats that require regular brushing and seasonally shed. They tend to bond more with one person in the family than with the entire group. Flat-Coated Retrievers require regular exercise, and chasing sticks and retrieving them from lakes make them think they're in dog heaven. These dogs are not good for apartment dwellers or those who are housebound. They need more exercise than can normally be provided under such circumstances. Other than these minor inconveniences, there are no known negatives about this dog breed.

Job Opportunities for Flat-Coated Retrievers

For people who are into hunting, Flat-Coats make wonderful companions. For those who love boating, these dogs enjoy the water and can serve guard duty to add extra comfort and security to those times spent on boats or yachts. Flat-Coats offer excellent protection for river barges and their cargo. These dogs are very good with children of all ages. Flat-Coats make excellent family pets. Teach them to fetch anything, and if you're into exercising, they enjoy jogging or biking with you. These are super dogs for seniors looking for home protection. And these even-tempered, wonderful dogs are perfect to take to nursing homes and hospitals to visit the infirm. Flat-Coats are very empathetic and reach out to these people. Watch their eyes if you want to see canine love expressed. They all but shout, "Don't worry, you're not alone. I'm here with you!"

Most Compatible Sun Sign: Cancer

One of the few animals who love the water as much as Flat-Coated Retrievers is the Cancer native! Both are mellow, life-loving, calm, compassionate animals. Like this dog breed, Cancer natives are domestic, understanding, sympathetic, diplomatic, strong, and purposeful. Cancerians are born under one of the most loving, giving signs in the zodiac. Equally, Flat-Coats are among the most loving, giving dogs in the canine world. Both are reserved. Both are loyal and have a quiet kind of zest for living. Cancerians encourage others to turn to them when they're in trouble or feeling poorly. Natives of this sun sign probably have more patience than any other in the zodiac. They also have tremendous tenacity. Both Cancerians and Flat-Coats enjoy pleasing others. The Moon rules the sign of Cancer and it has dominion over the moods of humans and dogs. Though these two are extremely compatible, it would probably be wise for Cancer humans to avoid adopting Flat-Coated Retrievers born under the sign of Cancer. Two moody animals in the same house could present difficult situations. The next best sign for Flat-Coats is Pisces.

FOXHOUND (ENGLISH)

Positive Traits

Slightly smaller than German Shepherds, Foxhounds are energetic, friendly, affectionate, and tolerant. Originally bred to be deer hunters, these dogs have been used by the British for over four hundred years as their primary canine companions on fox hunts. In the field, these Cosmic Canines are obedient. Foxhounds are of even temperament though they can be very energetic when inside the home, and so they must be trained as puppies about outdoor versus indoor behavior. These affectionate dogs are very attentive to their families and have big barks designed to warn off prowlers. When running with the pack on fox hunts, they work like surgeons—with discipline, endurance, and professionalism. These are good scent dogs and, if trained for it, could probably help Bloodhounds find lost people or escaped criminals. The first English Foxhounds were brought to America in 1738 by Lord Fairfax. The English variety of this dog breed is heavier—sturdier—than the American counterparts, yet they maintain their graceful appearance. When properly bred and trained, Foxhounds can be wonderful home companions. If, however, they spend their puppyhoods in stables or a kennel with other dogs (the pack), they will not make the transition to household living as family pets. Once a pack dog, always a pack dog, and in the family home, pack dogs can be quite destructive.

Negative Traits

Given the opportunity, Foxhounds yap constantly. One of the reasons they make such good hunters is their deep, baying voice (and they love to use it). Discourage unnecessary barking from day one. Do it without punishment, which discourages dogs from becoming good watch-and-warn protectors. If you do not control Foxhound barking while they are young, they will be so noisy as adults, they become unsuitable pets. This dog breed has a history of possible inherited deafness (have puppy hearing checked by a vet, find out about the hearing of the sire and dam, too). Though excellent Scenthounds, these are otherwise not the most intelligent dogs in the canine world. Once through the puppy months and trained, they are easy-to-keep-up dogs.

Job Opportunities for English Foxhounds

When properly bred, raised, and trained, these are obedient, quiet, and loving house pets. Good company while riding horses, going for jogs, riding bicycles, or taking long walks. Foxhounds need exercise. They are good watch-and-warn dogs (trained to guard, they can do it), excellent hunting companions, and possibly adequate search-and-find dogs. Foxhounds can be quiet, mannerly family companions, but it's not necessarily the personality style that comes most naturally to them, and they may need some help getting there.

Most Compatible Sun Sign: Virgo

Like these dogs, Virgoans are practical and down-to-earth. They are usually not showy people. There's very little tinsel in this sun sign's personality. What you see is real. Like Virgo human companions, Foxhounds are comfortable with reality. Natives of this dependable, self-contained, and commonsense sun sign instinctively know how to control Foxhound barking when they are puppies. This stops them from falling in love with the sound of their own voices before it begins. Virgoans are great listeners, but even they have their limits! Self-improvement is important to Virgo natives and what's good for the goose is good for the gander in this instance. Virgoans will commit themselves to giving Foxhounds the training they need to become good household members and will reap huge rewards for their trouble. Trained, these *Cosmic Canines* are wonderful household pets. Untrained, which politically correct Virgo humans would never permit, Foxhounds never reach their pet potential. Virgo natives are constructive, reasoned, tactful, discriminating, and active yet calm. And like Foxhounds, they are energetic, friendly, affectionate, and tolerant. All of these traits have high appeal to Foxhounds and are good for them, too. When Virgoans become overly sensitive, domineering, hard-nosed, or too critical, Foxhounds are likely to respond with a long yawn and take a nap until their human companions get back into a positive groove.

GERMAN LONGHAIRED POINTER

Positive Traits

Solid liver in color, these sturdy dogs (who are not at all like German Shorthaired Pointers) are enthusiastic hunting dogs and require exercise. If they do not get it, their high energy piles up to become tension that results in nervous temperaments. These dogs enjoy one primary human companion and, in family environments, there is a danger they will bond only with that individual. Longhaireds so enjoy hunting, it is likely that one-person bonding will occur with whomever accompanies them into the field. German Longhaireds are famous for their falconry and hawking skills. Their first love is hunting birds! They are fun-loving, relaxed animals. They are top-drawer water Retrievers and high-energy pets.

Negative Traits

Longhaired Pointers have too much energy to be penned up in apartments or small yards. These are country dogs who need lots of room to run and exercise. At the very least, they need large yards. Ideally, they should have some out-of-yard exercise several times a week. Their coats aren't very long and do not present grooming problems, but they do require brushing and their feathering takes some extra care. These dogs are first and foremost hunters and have the independent attitude that accompanies that status. They are not the best children's dogs or the most affectionate family pets. On the other hand, aside from their exercise requirements, they make few demands on members of their households. As family pets, Longhaireds are rather laid-back and have humorous personalities. They enjoy game playing with their human companions.

Job Opportunities for German Longhaired Pointers

If you like to spend time on the water, these dogs make wonderful boating companions. They enjoy playing retrieving games (take them to a lake and throw Frisbees into the water) and you can teach them to fetch just about anything. Good in the field as Retrievers or as falconers and hawkers. Longhaireds are easygoing family pets, but they are not the kind of dog who is happy curling up, night after night, by a crackling fire. They need activity!

Most Compatible Sun Sign: Scorpio

Like German Longhaired Pointers, natives of Scorpio love the water and are fun-loving and relaxed. They, too, are high-energy animals. Scorpions love a mystery (Scorpions *are* mysteries) and German Longhaired Pointers provide good puzzles to unravel. Both sun sign and dog breed are independent individualists, quick-thinking, and self-controlled, and both thrive on approval. Neither throws out the welcome mat for just anyone and both have very strong characters. Scorpions can be friendly but may choose not to be—very like these dogs. Both are determined, talented, decisive, and somewhat dignified. This sun sign has a dual nature and natives born under Scorpio can, like these dogs, be very good or very bad. Both are creatures of extremes and very little moderation. Obstacles mean little to either, and both can be their own worst enemies. These two are very much alike. Scorpions, however, are known to be sympathetic and empathetic, two things these dogs need to learn. And natives of this sun sign are among the most powerful in the zodiac. Longhaireds need that, too. The traits most admired by these dogs: Scorpion energy, dominance, and perseverance.

GERMAN SHEPHERD

Positive Traits

No dog breed loves its family more than the German Shepherd. Nor is any dog more willing to protect that family. Shepherds are extremely loyal, supremely intelligent, protective, and courageous. And they are very versatile and flexible. They have been outstanding Working and Herding *Cosmic Canines*, are unbeatable in the obedience ring, and have been used as guide dogs for the blind, police dogs, military dogs, and drug/explosive search dogs. They have been used as scenting dogs, trailing escaped criminals and lost children. Their very versatility is what makes them such good guide dogs for the blind. German Shepherds *need a purpose in life*—they need jobs. They have highly developed senses, mentally and temperamentally. Shepherds are ever vigilant, consistent, reliable, energetic, and watchful. This dog breed is known for its uncanny ability to assimilate and remember information. It goes far beyond the definition of a canine companion. This is one of the few breeds with the capacity to be pals to humans, too (and protective ones, at that). These dogs are so patient, it sometimes makes you wonder who is supposed to be the superior being. German Shepherds observe everything that's going on around them. They miss very little. They were not bred to brawl with other animals but to protect them. Yet they are dominant fighters when they need to be. Their value as police dogs is that they do not slash flesh when they bite (like Doberman Pinschers do). German Shepherds have a unique kind of dignity and do not offer friendship or love easily. Once offered, it will never be withdrawn. When you watch this dog's smooth, flowing gait, you can picture him in the fields, herding sheep or cattle. Like his personality, the gait is as smooth as glass, effortless, strong, and real.

Negative Traits

When Shepherd puppies first begin to show protective tendencies, they need to be taught not to overguard or overprotect. Though extremely affectionate, these are not lap dogs. Rather, they are working dogs who need a job, like Border Collies. These are noble dogs with a great deal of power and intelligence. Left untrained, they will dominate when the opportunity presents itself. German Shepherds need to be obedience-trained while puppies by firm, loving hands. Until they are well trained, they are not reliable around small children. With Shepherds, you get better results by rewarding positives rather than correcting negatives. Shepherds need their energies focused or else their good traits can become negatives. For every good potential, there are bad ones. Shepherds have dense, waterproof undercoats that need regular grooming. They shed seasonally.

Job Opportunities for German Shepherds

If dogs can do it, Shepherds can handle it, except being lap dogs (though I've seen a few try). German Shepherds are one of the few dogs intelligent enough to be taught to disobey commands they have learned—for example, a blind person tells the dog "forward" and an open manhole lies directly in the path of the dog and its blind companion. Shepherds can be taught not to go forward, to disobey. Other breeds either jump over the hole (letting the "blind" dog trainer walk into it) or refuse to move. German Shepherds make excellent military and police dogs, home protectors, drug enforcement dogs, trackers of lost people or escaped felons, and guide dogs for the blind. They are also among the best of herding animals and are good exercise companions. Most of all, they make the best of friends and are wonderful family pets.

Most Compatible Sun Sign: Aquarius

More geniuses have been born under the sign of the Water Bearer than any other, and natives of this intelligent, loyal sign are also patient, dependable, faithful, and kind. In fact, the Water Bearer symbolizes compassion for humanity. These two have so much in common, it would be easier to list their differences. Like these dogs, Aquarians are determined, quiet, and unassuming. And they are very versatile and flexible—people who can keep ten balls in the air at one time with seemingly little effort. Also like these *Cosmic Canines*, Aquarians *need* a purpose in life; they need a job. They are consistent, reliable, energetic, and not only remember but attract data. In fact, Aquarians sometimes seem to gain information through osmosis, right out of thin air. Also like German Shepherds, natives of this sun sign have a unique brand of dignity—it may be very unconventional, but it is branded by Aquarians as their own—and they do not offer friendship or love easily. Once offered, it is never withdrawn unless rejected. And though natives of the Water Bearer may not gush and ooze over their families, they love them deeply and will make any sacrifice needed on their behalf. They can be disorganized, scattered, arrogant, inflexible, fickle, and unfocused when going through negative cycles, but German Shepherds are so strong in these areas, they won't think anything of it. Sheps are more physical than Aquarians, and that's good. These people need something (like a good dog) to get them out of their offices and outside where they can smell the roses. German Shepherds do that for Aquarians. These two go together like mud and rain.

GERMAN SHORTHAIRED POINTER

Positive Traits

Shorthairs are proficient in the field. When it comes to hunting, they take it very seriously. They have a regal bearing and are strong, agile, powerful dogs. They are well-balanced, muscular, and beautiful animals. Shorthaireds are graceful, animated *Cosmic Canines* in the field and are adaptable. They work both on land and in the water with skill. They are, however, water dogs to their toes—well, to their webbed feet, anyway. German Shorthaired Pointers are a little better at obedience training than many hunting dogs—part of their adaptability and ability to focus. These are intelligent, affectionate pets with nothing standoffish or aloof about them. They make very good family pets and are easily trained for obedience.

Negative Traits

Shorthaireds need room to run. If their human companions are sufficiently attentive to take them for a good run three or four times a week (or a bicycle ride or chasing balls on deserted country roads, etc.), they will do fine in medium-sized houses and yards. This is not the best possible family dog, but for hunters seeking superior field dogs who are adaptable to family life and who readily express affection to all family members, German Shorthaired Pointers may be just the ticket. They are easy to groom. If raised around small children, Shorthaireds will do well with toddlers. If not, they, like most large dogs not raised around little ones, will do better around school-aged children. All large dogs should be supervised by an adult when in the presence of young toddlers and infants.

Job Opportunities for German Shorthaired Pointers

Wonderful bird dogs, hunting companions, and excellent Gundogs, Shorthaireds have keen scenting capabilities and are good trackers. They love the water and are excellent boating companions! People who like camping will have interested overnight guests—these dogs love outdoor motels. They are good family pets and personal companions, and excellent exercise partners. German Shorthaired Pointers are good for obedience hobbyists and can be taught to fetch anything.

Most Compatible Sun Sign: Pisces

Pisces natives take their jobs very seriously, just like Shorthaireds do when in the field. And natives of this Water sun sign love the wet stuff in which people swim almost as much as these dogs (although Pisceans do not usually have webbed feet). Pisces natives, like these dogs, are intelligent, affectionate, and very giving. People born under this sun sign are known to be neighborly, and like Shorthaireds there is nothing standoffish or aloof about them. Pisceans are peaceful, giving, imaginative, and controlled (yet exciting) to be around. They are primarily good with Shorthaired *Cosmic Canines* because they have warm, endearing personalities. These dogs are not assertive with people. They are settled and content with humans born under a sympathetic, compassionate sun sign like Pisces. These are gentle people with sensitive feelings who appreciate honesty when presented in a way that does not offend; both dog and sun sign are politically correct. German Shorthaireds are sensitive to the feelings of human companions. Pisceans enjoy the regal bearing of these dogs and will stand a little taller as a result. Because they are individualists who magnetically give and receive energy, Pisces humans have much to give and receive from these even-tempered pets. When Pisceans go negative (as all sun signs do from time to time) and become unsettled, dissatisfied, narcissistic, melancholy, and obsessive, the sad look in the eyes of these dogs can bring their guardians back to normal quickly. Pisces humans would never hurt another living being if it could be avoided.

GERMAN WIREHAIRED POINTER

Positive Traits

Retrieving Pointers were in great demand in Germany during the late 1800s and the Wirehaired was bred in response to that demand. They are handsome dogs, stable, who like to learn rules and follow them, and enjoy pleasing human companions. Wirehaireds are easy to train, have moderate temperaments, and are good Gundogs. They are also good with children and make wonderful household pets. Human companions particularly appreciate their desire to obey. These *Cosmic Canines* swim like professionals and are powerful and versatile, not just good family pets but also excellent hunters and good guard dogs who protect their families and their homes. Though they have excellent scenting powers, they are a little slower than some in the field, yet Wirehaireds have endurance and power. These dogs are some of the great individualists of dogdom. These *Cosmic Canines* definitely respond better to positive training that rewards and applauds doing the right thing while correcting but playing down errors every dog makes until trained. Once trained, Wirehaireds are among the best of family pets and protectors.

Negative Traits

These very active dogs need plenty of exercise. Wirehaireds have their own personalities, good or bad, and half of the fun of being their guardian is finding out who they are. They are, first and foremost, Gundogs who love to hunt (and are very good at it). Their coats are harsh and wiry and, though not long, do require some grooming. The coat is water-repellent and straight and harsh, lying quite flat along the dog's body for such wiry hair. These Pointers show an intelligent sense of determination, which, without good breeding or good training while young, can turn to stubbornness.

Job Opportunities for German Wirehaired Pointers

Water lovers, Wirehaireds make great boating companions and add a degree of security with their protection skills. These obedient dogs are super family pets, although if not raised around small children, they will be unused to them and will need to be supervised when with them. But this is true of all large, energetic dogs. Good trackers—what have you lost lately? Teach Wirehaireds to fetch everything from the newspaper to the kitchen sink . . . well, maybe not the kitchen sink (but close). Slow but enduring hunters and Gundogs. Reliable exercise partners.

Most Compatible Sun Sign: Scorpio

Wirehaired personalities are a bit of a mystery and that hooks Scorpio natives at the outset. Like people born under Scorpio, these dogs are very independent and great individualists. Both are talented, decisive, quick-thinking, persistent—and powerful. Scorpio natives are among the most powerful in the zodiac and, like these dogs, stable. While Scorpio humans don't particularly like to learn rules and follow them, they like others who like to learn the rules and follow them. Their Wirehaired pets fill that bill nicely. Handsome or pretty rather than glitzy or showy describes both dog and sun sign pretty well. No sun sign is more versatile than Scorpio. They are, in fact, known as the sign of extremes and have wide behavioral parameters that allow versatility and adaptability. Scorpion natives also thrive on approval. If half of the fun of owning Wirehaireds is finding out who they are, Scorpio is already in love with them (even if they've never met one). Both dog and sun sign love and are good with children. These are strong dogs easily capable of withstanding Scorpion negatives—willful, rigid, harsh, and faultfinding behavior. If Scorpio human companions become immoderate or uncontrollable, Wirehaireds will simply ignore them.

GOLDEN RETRIEVER

Positive Traits

These intelligent, gentle dogs are not only friendly and willing in the field, they are friendly and willing in the home, too. They love their families but are not good guard dogs. They are too easygoing and gentle of nature. They adore children. When properly bred, they have sound temperaments and are easily trained. Most of all, they are loyal. Golden *Cosmic Canines* will romp in the yard with the kids, go take a nap on a sick child's bed to make sure he or she doesn't feel ignored, go for a drive with you, or simply enjoy human companionship and some obedience training. They also like a day in the field, hunting. They are very adaptable pets! Goldens are among the most trustworthy of the canine world. They are happiest sharing the family room with those they love. They are sensitive to your feelings and expect the same in return.

Negative Traits

Goldens have long, smooth (or wavy) outercoats and dense undercoats. They shed all year but especially during spring and fall, and need to be groomed—a small price to pay for such endearing home partners. They require daily exercise to stay in the best of health. Goldens are not the most mentally focused dogs and may forget to stay where they are told if too much time elapses. Be calm (not harsh) when training them. They are very tone-of-voice sensitive and their feelings get hurt when human companions' voices are filled with vitriolic reprisal over small mistakes. Taurus natives are also voice sensitive—Taurus-born Goldens will be doubly voice sensitive. They respond better to positive approval than they do to criticism. Deemphasize the negative. Aside from these minor inconveniences, there are no known negatives about Golden Retrievers.

Job Opportunities for Golden Retrievers

They have an innate ability for (and love of) retrieving and will enjoy carrying the newspaper home or will (with your permission) wander around the house carrying an old slipper in their mouths. If you want your slippers delivered to you (unchewed, of course), Goldens will be glad to provide that service, too. They have been used as guide dogs, where they have been found to be gentle, eager, alert, and self-confident. They are wonderful family pets, great exercise partners, and are good travelers (in spite of their size). If you're looking for dogs for protection reasons, this is not the best choice. They will, however, bark and warn of strangers if trained to do so.

Most Compatible Sun Sign: Taurus

Practical, patient, and persistent are the traits of a Taurus or a Golden Retriever. Both sun sign and dog breed have a kind of endurance about them that is stable and reassuring. You just know they're always going to be there for you. Both are also faithful, friendly, and fearless. And they have loads of vitality—Goldens and Taureans are, more than anything else, vital. Goldens can become such an integral part of family life, they become essential to family happiness. The same is true of Taurus human companions. Both sun sign natives and dog breed are generous, soothing, peaceful, and somewhat reserved. Both adore family, are wonderful with children, and are totally trustworthy. When Taurus humans get into trouble, it's because they can be too easygoing and gentle of nature and have a tendency to make the easiest decisions rather than the right ones. Golden *Cosmic Canines* are like that, too. Both are voice sensitive. Taurus natives won't commit the ultimate Golden Retriever sin. They won't yell or use recriminatory verbal tactics to correct mistakes. In negative cycles, Taureans can become obstinate and dogmatic, materialistic and selfish. They can even become fearful—totally opposite to their usual fearless states. Goldens are patient and will wait out the bad moods.

GREAT DANE

Positive Traits

Of German origin, these dogs have been called elegant. And they have been called "distinguished." But as one royal Dane pondered the ultimate question—"To be, or not to be?"—so do people thinking about adopting Great Danes need to ask themselves some questions. How big is your yard? That's a good place to start. Your house? Your children? And your kitchen? Is it big enough for you and your Dane to turn around at the same time? If not, dinnertimes can be difficult, and eating is one of this *Cosmic Canine*'s favorite pastimes. Great Danes are not as independent as some other large dogs. They like to take part in family activities. Though their size is enough to intimidate anyone, Great Danes are too good-natured to be good guard dogs. They are easy to train and make excellent family pets (once children are of sufficient size not to be knocked over by such large dogs when they become playful—teenagers, at the very least).

These dogs are wonderful companions, slow to anger, who willingly—even readily—accept other pets. Great Danes are noble in spirit, quick on their feet, and have a lot of endurance. Because of their size, they must be obedience-trained (take them to class or get private sessions because it needs to be done properly) before six months of age. They are easy to groom and shed very little.

Negative Traits

Great Danes are not known for their longevity. And any dog this size can be intimidating, especially to young children. If there are older children in the home, be sure parental temperaments of Dane puppies are known before adopting them. Nips from small dogs because of temperament problems are one thing. Nips from mouths the size of a Dane's (even as puppies) can do real damage, especially to little ones. Improperly bred and left untrained, any animal of this size can make life pretty unpleasant. These are not dogs to have rough-and-tumbles with—they might take such games seriously. Feeding very large dogs can be costly, so review budgetary allowances.

Job Opportunities for Great Danes

Their beauty and smooth musculature make Great Danes wonderfully photogenic and great models. They are excellent exercise partners once obedience-trained. Unless leash training (at the very least) is accomplished, these dogs can go just about anyplace they want to go. Without training, Dane quickness, size, and strength make it impossible to put these good-natured dogs to work at meaningful occupations. They can just drag the person at the end of the leash from one point to the next. Their size prevents them from being good travel companions. Trained, they make gentle pets for households with older children; raised with school-aged children from puppyhood *and* trained, they are good family pets. Great Danes are truly gentle giants with wonderful temperaments. The only negative comments regarding their interaction with children are based on size, energy, and enthusiasm for life, not from temperament problems of the breed.

Most Compatible Sun Sign: Virgo

Like Virgoans, Great Danes project a sense of elegance and are easygoing and distinguished. And they have a mind for details—like asking all the right questions before adopting one of these fine pets. Both dog and sun sign are slow to anger and make wonderful companions. Natives of this sun sign are active, yet calm; constructive, yet tactful. Virgoans are the essence of political correctness—and so are these dogs. Virgo humans admire the nobility of these dogs. Virgo natives like to have others depend on them, and Great Danes are less independent than other canines. Self-contained, reasoned, and detail-oriented, Virgoans gather all the information they can about the best way to handle and train Great Danes. By doing so, they ensure these pets have the opportunity to achieve maximum potential. These sun sign natives are very analytical, logical, and observant and set very high standards of behavior. Without human companions who expect a lot from them, Great Danes have difficulty achieving all they are capable of achieving. Virgo dog guardians are down-to-earth and plain-speaking, which these dogs find easy to respond to and understand. Most important from the perspective of Great Dane *Cosmic Canines*: no sun sign produces more dependable humans than Virgo. And Virgoans are happiest when being of service to others, including their pets. Like these dogs, Virgo human companions enjoy involvement with whatever makes up their life environments. This is a pragmatic sun sign and those born under it will find pragmatic Great Danes high on their list of favorite hobbies.

GREAT PYRENEES

Positive Traits

This beautiful, white snowball of a gentle giant (32 inches at the shoulder, 130 pounds) is docile, loving, and thinks children are the greatest thing since dog kibble. Inconsiderate teasing doesn't even bother Pyres. It's hard to say enough good about this dog breed of French royalty and nobility—and it's equally hard to say exactly where the Great Pyrenees originated. Most people think their ancient lineage is Asian. These *Cosmic Canines* were used for guard duty at the Château of Lourdes, France, in the early 1400s and accompanied jailers on prison rounds. They were given places at the château in sentry boxes, with armed guards. Wonderful family pets, they are loyal, devoted, loving, and they understand humans very well. Great Pyrenees dogs can be kept indoors or out and they get on well with other animals. Slow to anger, courageous and generous, this is one of the kindest members of dogdom. It was said by *Cynographia Britannica* in 1800 that "[in] a family, he will permit the children to play with him and suffer all their pranks with offense." These dogs have the patience of Job, the gentleness of the lambs they have historically protected and herded, the loving nature of saints, and, like all herding dogs, are highly independent. Their sweet side does not diminish their nobility, courage, faithfulness, and working abilities.

Negative Traits

These are working dogs who are happiest with a job. People who don't have herds of sheep for Pyrenees to move around and protect should train them in some endeavor. Pyres do not like strangers who take liberties, so don't give your friends keys to come and go as they wish in private homes, unless these dogs are safely ensconced in well-fenced backyards. These dogs need plenty of space (they are not apartment dogs), exercise, and regular grooming. Their white (sometimes patched with gray or tan spots) coats are of medium length and they have thick undercoats, shedding seasonally. Pyres are not the easiest dogs to obedience-train, but with persistence they do learn their lessons and household manners. Because of their size, obedience training needs to start prior to six months of age. They are too docile to be good guard dogs, but their very size deters many would-be prowlers.

Job Opportunities for Great Pyrenees

Since these dogs herded sheep for hundreds and hundreds of years in the mountains of France, those instincts still run strong. These are wonderful ranch and farm dogs (where herding jobs for dogs are still available). They are courageous enough to deal with the wolf attacks on livestock faced by Western ranchers while maintaining their gentleness as family pets after a hard day's work. Pyres are problem-free exercise partners who will not try to fight with other animals along the exercise route. Among the best of all dogs for children and multiple-pet families.

Most Compatible Sun Sign: Leo

Kind, warmhearted Leos are the perfect human companions for these loyal, devoted, loving dogs. Like the Great Pyrenees, Leo dog guardians are indoor/outdoor animals and get on well with others—people and canines. Natives of the sign of the Lion are also known for being self-conscious, forceful, vital, and loving individualists. The Pyre's slowness to anger is good for Leo human tempers, which, like dogs of war, sometimes slip their leashes a little too easily. Lions are also courageous, like these *Cosmic Canines*, yet are known for their kindness and generosity. Leo natives are generous and make good friends capable of understanding how best to give to these large, docile dogs. Leo natives are not known for their patience, and Pyrenees patience adds to the total human-pet relationship, as does Pyrenees gentleness (not one of the outstanding traits of Leo humans). Both, however, bring loving natures and noble characters to these relationships. Sun sign and dog breed are very independent. Leo humans are energetic, sincere, and faithful to friends, which are also traits highly compatible with Great Pyrenees dog attitudes.

GREYHOUND

Positive Traits

Faster than a speeding bullet, as aristocratic as Louis XIV, Greyhounds are built for speed These racing kings of dogdom are also adaptable, affectionate, and good with adults and older children who have been taught dog manners. One of the few things that will make a Greyhound snap is being teased, and a snap from one of these dogs can be devastating. With people, Greyhound *Cosmic Canines* are gentle and loving. These dogs are fast, fast, fast. In controlled, predictable environments, Greyhounds are even-tempered and affectionate, though they are happiest (and most predictable) in the hands of dominant handlers. They are among the most graceful and powerful of dogs. Their history was written in the hot Egyptian sands. Carvings strongly resembling elegant Greyhounds found in Amten's tomb, circa 2900 and 2751 B.C., give proof of the ancient nature of this breed. These dogs have been friends to humans for thousands of years. The only question to ask concerning this breed is: "Should I adopt a Greyhound?" The only answer is: "If you control your household environment." In predictable environments, there are no better pets than Greyhounds. They are loyal, gentle, and loving, but they need human companions capable of commanding these relationships. That is accomplished by controlling the household environment.

Negative Traits

I watched one day while three year-old Greyhound puppies turned on their brother, the fourth of the litter, over nothing. He just happened to be the runt. Within less than a minute, they had killed him. Though normally happy-go-lucky, energetic dogs, Greyhounds can react unreliably when faced with rapidly unfolding, unpredictable situations—like teasing or teenage roughhousing. In the above incident, the fourth puppy did something to aggravate one of his siblings, got nipped, and nipped back. All three siblings joined in the attack against him. When living in family environments, Greyhound behavior in the face of the unpredictable can't be taken for granted. Will your teenagers let their friends tease the dog? If so, get another pet. Greyhounds are called "the most misunderstood" canine. They have a natural instinct to chase small, fast-moving objects, and they *must* have exercise to maintain their health Speaking of health, Greyhounds have a tendency to be arthritic or to have bouts of rheumatism. These are not good dogs for multiple-pet households. If you understand their strengths and their weaknesses and don't tempt fate by trying to change the proud genes they carry, if you are not intimidated by strong, powerful dogs who are not always predictable in uncontrolled circumstances, then Greyhounds make wonderful pets.

Job Opportunities for Greyhounds

Greyhounds entertain millions of people annually with their graceful, powerful racing skills at dog tracks around the country. They make great corporate logos, company names—taken a bus cross-country lately?—and symbols for advertisers wanting to project speed, symmetry, strength, and independence. Greyhounds have the keenest eyesight of all canines, and when properly bred and trained, they make wonderful guide dogs for the blind. They are good exercise partners when the environment is controlled (free from other animals, especially cats and other dogs) and the dog has been properly leash-trained. For the right human companions, Greyhounds are loving, gentle pets.

Most Compatible Sun Sign: Gemini

Like these dogs, Gemini human companions are adaptable, changeable, multifaceted, and diverse. They are also bold, assertive, quick, and forceful. These two sound a lot alike, don't they? They are! Gemini natives are the most misunderstood sun sign because of the dual personality of natives born under the sign of the Twins. Geminis are nature's way of exemplifying that all human beings have more complex personalities than the one they put forward publicly (from working to dating to marriage and parenthood) Greyhounds also have dual natures: a sporting nature (created by humans for their enjoyment) and their natural pet nature. These dual natures make them the most misunderstood canines in dogdom. Like Greyhounds, Geminis are inquisitive, functional, confident, and refined. These *Cosmic Canines* are physically agile and Gemini natives are mentally agile—a perfect combination that ends up making both dogs and humans stronger life-forms. Natives of the Twins have a lot of get-up-and-go (just like Greyhounds) and can, depending on their moods, have short fuses on their tempers. These two even share a lot of the same negatives: anxiety, belligerence, aloofness, moodiness, and restlessness, and they go through periods where they are very high-strung. Gemini humans and Greyhound dogs share more than the same first initial. These two work together like contractor and builder (or they should). Gemini humans are the contractors, directing the efforts of Greyhound builders.

IBIZAN HOUND

Positive Traits

A companion to Hannibal when he invaded Italy, amber-eyed Ibizan Hounds come in both shorthaired and wirehaired varieties—both with thick coats. Their ancestry is similar to that of Pharaoh Hounds. Ibizans have kind dispositions, are excellent with children, and are good for multiple-pet families because they get along well with other animals and seldom start fights. They are intelligent and seldom aggressive. Overall, they are wonderful house pets. Ibizan *Cosmic Canines* are both scent and sight hunters and are excellent Gundogs. Strong and flexible, they make good watchdogs. They are clean, friendly animals who are good-natured and happy.

Negative Traits

These friendly animals have sensitive feelings and can be easily hurt. In addition to having superior sight capabilities, Ibizans have exceptional hearing. Do not shout at them and be careful what tone of voice you use. A careless comment said in an exaggeratedly negative tone of voice may result in your Ibizan walking around with his large, upright ears flattened against his head (expressing hurt feelings). Wirehaireds need more grooming than shorthaireds, but nothing major or difficult. Ibizans resemble Greyhounds and are likely related to them, and just like those speedsters, they need a lot of room for exercise. Ibizan human companions need enough time to make sure these dogs exercise in large yards daily and get twice-weekly, half-hour trotting sessions outside the yard.

Job Opportunities for Ibizans

Ibizans are sight-and-scent small-game hunters and Gundogs. They are excellent household pets, especially for families with children. As with all large dogs (and regardless of how mild canine temperaments are), involvement with less than school-aged children should always be supervised. Obviously, Hannibal thought them good travelers, but he was using elephants for transport, not cars. They are a little big to be good travel companions. Excellent exercise partners after being leash-trained.

Most Compatible Sun Sign: Capricorn

Both of these animals are kind, balanced, fair, diligent, and persistent. Like these dogs, Capricorns are self-reliant, independent, and patient. They get along well with others and though they are very capable of defending themselves, are seldom the ones to start fights. These *Cosmic Canines* may be a little more flexible than natives of this sun sign, who, when they have opinions, tend to think the world ought to agree with them But those born under the sign of the Goat love progress, and flexibility is something they can learn from Ibizans. Both dog breed and sun sign are intelligent, friendly, good-natured, and happy. Ibizans have mild temperaments that can withstand negative Capricorn sadness, suspicion, and cold and aloof behavior when it rises to the surface. Their amber eyes may fill with questions when their Capricorn companions get impatient with them or become nervous. They, like Capricorns, are patient animals, though, and rejoice when negative phases pass and Cappies return to their fair, balanced, practical ways.

IRISH WATER SPANIEL

Positive Traits

The Irish Water Spaniel's lineage goes to ancient times. These strong, sturdy *Cosmic Canines*' senses of humor and bold, eager attitudes have given them reputations as comedians. They don't know the words *shy* and *retiring*. They are brave, easily trained, even-tempered, and have very adaptable intelligence (they easily learn things beyond those for which they were bred). They can be very affectionate, have a lot of energy, and are friendly and tolerant of people they know. Irish Water Spaniels are loyal to their families—if trained to hunt, they are particularly loyal to those with whom they work—but they do not like strangers. These dogs have a lot of common sense and make good guard dogs. They have deeply affectionate natures, are excellent Retrievers, and are strong, fearless swimmers. Overall, Irish Water Spaniels have commonsense temperaments with a lot of energy, enthusiasm, and courage.

Negative Traits

Known more for their hunting skills than household charms, there is little to report about Irish Water Spaniels as house pets because not much has been said about it. These dogs are, first and foremost, bird dogs. Their coats are masses of short curls and tend to pick up field debris—thorns and other plant life. They can work in brush country, but owners will be picking stickers out of their coats for a while. Their coats are long and lie in tight ringlets. They require a lot of grooming beyond the norm. Other than having a tendency to be one-person or one-family dogs who don't trust strangers, there are no negative comments about this breed. Their high energy levels combined with their zest for life (and up to sixty-five pounds in weight) indicate they will do best around older children and should only be around toddlers on a supervised basis (regardless of wonderful temperaments).

Job Opportunities for Irish Water Spaniels

Being Gundogs and wet Retrievers are the first loves of these dogs. Good obedience-training companions and exercise partners. With the right breeding and training, Irish Water Spaniels make delightful home companions (but they do require human friends with dominant personalities who are unafraid of animals with so much energy). Teach these dogs to fetch just about anything. They are not good travel companions because of their size, energetic temperaments, and such. When properly trained, Irish Water Spaniels are good guard dogs, especially for nights spent on board boats of any size.

Most Compatible Sun Sign: Aries

Strong, sturdy, sense of humor, bold, eager—these words, used to describe Irish Water Spaniels, can just as easily be used to explain Aries natives. Nor is there anything shy or retiring about natives of the Ram. Aries's ruling planet, Mars, gives courage to those born under this sun sign (along with energy, geniality, intelligence, and common sense). It's easy to see why these two are so compatible! Aries natives are not known to be very affectionate, but they are known for their humor and strength. One of the bywords for those born under this sun sign is "sociable," which blends nicely with Irish Water Spaniel's "friendliness." Those ruled by Mars aren't the most tolerant of the zodiac, but they can learn tolerance from these *Cosmic Canines.* These Irish dogs will be the best possible audience for Aries antics as entertainers. Both dog and sun sign are strong and have a lot of energy, enthusiasm, and courage to share with one another. During bad moods, Aries natives can be pretty headstrong and impulsive, aloof and distant, and domineering—maybe that's why Irish Water Spaniels were designed to be so tolerant. These dogs know a good thing when they see it and will (impatiently) wait for Aries companions to return to the sunny side of the street.

IRISH WOLFHOUND

Positive Traits

"All Rome viewed them with wonder." This is a very old breed and the tallest of all dogs (from 31 to 34 inches at the shoulder, weighing up to 125 pounds). They are quiet, affectionate animals and aren't pushy about expressing their feelings. Marvelous with older children, they are happiest as house dogs. They're just . . . amiable. Irish Wolfhound *Cosmic Canines* are not aggressive. In fact, sometimes they are not even assertive. They are intelligent and slow to anger, but not so slow when it comes to stubbornness. Irish Wolfhounds definitely have minds of their own. They are intensely loyal to their families. These dogs like to take life slow and easy and, to exemplify that lifestyle, are friendly and obedient. The very size of Irish Wolfhounds gives them a commanding presence.

Negative Traits

Irish Wolfhounds are very big and need room to roam—more room than is available in the average suburban backyard. These are country dogs! And you need to consider your food budget, too. Big dogs eat a lot What you give is what you get with these dogs. If you are kind, they will be kind to you. Before trying to abuse Irish Wolfhounds, humans need to be sure their insurance is paid up. What goes around comes around with members of this canine breed. The size of these dogs deters unwanted visitors, but they are not good guard dogs. Because of their size, Irish Wolfhounds must be controlled by human companions, and because they get big at a very young age, the process of teaching control and discipline must begin during early puppyhood. The younger the puppy when trained, the more important for the trainer to understand how to achieve objectives through praise rather than correction. These Hounds can give a whole new meaning to the term *laid-back*; they can become so indolent that they may need to be forced into daily exercise. Irish Wolfhounds are just too big to be good with small children. Temperament has nothing to do with it. The size of these dogs simply overwhelms many preteenagers. And it is impossible to teach very young children that these particular dogs must be treated kindly at all times or they will react negatively. When they play with older kids, they can be a little too rough-and-tumble.

Job Opportunities for Irish Wolfhounds

Bred to hunt wolves, Irish Wolfhounds have also hunted wild boar, elk, deer, and other large game. They are wonderful companions around campfires during hunting season—be sure they are dressed in luminous orange or hunters may mistake them for deer (they are close to the same size!). For the right families, these dogs make wonderful pets. They can be good exercise partners (if you can lure them away from their naps) and are deterrents to prowlers because of their size. Irish Wolfhounds should qualify nicely for movie roles and modeling jobs that require large dogs with loving personalities and outgoing attitudes toward people. Corporations wanting to send messages to consumers about how strength can be tempered with compassion should hire Irish Wolfhounds as models.

Most Compatible Sun Sign: Sagittarius

No sun sign is more amiable nor produces natives with more friends than Sagittarius. Like Irish Wolfhounds, Sagittarians are assertive, not aggressive. Neither sun sign nor dog breed would use superior strength or size to compete unfairly—to bend others to their will just for the sake of winning. Both view competition as an honorable contest that should enhance the character of all participants. Both sun sign natives and these *Cosmic Canines* are intelligent and slow to anger, and the joyful, hopeful, and confident Sagittarius human attitudes help these rather indolent dogs come to life. Natives of this sun sign are known for their single-minded, purposeful, freedom-loving personalities and are more than a match for Wolfhound stubbornness. Sagittarians understand and respect loyalty, and their active, honest, giving, and sincere attitudes will be innately understood and appreciated by these dogs. And Saggie cycles of negative behavior—restlessness, nervousness, defiance, irritability, and dominance—won't be imposed on Irish Wolfhounds. Sagittarians are too giving and sincere, in addition to being too smart, to impose onto these gentle giants their momentary lapses into life's negative side.

KUVASZ (TIBETAN, SLOVAKIAN, HUNGARIAN)

Positive Traits

These beautifully proportioned dogs have a coat and a half—flowing, all white, long, and plush. They somewhat resemble Newfoundlands, but the Kuvasz is a much older breed and more assertive. The Kuvasz is tough and can be fierce when protecting families (or herds of cattle or sheep). They are excellent guard dogs with well-honed protection skills—sometimes with only one person (which, in family settings, must be discouraged). These *Cosmic Canines* are loyal and devoted to human companions, bonding closely with their families. Translated, their name means "guardian of the peace" and they are sufficiently trustworthy to deserve the name. Trustworthy, in fact, is one of the best words to describe this dog breed. The Kuvasz is intelligent, easily trained, and maintains the sense of independence reflective of dogs bred to herd These dogs are natural herders but have also been used for big-game hunting. At 26 inches in height at the withers and a maximum 120 pounds, the Kuvasz is a very large dog—his long, white coat making him appear even bigger than he is.

Negative Traits

To be enjoyable household pets, the Kuvasz must be taught obedience and discipline while small puppies. After six months of age, their very size makes effective training difficult. Untrained, they can be unhandleable. Their inclination to be one-person dogs must be discouraged and directed to include the entire family. Because once this dog bonds it will very likely not bond with another human companion, adopting a Kuvasz should be viewed as a lifetime commitment. All this hair means a lot of shedding and brushing. When necessary or when threatened, the Kuvasz can be ferocious. Left untrained or improperly trained (that is, by brawn rather than brain), Kuvaszes can be dangerous household pets when placed in proximity to small children—all that energy, all that height and weight. When properly bred and trained, it is hard to beat these dogs as top family companions. These very large dogs need a lot of space for day-to-day exercise and they have appetites reflective of their size. Make sure your budget can handle their feeding needs.

Job Opportunities for Tibetan, Slovakian, and Hungarian Kuvaszes

Their herding instincts still run strong, and they can be easily trained to perform that function, for which they were originally bred. Once trained, Kuvasz dogs make good exercise partners (though the environment should be controlled). They are too large to be good travel companions. When properly trained, they are excellent guard dogs. When improperly trained, they are dangerous guard dogs. The Kuvasz makes a wonderful family companion—among the best, in fact—for the household that can make (and keep) a true commitment to obedience-training this pet. Everything depends on training and a well-bred temperament.

Most Compatible Sun Sign: Scorpio

Loyalty and devotion are two traits at the heart of Scorpio personalities. They can be as fierce as these dogs and as loving. Scorpio humans don't bond with a lot of people either—just a chosen few. Natives of this sun sign can have tremendous strength of character, like the Kuvasz. On their positive sides, Scorpion natives are extremely trustworthy. Kuvasz dogs enjoy the optimistic outlooks of these zodiac natives and respect the power and strength that go along with being Scorpions. They also appreciate (and relate to) Scorpion intelligence, decisiveness, persistence, dignity, and determination. Both dog and sun sign are independent types who, under the right circumstances, can be the most tranquil of beings or, under the wrong circumstances, uncontrollable. Because it is impossible to put Kuvasz dogs into tidy, neat categories of any kind, they present a bit of the unknown for mystery-loving Scorpion natives to solve. Like natives of this sun sign, others seldom react to Kuvasz dogs with neutrality. They either love or dislike them. Dominant, forceful Scorpio is the right sun sign for dog-guardian compatibility.

LABRADOR RETRIEVER

Positive Traits

Labs are very versatile—much like Golden Retrievers—and make good guard dogs. They are among the best of family pets—are very kind and gentle with children. Even more important, well-bred, properly trained Labs can be trusted with children of all ages. Their normal temperaments are moderate. Poor breeding techniques can, however, damage the temperament of any dog breed. Labs are also excellent Gundogs and have proven to be good guide dogs for the blind. They have proven themselves as war dogs by detecting land mines and jumping by parachute into battlefield areas. And they earned their badges as police dogs, too. Their loving natures make them ideal family pets. They are fussy about being mannerly and are just as kind, soft, and warm as they look. Lab *Cosmic Canines* are very intelligent and easily trained, provided their trainers are smarter than they are. They are strong and active dogs who love chasing balls and sticks thrown by their families. When they get to retrieve something from the water, they're in doggie heaven! Labs thrive best on praise, not correction, so when you find them doing the right thing, enthusiastically tell them what good dogs they are. Maximize the positive, minimize the negative. Three key words for Labs: devoted, dependable, intelligent (delightful, too).

Negative Traits

Labs tend to have a "lead, follow, or get out of the way" mentality. They are large dogs and have assertive (though gentle) personalities. It is important for human companions to take charge, though not forcefully. If you know how to teach (or can learn), this dog really loves growing and learning, but beware. He'll test you, every now and then, just to make sure you're paying attention. Labs need regular exercise and grooming and their ear flaps need regular cleaning. Aside from these minimal negatives, there are none known.

Job Opportunities for Labrador Retrievers

Labs are great assets—company and protectors—on boats (and they love the water and won't drown if they fall overboard) They are excellent company for barge and fishing boat captains and provide wonderful onboard protection services. They are good guard dogs and protectors of children, too. These dogs are among the best, most devoted family pets you can adopt. Regardless of size, Labs are good travel companions and excellent exercise partners. Professionally, they do well in police work and in the military, as guide dogs and as hunting dogs. Take them to hospitals to visit those who are sick and confined—they are very empathetic!

Most Compatible Sun Sign: Cancer

These two grow from the same roots. Trust is important to both and each is equally worthy of it. Cancerians are known for their love of children and the water, and are the most domestic of all sun signs. Both dog and sun sign have moderate temperaments. Natives of the Crab are gentle, dependable, loving, intelligent, kind, and mannerly. They are strong, active, and notably tenacious. They are known for their sensitive natures, determination, understanding, empathy, self-reliance, and rationality. The calm, strong, purposeful, and compassionate personalities of Cancer natives are very good for Labs, who need these things. Labs thrive on praise and Cancerians happily give it in very positive ways. This sensitive sun sign has strong leadership capabilities—just what Labrador Retrievers need! They are also among the most loving of all sun signs—also what loving Labs need. In negative cycles, Cancerians can be fearful, defensive, selfish, self-serving, worrisome. Having Labrador pets around helps them through their bad moods. When Labrador Retrievers look deeply into the eyes of human companions with loyally questioning looks, it's hard to stay negative.

MASTIFF

Positive Traits

Mastiffs exude power and strength. They are massive of build and one word describes their appearance better than any other: imposing! Julius Caesar was so impressed with these dogs he described *Cosmic Canine* Mastiffs as "fighting like soldiers beside their masters" when Rome attacked Babylonia. They come in apricot, silver, or fawn colors, stand up to 30 inches at the shoulder, and weigh an average of 180 pounds. These are not dogs to mess around with in family environments. They are excellent guard dogs unless inbred, which can double aggressive genes, or unless their human trainers equate "mean dog" with "guard dog." Mean dogs of any breed make terrible guard dogs. They are as likely to attack family members or friends as they are to attack prowlers. This is particularly dangerous when the dogs involved are as big as Mastiffs and as naturally protective. This ancient dog breed is brave, intelligent, loyal, and quietly dignified. And they are devoted to their human companions. Not only have they served as herders, they have hunted wild horses, lions, and other formidable animals. And they were guard dogs in ancient Babylonia. They have a fighting history, having been paired off with gladiators, bulls, bears, lions, and tigers. They are powerful and very agile for their size. They also have big appetites, especially for such otherwise noble-looking beasts.

Negative Traits

Mastiffs are not good city dogs. Their sense of nobility requires they have estates to protect or on which to herd and protect lesser animals. They are suspicious of strangers, and need a lot of exercise and lots of room in which to get it. Like many large and popular dog breeds, there is a history of hip dysplasia problems. Be sure to get X rays of both parents as well as a breeder guarantee. These dogs are too big to be good companions for children. They prefer the predictable behavior of adults. Mastiffs aren't the most sociable animals in the world. Training must begin at an early age and be ongoing until good obedience habits are learned. Whenever you feel inclined to skip a training session, just think of the Mastiff's fighting background and tell your aching feet they can get through another twenty minutes while you teach these young dogs how to behave.

Job Opportunities for Mastiffs

Make icons of Mastiffs and bury them under the entryway to your home as the ancient Assyrians did to prevent evil occurrences. When properly bred and professionally trained, Mastiffs make excellent guard dogs. They serve as great company logos if the objective is to present a strong, noble, and dominant image. Because of their ancient military roots, Mastiffs would be good symbols for any armed force. Trained to herd sheep, cattle, or horses, Mastiffs could probably still handle it. They are too big to be home or travel companions or exercise partners.

Most Compatible Sun Sign: Aries

The most common words used to describe Aries natives are resolute, forceful, and strong. These same words serve nicely as root descriptions of Mastiffs. Aries natives are also brave, intelligent, and energetic, and their dominant personalities make it impossible to ignore them. Like those *Cosmic Canines*, natives of the Ram are independent and energetic. And they have endurance—the kind that allowed Mastiffs to herd flocks, hunt wild horses and lions, and fight gladiators, bulls, bears, lions, and tigers. Both Aries natives and Mastiffs firmly believe that they control their own destinies, and Aries bywords are "life is action." With both dog and sun sign, what you see is what you get—no phoniness or hidden agendas here. Like Aries natives, people either like Mastiffs a great deal or want nothing to do with them. There is no sense of ambiguity toward either these dogs or this sun sign. These two even share some of the same negatives Both can be headstrong, impulsive, high-strung, hypersensitive, aloof, domineering, and unfeeling. It is up to their human companions to control the negative moods of dog and self. These two have a great deal in common—good *and* bad!

NEWFOUNDLAND

Positive Traits

It's been said that Newfoundlands have all the virtues of humans without any of the vices. These gentle giants are excellent watch-and-warn dogs and shine in their role as protectors of children. Newfoundlands enjoy playing baby-sitter and, when properly bred, usually do not react aggressively to small, curious fingers (nor to prowlers, but they will warn you of unwelcome strangers). They are marvelous with young ones and are thoroughly reliable companions. They are slow to attack but are fierce when provoked. They are strong and solid, but their best traits are their intelligence, loyalty, and sweetness of character. Newfoundland *Cosmic Canines* evolved from fishermen's dogs and are wonderful, strong swimmers—they have webbed feet to help propel them through the water. They have heart and character, style and grace; they are the kind of friends who stay by the side of their human companions through good times and bad. They have a kind of magnificence about them that any politician would envy and a dignity all bureaucrats should study. They are, to say the least, imposing.

Negative Traits

No negative traits about this dog breed are known. Their size may intimidate people and make them difficult dogs to raise around toddlers. It would break a Newfoundland's heart to harm a family member, but it is sometimes difficult for big, growing, and exuberant puppies to control their movements. The more limited the space, the more difficult the problem. Newfoundlands have fairly long black hair with heavy undercoats. They shed and need to be brushed regularly, with an occasional visit to professional groomers. Unless Newfoundlands are poorly bred and have resulting bad temperaments, unless they have been abused (they are very sensitive to unkind treatment), this is about all the bad that can be said. Their life expectancy is shorter than that of smaller dogs. These dogs are a delight! Newfoundlands may be too friendly to be good guard dogs. Because of their size, obedience training must begin at an early age.

Job Opportunities for Newfoundlands

Tell the cast of "Baywatch" to move over because Newfoundlands are natural lifeguards. They have been used as water-rescue dogs and make wonderful company if your private yacht is large enough to accommodate them It adds a whole new concept to the words *travel companion.* They are among the best of the canine world to serve in roles as friends to humans and family pets. Newfoundlands would make good models for corporate logos or advertising campaigns where a company image of strength, compassion, dignity, intelligence, and loyalty needs to be communicated to consumers.

Most Compatible Sun Sign: Leo

It is impossible to describe the character of those born under sun sign Leo without using the words giving, vibrant, strong, warmhearted, and noble. Though the words used to describe Newfoundlands are somewhat different, the meanings are very similar. The words *imposing* and *magnificent* are also used when describing Leo—and Newfoundlands. Both dog breed and sun sign have heart and character, style and grace. Leos especially have style. These warm and loving dogs will enjoy the magnetism natives of the Lion bring to the lives of all they know. They will respect Leo's sincerity, faithfulness, and sympathetic nature. And they will appreciate it, too, because Newfoundland character is imbued with these same strengths—strengths that may present themselves more quietly in the dog than in sometimes effusive Leo natives, but the same strengths nonetheless. Leo humans will appreciate the strength, loyalty, intelligence, and sweetness of character Newfoundlands bring to this relationship. The sometimes insecure Leo will find this dog breed's commitment to friendship through good times and bad particularly appealing. Newfoundlands have sufficiently strong personalities to withstand Leo's occasional bouts of ego and self-doubt, which can result in authoritarianism. These dogs will wait it out.

NORWEGIAN ELKHOUND

Positive Traits

Though called a Hound, the Norwegian Elkhound isn't one—a Hound, that is. In Norwegian, his name (*elghund*) means "moose dog." His breed is an old one—dating from about 4000 B.C. Skeletal remains of these dogs have been found by the sides of their Viking masters. Since Vikings believed what they took with them at burial accompanied them to Valhalla, it is a meaningful indication of the high esteem in which these dogs were held by these ancient warriors. These pets are reliable and they learn quickly. Elkhounds are beautiful, self-confident, energetic dogs who are friendly to people they know. All of these qualities make them good household pets. They are odorless, reliable with children, and sensible guard dogs. Elkhounds are happy, loyal, and devoted to their families—particularly the one person with whom they bond. They love the outdoors and, above all, are outstanding game hunters (Elkhounds can trail an elk or deer by silently creeping after them on their stomachs). As hunters, they are unique—they bay or can work silently and they are known to have dodged attacks by mountain lions and bear. This is a very versatile dog, both as a hunter and as a family pet. These dogs are usually friendly, even though they have very independent personalities.

Negative Traits

Norwegian Elkhounds require exercise, so you need the space for it. They also need firm but gentle discipline in puppyhood or they can mature into overly assertive dogs. When properly bred and trained, these dogs are calm and deliberate. Because of their size and energy, Norwegian Elkhounds need adult supervision when playing with toddlers. Once trained, however, they are wonderful with older children. Their thick gray coats require regular grooming. Aside from these minimum negatives, no others are known about this dog breed.

Job Opportunities for Norwegian Elkhounds

Get this dog a job on the television series "Tales from the Crypt" and give him a role that requires a baying wolf on the night of a full moon in a cemetery. Elkies bay and, with a little makeup, can easily be made to look like El Lobo, the Wolf. Good exercise partners and excellent family protectors and companions. These dogs are among the best at hunting game—deer, elk, or moose—and Californians having trouble with wildcats would do well to take an experienced mountain-lion hunter like the Norwegian Elkhound along with them as they go for a jog.

Most Compatible Sun Sign: Taurus

Aside from Librans, no sun sign natives appreciate beauty more than Taureans. And the more down-to-earth the beauty, the more practical Taurus natives appreciate it. Elkhound *Cosmic Canine* beauty issues forth from self-confidence that results from being tried and proving true. Natives of this sun sign respect Elkhound reliability and appreciate their loyalty—and their common sense. Like these dogs, humans born under the sign of the Bull are sensible and trustworthy; rather than offering friendship to all, they reserve it for those they know and truly admire and respect. The Taurus-born are a bit reserved, quite sincere, and powerful people (once they learn how not to abuse their power—power abused is power lost). These self-confident dogs have an innate understanding of such traits (perhaps it's karma from their ancient roots). Elkhounds appreciate Taurus tendencies to be happy, loyal, and devoted and respect natives of this sun sign for their fearlessness (perhaps reminding them of Odin's brave deeds). Both dog and sun sign are companionable, enduring, tenacious, and, generally, at peace with themselves. The dog may be a little more independent than the human companion in this match Norwegian Elkhound independence and loyalty can withstand Taurean temperaments when they become obstinate, dogmatic, selfish, temperamental, and despondent. And, of course, stubborn.

OLD ENGLISH SHEEPDOG

Positive Traits

About two hundred years old, this dog breed is absolutely excellent with children, gets on well with other animals, and has an overall sound temperament. Bred to be drovers of sheep, Old English Sheepdogs have also been used to herd cattle. These dogs make devoted friends, make good guardians of children, and have sound, sensible temperaments. They are good watch-and-warn dogs, but are too friendly to be guard dogs. The normal Old English Sheepdog temperament is quiet, loving (and lovable), intelligent, and affectionate. These dogs love their homes—truly, their homes are their castles. They don't roam, they don't fight, and they are very intelligent and affectionate. Even though the size of Old English Sheepdogs might give human companions pause, they really are good house dogs. They are quiet and have perfect temperaments for families of all sizes and ages They will happily pull kids around in wagons or on sleds, and if their human companions will commit to a good daily exercise regime, they can make do in even average-sized yards. They have a great deal of staying power and stamina and, like all herding animals, can be a bit independent.

Negative Traits

There are no drawbacks known about this breed. Grooming is no more difficult for Old English Sheepdogs than for any other long-haired breed. They must be brushed regularly and taken to professional groomers for occasional trims. They are not good guard dogs but if trained to watch and bark warnings, they will happily do so. Because of size, obedience training must begin at an early age.

Job Opportunities for Old English Sheepdogs

Movie stars, models, sheep and cattle herders, Old English Sheepdogs are, most of all, loving pets and faithful family companions. These dogs are good exercise partners but are too big to be good travel companions. This homebody would rather be in the family room anyway. Sled-pulling, wagon-tugging child's playmate—or Hollywood's new star. These dogs are not horses, and toddlers riding on their backs should not be permitted.

Most Compatible Sun Sign: Libra

The three primary traits associated with Libra humans are equally innate to the personalities of Old English Sheepdogs: devotion, intelligence, and affection. Both make devoted friends, both love children, and Librans' balanced approach to life has great appeal to sensible Old English Sheepdog temperaments. Libra human companions go out of their way to avoid making enemies—very much like these dogs, who are too friendly to be good guard dogs. Like the Old English, Libra natives are quiet, loving, and friendly. Also like these dogs, Librans (along with Cancerians and Taureans) love their homes more than other signs of the zodiac do. Kind, amiable Libra is the natural companion for Old English Sheepdogs. Both dog and sun sign can charm the gills off fish and neither likes fights or upheaval of any kind, except when Librans go through negative cycles. Then they can be combative, insensitive, thoughtless, and undisciplined. Nothing will snap Libra out of being insensitive like the trusting, friendly eyes of loving Old English Sheepdogs, patiently waiting for the kind, loving friend they know to return.

OTTER HOUND

Positive Traits

Above all, these dogs love people, love to go hunting with them. Originally bred during the time of England's King John (1199–1216), these *Cosmic Canines* can also trail game. They have appealing personalities, are friendly (sometimes too enthusiastically so), responsive to attention and affection, and, when trained, are gentle—even patient—with children. Though amiable (actually, they love to have fun), Otter Hounds were bred to run with a pack and to kill their prey. If people would keep this in mind during their relationships with these dogs, Otter Hounds might be less unpredictable and offer fewer surprises. They do adapt to home living (though they prefer country to city life). Otter Hounds are a bit independent but have a merry outlook on life. They are outstanding swimmers, with webbed feet to help with their dog paddle. Once they understand family life and the behavior it requires, they are unfailing in their devotion to human companions.

Negative Traits

Attitude-wise these dogs are hunting Hounds first, house pets second. They are not ideally suited to city or suburban life. They are not good guard dogs, but will watch and warn if trained to do so. Otter Hound undercoats are oily (waterproof, to be sure) and the outercoat is hard and crisp. They require regular brushing and an occasional visit to the beauty shop. Otter Hounds can be difficult to train for any activity other than that for which they were bred: hunting. They should never be off-leash outside their homes and yards—if a cat or squirrel runs in front of these dogs, they will be off like a shot after them. Old genes die hard!

Job Opportunities for Otter Hounds

They do best that which their name defines. Though the approximate size of German Shepherds, these dogs can best be defined as "cute." They could be the next filmland discovery. With Bloodhounds somewhere in their backgrounds, Otter Hounds have good scent capabilities and make good drug detection dogs. Teach them to fetch whatever you want brought; with a good leash and choke chain, they make good exercise partners. They are not the best travel companions or guard dogs.

Most Compatible Sun Sign: Pisces

Receptive Pisces humans love responsive Otter Hound *Cosmic Canines*. Both flourish on the attention each gives the other. Affectionate natures shared by both will be an added bonus. And peaceful Pisceans have a calming effect on energetic Otter Hounds. The patience expressed by these canines is likely to fascinate imaginative natives of the sign of the Fishes. Like this dog breed, Pisces natives are gentle and amiable, warm and neighborly. Pisces humans can be exciting and fun-loving, and Otter Hounds share and enjoy these traits. Another thing these two share is their unpredictability. Pisceans are quite capable of surprising those who think they know them. Otter Hounds are independent; Fishes natives are individualistic. These two go well together, even including their love of the water. Pisceans are giving, sensitive, and compassionate, and Otter Hounds will be drawn to them like magnets, even when these human companions become dissatisfied, afraid, obsessive, excitable, and melancholy. Otter Hounds maintain their devotion, even during negative times. That's loyalty!

PHARAOH HOUND

Positive Traits

This is one of the oldest domesticated dogs in recorded history (some say 4000 B.C.; others, 3000 B.C.). They are affectionate, happy dogs—and they show it. Their noses and ears blush when they become stimulated, either from happiness or expressions of affection. They have large, deerlike ears and they are beautiful, elegant animals who, when they pose for cameras, look graceful and dignified. Powerful, too. Though in the field Pharaohs are excellent hunters, in a family setting they are very playful. It is said these *Cosmic Canines* have senses of humor that make them interesting, fun companions for children. Like the Greyhounds they somewhat resemble in build, Pharaohs are fast, fast, fast. They are also intelligent, af-,fectionate, and, as an added bonus, odorless. They are versatile hunters, capable of finding their prey using either scent or sight. These dogs have lived in structured societies with human companions for centuries and express a natural affinity for people. They are freedom-loving animals whose theme song might well be "Don't Fence Me In." Their short tan or chestnut coats make them easy-to-care-for pets.

Negative Traits

Pharaoh Hounds are about the size of German Shepherds and sometimes their energy can get a little intense. Thus, to be safe, they are not the best dogs for very young children (they should be at least of school age). When these dogs are in the presence of younger children, an adult should supervise. Pharaohs do not trust strangers (who can range from your best friends to prowlers) and can be overly assertive when company calls. Provide them with a "time out" room or outdoor structure where they can be placed whenever "strangers" (to the dog) are on the premises (including children's friends), and that problem is solved. Pharaohs need training when young or they can be too assertive to be good guard dogs.

Job Opportunities for Pharaoh Hounds

If you lose something, put your Pharaoh to work finding it for you. Or if you want to find something—like birds or small game—Pharaohs can help. They are excellent hunting companions. These dogs can use both scent and sight and make excellent drug search and immigration control dogs. Teach these pets to fetch anything within reason and they will blush with pleasure when you praise them for bringing your paper (or whatever) each day. They are good exercise companions once obedience training has been completed. Wonderful pets for families with school-aged children.

Most Compatible Sun Sign: Scorpio

Powerful, dignified, versatile Scorpio human companions go well with these affectionate, happy *Cosmic Canines*. While Scorpion noses and ears do not blush when they become excited, natives of this sun sign are known for their expressions of affection, and when Pharaoh Hounds blush, Scorpions' love of mystery will be tweaked as they try to figure out why. And, like Pharaoh Hounds, Scorpions do not like the possibility that someone might ignore them! Also like these dogs, these sun sign natives need to learn discipline at a young age. Otherwise, they can live life with devil-may-care attitudes that are harmful to them. This dog breed's playful nature appeals to this sun sign's need for entertainment. Both sun sign and dog are intelligent and affectionate and both are freedom-loving. The strongest common base between these two is their mistrust of strangers. Natives of Scorpio are, like Pharaoh Hounds, frightened by few things, and neither offers trust to others until each person has been tested and found worthy.

POINTER

Positive Traits

As Hunters, these dogs are hard-driving and they tend to business. Every inch a Gundog, Pointer *Cosmic Canines* are clean-limbed, solid—even elegant in their aristocratic grace. There is no coarseness associated with these dogs. Though they are suitable as pets, their greatest interest in life is hunting. They love the field and sharing moments in it with their favorite human companions. They are even-tempered and have kind dispositions. Though they make good family pets (when properly trained they can be very gentle), they'd rather be hunting. Few sporting breeds are more alert, hard-driving, or have more stamina and courage than Pointers. They are loyal and devoted to owners and are possessed of a lively kind of independence. To human hunters, there is nothing prettier than Pointers in pose, one front leg raised, tail standing stiff and straight, eyes filled with concentration, and flesh somewhat atremble. At no time are their muscular bodies more graceful, elegant, or filled with a sense of purpose. Pointers are intelligent and are relatively easy to train.

Negative Traits

If training is ignored, Pointers (like most dogs) can be stubborn and self-serving. These dogs require exercise and sufficient yard room in which to get it. If there is no outlet for their substantial energy, it turns to nerves. They are not the best dogs for small children. Other than these few minimal comments, there are no known negatives about Pointers.

Job Opportunities for Pointers

There is no better scent bird dog in the field than a Pointer. They love fieldwork and make excellent companions for bird hunters. Properly bred and trained, they are loyal, devoted family pets. They are suitable companions for obedience-training hobbyists and, once trained, they make excellent exercise partners. They are easy to care for and, though large dogs, good travel companions.

Most Compatible Sun Sign: Gemini

Pointer *Cosmic Canines* have dual personalities, just like sun sign Twins. Geminis can be happy, charming, adaptable, sensible, and confident—so can Pointers. Or they can be jittery, overconfident, belligerent, inconsistent, and aloof—so can Pointers. And there is a bit of aristocratic elegance about both these dogs and natives of this sun sign. Both are even-tempered, have a lot of energy, and need outlets for it or they become stressed and nervous. Like Pointers, Geminis are turned off by coarseness—this is the strongest compatibility tie that exists between these two. Both can be loyal and devoted; both are very independent creatures. Each has an innate understanding of the other. Just as Pointers love having a purpose in life (which they realize when hunting), Geminis also need life purposes (they are just too functional to be happy without them). Natives of Gemini are alert, assertive, confident, and forceful—just the right mixture to control and train Pointers to be good family pets. Without training, these dogs never achieve their full potential.

POODLE (STANDARD)

Positive Traits

Everyone knows Standard Poodles have great eye appeal, but not everyone knows they are very talented Retrievers who love the water and are strong swimmers. In the field, Poodles have great stamina. Properly bred Poodles have good and even temperaments, are intelligent, make the best household pets, and bring to their families their own unique sense of fun. These dogs learn things faster than other breeds. In my experience, some Poodles can learn in one-third less time than a German Shepherd or Doberman Pinscher. And Poodles love obedience training. They have good and even temperaments and intelligence. These *Cosmic Canines* are dignified, when they aren't clowning. Even then, their sense of self-confidence shines through Poodles seem to have a sixth sense that tells them what pleases their human companions.

Negative Traits

Poodles are active dogs who can overwhelm toddlers with their energetic expressions of love and affection. These personality kids are filled with energy that can be easily controlled with in-depth obedience training. If you can commit to training a Poodle and will keep that commitment, these dogs are for you. They are the best possible pets for children of all ages. One of the first lessons Standard Poodles need to learn is not to jump on people. Don't let them start this habit, even as puppies. As adults, they can weigh upwards of seventy pounds, and loving people and having a great zest for life, they think planting their front feet firmly on human bodies is a great way to let you know they care. If you mind spending money and time in doggie beauty salons, you will do better with another dog. These are not dogs you can ignore. They need attention. Without it, they become moody and sad. Poodles have a tendency toward rheumatism and arthritis (which explains the historic reason for Poodle cuts—traditionally, long hair was left over the joints to help prevent rheumatism when Poodles took to cold water while hunting).

Job Opportunities for Standard Poodles

Aside from certain breed-specific activities (tracking, flushing, pointing, etc.), if other dogs can do it, so can Standard Poodles. It's a good rule of thumb. They are performers supreme—in circuses, parades, movies. Poodles are wonderful scent dogs and can be used to track or trail, as drug search dogs, and as guide dogs for the blind. They are great obedience-training pets and human companions. Once trained, there are no better exercise partners. Until they are trained, though, they are just too exuberant and filled with energy to take them out in public. They are wonderful travel companions, regardless of size.

Most Compatible Sun Sign: Aquarius

Individualistic and intelligent, Aquarians truly appreciate the positive traits of Standard Poodles. Dog breed and natives of this sun sign learn faster than others and value knowledge above almost everything else. Both are very likable and neither has a malicious or petty bone in their bodies. Natives of the sign of the Water Bearer are even-tempered, have a unique concept of just about everything, and have imaginations supreme—traits shared by Poodles. It won't be hard for those born under this sun sign to daydream about their Poodles performing in the circus or in front of movie cameras. Like Poodles, Aquarians are often misunderstood. Just as some people downgrade the intelligence and capabilities of Poodles because of what they perceive to be a rather silly haircut, some people just don't take Aquarians seriously because these people tend to think twenty years ahead of current times. ("As Aquarians think today, so will everyone else in twenty years," as astrologers say.) The sign of Aquarius brings with it some very important personality traits helpful to Poodle development: patience, loyalty, determination, dependability, kindness, and sincere honesty. This is a sun sign with whom these dogs can relate, even when these humans become disorganized, arrogant, inflexible, and unfocused as they transit through negative cycles.

RHODESIAN RIDGEBACK

Positive Traits

From Zimbabwe and also known as African Lion Hounds, Rhodies are friendly and affectionate, obedient and good with older children. Though their wrinkled brows make them look worried (or like they're about to ask a question), they are energetic, have a cute sense of fun, and they rarely bark. Rhodie *Cosmic Canines* are powerful, muscular Hounds who enjoy spending hours curled lazily at the end of their human companions' beds or lounging beside them on the patio. They are likely to be stretched out, catching some rays. Rhodies like to lean against people or to sit on their feet. They scoot their backsides between people's legs as they sit on couches, raising their back legs off the floor to "sit" with them as they watch television. They are known to be gentle guardians of homes and excel in guard duties. They are profoundly loyal and enjoy playing games wherein they change their normal personalities—Lassie, today; Rin Tin Tin, tomorrow. Is it personality—or split personality?

Negative Traits

Though not aggressively distrustful of strangers, Rhodesian Ridgebacks remain suspicious of people until the dog, not the human companion, is satisfied the visitor is a friend. They are good with children of school age. Though not the easiest dog to obedience-train, Rhodies never forget what they learn. Left untrained or spoiled, they can be stubborn and self-indulgent, and lack of training makes them unsafe around young children.

Job Opportunities for Rhodesian Ridgebacks

Rhodesian Ridgebacks, like Norwegian Elkhounds, are good dogs to have along when jogging in rural areas where wildlife is making unexpected appearances and endangering humans. Due to overpopulation and food shortages in their normal habitats, bears and mountain lions have surprised (injured and killed) more than one unsuspecting jogger. Rhodies got their nickname by annoying lions and luring them toward hunters, so they make great exercise partners and are, in general, wonderful companions. People who like to camp or otherwise enjoy the outdoor life enjoy taking Rhodesian Ridgebacks with them; they enjoy campfires as much as family room hearths. When properly bred and trained, Rhodies make excellent guard dogs. They do well at all occupations requiring courage, loyalty, and stamina.

Most Compatible Sun Sign: Leo

Forceful and magnetic, warmhearted and loving, friendly and able to show affection, natives of Leo the Lion are the most natural of human companions for Rhodesian Ridgeback *Cosmic Canines.* Leonine types are generous, vital, noble, and, most of all (relative to compatibility with this dog breed), powerful. No one has more energy than Leo human guardians and few are capable of enjoying life more. Rhodesian Ridgebacks require both power and energy. Leo humans have fun and totally appreciate pets with a sense of humor. Lion natives are born with a sense of imagination second only to, perhaps, Aquarians and a sense of drama second to none. They will truly enjoy it when Rhodies take on different personalities as a means of humorous game-playing. These powerful, muscular dogs require human companions strong and tenacious enough to control and lead them into enjoyable family life. Leo natives can handle that job. Those born under the sign of the Lion thoroughly enjoy the attention these dogs show human companions. Leo humans innately understand that attention from others is their due, which is why so many of them make fine performers. Just like these dogs, if Leo natives are ignored as children or, worse, spoiled, they can be stubborn and self-indulgent. These two have a great deal in common, though there is nothing "common" about either.

ROTTWEILER

Positive Traits

Working for the early Romans, Rottweilers took part in Rome's battle against central Europe. They needed strong, durable herding dogs to help them get cattle, sheep, and goats across the Alps. Reliable Rottweilers got the job. This dog breed is close to two thousand years old. In addition to herding and guard work (at which they excel), they have been utilized as draft dogs, pulling considerable weights. Rottweiler *Cosmic Canines* have also served as members of police K-9 units. When properly bred and trained, they have good temperaments; are intelligent, friendly, capable, and affectionate; and are reliable working dogs. Their courage has been tested and proved. Rottweilers normally don't get excited easily (a most desired trait for guard dogs), are independent, and always maintain a certain sense of modest dignity.

Negative Traits

These dogs need jobs and a sense of purpose. They also need exercise or all of their powerful energy turns into nervous tension (which results in aggressive dogs). This, along with poor breeding (and naive, macho owners who think abusing dogs makes them good for guarding) are one of the primary reasons we see occasional newspaper headlines about a normally calm Rottweiler attacking someone. According to the National Animal Control Association, this dog breed is second only to Chow Chows in the number of reported human bites each year. Rottweilers are very intelligent and require owners who are at least as intelligent as they. Further, if these dogs sense human fear, it can motivate them to become aggressive where they otherwise would not be. Because children do not hide their fears, these are not good dogs for them (even though Rottweilers love families and children). Rottweilers need to be trained while young. They need firmness, not bullying. They do not tolerate abuse well and when it happens, they remember it for a lifetime. They should never be tied up. Their independence requires the freedom of a large yard. They are better country than city dogs.

Job Opportunities for Rottweilers

Rottweilers are good at protective work of any kind—patrol, search, and drug enforcement. When properly bred and trained, they make excellent guard dogs. Once obedience-trained and totally under the control of the human companion at the other end of the leash, Rottweilers are wonderful exercise partners (especially in the country where meetings with stray dogs who mistakenly think they can successfully challenge a Rottweiler are minimized). They are not the best dogs for average family companions who have no dog-handling experience. They are great doggie models for corporate logos when the desired image is power, courage, dignity, and dependability. Rottweilers are excellent herding dogs and draft animals.

Most Compatible Sun Sign: Scorpio

No sun sign is more reliable, powerful, or courageous than Scorpio It takes all three to control and train Rottweilers—to put their puppy feet on roads to happy lives as family pets. Dependable Scorpio humans achieve the job with dignity, intelligence, and friendliness. Scorpio natives are very self-controlled and are more capable than any other sun sign of not showing fear. That is important with Rottweiler *Cosmic Canines*. People born under this sun sign are optimistic and decisive (and they think very quickly, too—another necessity with Rottweilers). And they are determined. These are all traits Rottweilers need and respect. Both dog breed and sun sign are known to be independent creatures. If the human part of this relationship isn't stronger (and more flexible) than these very strong *Cosmic Canines*, training efforts will fall short of the desired end. Human natives of Scorpio have no problem controlling these dogs, who, if not trained, can become irresistible forces. Inherent Scorpion intelligence tells these human companions not to mistake abuse (which can make dogs mean) with training Scorpion humans need to put leashes on negative moods that encourage them to be willful, rigid, harsh, and uncontrollable until after training sessions are over. Once trained, Rottweilers won't mind these infrequent moods that go hand in hand with being Scorpio humans.

SAINT BERNARD

Positive Traits

It is impossible to give a specific date when these dogs first came on the scene as a documented dog breed. Records of them first appear at Great Saint Bernard Pass, a sixteenth-century Catholic hospice in the Swiss Alps. Monks were their initial human companions and they took these *Cosmic Canines* along with them on mercy missions The monks found them to be good at finding snow-covered trails. This breed's sense of smell is well developed, and Saints have an unerring sense of direction. The monks used them to help find people lost in mountain snowstorms. Saint Bernards have saved literally thousands of humans. They adore children, are easy to train (they served in the military during World War II), are supremely intelligent, and European dog enthusiasts believe Saints function acceptably in social circles. They are powerful but considerate, loyal, and affectionate. In a word, these dogs are kind. They are steady. They make wonderful companions for children—their temperaments are ideal, but be careful of their size.

Negative Traits

There are few negatives associated with Saint Bernards. They are not as long-lived as other breeds. And like German Shepherds, Collies, and other popular large dogs, they have been inbred, causing resultant hip dysplasia problems. Ask to see X rays of the parents' hips and for a "healthy hips" guarantee from breeders. These are gentle, loving dogs, but even gentle, loving dogs can knock toddlers over when they are this big and energetic. They adapt nicely to suburbia but need large yards. Saints are not good guard dogs. They care for all people, not just lawful ones.

Job Opportunities for Saint Bernards

"Oh what fun it is to ride in a one-dog open sleigh . . ." If you live in a winter climate, your Saint will enjoy being hitched to your child's sled (wagon in warm climates) to pull kids around the backyard. Such sport offers them much-needed exercise. These dogs are second only to Bloodhounds in their ability to find people. They are number one at finding them in winter storms. Saint Bernard models make great corporate logos for companies seeking to present an image of compassionate strength, intelligence, and loyalty. For people whose yards are large enough and who aren't looking for guard dogs, Saints make wonderful family pets and exercise partners.

Most Compatible Sun Sign: Libra

Both Libra humans and Saint Bernard dogs have a true sense of consideration, kindness, and appreciation for others. Interestingly, they also share a keen sense of smell and a balanced sense of direction. Librans are known for their epicurean talents (you can't be a great gourmet without a great nose) and their balanced approach to life. Balance is the key to having a good sense of direction. Libran human companions are also known for their intelligence and social skills. Like these dogs, natives of this sun sign are, well, sociable. Both are amiable, intuitive, restful, calm, and humane. No wonder they are so well liked! Both are big on compassion, too. These two have much in common! Saints love to learn and Libran humans are good teachers. They teach by using their perceptive, generous, and pleasant natures. Those born under the sign of the Scales appreciate the gentle (Librans are known for their gentility), loving, and loyal temperaments of Saint Bernards. Almost all of the innate personality traits of these dogs are important to Librans. This is a loving pet–human companion relationship waiting to happen. It will be an affectionate, steady world for these two!

SALUKI

Positive Traits

Few canines can keep pace with Arabian horses, but Salukis have a history of having done so. Known as Royal Dogs of Egypt, Salukis are among the oldest domesticated breeds of dog. It is said pictures of them appear in Egyptian tombs from as early as 5000 B.C. They have been valued trophies to the Arab people for generations. This dog breed is the source of much religious discussion. Islam classifies dogs as "unclean," yet Salukis have been declared sacred. Muslims have called them "noble ones" given to the people by Allah for their amusement and protection. In the early years, Salukis were the only dogs allowed to sleep on the carpet of a sheikh's tent. Four or five thousand years ago, they were so highly respected that their bodies were often mummified (like the bodies of pharaohs, themselves). Saluki *Cosmic Canines* are faithful dogs who are gentle companions (with children, too) yet have the sound judgment to be excellent guard dogs. They are healthy and intelligent. As an added bonus, they are also odorless (no wonder they got to sleep on the sheikh's carpet). Salukis were bred to sight-hunt everything from rabbit to wild boar to fox and are known for their keen vision. They have raced on special tracks with mechanical rabbits but, unlike Greyhounds, were required to jump hurdles at intervals. In short, these dogs are intelligent, gentle, dignified, trustworthy with children, and affectionate (without being too assertive about it). They appear graceful and well balanced. Their hunting genes run deep and they will most enjoy homes where they can be both protective, loving pets and skilled hunters. These dogs are elegant.

Negative Traits

Salukis are large dogs—upwards of twenty-eight inches at the shoulder (for males). They have feathering, which means some long hair, and that means regular grooming. They need room for daily exercise. Aside from these minimum inconveniences, there are no known negatives about Salukis.

Job Opportunities for Salukis

No dog breed has a longer history of being good, gentle, loving best friends. Nor have hunting dogs had a more lengthy test of time—and passed with flying colors! Salukis are excellent at both jobs. For people who want good guard dogs who are also trustworthy with kids, Salukis are a good choice. They are enjoyable, reliable exercise partners who, when properly bred and trained, never start fights with other leashed dogs while jogging with companions around the neighborhood. Teach them to fetch slippers and newspapers, but most of all enjoy them in the family room!

Most Compatible Sun Sign: Aries

Competitive Aries, first sign of the zodiac, understands wanting to be first better than any other sun sign. Like these dogs, they are known for their intelligence, their humorous approach to life, and their sensible, strong personalities. Well-balanced Aries natives not only understand winning, they are energetic and have genial, amusing personalities—they are known for their social skills. Like these dogs, they never sulk when they lose, they just become more resolute about winning the next time out. Aries natives communicate well, are independent, and are decisive—traits both understood and needed in human companions for Salukis to grow into their potential. These dogs offer natives of this sun sign a sense of nobility, gentility, and dignity—traits for which Ariens are not known yet respect and appreciate in their pets. The Aries born, like Salukis, are affectionate without being assertive. They are protective and healthy, energetic people who need healthy, energetic pets. These two get along very well indeed!

SCHNAUZER (GIANT)

Positive Traits

Like good, dark lager beer, Schnauzers trace their roots to Bavaria. These are hardy, happy, and very powerful dogs. Their musculature is admired by anyone interested in bodybuilding and this dog breed is one of the most vigorous in dogdom. Giant Schnauzers give every appearance of power and strength and possess both in abundance. They are Working Terriers, historically used to herd and drive cattle (and they've served as ratters). When Ford pickups replaced drover dogs, Giant Schnauzers changed jobs and became guard dogs. They are fearless and, undaunted by danger, are fine watchdogs. Giant Schnauzers have served as police and military dogs and are alert and reliable. Quick and daring, Giant Schnauzers are hardy and vigorous, both mentally and physically. They adapt well to almost all living conditions and all kinds of weather. These *Cosmic Canines* usually have calm temperaments, but can get hyper when excited. Interestingly, their smaller brethren—Miniature and Standard Schnauzers—require more exercise than their Giant counterparts to prevent tension and stress.

Negative Traits

Slow to mature, Giant Schnauzers are friendly but wary of strangers. When friends visit, these dogs should be allowed to decide when they are ready for affectionate pats. Giant Schnauzers have woolly undercoats and they shed; they do need professional grooming, though infrequently. Without adult supervision, this dog can be too enthusiastically energetic to be good around children until they are of school age. Giant Schnauzers may, like any Terrier, react to sudden and erratic movement. For that reason, they may not be the best pets for toddlers, who have a tendency to make unplanned, sudden moves. These are loving dogs with wonderful temperaments, but they are large and are genetically programmed to react fast to erratic movement! And they are excitable. Happy, excitable dogs the size of Dobermans who react to unplanned movements are not the best pets for toddlers. When together, these two should be supervised by adults.

Job Opportunities for Giant Schnauzers

Schnauzers are wonderful protectors who truly become members of the family. They are particularly protective of children. These dogs are loving pets who share their sense of élan for life with those they love. They will find careers with potential in all police and military canine jobs. Schnauzers make super exercise partners, travel companions, obedience-training students, and show dogs. And, of course, they make wonderful advertising models and television and movie stars.

Most Compatible Sun Sign: Sagittarius

One word sums up very well why natives of Sagittarius and these *Cosmic Canines* are so compatible: enterprising. Natives of the Archer and Giant Schnauzers will, once they make up their minds to do something, find a way to do it. Both have joyous, hopeful attitudes toward life and are confident they can make dreams come true. Sagittarians can be extremely purposeful and single-minded, and so can these dogs. Both are frank, honest, giving, and sincere. Sagittarians are known for their loyalty, affectionate natures, and need for freedom. These traits blend well with Schnauzers' calm temperaments, faithfulness, and adaptability. Natives of this sun sign and these dogs are equally healthy and hardy, energetic (Sagittarian energy turns to tension if they get insufficient exercise) and intelligent—two mentally and physically fit specimens. Interestingly, Saggies are also slow to mature—much of their youth is spent dreaming and aiming for the stars. Sagittarians enjoy the good-natured, playful temperaments of these dogs and will think they are great company around campfires (and the hundreds of other places Sagittarians want to explore). Schnauzers will particularly appreciate the devotion, self-reliance, and freedom-loving lifestyles of Sagittarius natives. They won't even mind when these human companions become negative—restless, overactive, nervous, tense, and irritable—because dogs, especially positive ones like Schnauzers, can always see through human frailties (the basis of our negative sides) to the real person.

SETTERS (IRISH, ENGLISH, AND GORDON)

Positive Traits

IRISH SETTERS: Beautiful Irish Setters think your children belong to them. Few dogs exceed their gentleness with young ones. Irish, English, and Gordon Setters are all agile, very lively, and are . . . well, just happy! Irish Setters are graceful, sweet, versatile, and, in modern times, more show than Hunting dogs. Their beauty and happy attitudes did them in, making people prefer them more as pets than as hunters. Don't let their gentleness with children fool you, though. They can be bold, tough, and are very loyal. They aren't terribly independent, though Irish Setters really need human companions and have ever since they came into being in Ireland in the fifteenth century.

ENGLISH SETTERS: Less demonstratively affectionate than Gordon and Irish Setters, English Setters are reliable and make great family dogs Children love them—and it's mutual. One so very English thing that can be said about these dogs is "they are useful." They are also quite beautiful. English Setters have quiet, sweet personalities and are very lovable.

GORDON SETTERS: Affectionate but not as aesthetically, sleekly beautiful as their Irish and English cousins, the beauty of these *Cosmic Canines* lies in their substance, intelligence, and cosmopolitan gait. Great hunters, Gordon Setters are quiet, dignified, clean, and very gentle with children. Their tails may wag constantly, they are mannerly and eager to please, but Gordons do not trust strangers and will not try to make friends with every guest or visitor.

Negative Traits

Gordons jealously guard their families and may be aggressive with other dogs—not the best multiple-pet family dog. Irish and English Setters love everyone too much to be good guard dogs. English Setters need attention and do not thrive when left to their own devices too often. They love to be in the company of people and other dogs. Irish Setters can be roguish and self-willed, sometimes preferring to make their own deci-sions rather than obeying commands given by their human companions. All Setters need regular exercise to maintain their highest level of health and happiness.

Job Opportunities for Irish, English, and Gordon Setters

Child protectors (they'll try to baby-sit if you don't watch them), fun and easygoing exercise partners, loving family pets supreme, graceful and beautiful additions that enhance the image of your home, English and Irish Setters are good for multiple-pet families, and all three breeds make wonderful photographic models. Irish Setters can be too excitable with-out obedience training, and all three respond well to training. When properly bred and trained, all three make a day of hunting even more en-joyable. They work well and very compatibly in the field. Gordon Setters make good protectors and are excellent hunters. English and Irish Setters are not good guard dogs.

Most Compatible Sun Signs: Cancer, Virgo, and Aquarius

IRISH SETTERS: Like natives of Virgo, Irish Setters just strive to be happy. There is a basic kind of innocence about both of these animals. Virgoans, like these dogs, adore children and are very gentle beings. Virgo natives can gain much from relationships with these dogs; these are peo-ple who need to be needed, and Irish Setters are more dependent on their human companions for happiness than many other dogs. Virgoans are self-contained and enjoy the élan these dogs bring to their human com-panions. They can learn from it (and Virgo natives love to learn). Gentle Virgoans, like these dogs, can be pretty tough when circumstances re-quire it. Irish Setter versatility is good for these humans who can get too precise, detailed, and reasoned—Setters know everything cannot be solved with mathematical equations. Irish Setters truly appreciate active yet calm Virgoan personalities. These two are a good match.

ENGLISH SETTERS: These dogs will fall in love with Cancer natives (who will love them back). Above all, both are reliable and very loving—

not assertively or overtly affectionate, but very loving. Family is very important to both, and perhaps the only beings who love children more than English Setter *Cosmic Canines* are Cancer natives. Both have quiet personalities, quiet natures, and enjoy being of service to humankind. And both are sensitive to hurt and require personal attention from those they love. Remember, Lassie's personality was patterned after the personality traits of the sun sign Cancer. Can you imagine a better companion for these sweet-natured dogs than Lassie?

GORDON SETTERS: A lot like natives of the Water Bearer, both Aquarians and Gordon Setters are quiet, have substance, and are intelligent. Though they are not as glitzy as other Setters or sun signs, both are dignified, affectionate (but not assertively so), mannerly, and easy to please And neither gives trust easily or often. Just as Aquarians can be loners, Gordon Setters tend to walk the road less traveled, too. They aren't always friendly with other dogs (as Aquarians are not always friendly with everyone) just for the sake of being friendly. Gordons are a little more aloof than their English and Irish cousins—and natives of the Water Bearer have been called indifferent. Both sun sign and dog breed place more emphasis on substance than appearances. They are very much alike.

SWEDISH ELKHOUND

Positive Traits

Swedish Elkhounds (Jamthund, in Swedish), sometimes referred to as Norwegian Bearhounds, are taller and heavier than their close relatives, the Norwegian Elkhounds. They are very popular in their homeland, serving as both hunting and family companions. If you've ever had someone dote over you, you will have some insight about how these dogs express their affections toward family. These *Cosmic Canines* dote! In addition to being loving, they are brave, have balanced temperaments, and, when properly bred, can be trained to be excellent guard dogs They are, first and foremost, hunters of moose and other four-legged wild game. These Swedes have a lot of staying power, which, combined with a bit of natural derring-do, puts them a few steps ahead of most dogs used by humans to help them hunt wild game. Swedish Elkhounds are bold, have a great deal of energy, are loyal but calm, and are very agile.

Negative Traits

Swedish Elkhounds may be too assertive for young families. If they are specifically raised to be family dogs and are trained to be pets rather than hunters, they make wonderful (though energetic) family companions. Raised from puppyhood with toddlers around, these are wonderful dogs for children of any age. If children make their entry into your household after a Swedish Elkhound has reached maturity, playtimes with less than school-aged children should be supervised. They need substantial exercise to keep their energy levels properly contained—unspent energy can turn into nervous tension. Their coats require regular brushing.

Job Opportunities for Swedish Elkhounds

For those who live in the country, particularly the mountains, these are great household pets. Because of migration of the wild bear population to people-populated areas, Swedish Elkhounds offer particularly meaningful talents. These protectors never let human companions walk unknowingly into their kitchens to find Papa Bear rummaging through cabinets. Human companions should take Swedish Elkhounds with them to hunt deer, elk, and other game. Not only will they amuse and protect you, they will help you get your limit. Elkhounds are great exercise partners and companions for seniors. They are among the best canines to take along on overnight camping excursions.

Most Compatible Sun Sign: Libra

The best doters in the zodiac are born under the sign of the Scales. They are very idealistic and doting is a natural part of such a nature. With idealist personalities goes kindness, amiability, pleasantness, generosity, and politeness. Swedish Elkhound *Cosmic Canines* and Libra personalities are loaded with these items. In addition to being loving, both are brave, have balanced temperaments, and, above all, always stay calm—or try to. No sun sign natives seek to create auras of harmony more intensely than Librans. It's just their nature. In the midst of huge family fights, Librans ask everyone, "Can't we all just get along?" They are likely to light some candles and turn on relaxing music, too—if they can't create harmony one way, they'll find another. Both dog breed and sun sign are very intelligent, energetic, and balanced. Elkhounds are bold dogs, a concept with which Librans sometimes have difficulty and one about which they need to learn. Elkhounds are good teachers! Exposure to Swedish Elkhounds is a positive experience for these sun sign natives. Also, Librans are known for their appreciation of beauty. These are beautiful dogs who, along with all the other compatible factors between these two, light appreciative candles in the eyes of Libra natives.

VIZSLA (HUNGARIAN POINTER)

Positive Traits

Right out of the Middle Ages, golden rust Vizslas are Hungary's national dog. They are first-class Gundogs as well as excellent family pets. Vizsla *Cosmic Canines* are gracefully but powerfully built and have keen scenting abilities. They are supple, very intelligent, and easily trained. Vizslas are distinguished-looking dogs (slim and supple) who are congenial, gentle, and energetic. There is nothing shy about them. They enthusiastically give outward displays of affection to human companions. They are fearless and have strong, protective instincts that, when combined with their gentle natures, make them excellent guard dogs. They thrive on learning and take to obedience training as naturally as they take to the water when retrieving the fowl they hunt so well. Vizslas are very clean dogs Their short-haired coats make them easy to groom.

Negative Traits

No drawbacks known. Vizslas are, however, large, energetic, and lively dogs and, unless raised with very young children, should be supervised when around them. They need exercise or their energy becomes tension.

Job Opportunities for Vizslas

Good boating companions who add an element of protection to days on the water. Rent them out to barge captains who can benefit from having Vizslas guard their cargoes. These are great Gundogs, water Retrievers, and small-game hunters. Vizslas are energetic household companions who, gently yet assertively, make excellent guard dogs. One of the best exercise partners and obedience-training dogs. Because of temperament and ease of care, these dogs are good travel companions, regardless of their twenty-four-inch shoulder height.

Most Compatible Sun Sign: Leo

To Leo the Lion, love is everything! These sun sign natives thrive on the enthusiastic and open displays of affection shown by Vizsla dogs to family members. Leo natives tend to be sentimental and loyal, and are strongly protective of those they love—very like these dogs. Both dog breed and sun sign natives are intelligent, vital, energetic, and neither has a problem with being shy. Vizsla gentleness has a positive influence on their human companions, helping them be less intense. Leo is the sign of actors and the stage eyes of Lion natives fully appreciate the graceful, powerful, supple physical attributes of these dogs. Those born under the sign of Leo may wonder how a work of art can maintain such an air of dignity while being so openly affectionate yet unpossessive. In truth, these Vizsla traits are precisely what Leo humans want to emulate (and when they get their egos and insecurities out of the way, this is the true Leonine nature) Both are congenial animals with giving natures, and like Lions, Vizslas are fearless and have strong, protective instincts. Each will be able to bask in the other's positives—Vizslas enjoy Leonine popularity and vibrancy. They appreciate natives of this sun sign whose natural leadership skills make them wonderful teachers—Vizslas live to learn and Leos love to impart knowledge. Leo human vivacity can become overbearing and require strong personalities like that of Vizslas, who are capable of maintaining personal identities while basking in this sun sign's strong vitality.

WEIMARANER

Positive Traits

Nicknamed Silver Ghost or Gray Ghost, Weimaraners are hunters of small game and enjoy tracking both large and small game. They are fine Gundogs. Where these *Cosmic Canines* really shine, however, is in the home as family pets. They are beautifully powerful dogs and are easily obedience-trained, provided their human companions are strong enough to handle them. They make good pets (but would rather work), and their moderate temperaments, combined with their intelligence, make them good guard dogs and home companions. Weimaraners are sharp, fearless, friendly, protective, and, once trained, very obedient. They are bright and enjoy personal yet unique relationships with each family member. Perhaps this breed's middle name should be "Freud" because Weimaraners are known to seek out each person's unique personality and either like or dislike each individual for who they are rather than just accepting them as members of a group. Once they bond with a member of the family Weimaraners are very devoted. They are wonderful, active dogs and enjoy involving themselves with children (who should be preteens before being trusted to play with these dogs unsupervised for long periods). They are very energetic animals. These dogs shed little and need minimum grooming.

Negative Traits

Weimaraners, like German Shepherds and Border Collies, *need* a purpose. Without one, they are like human workaholics without jobs—unhappy and unfulfilled. Weimaraners also need owners who are firm, purposeful, and clear in giving directions when training—and training needs to start early. As hunting dogs, they are independent. All of this dog's power combined with an independent attitude means early and firm discipline—not abuse, discipline. They need to know who makes the decisions and that it's not them. Weimaraners need exercise; they have boundless energy. They need a lot of *supervised* freedom.

Job Opportunities for Weimaraners

In the field, these dogs can be used as Pointers, trackers, or scenters. In addition to small game, they've been known to hunt birds. They are very adaptable dogs! Weimaraners are loving, devoted family companions and can be easily taught to fetch papers and slippers. Good dogs for obedience-training hobbyists. They adapt well to life on the water and should be good boating company. Excellent exercise partners. Easy-care travel companions, regardless of size.

Most Compatible Sun Sign: Sagittarius

Let's face it. Sagittarians are attracted to anything with nicknames like Silver Ghost and Gray Ghost. It's just part of the nature of those born under the sign of the Archer. These dogs need strong human companions, and Sagittarius humans offer that strength—and temper it with humor and a love of life that Weimaraners enjoy immensely. Weimers may be puzzled, wondering how humans who are so imaginative and cheerful, so honest and open, so friendly and well liked, can also be so down-to-earth practical. But that's Sagittarius for you. An enigma. Like Saggies, Weimers are friendly and well liked, keenly intelligent, and these dogs will not only understand the competitive nature of those born under this sun sign, they happily partake of it. Weimaraners are basically honest, too, and appreciate infamous Sagittarian directness of speech There will be no confusion about what these human companions want Weimaraners to do, which will suit Weimers to a "tee." Saggies really enjoy these dogs because they can take them anywhere and know they will function well—at overnight campsites or posh affairs, these dogs are at ease, moderate of temperament, obedient, and friendly. Weimaraners aren't just pretty faces (which Sagittarians respect, a lot), they want to contribute, too. They happily serve as protectors when needed, companion and friend when possible, and when those born under this sun sign need their independence and freedom away from everyone and everything, it won't cause Weimers any kind of problem. Quite simply, these two belong together.

PART THREE

AN EXPLANATION OF DOG SUN SIGN PERSONALITIES

6

ARIES

SIGN OF THE RAM
(WARRIOR OR EXPLORER)
March 21 to April 20
First zodiac sign, first of three Fire signs,
first of four Cardinal (Leadership) signs
SYMBOL: The Ram
ASTROLOGICAL RAM SYMBOL: ♈
PART OF THE BODY RULED BY ARIES: The head (consciousness)
GEMSTONE: Diamond
COLOR: Red
METAL: Iron
RULING PLANET: Mars

THE ARIES PUPPY

Positive Traits

Male or female, large or small, these puppies are first to the feeding dish, first to get into trouble—in fact, first to do almost everything and anything! Aries the Ram is the first of the twelve sun signs. They like being first. It's their birthright, after all.

When you see puppies always on the go and filled with happy energy,

243

chances are it's Aries exhibiting enthusiasm for life. That's what they do best. It's part of their carpe diem—seize the day!—attitude and lifestyle.

Competitive and assertive are the two most popular words on the wavelengths of little Rams. Ariens settle down with maturity, but they are the gangbuster kids on the block as puppies. These youthful canines are intelligent and energetic from the day they draw their first life-loving breath.

Ariens have two speeds: full speed ahead and dead to the world. Sometimes natives of the Ram, especially puppies, just don't know when to stop. They must be shown. Like a popular television commercial for batteries, Aries puppies just keep going and going and going. When they run out of energy, they drop into a deep, restful sleep until they revive.

Aries canines are usually solid, sometimes stocky. Everything they do has an air of uniqueness. They are forceful and strong-willed. You can't ignore them. They skillfully entertain everyone. It's hard to ignore great communicators! Aries is also one of the most dominant sun signs in the zodiac. Their personalities are softened by originality, humor, and amiability.

The first sign of the zodiac, Aries represents birth and always maintains a bit of unreserved puppy enthusiasm. When Aries puppies grow old, human companions will still be able to see the puppies they once were.

Owning Aries puppies is a little like being an artist. The puppies, within certain idealistic parameters, become what human companions paint. A Renoir? Picasso? Lassie? Rin Tin Tin? Cujo? What Aries puppies become depends on you. They have all the potential in the world!

Negative Traits

It's true: Aries puppies have tremendous potential. How the potential gets developed largely depends on the people who adopt these adorable pets.

If they find whining gets what they want, look out. Remember when Aries native Nikita Khrushchev banged his shoe on the podium at the United Nations? He got a trip to Disneyland.

Human or canine, it is difficult to force Ariens to do anything. They may do something when forced to, but this puts out their fire, the core of this sun sign's charm! What's the solution?

Loving-kindness, a good plan, and enough resolution to complete the plan. Emphasize praise for positive behavior, correct but otherwise ignore bad behavior. Correction and discipline should not be ignored—to do so spoils Aries dogs, and spoiled dogs can become problem dogs. Aries puppies hate being ignored, so when they do something wrong, correct and then ignore them. They so enjoy the praise they get for doing things right!

Ariens are so charming and enthusiastic! It's hard to say no or discipline clowns who smile while tears run down their faces It's why so many Aries pets don't get the discipline they require. Their charm gets them what they want rather than what they need.

Tips for Human Companions

Love can be difficult to express between humans and pets. It requires attention, affection, education, warmth, approval, disapproval, and discipline.

Praise, gentle petting, and the warmth of companions' voices express human love to puppies. They lick our faces and hands. But love isn't just happy expressions. It also includes responsibility. It can be difficult to balance positive displays of affection with needed behavioral corrections, but it must be done. Love demands it.

Discipline is not a natural part of Aries puppy or adult life until loving owners teach them. They enjoy learning discipline almost more than any sun sign, but it does not come to them naturally. Untaught Aries dogs never achieve full potential. What a shame! They have so much!

THE ARIES DOG

General Personality Traits

Headstrong Aries dogs, when properly trained, are joys as long-term adult pets. Untrained, they are pampered, spoiled, and refuse to see companionship as a two-way street. They can be pretty self-serving when left undisciplined Don't allow it. Train them. When you do, you will have one of the best pets in the world!

Aries dogs do not follow the crowd. They are individualists. They look forward, seldom back. Disagreements occur in all relationships, even between humans and canines. Don't hold grudges with Aries. They don't.

When human companions are sorry for a thoughtless action, Aries dogs can sense it. An apology and some much-loved ear scratching puts you back in their good graces. If the apology isn't heartfelt, they'll know it It's hard to fool perceptive Aries. These *Cosmic Canines* are very honest. Some say Arien destiny is to seek truth—and find it

These pets like to gain approval and do not enjoy being yelled at every time they jump into the laps of your friends (if they're small) or plant their feet in a friendly, firm way on visitors' chests (if they're big). Chances are family friends won't enjoy it a great deal either. Training is the answer.

Ariens are go-getters, natural-born enthusiasts. Their friends, both two- and four-legged, had better not be easily intimidated. Natives born under the sign of the Ram don't try to intimidate. It just happens. It seems to emanate from their strong, energetic personalities.

Arien attitudes may make them seem like dogs who don't need much tender, loving care. They are strong and independent. They are always there when others need something. Surely, such strong animals don't need much? Nothing could be farther from the truth. Their wandering hearts need a warm, secure place.

These dogs can be the source of many amusing moments. They have a lot of personality, and they use it. The thing Aries dogs prize most is the praise and love of human companions. Your love is like Olympic gold to them.

Aries: Preventing Problem Dogs

Begin the Aries discipline process by making sure they understand that no means *"No!"*

Aries canines enjoy being held to high standards by human companions and enjoy working to gain approval. They spoil easily and all spoiled dogs can become problems.

Will their human companions understand that love sometimes means teaching manners to curious, active pets? Some people think it compassionate to avoid training and discipline. Yet few trained, disciplined canines end up in pet shelters awaiting euthanasia. Untrained dogs are not compassionate by anyone's standard.

Uniformity of discipline is important to Aries puppies. Emotional disturbances and training problems occur in all canines when rules have not been established. Have a plan so all family members know when to say no and, especially, when to say, "Good dog!"

It's true that naturally positive traits of Aries animals—both human and canine—include the need for independence and freedom. Don't, however, confuse independence with selfishness or freedom with license. They are two different things.

The more energetic, intelligent, forceful, and assertive the traits bestowed by a sun sign, the more important obedience training becomes. Aries is one of the most assertive, forceful sun sign pets in the zodiac. Enough said?

With sufficient positive attention and discipline from human companions, there are no better pets than Aries dogs.

Job Opportunities for Aries Dogs

Many astrologers have spoken of the appeal—the almost psychic pull and attraction—of Aries humans to military careers. In fact, there are more Ariens in the world's militaries than any other sign. Maybe Aries natives instinctively know they need discipline, so they seek it from this external source.

Combine the need for discipline with Arien courage, alertness, and intelligence and you've got the makings of good military personnel. Military and police officials, organizations that train dogs for the blind, and drug enforcement agencies would do well to recruit Aries dogs.

This is a good sign under which to plan the birth of racing Greyhounds, and Aries canines have a natural sense of showmanship that reflects well in America Kennel Club competitions.

Overall, Ariens are happiest with a purpose. It's a little easier for humans than our four-legged friends to seek and identify life purposes. So Aries canines depend on human companions to help them realize their abilities. One of the highest canine purposes is serving those they love. Sometimes canine values and those of human beings have a great deal in common. This is one of those times.

If you're a couch potato, you'll find life with less assertive, competitive *Cosmic Canines* more to your liking. Humans looking for companions to take on camping trips, guard their homes, or take on long walks will find Aries dogs their cup of tea!

COMPATIBILITY GUIDE FOR ARIES DOGS

Air Sun Signs

GEMINI human companions are usually gregarious and outgoing. Those two things alone are a good start for explaining why they are good for Aries dogs. Like Ariens, Geminis are assertive, bold, and confident and as a result are unlikely to be intimidated by these canines.

These two are very good together. Gemini human companions are very functional and sensible. They understand why training and discipline are important. Though inexperienced trainers, confident Geminis will not hesitate to pick up a leash and choke chain to begin the process.

LIBRA humans are kind and amiable and share with Aries dogs sensible, social attitudes and intelligent, logical minds Both are very bright and outgoing.

Librans like harmonious relationships and Ariens like decisive human companions. Therein lies the rub between these two. Aries dogs will likely think Libra's refined nature a bit different from their own roughhouse, competitive personalities.

Librans are compassionate and humane. Those too humane to train their dog should get another pet.

The biggest Aries pet problem with Libra companions is the lack of decisiveness. Canines interpret delayed decisions as human weakness. Assertive Aries may try to make decisions for Libra companions. Or they may become confused and insecure. Ariens need clearly defined guidelines to be happy. If Librans can be decisive as pet owners and let down their hair—be a little rowdy with Aries dogs—these two can be very good together.

AQUARIUS humans are compatible with Aries dogs. Sometimes, however, forgetful Water Bearers may need to make a list to remember all of the daily details involved in caring for their pets.

Aries dogs benefit from Aquarian patience and determination. Ariens innately respect loyalty, and Aquarians offer it in abundance. Natives of the Water Bearer are faithful and they motivate trust. Aries appreciates both. Aquarians need to avoid disorganization, stay focused, and shrug off occasional bouts of aloofness—let their enthusiasm for life shine through. Aries can help with this last item. These *Cosmic Canines* are good for sometimes-too-serious Aquarians.

Earth Sun Signs

TAURUS humans are likely to find Aries difficult to understand These two sun signs are, in many ways, opposites.

Taureans tend to be practical, solid, vital, patient, enduring, and matter-of-fact.

Aries is never matter-of-fact about anything, and the concept of practicality is a distant dream. Frankly, Taurean practicality gives Aries dogs a needed dose of pragmatic reality.

Taureans are famed for stubbornness—a trait for which energetic Aries dogs don't have time (or respect). It sounds like these two shouldn't get along at all, but they do!

Freedom-loving, headstrong, competitive Aries may not understand why Taurus is so determined, or why the Bull's generosity is so objective, but will sense the tremendous vitality of these sun sign natives. These two can establish supportive relationships.

VIRGO humans are not known for their ability to command. There are exceptions, of course. You must be able to command Aries dogs to earn their respect. Virgoans may be somewhat delicate in nature. Charge-ahead Aries dogs just don't understand refined humans who don't like to roughhouse.

Natives of the sign of the Virgin are the most tactful in the zodiac and Ariens don't know how to spell the word *tact.* Virgo natives are calm; Aries is about as exuberant as Mount St. Helens on eruption day.

Though these two are opposites, they bring new learning opportunities to one another.

CAPRICORN natives are natural leaders with whom Aries dogs are compatible. However, Capricorns will need to move faster than their usual one step at a time or they will drive barge-ahead Ariens crazy. These two define forward movement quite differently.

Aries dogs want pals. Capricorn natives are sometimes loners and need to be sensitive to the need this dog has for friendship.

Cappies are precise and exacting—two other traits for which Aries dogs have little patience. Capricorns are balanced, fair, precise, careful, diligent, and calm. The calm part is good for Aries dogs. The other traits must be carefully communicated for good relationships to result.

Water Sun Signs

CANCER pet owners have an innate sense of gentility. Aries dogs have a natural sense of exuberance. Careful, controlled Cancerians can learn from the Aries sense of joie de vivre and spontaneity.

Arien competitiveness often does not allow outward expressions of strong personal attachment. They feel attachment strongly, but are not as

250 · Cosmic Canines

expressive about it as Cancerian humans. Cancerians can be pretty quiet. Aries has a go-go personality. This may grate on strongly attached, calm, and loving Cancerians who need outward expressions of affection.

Cancerians can be sensitive and domestic. They are also determined and resolute; most notably, they are tenacious. And you can add self-reliant and rational to the list (along with strong, purposeful, and calm). Cancer humans have a great deal to offer Aries dogs.

SCORPIO humans are likely to expect their pets to relate to them. Aries dogs will likely expect human companions to relate to them. They are so different, neither will have realistic views of the other. Both will be disappointed by the lack of unintentional responsiveness each gives the other.

Scorpion humans don't give their trust easily, and neither do Aries dogs. Add to that the Scorpio need to maintain a sense of mystique. Aries dogs may find it difficult to trust and bond with a mystery person.

Like Aries dogs, Scorpions thrive on the approval of others. Good or bad, the Scorpio character is very strong. They are among the most powerful of all sun signs. A lot of things Aries dogs need, Scorpios have in abundance—like leadership.

PISCES Water can put out Aries Fire, but doesn't have to. Pisces humans are magnetic, attracting to themselves the energy vibrations of others—and Aries emits a lot of energy.

Aries dogs are outgoing, energetic, and have highly entertaining, humorous personalities—all traits appreciated by one of the zodiac's greatest actors, Pisceans. Natives born under the sign of the Fishes appreciate many Arien traits.

Human Pisces are peaceful, accepting, sympathetic, compassionate, and sensitive. These are all traits that can broaden the personalities of Aries dogs, helping them become kinder, gentler *Cosmic Canines*. This can be a very compatible relationship from which both parties benefit.

Fire Sun Signs

ARIES is a very strong, positive birth sign. Two living entities with the same strong, positive traits can be very good—or very bad.

For example, neither Aries humans nor dogs like to lose. Human companions need to be sensitive to the dog's need to win every now and then. Both dog and human are independent—in the best personal relationships, a little dependence is nice.

If natural Aries human emotions are kept under control—being head-strong, impulsive, high-strung, hypersensitive, jealous, and impatient—they and their Aries dogs will get along fine. With a little thoughtfulness, Aries humans can establish lasting relationships with Aries dogs

LEO humans may find themselves in competition with Aries dogs for center stage—a position these humans seldom relinquish to people, let alone pets. Leonine practicality, however, makes this combination exceptional. Practicality is one thing Aries lacks but Leo has in abundance.

Aries natives live in the mind, Leo humans live in their hearts. This combination offers the opportunity to join the mind with the heart—pretty dynamic! Natives of the Lion are forceful, magnetic, vital, kind, warmhearted, and loving. Add to that a high energy level, the capacity for faithfulness and sincerity, and a generous personality, and you'll see why these dynamic *Cosmic Canines* are so happy with Leo humans.

With Leo companions, whatever Aries dogs want (or need), Aries dogs get! This is as close to perfect as it gets.

SAGITTARIAN impulsiveness and Sagittarian love of competition both have great appeal to Aries dogs. The only danger here is too much fire—too little thought, too much action. Both Ariens and Sagittarians are Fire signs. Every living thing needs to slow down and refuel, but these two need someone to point that out.

Sagittarius owners are firm and decisive (which Aries dogs need), impulsive and happy (which these canines love), and understand competition (on which Ariens thrive). Human Sagittarians will have to understand the Aries need to win every now and then, but that's no problem to sensitive Archers. Sagittarian humans find a true soul mate pet in Aries *Cosmic Canines.*

7

TAURUS

SIGN OF THE BULL
(MANUFACTURER OR BUILDER)
April 21 to May 20
Second zodiac sign, first of three Earth signs,
first of four Fixed (Power) signs
SYMBOL: The Bull
ASTROLOGICAL BULL SYMBOL: ♉
PART OF THE BODY RULED BY TAURUS: The throat and neck (controls the way
the head turns)
GEMSTONE: Emerald or moss agate
COLOR: Indigo blue
METAL: Copper
RULING PLANET: Venus

THE TAURUS PUPPY

Positive Traits

Warm and affectionate; the salt of the earth; calm, natural, warm, magnetic, and charming—these are all words used by astrologers to describe

Taurus. But there are very practical minds beneath those warm eyes glowing with affection.

Taurus puppies need loving, secure environments. Only then can they be calm, warm, magnetic, and charming. In other words, to be loving, Taurus pets need to be loved. To be calm, they need security.

When you train, feed, love, and praise Taureans, don't do three other things at the same time. Human companions may think they've shown puppies love and attention, but Taurus canines don't think so. When giving love and attention, do just that. Focus on them, not the kids, the dinner dishes, or telephone conversations.

You can expect Taurus puppies to be committed to a purpose. Few animals are more tenacious. If they could talk, they would make wonderful bill collectors; they make great search-and-scent dogs (a job where persistence pays).

Bloodhounds born under the sign of the Bull *never* give up the search. If Taurus noses tell them to, German Shepherds will search diligently for illegal drugs in airport luggage until they find what they're looking for.

Taurus puppies grow best when surrounded by love. As important as love is to most other sun signs, it is critical with natives of the Bull. They feel crushed without it. And your definition of love must be healthy if you want a healthy, well-adjusted dog. Without positive love, Taurus dogs can become neurotic.

These are loving, gentle animals. They are smart and love being of service to others. Taurus puppies of any breed have temperaments more settled than dogs born under other sun signs.

If a breed is considered genetically friendly to little people, then Taurus puppies are perfect for small children. They may have typical puppy energy and zest for life, but they are not likely to knock little ones over with unbounded, uncontrolled energy.

One of the physical traits associated with all Taurus natives is beauty. They make excellent show dogs, thriving on recognition for their accomplishments. When they do something right, be a good audience. Applaud and get encores.

Negative Traits

Taurus canines can be led to water but cannot be made to drink. Stubborn can be their middle names. These are sturdy, quiet, and loving animals, but they do not handle confrontation or conflict very well.

If training sessions are confrontations, you will lose. You may win a battle here and there, but you will lose the training war. Presenting Taurus dogs with conflict in their versus your objectives is like waving a red flag in front of that mythological Bull.

When correction is required, don't avoid it. When Taurus puppies do something wrong, they need to be made aware of it, sensitive feelings aside. But don't make a big thing out of it. Mistakes are like business—impersonal. Praise is personal and deserves enthusiastic support. If people use communications skills—voice, touch, enthusiasm, attitude—these dogs are bright. They get the message and enjoy the praise.

If praise is given in a dull monotone—a moderately enthusiastic "good dog"—and corrections are emotional scenes, what gets emphasized: doing things right or doing things wrong?

Taurus puppies and dogs can be possessive Discourage it. They are susceptible to jealousy biting. Possessive dogs raised on love and praise can be very good home protectors. Raised on negative corrections and too little approval, possessive dogs may become jealous and self-protective. Mean dogs are not good guard dogs. They are dangerous—to everyone (prowlers, small children, and family friends).

When it comes to Taurus temperaments—both human and canine—they are a little like empty vats. Fill them with love. It will be returned a hundredfold. Fill them with inconsiderate treatment and that, too, will be returned.

Untrained and undisciplined, Taurus dogs become possessive, sometimes bullies. Trained and loved, they are among the best pets for the entire family, including small children.

Tips for Human Companions

Make these pets part of the family. Give them a cause and they won't become rebels. Give them responsibility—get the newspaper, find your slippers, be a jogging partner. They like to share. Put these four little paws on a path with a positive purpose and all the wonderful, positive canine traits of this strong sign will unfold before your very eyes.

They don't like change. When human companions move to new homes, comfort them. They may not show it—they like to be brave—but change causes insecurity. Insecure Taureans are unhappy puppies.

Give them a little extra cuddling and keep everything as nearly the same as possible—feeding and training schedules, familiar toys, and blankets or pillows. Don't put everything in the laundry before moving. It washes the old familiar smells off doggie possessions. After human companions have settled the new home and Taurus puppies become accustomed to new scents, do as much canine laundry as you like. Little things mean a lot to Taureans.

Taurus dogs are reliable and gentle. Provided they are not breeds with genetic inclinations to distrust strangers, they won't bite guests who visit. Strangers sneaking around in the dark are another matter. This home and yard belong to Taurus, the *Cosmic Canine.*

Taurus dogs tend to have possessive streaks. Take a few extra precautions. One of the first things dogs become possessive about is the cars in which they ride. Cars have familiar human companion scents and are smaller than yards or houses. They are more easily "possessed."

These dogs have no appetite problems But, the older Taurus dogs get, the more carefully their appetites and what they eat to satisfy them need to be watched. This inclination to gain weight means adhering to specific feeding schedules (which do not include table tidbits).

As Taurus dogs grow older, their easy, laid-back personalities reject exercise and, combined with weight gain, can cause a health problem. Put them on regular exercise schedules. Take leashed Taurus canines jogging. It's good for them and they love the attention and time gained with you.

THE TAURUS DOG

General Personality Traits

There are five ways to get to Taurus dogs: through their senses of touch, scent, sight, hearing, and taste. Keep these five things in mind as you plot ways to train little Bulls—er, puppies. This is a trait Taureans share with Cancer canines. If corrections leave more of an impression on their five senses than praise, you are reinforcing the wrong thing.

To Taurus canines, life is a feast that involves all tactile senses. Very few things frighten these animals and, if they had one, they'd give human companions the shirts off their backs.

Generally not worriers by nature, Taurus dogs have personalities all their own. They aren't live wires, but they won't get into much mischief either.

They are steady, patient, enduring, intelligent, and entertaining performers. Taureans have enduring vitality. Even so, they are good apartment dogs. It's a good sun sign under which to adopt energetic Terriers or Toy breeds. Sun sign Taurus has a calming influence on dogs with active genes.

If you want your morning paper delivered from the driveway to your living room each day, Taurus is the right dog for you. They seldom forget obligations or commitments. These *Cosmic Canines* are capable of enduring faithfulness and are very loyal. Equally, they demand the same traits of their human companions.

If you want to adopt an older dog who is house-trained, adopt another sun sign. Once Taurus puppies bond, the danger they may not rebond is pretty high. They may even mourn and show extreme emotional distress if separated from the first human companion with whom they bonded.

The Hollywood version of pets pining away at graves of loved ones was probably motivated by either Taurus or Cancer pet behavior.

When seeking an older pet, look through the breed data to find dogs who don't have particularly strong bonds with their first human companions. If particular breeds of dog list difficulty with second human companion bonding, the tendency is doubled when such dogs are born under the sun sign of Taurus the Bull.

Taurus: Preventing Problem Dogs

A full dog obedience training schedule should not be started with Taurus puppies until six months of age. When adults, these dogs are vital and strong. When properly bred and taught needed lessons as puppies, they evolve into very secure dogs. As puppies, however, they can be insecure, so don't start training sessions too soon.

Leash training, however, can be easily accomplished when they are only four months old. This exercise teaches puppies not to pull against a leash. Good leash training allows dogs to walk anywhere close to human companions—left or right side, slightly ahead or slightly behind so long as they keep their eyes on their human companions and can immediately respond to any change of direction.

There is no doubt Taurus dogs have the strongest wills of any sun sign life-form. If you break their will, you will also break their spirit. Determination and tenacity can be used to achieve what you want. By using praise (or withholding it), you can make Taurus puppies determined and tenacious about doing what you want rather than what they want.

There is only one way to Taurean heads and it's through their hearts.

Praise gets their attention more effectively than retribution. It's the old vinegar and honey story. Watch your puppy for what they do right. Praise them when the happy event occurs.

Puppies need to be corrected. No doubt about it. They are going to have potty-training accidents on living room carpets. It's part of raising puppies just like potty training is part of raising children. Watch your own performance and grade it. For what do you show more verbal and physical enthusiasm? To which do you give more emotional response: correction or praise?

Job Opportunities for Taurus Dogs

Just as human Taurus natives find fulfillment in positions of service to society, Taurus dogs find fulfillment as guide dogs for the blind and from sniffing for drugs and explosives at airports and points of immigration. They are excellent police dogs, military guard dogs, and business guard dogs. They make wonderful protectors.

They need to be of service. Praise is a strong motivating force for Taurus canines. Their vitality, calm temperament, and tenacity make them superior performers. Take Taurus dogs to visit people who are confined— to Veteran's Administration or children's hospitals, to nursing homes or hospices. Taurus pets reach out to humans in troubled times.

Looking for a dog to take to a séance? Taurus dogs fill the bill! Natives of this sun sign are so intuitive, Taurus humans often serve as mediums when people seek to contact those "on the other side"

COMPATIBILITY GUIDE FOR TAURUS DOGS

Air Sun Signs

GEMINI owners and Taurus pets can be friends, strangely enough. Gemini's worship change as a lifestyle, but are not pushy about it. They won't insist Taurus pets accompany them on butterfly sighting adventures or African safaris. The buoyancy of Gemini humans can be good for Taurus dogs. At the same time, Taurus pets calm those around them and can bring out the quiet side of Gemini, giving them relief from their always logical, always analytic personalities.

The rapid personality changes for which Gemini humans are noted may make Taurus canines (who function on the basis of intuition and instinct, not human logic) feel uncertain, moody, and insecure. Taurus natives do not like surprises.

LIBRA owners and Taurus pets have little in common, but each has a certain gentleness and sense of fair play. Both are serene. All Taurus animals are practical and down-to-earth, motivated by objective physical wants and needs. Librans tend to be impractical, motivated by subjective ideals.

Dogs are, by nature, objective—they want food, water, training, love, attention, and fun. Add a Taurus sun sign to that mix and a very objective animal results. Objective dogs with subjective human companions may have difficulty bonding.

Both are ruled by Venus and have been gifted with an innate appreciation for beauty. Both are sentimental, warm, and calm.

AQUARIUS owners and Taurus pets are drawn to one another. Water Bearers run on mental energy, are assertive, and, though dominant, are not physically forceful. The calm and peace of Taurus Earth can benefit intense Aquarians. Both are peace-loving, both are determined.

Winter-born and somewhat distant Aquarians may withhold the physical displays of emotion so needed by Taurus pets. Neither understands the other in this regard.

On-the-go Aquarius humans may not be home as much as stable Taurus *Cosmic Canines* prefer, but Taurus canines find this sun sign's loyalty, faith, and sense of humanity heartwarming.

Earth Sun Signs

VIRGO human companions understand Taurus pets immediately. From the start of this relationship, these two will be old friends. They are on the same wavelength.

Virgo pet owners may try to dictate rather than command, manipulate rather than motivate. Taurus *Cosmic Canines* are too honest and straightforward to appreciate dictators or manipulators.

Virgoans love details. It is good for Taurus pets. It helps them focus. In turn, the peaceful nature of Taurus comforts Virgo pet owners. Virgoans understand the drive Taurus animals have to serve those they love.

CAPRICORN and Taurus are magnetic signs; both draw attention to themselves. Each is drawn to the other. Taurus dogs love Capricorn fairness, self-reliance, and calm. Cappies need their legendary patience with Taurus puppies.

Both are Earth signs. These two may be bored because they have so much in common. Both are down-to-earth about relationships. Both are open, independent, and persistent.

Every Capricorn should have a Taurus dog.

TAURUS with Taurus is too much determination, too much practicality, too much objectivity, too much vitality. Taurus can be obstinate, dogmatic, lazy, fearful, selfish, and indecisive. Taurus with Taurus is okay during positive cycles, less than desirable during negative ones.

Water Sun Signs

CANCER humans and Taurus dogs don't produce the most exciting relationships in the world. Life is quiet and enjoyable for both. The relationship is intuitively supportive. Cancerians and Taureans are sensitive and domestic, and this relationship will be home-based.

Cancer Crabs are as tenacious as Taurus Bulls, but both achieve their ends in different ways. Cancer is one of the few sun signs that can out-stubborn Taurus, but Cancerians provide the gentle physical expressions of love Taurus *Cosmic Canines* need. These two are good together.

For multiple-pet households, Taurus/Cancer combinations work nicely.

SCORPIO and Taurus are usually compatible sun signs in the human world, but it may not work between dogs and humans—both are possessive and tend to be jealous.

Taurus is very open, direct, and honest. What you see is what you get. Scorpions have a natural mystique. It baffles natives of the Bull, who don't trust what they can't really know.

These practical dogs see things for what they are and attach little to making mysteries out of the easily identifiable.

PISCES humans, like Taurus pets, can be good, solid friends; each appreciates the other. Pisceans are quieter than Taureans, but both have settled, laid-back temperaments. There is harmonious accord but little action between these two.

Pisces has an ongoing conflict, seeking true identity and meaning. Taurus canine calm is a positive influence. Pisceans are giving, Taurus dogs love receiving. Both get their feelings easily hurt.

All in all, these two should be great pals with a lot in common. Taurus Earth is nurtured by Pisces Water. Taurus pets enjoy the imaginative Piscean approach to life. Pisces natives are sympathetic, sensitive, and compassionate. Will they give Taurus puppies needed discipline?

Fire Sun Signs

ARIES humans and Taurus dogs are an unlikely mutual admiration society. What appears right to one appears wrong to the other.

For example, Aries humans are not possessive. Taurus dogs may view this trait as not caring and think they did something wrong. To Ariens, possessiveness is a negative. To Taureans, it is a normal way of expressing love. These two just don't express emotions the same way.

Aries communicates well, is entertaining and humorous. These two get along, but Aries humans will have to make some adjustments.

LEO pet owners may be too assertive, full of life, and independent for Taurus pets. Leo humans assume they own center stage. Taurus dogs may resent it, become jealous. To Taurus dogs, sharing the spotlight means sharing their favorite person.

All Leo natives have to do to get attention is walk into a room. Taurus natives have to work for attention. Taurean pets will enjoy the warmth of Leo's spotlight, even if it isn't theirs.

Leo humans are warmhearted and Taurus canines bask in the heat. Lion natives are generous, sympathetic, and kind. Taurus dogs appreciate Leo's outward expressions of love. Like Taurus canines, Leo humans are known for their vitality.

SAGITTARIUS humans and Taurus *Cosmic Canines* are quite different personality types. Sagittarius humans appear unpredictable to security-motivated Taurus pets. These two can be friends, but Sagittarians can drive Taurus to total anger.

No sun sign is more competitive or on-the-go than Sagittarius— certain to upset stable, down-to-earth, laid-back Taurus.

To make friends with Taurus dogs, Sagittarians need to emphasize their joyful, hopeful, happy disposition and to downplay their freedom-loving natures. Taurus dogs love Sagittarius honesty, sincerity, loyalty, and their happy dispositions.

8

GEMINI

SIGN OF THE TWINS
(EXPRESSER OR ORIGINATOR)
May 21 to June 20
Third zodiac sign, first of three Air signs,
first of four Mutable (Wisdom) signs
SYMBOL: The Twins
ASTROLOGICAL TWIN SYMBOL: Ⅱ
PART OF THE BODY RULED BY GEMINI: Arms and lungs
GEMSTONE: Aquamarine, beryl
COLOR: Yellow
METAL: Quicksilver
RULING PLANET: Mercury

THE GEMINI PUPPY

Positive Traits

Gemini puppies have the capacity to offer more pleasure—and challenge—
to human companions than many pets.

From birth, Gemini strength revolves around communication and expression. Puppy Twins won't have difficulty letting you know how they feel. They are downright clever!

When you hide their favorite toys, Gemini puppies look in places they have never taken toys . . . and keep looking until they are found. They are smart. They are logical. They are curious. They are secure. They find challenge exciting. They love the opportunity to solve puzzles. And they are persistent.

Gemini puppies tend to go—and go and go. They finally drop from exhaustion, sleeping very soundly. Then they go and go and go again. They do, however, stop before exhaustion makes them ill.

They are self-reliant and may not wait for directions. They get along best when people provide strong leadership (not to be confused with dictatorship). Gemini canines communicate what they want by acting out roles: "Here's what we're going to do; that's okay, isn't it?" They aren't shy or retiring. Especially when it comes to what they want. Gemini canines can't verbalize what they want, but they do give excellent clues.

No young canines need human support and direction more than Mercury's Twins. Without discipline, Gemini natives stand little chance of achieving their potential. The adult dogs into which they grow can thank humans who cared enough to teach them proper behavior—the same people they resented during the teaching process.

Are these puppies always going to be energetic? They mellow with age. All dogs become more controlled (and controllable) as they mature Just like people.

Some dog breeds are more laid-back than others. Some Hound breeds can be pretty nondynamic. Being born a Gemini adds zest to otherwise lethargic animal personalities.

Puppies born under this sun sign are quick. Terriers are particularly known for their responsiveness to erratic movements. These traits are emphasized in Gemini dogs.

Playful Gemini puppies grow into forceful, bold, assertive dogs. They need training as puppies to make comfortable transitions to canine adulthood. Teach them to be responsible. These are intelligent animals, so don't use demeaning training techniques.

Unlike more passive sun sign natives, Gemini canines enjoy enthusiastic praise. They won't find hardy slaps on their shoulders and rough-and-tumble wrestling unrefined. As puppies, they thrive on exuberant expressions of approval.

One negative Gemini trait is self-indulgence. People who indulge

Gemini puppies may find they have adult tigers by the tail. Indulged Gemini canines can be moody, high-strung, aloof, and remote.

Dogs do not use human logic nor are they analytical. They function on intuition and instinct. Their intuitive and instinctive skills evolve as human companions train them. If they have more negative than positive life experiences, they exhibit more negative than positive sun sign traits.

Versatility is an innate part of changeable Gemini personalities. They can be great hunting companions in the morning and jog alongside the kids on their Roller Blades in the afternoon. Not all canines are quite so flexible.

Negative Traits

The sign of Gemini is personified by the Twins. Each represents a different personality within Gemini natives. No puppies are more charming (or cantankerous), charismatic (or remote), practical (or exotic), sensible (but impetuous). They're not being psychotic, just Geminis.

They are happy one moment, sad the next; loving one moment, distant the next; energetic one moment, worn-out the next. These little pets express feelings openly one day, are self-absorbed the next. Welcome to the dual personality of the Twins! You'll never be bored!

Gemini pets may have difficulty making commitments to family. It's not insecurity, nor is it a phobia. It's just the internal explorations of Gemini before making decisions. Once commitments are made, they are honored.

Because their personalities change so much as they learn and grow, these pets frequently appear fickle. Astrologers have called Geminis "emotionally cold." At the very least, those born under this sign are restless. Their loves in life can appear to change as quickly as the weather. They don't, really; they're just curious about everyone and everything.

Tips for Human Companions

These puppies chew on shoes, old (or new) socks—whatever you leave behind for them. Left alone too much, Gemini dogs may develop bad habits. Solution: Don't leave them alone too often until they have been taught good habits. When you do leave them alone, don't leave chewables in the room.

Find a safe haven for both your possessions and the puppy. Gemini puppies behave responsibly when you set a good example. On nice days, leave them in the yard when they're alone. On bad days keep them indoors in containment centers—such as a baby's playpen.

When Gemini pets need rest, let them sleep as long as their instincts tell them. Don't waken them to meet food or training schedules. Provide dinner and training when they are mentally and physically up for it.

There is no other sign of the zodiac for which *not* adhering to feeding and training schedules because puppies want to sleep is recommended. This happens to be a unique Gemini trait. It requires exceptions to rules.

If Gemini puppies don't pay attention during obedience sessions, it's usually because trainers present the wrong messages. Catch the interest of your young pupils. Make training fun and less of a learn-by-rote exercise, and Gemini puppies are exemplary in their concentration. These are very intelligent animals and need to be treated that way.

Don't show Geminis the entire picture when you want them to do something. It helps get their interest. Let them help you solve "the mystery." It helps them concentrate if they're involved in finding solutions.

THE GEMINI DOG

General Personality Traits

As these dogs mature, their energy mellows a bit. Properly trained, Gemini canines are supreme pleasures to pet owners who appreciate *Cosmic Canine* intelligence and enthusiasm for life.

Chances are, dogs with shining, curious, wandering, intelligent eyes are Geminis. When surrounded by activity, Gemini eyes seldom stay fixed on the same object. Yet one to one, they can stare humans down. Not many dogs engage in the human activity of sustained eye contact.

Gemini attention moves from one wonder of nature to the other. These pets are curious about everything. Like Scorpio natives, they love mystery. Unlike Scorpios, they are not, themselves, mysterious.

Above all, these dogs are functional. And they need to be. Being useful is part of their nature. Several dog breeds—German Shepherds, Border Collies, Newfoundlands, and Rottweilers, to name a few—carry genetic traits that make them need jobs to be happy. If dogs who need jobs are Geminis, the need to functionally fill a purpose is doubled. It may be getting your newspaper or slippers each day. It may be protecting home and family. Whatever it is requires training. Do you have the time?

If Gemini pet behavior offends you, buy a choke chain and leash. At four months of age, teach leash training. Properly done, it makes dogs aware of and responsive to the human companions holding their leashes At six months of age, begin obedience training.

There is always a kind of joyous excitement surrounding animals born under this sun sign. And Gemini dogs always think fast on their feet—all Twin eight of them. They are very curious.

This dog's mission is self-expression, which is one reason so many human Gemini natives are stars in the entertainment industry. As natives of the Twins mature, they become highly versatile, intelligent, and adaptable pets. To humans who value these qualities, Gemini dogs are loyal, loving companions.

Gemini: Preventing Problem Dogs

When they get proper attention, Gemini puppies grow to be the very best companion dogs possible. Human or canine, if they can't find outlets for their energy, they can suffer emotional breakdowns (Marilyn Monroe, for example).

To motivate Gemini dogs, get them psychologically ready. Exercise is the answer. If too much physical energy gets bottled up because of too little exercise, they won't concentrate well and training sessions are meaningless. Take them for a jog.

Adult Gemini personality traits include quick responses (they make great bird dogs), confidence and assertiveness, common sense that's as practical as dirt, courage, changeable moods, adaptability, and dominance. Dog breeds known to have genetically assertive behavior (e.g., Mastiffs, Bullmastiffs, Rottweilers, Doberman Pinschers) will be more assertive when born under the sun sign Gemini.

Breeds described as being unpredictable and changeable will be more so. Dogs known to respond quickly to unpredictable movement—Terriers, for example—will have faster responses if they are Geminis. Check dog breed data and combine it with astrological insights to find your dream dog.

Job Opportunities for Gemini Dogs

Families on the go find Air sign pets perfect for their wandering ways. Geminis love change! Camping? Summer and winter homes? Gemini dogs think it's a great adventure. Some dogs are disconcerted by moves.

Anything that keeps their curiosity skills honed is fine with Mercury's

Twins! With Geminis, the grass is greener on the other side of the fence, the world more interesting on the other side of the ocean.

Depending on breed (size, genetic traits, etc.), Gemini dogs make wonderful police, search, and drug-sniffing dogs. They have the courage, confidence, common sense, and physical strength for it. And, of course, the intelligence.

Provided no breed limitations exist, Gemini dogs are among the easiest to train for almost any canine function They can be easily trained to bark at strangers. You may first have to define a stranger, however—who is acceptable and who is not.

Gemini dogs of appropriate breeds make excellent guide dogs for the blind. They are confident, dog-logical, multifaceted, inquisitive, and refined (especially helpful when guide dogs enter public restaurants). They find being useful to people a shining star of which to be proud It gives them the purpose they need to be happy.

No matter how young or old, Gemini dogs are puppies at heart. They love life. They love children. Geminis have a special kind of sympathetic friendliness. They'll be there when children have hurt feelings. They instinctively know when something is wrong and will lick away tears brought about by hurt feelings.

COMPATIBILITY GUIDE FOR GEMINI DOGS

Air Sun Signs

GEMINI humans who adopt Gemini puppies might check the biorhythms for both. Determine if the two Twins have compatible cycles. It isn't fun when both belligerent and moody Gemini Twins emerge simultaneously.

Both members involved in this relationship are forceful, confident, bold, and changeable. If human Geminis control their sun sign canine compatriots without being too dominant, too confident, or too forceful, this can be an excellent match.

LIBRA natives analyze everything. Indecision drives Gemini dogs bonkers (and gives them an excuse to usurp human companion authority).

Natives born under the sign of the Scales are restful and calm; Geminis are assertive and action-oriented. A little Libran calmness is good for them. Librans are balanced and harmonious, Geminis are changeable and forceful. Both are refined and sensible. There is a bit of opposites attracting here, but these two get along well provided Libra takes charge and maintains control.

Gemini dogs thrive on the amiable, courteous, generous natures of Libra humans, but more assertive breeds may mistake gentleness for weakness. Gemini canines assert themselves when they think humans are wimps. Librans are not and, with true Libran pleasantness, will educate Gemini dogs who think they are.

AQUARIAN pet owners understand the mental energy of Gemini pets. If they aren't disciplined, however, they may not keep training and feeding schedules. Natives of the Water Bearer can be forgetful geniuses when other things catch their attention.

Gemini pets require schedules in order to mature properly. These personalities are compatible but discipline is the key—Aquarian self-discipline. These two have a great deal in common intellectually and they communicate well. If any sun sign can "handle" Gemini dogs, it's Aquarius.

Natives of both sun signs enjoy change. Gemini canines are attracted to Aquarian loyalty, kindness, honesty, and sincerity. Natives of the Water Bearer motivate trust. Gemini dogs find them reliable and dependable, except when they forget things, of course.

Earth Sun Signs

TAURUS pet owners find Gemini dogs with so much dominant energy, it may unsettle them a bit. Taurus is one of the most vital sun signs in the zodiac, but vital and dominant energies are two different things.

Geminis need to explore. Taurus natives are usually most comfortable with the familiar. Taurus pet owners may wish Gemini pets would lie by the fireside more often. Taureans enjoy peaceful, quiet environments. Geminis find peace in activity. The two signs are opposites in several ways.

These two have equally compatible traits, too. Natives of the Bull are patient, enduring, and reliable—all traits Geminis need (they don't possess them). Taureans may not like the traits that make Gemini such attractive pets. Gemini natives don't understand living beings who don't compete for everything, for example.

VIRGO humans and Gemini canines are almost total opposites, and not the kind of opposites that attract, but the kind that just don't understand one another.

Virgo humans tend to be self-contained; it's difficult for Gemini dogs to be contained about anything. Natives of Virgo are precise, detailed, introspective, and tactful. Gemini dogs are changeable, forceful, bold, assertive, and confident—they are not known for self-insight or tact.

These two do have some things in common: common sense, reason, and their need to serve humanity. Calm, retiring Virgoans, however, have little else in common with charge-ahead, outgoing Geminis.

CAPRICORN natives know slow and steady gets the job done (and done without error). They aren't opposed to speed, it's just not their nature to think of movement as fast forward. Geminis live life in the fast lane. They like it there; they thrive there.

Capricorn pays attention to detail, is careful, calm, determined, and patient. With discipline, Gemini canines can do these things, but they don't enjoy them. These two really don't have conflicting personalities, they just don't have many common interests in or reactions to life.

Both are independent and intelligent, and these two traits can take relationships a long way.

Water Sun Signs

CANCERIANS are sensitive, home-loving, and empathetic. Geminis are not. These two sun signs get along well not because they're alike but because their differences strengthen, rather than weaken, relationships. Though not the most compatible combination between humans, between dogs and humans it's good.

Some opposites attract because of negative differences; others, because of positives. With Cancer humans and Gemini dogs, it is an opposite attraction of positives—but requires patience and understanding nonetheless.

Gemini dogs will undoubtedly try the patience of Cancer pet owners, but they'll lose. Cancer the Crab is known for patience and tenacity.

SCORPIO humans can have very nice relationships with Gemini dogs—probably the best of the three Water signs. These people don't hesitate to make decisions and have great strength of character. They are born under one of the most powerful signs in the zodiac. Gemini *Cosmic Canines* respect decisiveness, power, and character.

Scorpions are quick thinkers, too—an asset with mentally alert Geminis When Gemini pets turn cool, aloof shoulders to them, Scorpions will be amused, not hurt.

Curious Gemini will fall head over heels in love with Scorpion mystique. It fulfills Gemini's need to solve puzzles every day. With Scorpio human companions, Gemini dogs won't even have to leave home to find a mystery to solve.

PISCES pet owners won't understand why Gemini dogs lack patience with repetition. To them, it's a necessary part of learning. They're right. Repetition is *one way* to learn. Always exuberant Geminis lack patience. Repetition bores them.

There is mutuality here, though. Both are original and imaginative. Both are individualists. These two aren't the best together, but it's not impossible provided Pisces humans don't try to remake their pets into their own image. Geminis can't change their positive qualities, nor should they be asked to.

Fire Sun Signs

ARIES human companions are quite capable of providing the leadership required by Gemini dogs. Though patience and persistence are not Arien strengths, they understand the need for both—especially during training. If there's one thing Aries natives understand, it's the need for militarylike discipline during maneuvers.

Gemini dogs appreciate uncomplicated Aries. Both understand competition and move fast, and Ariens have sufficient energy to keep up with Gemini pets.

Both are sensible, strong, good communicators, and Ariens have such humorous outlooks on life, it helps intense Geminis take life a little less seriously. Aries humans are known to be determined people. These two are a good match!

LEO humans won't have to compete with Gemini pets for attention. Gemini loves competition but enjoys the contest for its own sake. It brings out their best. However, like Leo personalities, Gemini presence commands attention. If Leo pet owners share the spotlight, this is a compatible match.

Human Leo magnetism draws curious Gemini dogs to them. These human companions happily support their pets when they express personality quirks along the road of life.

Leonine strengths include personal forcefulness—they can persuade anyone to do anything. They are warmhearted and loving pet owners. Like Gemini dogs, they are great individualists. Call this combination the "Dynamic Duo."

SAGITTARIUS and Gemini together can be too intense. Relationships that are too intense are too serious for carefree Saggies. These humans have a wonderful sense of humor, which helps keep Gemini pets from taking themselves too seriously Gemini sensitivity and intelligence may be socially offended by the well-known Sagittarian trait of being too frank—open mouth, insert both feet.

Sagittarius pet owners are bright, confident, happy, and purposeful. Gemini dogs always know where they stand Saggies are not only frank, they are honest, giving, and sincere. They are free spirits who won't try to control Gemini pets (who react negatively to control). This relationship can be the very best in the zodiac. If not, it will probably be the worst.

9

CANCER

SIGN OF THE CRAB
(INSTRUCTOR OR PROPHET)
June 21 to July 21
Fourth zodiac sign, first of three Water signs,
second of four Cardinal (Leadership) signs
SYMBOL: The Crab
ASTROLOGICAL CRAB SYMBOL: ♋
BODY PART RULED BY CANCER: Stomach, breasts
GEMSTONE: Moss agate, emerald
COLOR: White, violet
METAL: Silver
RULING PLANET: Moon

THE CANCER PUPPY

Positive Traits

Human companions will make Cancer puppies happy if they are sensitive,
giving, loving, and stable. People who think owning dogs means putting

them in the yard and feeding and watering them daily (and patting their heads when the trash is taken out) will do better with another pet.

The song "Like a Rock" expresses well Cancerian love. They, like their ruling planet, the Moon, are changeable, but their love is solid as a rock—so strong, it makes these puppies vulnerable.

No pets have more capacity to be sympathetic and understanding. Treated lovingly and with respect, they are self-reliant, reserved, and, generally, quite calm.

The only thing aside from bad genetics that makes Cancer puppies grow into negative dogs with attitude is negative adult human companions with attitude. Loved and thoughtfully trained when young, these puppies grow into secure, enjoyable, disciplined adult dogs capable of giving families more loyalty and love than many sun sign dogs.

There is a personality trait unique to all Cancer Crabs. Each time they are abused or hurt, they add to their Crab shells. Too many hurts or too much abuse results in dogs who let no feelings penetrate their armor.

Cancer puppies tend to be naturally shy. It isn't a psychological fault. It's Cancer's way of dealing with constant conflict between feeling vulnerable and needing to protect against hurt. As they live through hurt with the support of loving friends, they grow secure, developing very strong character.

The love of positive Cancer dogs encompasses everything in their lives: their homes, families, neighborhoods, friends, food, and anything else with which they come in contact. Cancerians feel something about almost everything. Apathy is not part of their makeup. They care. Such is the impact of the Moon.

Cancer puppies want to please and are happy when others smile and laugh at their antics. Give them ammunition to behave in pleasing ways; they'll do the rest. What ammunition? Your enthusiastic approval for good behavior and kind, supportive discipline for bad behavior.

When Cancer puppies show symptoms of fretting or worry, gently reassure them. Hold and pet them. Make sure they know you're okay. They worry less about themselves and more about those they love.

These are among the most domesticated *Cosmic Canines* in the zodiac. They are reliable, thrive on human companion approval (and are thus responsive to praise-based training), and have strong canine instinct and intuition.

Cancerians are very voice-sensitive. Loud-voiced human anger hurts not just their ears, it hurts their feelings as well. When things become loud and disorganized, show them lots of affection. Discipline them, gently and kindly—but firmly. Human companions not in control of their tempers are not the best human companions for Cancer puppies.

These are not weak or difficult dogs. Lovingly raised Cancers have the potential to become strong leaders. They have sensitive feelings, remember the hurts of youth and forget the positives, but they are fair and forgiving. They can be either the strongest, most loving and pleasing dogs in the zodiac, or the worst. It depends on how they're raised. Good genes help, too.

Negative Traits

The Moon has long served as the symbol of love. It is typical of the loving, changeable Cancerian nature. But, like the Moon, these natives have a dark side.

These puppies are perfect examples of: Hurt me once, shame on you; hurt me twice, shame on me. Like all puppies, Cancer *Cosmic Canines* are curious. Beachgoers who have seen land crabs sidle across the sand understand how Cancerians love to explore.

No animal can leave the nest and begin using baby hands, doggie noses, or crab claws to explore the big world without getting those appendages into trouble. Sensitive puppy feelings get hurt. A caring human companion can truly "kiss the hurt and make it go away" with these puppies.

This should point out how important a loving environment is, one in which training and the development of good habits has been made a strong priority. Without these things, Cancerians frequently become trapped by their own mood swings.

Tips for Human Companions

Cancer puppies can be very tenacious. Remember, once the crab gets its claws on something, it can be very determined to hold on to it. In real life, once a crab gets something between its claws, it will let the claw be cut off before giving up what it's holding.

Untrained Cancer puppies get yelled at for misbehavior and mistakes. Each yell helps Cancerians build shells to protect themselves from the hurt. The second yell will not be as effective as the first, and the third will be even less so as the Crab adds to its shell.

It is especially important not to insult Cancerian intelligence. To strike Moon-ruled pets with human hands (or anything else) emotionally devastates Cancer puppies. Hands are for praise and love.

THE CANCER DOG

General Personality Traits

When properly bred and raised, these are ideal adult pets. The loyalty and love they show their families make them one of the best possible pets with whom to share life. Their flexible, calm, and strong personalities make them the best friends. Their loyalty makes them wonderful protectors. Their love of travel means they won't mind moving. They'll have a little period of adjustment, but moving won't devastate them. Cancerians are glad to go wherever human companions go because that is where these *Cosmic Canines* want to be.

Their patience makes them wonderful companions for children. Cancer *Cosmic Canines* are absolute joys to little people. Their loyalty is the thing of which books are written. Lassie, as portrayed in the movies, is a perfect example of the loving Cancer nature: loyal, smart, prophetic, patient, proud, fretful when worried, and extremely loving.

Mark Twain patterned the character of Tom Sawyer after typical Cancerian personalities: adventurous, but easily hurt; considerate, but a normal child who occasionally disobeys adult direction; intelligent, but sensitive to the ideas of others.

Early memories and old habits are ever with these pets. People who adopt older dogs might find other sun sign pets have an easier time rebonding. Even if Cancer dogs are raised by loving human companions, they form very strong bonds with their first family and remember them for life.

Certain dog breeds have the same rebonding difficulty. Read the breed information. Do not adopt Cancerian dogs of breeds known to strongly bond with their puppyhood human companions. Such pets may never rebond.

Canines function on intuition and instinct. You can trust the instincts of dogs born under the sign of the Crab. If a Cancer dog doesn't like one of your lifelong friends, the dog senses there is something to dislike. You might want to count the silver when this particular friend leaves. Cancerians tend to be social animals who like people unless some sixth sense makes it impossible to trust them.

As puppies, Cancerians are motivated to gain approval. Security is number one on their list of priorities. As Cancer puppies grow to adulthood, they become comfortable and secure, masters of their own fates. If abused as puppies, that wonderful gift of maturity will be withheld from them.

Emotionally healthy adult Cancer dogs are very strong—like tempered steel. They have leadership qualities but never lose their gentle, loving attitudes—their hallmarks as puppies. Cancer canine youths are shy. As adult dogs, they appear shy, but they're not. They are merely very self-contained.

Young Cancerians are known for their need to wander (check the breed data—numerous breeds of dog wander; don't double up on this tendency), but when grown they need a place to come home to, a place where they are loved, where they can love others. Cancer puppies can be changeable; adult Cancer dogs are happily settled and have all four paws on the ground.

Changeable, restless Cancer dogs love domestic tranquillity. If your home is loud and boisterous, yelling at one another one moment, hugging and kissing the next, Cancer pets will have to make some adjustments (during which they may fret).

They can literally make themselves physically ill from worry, so domestic tranquillity is the best recipe for contented Cancer canines.

These dogs have the ability to wait for what they want. Just as Taurus is synonymous with stubborn, Cancer is synonymous with patience and tenacity. These combined traits can make it difficult to beat them at waiting games.

Give Cancer pets time to dream their dreams, treat them in positive ways—as if you are absolutely certain they have the ability to make their dreams come true (having those they love believe in them is very important)—and they may surprise you by becoming famous. Like Lassie. Or Tom Sawyer.

Cancer: Preventing Problem Dogs

The best way to motivate Cancer dogs to do anything is through their senses of smell, touch, hearing, taste, and sight. They respond to what their senses tell them.

Cancerian canines have highly sensitized hearing (one of the reasons they make such wonderful guard dogs). Certain dog breeds also produce hearing-sensitive animals. Check the breed data, and if you're thinking of adopting a dog born to a hearing-sensitive breed, make sure it's a sun sign other than Cancer. Otherwise, family behavior and corrections in voices louder than whispers will get an overreaction.

"Get out from under that bed!" If you shouted, you've already lost Cancer's attention. They're focused on the ringing in their ears. These dogs are emotionally stable and can easily take disagreements. Aching ears are another matter.

When Cancer canines decide something, they stick to it. Make sure their decisions are wise and compatible with your wishes. It's much easier to point Cancer's feet on the right path than to continually correct them—the crab shell again.

Treat their sensitivities with understanding, but don't overlook bad behavior when it occurs just to avoid hurt feelings.

Just remember: If you shout, you've lost the bout!

Job Opportunities for Cancer Dogs

No dogs make better or more loving family pets and protectors than these.

When properly bred, well-raised Cancer dogs make perfect police protection and search-and-seize dogs; they are intelligent, patient, and calm, and once they know what is expected of them, very logical performers. Once they undertake a search, Cancerian persistence and tenacity take over; the search will, if at all possible, be completed.

Cancer dogs make wonderful guide dogs for the blind. They are great hunting and travel companions, and are trustworthy exercise partners—unless genetics says otherwise, Cancer dogs will not be aggressive toward other animals along your jogging route.

These Water sign natives make great company (as well as protectors) for boat owners who take to lakes (or rivers or oceans) on weekend trips or long vacations. Cancerians love to travel by water!

Their sensitive natures make them perfect for the disabled and shut-ins, or for hospital and nursing home visits to people confined in bed because of illness.

COMPATIBILITY GUIDE FOR CANCER DOGS

Air Sun Signs

GEMINI humans are competitive and may turn off calm Cancer Crabs. "Does someone always have to win?" the Crab asks. Gemini usually answers yes.

These two signs share one unsettling trait: Both are changeable. With Gemini, it is Mercury's Twin personalities; with Cancer, the influence of the ever-changing Moon It can be confusing. Human companions may feel they don't know their pets; Cancer dogs may feel they don't know their human companions Both are always changing!

Gemini humans are quick and forceful. Cancer dogs are calm and patient. Both are sensible, logical, and functional. Though alike in some ways, these two are opposites—not in personality, but in the way personality traits are exhibited.

AQUARIANS are too on-the-go for stability-loving Cancer. But these two do have much in common—patience, intelligence, kindness, thoughtfulness—they just express them differently. If someone is hurt, Cancer dogs show compassion and understanding with a lick on the face or hand. The dog all but says "lean on me."

Aquarians leap into action, find the source of the hurt, and remove it. If there's time, they'll express compassion and understanding, but it's second on their priority list. As a result, neither recognizes the other's positive traits. There won't be conflict—both signs are too quiet and humane for that. Neither will there be much understanding.

LIBRANS like balance and harmony, are kind, amiable, and courteous—very like Cancer natives. Humans born under this sun sign are sensitive, perceptive, and see the hidden agenda so many Cancer natives carry

Because of Libra's agreeable, pleasant nature, personal differences between these two are minimized. Libra humans and Cancer dogs can have wonderful, growth-oriented relationships.

Earth Sun Signs

VIRGO humans, like Cancer dogs, are very security-motivated and sensitive. Too much sensitivity can mean too little understanding and withheld but needed discipline.

Sometimes, having two sensitive types in one relationship means hurt feelings. Virgoans are warm, loving, humorous. They happily serve others—another point of compatibility. These humans appreciate the quiet strength of Cancer pets.

Virgo humans need to watch their tendency to criticize. Canines don't understand words, but they understand voice tone. Nagging voices and hearing-sensitive Cancer pets don't mix.

CAPRICORN humans are good *for* Cancer dogs. They are opposing

278 · Cosmic Canines

sun signs, and opposites attract. Opposites, however, also create friction. As Cancer's opposing sign, Capricorn has strengths that are Cancer's weaknesses. Equally, Capricorn's weaknesses are Cancer's strengths.

Capricorn humans are humorous. Like all Goats, to them progress means one step at a time and straight ahead. Cancer Crabs usually sidle, reaching objectives circuitously. Each gets where they're going in different ways.

Goat natives help *Cosmic Canine* Crabs reach beyond security needs and help them develop the deep base of talent Cancer canines keep so well hidden. These two are the best!

TAURUS human companions may exhibit traditional sun sign stubbornness, and it puts a fly in the ointment. That's about the only thing that causes conflict between the two, though.

Taureans do not challenge Cancer sufficiently, and Cancer dogs do not grow as much with these humans as with others. Overall, this is a peaceful relationship.

Both sun signs are practical, solid, patient, persistent, peaceful, and - sincere. Each is generous, reserved, and friendly, too. In negative phases, Taureans can be obstinate, dogmatic, selfish, fearful, stubborn, and indecisive. Cancer dogs resist stubborn opponents—and often win. Otherwise, this relationship is just about perfect.

Water Sun Signs

SCORPIO humans are ideal companions for Cancer pets. Like Cancer dogs, Scorpions don't live or die over won/lost columns (like Air and Fire sun signs do).

Scorpio natives draw Cancer canines out in subtle ways—like helping Cancerians through feelings of insecurity. They urge them to grow beyond fears and overcome them.

Scorpios are good with children and Cancer has great personal need during youth. Positive Scorpio natives are talented, decisive, quick thinking, persistent, tranquil, dignified, and friendly. Cancer dogs thrive when sharing relationships with positive Scorpions.

PISCES human companions make excellent owners of Cancer *Cosmic Canines*. Pisceans are quiet, strong, and make Cancer pets feel loved, needed, and protected. This, in turn, motivates these dogs to love, need, and protect.

Pisces natives share Cancer's security needs, and these dogs learn from the personal sense of individuality that is so much a part of these humans. Pisces natives have a special kind of magnetism that motivates dogs to trust them. And peaceful Pisceans seldom raise their voices—a trait appreciated by these *Cosmic Canines'* sensitive ears.

Piscean compassion, tenderness, warmth, and sympathy add icing to the cake. It's a cake Cancer dogs enjoy for life.

CANCER people are strong, understanding, sympathetic, and compassionate people. They have unique insights into Cancer dogs.

Relationships between two members of the same sun double up on negatives as well as positives, though. In negative phases, Cancerians are fearful, defensive, selfish, worried, and emotionally moody.

Too much understanding and empathy can result in lowered behavioral expectations and too little discipline. Cancer dogs need high hopes and a disciplined lifestyle.

Fire Sun Signs

ARIES companions for Cancer dogs may be a little more exuberant than these pets find appealing, but Cancerians can learn about being spontaneous from their Aries friends.

Ram natives feel attachment strongly, but are not expressive about it, which may leave Cancer *Cosmic Canines* asking, "Does he/she really care?" Cancerians can be pretty quiet. It won't bother Aries at all—the only thing that bothers the Ram is being expected to be quiet.

Cancerians are tenacious and self-reliant, and they have a lot of common sense. Aries humans can learn from these dogs, but will they?

LEO humans can have meaningful relationships with Cancer pets. They are open about everything, enjoy being on stage, and thrive on winning.

Cancer isn't a highly competitive sun sign, but Leos view competition differently than other people—winning is their right, not a game of chance. They expect the world to deal with them on their terms

Leo humans make Cancer dogs reach for life experiences they would pass by if not for this relationship. They help Cancer puppies gain self-confidence and overcome too large security motives. They help these dogs face life with a little less intensity. Leo people bring out Cancerian humor—not an easy thing to do.

SAGITTARIUS humans are filled with the spirit of competition (a concept little understood by Cancer natives). They may be a little too direct, too rowdy for Cancerians.

Sagittarians never mean to hurt the feelings of others! It's just the natural result of their very honest natures. Getting hurt by too much directness is equally as natural to Cancer pets.

Saggies do share a lot of compatible traits with Cancer natives. Both are devoted, giving, sincere, and affectionate. To Saggies, devotion is expressed by granting total freedom—a trait likely to make Cancer dogs feel unloved. This is not the most compatible relationship.

10

LEO

SIGN OF THE LION
(RULER OR ROYALTY)
July 22 to August 21
Fifth zodiac sign, second of three Fire signs,
second of four Fixed (Power) signs
SYMBOL: The Lion
ASTROLOGICAL LION SIGN: ♌
PART OF THE BODY RULED BY LEO: Heart
GEMSTONE: Ruby, diamond
COLOR: Orange
METAL: Gold
RULING PLANET: The Sun

THE LEO PUPPY

Positive Traits

Who wants to share life with a Lion? Remember, Leo *Cosmic Canines* are born to royalty. When properly raised, these pets rule with as much graciousness as Leo native Ethel Barrymore, queen of the Broadway stage.

Among fellow canines, Leo natives take the lead—as sled dogs, in the field hunting, guarding and protecting, leading the blind, or just being loving (and loved) family pets. Then there are the circus, the stage, the movies . . .

You are probably talented, intelligent, witty, warm, and loving if these pets see anything worthy of their attention. It's a bit of a moot point, anyway. Natives of this sun sign expect everyone to be attracted to them. It's the way of royalty (canine royalty, anyway).

All animals born under the sign of Leo show little or no hesitation when making decisions, even tough ones.

"What decisions?" you ask. "I make the decisions around my house. No dog, Leo or otherwise, is going to make any decisions."

Tell that to Leo dogs when they decide to pout or stop eating or start having potty accidents in the house because you brought the new baby home and their feelings got hurt because they lost the attention. Will they adjust to your precious surprise? If you are aware you are dealing with Leo the Lion's ego and involve your dog in the event when you bring the baby home, everything will be just fine.

Tell Leo dogs they don't make decisions when you have friends in for a social evening and, after a few drinks, someone pats the dog's head too hard, telling him what a "good dog" he is. Will he snarl, or grin and bear it?

Most dogs, of whatever breed, are, by nature, team players, though there are some exceptions (see breed data). Leo canines actively try to become family members. Should they welcome your friends? Should they warn you of character flaws when their instincts sense them? These are the kinds of decisions all pets make.

When you picture a lion, proud head thrown back, mane blowing in the wind (you may even hear strains of the song "Born Free" playing in the background), you are picturing typical self-images that Leo natives have of themselves (human or canine). No matter the breed of dog, Leo hair is usually luxuriant and gets a lot of attention. Even if it means, as was rumored, keeping Air Force One on a Los Angeles runway over a haircut.

They are filled with joie de vivre, expectations of great things, pride, and self-confidence. Leo dogs are wonderful for and enjoy being in the conformation show ring. Remember, they are at home in the theater!

Leos have very high energy levels. Some Leos are seldom sick or recover from illness quickly. Others always seem to be ill and never quite recuperate from one thing before getting another.

Most puppies thrive on pleasing their companions. Leos thrive on being pleased by them. They have wonderful ways of making you think you're very special because you're smart and attend to them so well. They give you special looks, cock their heads to one side, and give a little whine of approval, pick up a paw and put it on your knee—you'll swear they're smiling!

They are equally open when showing their displeasure. These puppies love life too much to become nasty or mean. They simply ignore you when you fall off the top spot on their Hit Parade.

These *Cosmic Canines* appear to be sincere about everything—their love for you and their homes, their need for action, their stubbornness, their pride. Leo natives are generous and openly show their emotions. Whatever they have to do to get the positive attention they want, they do.

Lions have great perseverance. To train them well, get (and keep) their interest. Some sun sign natives can learn by rote. Leo cannot. The best way to stimulate Leonine interest is through affection that makes them enjoy spending time with those they love. Self-serving? Sure. But it works.

Negative Traits

Good obedience training is critical to Leo puppies. They are so impulsive! Good training gives guardians control It can keep exuberant dogs from running in front of oncoming cars.

When trained, these cute, charming, and vivacious puppies grow into strong adult dogs. Left untrained, they become insecure, impulsive dogs who are vital, forceful, and dominant.

Leo puppies who know concerned owners will correct their impulsive behavior fall back on native intuition. That's a healthy place for Leo canines to be. They have a lot of positive intuition.

These canines may become aware of prowlers before they get into your house or yard—the best kind of guard dog! Leo dogs may also sense the arrival of guests moments before the bell rings. They are very intuitive.

From the first day Leo puppies enter their new homes, they must learn to earn their thrones. Teach them dominion over others is not a gift but a privilege to be earned.

Unfortunately, Leos (puppies or princes) behave as if majesty is a gift and exhibit confusion when others do not bow to their royal bearing. The truly regal have no idea where their sense of royal self comes from. It is an attitude. A bearing. A royal persona. It simply *is*—and it is very Leonine.

Tips for Human Companions

Leo is a Fixed Fire sign and has a great deal of energy. Once ideas have been formed, Leos have a great deal of persistent energy to help them hold their ground. Make sure the right ideas—your ideas—are the ones your Leo puppy forms. That way, your puppy will be stubborn about behaving precisely the way you want.

Leo puppies prioritize their energy in a way that ensures their enlightened self-interest. Most of the "partnering" they do involves self-interest (a canine leadership trait).

Being restricted in apartments may cause Leo canines to become moody. They love freedom, change, and space. All are difficult to achieve in confinement, regardless of the dog's size. Take them for regular visits to the country.

All Leos love getting their way. They will use manipulative tactics. They can be trained and disciplined, but they never stop trying to get their way. It's best for everyone, isn't it?

How do dogs manipulate humans? By whining, barking incessantly, pouting, eating little or nothing, having sanitary accidents, becoming lethargic, and so on. Until they learn that these tactics will not work, they use whatever behavioral tool they have at their disposal to get their way.

They are equally honest and sincere in their rejection of being manipulated. A double standard? Hypocritical? Sure, but no one has yet figured out how to explain hyprocrisy to *Cosmic Canines*.

This is a powerful, forceful sun sign. Every time you're tempted to spoil your Leo puppy, when you've given him a command and he disobeys you, ask yourself this: When the dog reaches his full weight and height and is no longer a little puppy but a full-grown dog, do you want him to respond to your commands?

THE LEO DOG

General Personality Traits

Families on the go need Leo dogs to take with them. They enjoy any adventure—wherever and whenever.

They don't want to be left out when you have friends over for dinner and will mind their manners if that's the price of admission. They will entertain you and anyone else who notices them.

What kinds of talent do canines have? Lassie, after all, was patterned after the Cancer personality. Perhaps Leos, with all of their gusto, are more reminiscent of Rin Tin Tin. It's easy to relate Leo's derring-do with Rinny as he loped from one crisis to the next, solving crimes and saving people. Leo dogs make wonderful Rin Tin Tins. Remember, Leo natives always play roles, even when they are sincere. If you want to understand them, you must understand this.

Leo *Cosmic Canines* carry themselves nobly. They are faithful, sincere, and earnest.

When properly bred and well-trained as puppies, Leo energy is positive. These animals look for reasons things can be done; competition excites them. Obstacles represent opportunities to grow, not disadvantages. But they can fool you.

For example, Leo's acting skills lead you to believe house-training is a done deal. You've been successful and the puppy knows where to relieve himself. The Leo puppy knows it's not on your off-white bedroom carpeting. It's snowing outside. When you run to the grocery store, you leave Spot at home. While you're gone, he decorates your carpet with a commemorative memento.

The dog knew he was doing wrong. He did it anyway. Why? Why didn't he use the doggie door to your backyard? Leo natives see their mistakes as your fault. It's Leo logic—faulty though that may be. You should never have left him alone. If you had taken him with you, if you had not ignored his need to go with you, he would never have had the urge to purge where he did.

This kind of stubbornness is different from what most pet owners are used to handling. It is not stubbornness, actually. It is a refusal to accept reality, to be held responsible for unacceptable behavior. Ask not for whom the world turns, Leo dogs think it turns for them.

Leo: Preventing Problem Dogs

Leos gain strength and energy from the sun They do better in sunny Denver with its infrequent snowstorms and bright sunny days, than in cloudy, overcast Seattle with its mild but cloudy climate

Forward motion comes naturally to Leo dogs. These *Cosmic Canines* bond with humans who like walks in the park, overnight camping trips, boating weekends, travel of any kind, competing in dog shows, and they like people who play games with them. For Leo, togetherness is the glue that bonds.

Be sure a disciplined set of standards is in place. Is it okay for him to clown around, running through the house knocking over things (and small children)? No, it is not. But his supreme acting skills will have you laughing so hard, it will be difficult to correct him.

Swallow your laugh, turn your back, and regain control. Then give a good verbal correction. Place your Leo puppy in isolation. The ultimate punishment for Leos is to remove them from their audiences.

Job Opportunities for Leo Dogs

It is under the "Help Wanted" category that Leo *Cosmic Canines* shine. Their vital, forceful, and assertive personalities, blended with warm-hearted, loving, sincere, and sympathetic natures, make them naturals for almost any canine job.

Their vitality and staying power make them excellent sled dogs. Their independence gives them an edge as hunting partners. Their perseverance and energy—not to mention intelligence—make them excellent guard and protection animals.

As guide dogs for the blind or as family pets, Leo canines are tops. They are generous and love giving to human companions.

For those who want to be stage mothers to their canines, Leo *Cosmic Canines* make great actors. There are jobs waiting at Ringling Brothers, on Broadway, and in Hollywood.

COMPATIBILITY GUIDE FOR LEO DOGS

Air Sun Signs

GEMINI guardians with Leo pets are a good combination since both have a lot of energy. Twins and Lions enjoy change and challenge, and both are intelligent animals.

This relationship works best with Gemini human guardians and Leo dogs rather than vice versa These two have a lot in common; both are forceful, quick, curious, bold, assertive, and sensible.

During negative cycles, both sun signs can be self-indulgent and overconfident. It causes too much focus on self. Both sun signs are too positive by nature to be negative for long, though.

LIBRA human guardians are smart and humorous. When Leo dogs act like royalty, their owners laugh—kindly and thoughtfully, as Librans are wont to do—and scratch the dog's ears.

Leo dogs find Libra human guardians balanced, kind, amiable, perceptive, and as intuitive as they are Libra humans help Leo dogs use their heads; Leo dogs help Librans use their hearts.

These two get along, but there is a subtle tug of war for control. Once compassionate Libra pet owners realize too much sensitivity can ruin strong-willed dogs, Leo dogs get trained.

AQUARIUS and Leo are opposing signs. Confusion can result because they express things like love and approval differently. Leo dogs communicate emotionally; Aquarian guardians, intellectually.

Water Bearers have a lot of what it takes to make Leo pets happy. They are determined, patient, quiet, and loyal—except for the quiet part, a lot like Leo.

The strongest compatibility factor for these two: Aquarian guardians enjoy teaching, Leo dogs love learning. After getting used to one another, this is a good combination.

Earth Sun Signs

TAURUS human guardians find amusing Leo's need to be noticed, until guests in their home try to ignore the dog (which ensures Leo attention). Socially correct Taureans may find it disconcerting.

Taurus and Leo are both Fixed suns signs—powerful. Leo doesn't like to be outdone. All monarchs do better with equals as companions (but history tells us honesty with royals can cost you your head).

These two sun signs have things in common: Both are solid, faithful, friendly, reliable, and sincere. Taurus human guardians should avoid trying to turn Leo dogs into Taurus personalities. It is not to this *Cosmic Canine*'s liking.

VIRGO owners and Leo dogs get along. It may not be the most exciting relationship, but it will be solid and lasting. Virgoans were born to serve; Leo was born to be served. It works.

Virgoans respect Leo's strong points and these dogs are quite comfortable in Virgo homes. Virgo natives offer pets a peaceful, warm, and loving environment.

Virgos who companion with Leo dogs should consult breed data.

Make sure the genetic temperament is not too assertive. Dominant breeds become more so when born under the sign of the Lion, and Virgo is not the most dominant of sun signs.

CAPRICORN humans and Leo dogs represent different views of how to live life.

Can the tortoise and the hare understand, let alone appreciate, one another? Capricorn's greatest strength is moving forward one step at a time—a big problem for charge-ahead Leos. Like the hare, Leo wants to run at full speed.

While these two are opposites, they can learn from one another. A little Leo charm can benefit Capricorn, and Leo dogs profit by learning the Capricorn philosophy: Haste makes waste.

These two get along nicely. Animals are drawn to and trust natives of the Goat. Cappies are balanced, fair, persistent, calm, patient, and determined—all good for Leo dogs.

Water Sun Signs

CANCERIANS not only get along with Leo pets, they may be the best guardians in the zodiac for them! The most significant thing shared by Leo dogs and Cancer humans are their ruling signs—Sun for Leo, Moon for Cancer. Both rulers provide light, warmth, and growth; one rules day, the other, night.

Cancerians love their homes and Leo dogs appreciate the graciousness of lifestyle—especially the gourmet fare—these guardians provide.

Crab natives, ruled by the symbol of love, the Moon, are affectionate, but they may have difficulty showing it. Leo dogs can teach them to express love; will, in fact, insist they learn. These two can be an ideal match!

SCORPIO can be too secretive for some sun signs, but mystique won't bother intuitive Leo dogs who see through any disguise to the real person. Though a difficult combination for humans, between human guardians and their canine pets, it's dynamic.

Both are decisive, friendly, self-controlled, and have great strength of character. This human-canine combination produces optimism. If Scorpion humans can view life through Leonine eyes and not try to dominate a dominant animal, this relationship may be a mutual admiration society.

PISCES humans offer Leo dogs homes that are peaceful, accepting, exciting, and warm. Natives of the Fishes are individualists. Their magnetism attracts others and their feelings. They are sympathetic and imaginative. All are traits compatible with Leo natives (human or canine).

Pisces human guardians, however, express things in ways difficult for Leo to understand—for example, sympathy to Leo is "oohs" and "ahhs," baby talk, and rubbing of the ears. To Pisces, sympathy is meaningful compassion and understanding. It is tenderness and sensitivity.

If Pisces can learn to say "ooh" while being compassionate and understanding, these two will be fine together.

Fire Sun Signs

ARIES and Leo (in human form) compete for center stage. Competition between these two, however, is healthy. Aries pet owners know that when their Leo dogs win, they do, too. It's a little like watching your child's Little League team take the state championships.

Humans born under the sign of the Ram are intelligent, energetic, humorous, resolute, amiable, independent, and decisive. No wonder, competitive factors aside, these two get along so well. They share so many personality traits.

Few misunderstandings occur between Leo dogs and Aries human companions.

LEO owners with Leo dogs? It can work a lot more effectively with human companions and dogs than human with human.

A relationship between two Leos is like the marriage between two egocentric superstars. Each expects appreciation and adoration from the other; it can be hard to give when you are focused on getting.

If the human half of this relationship is mature and has gotten past the self-centered ego of youth, one Leo dog and one Leo human can be real buddies.

SAGITTARIAN human companions and Leo dogs have great fun together. Leos love Sagittarian spontaneity and Saggies appreciate Leo's talent and aren't threatened by it. Rather, as all secure people do, they admire it.

Tender Leonine egos may fall victim to careless Sagittarian honesty, but dogs understand what people mean rather than what they say, so no hurt feelings result.

Saggies are confident (which Leo dogs respect), self-reliant, purposeful, loyal, and affectionate. In short, Sagittarian humans are the best possible companions for Leo dogs.

11

VIRGO

SIGN OF THE VIRGIN
(PUBLIC SERVANT OR CRITIC)

August 22 to September 21

Sixth zodiac sign, second of three Earth signs,
second of four Mutable (Wisdom) signs

SYMBOL: The Virgin

ASTROLOGICAL SYMBOL OF THE VIRGIN: ♍

PART OF THE BODY RULED BY VIRGO: Bowels, liver, pancreas/the digestive system (sun sign Cancer rules the stomach)

GEMSTONE: Pink jasper, hyacinth

COLOR: Yellow

METAL: Quicksilver

RULING PLANET: Mercury

THE VIRGO PUPPY

Positive Traits

Known for the detailed, fine, handcrafted watches they make, the Swiss patron sun sign is Virgo the Virgin (known for attention to detail). Don't mistake a love of detail for "boring personality," though. Virgoans can be quite unpredictable, too. They keep life interesting.

Like all puppies, Virgoans need warmth and loving attention to grow into secure adult dogs. Unlike all puppies, they need to *know* it's right to return love, to openly express their love.

Virgo represents transition from the irresponsible to the responsible, from the quickness of mind and idealistic views of youth, to the pragmatic caution and wisdom of age. Youth, by its very nature, is a transitional state. Virgo *Cosmic Canines* come to this planet with an instinctive need to gain wisdom and become responsible. When young, they try to achieve that objectively by eliminating risk. It can't be done, of course, but they try, then they move on to more realistic measures.

Ruling planet Mercury supplies ample intelligence to its subjects. In Virgo (this planet also rules unpredictable Gemini), Mercury gives its natives a big dose of common sense and practicality, intelligence and the love of learning. In a nutshell, that explains Virgo canines.

They are industrious—the workers of the world—fastidious, studious, and practical; having fun isn't one of their basic hot buttons. Only when their guardians play with them do they learn how to have fun. Adult Virgo dogs who haven't learned to play are intense.

To have dogs with well-rounded personalities, make your Virgo pet think enjoying life is part of his or her job. That's how centered these sun sign natives get on what they perceive to be their "life's work."

Workaholics are workaholics. Addiction to anything removes joy from partaking of it. These are the workers and craftspeople of the zodiac. They need to learn there is value in fun and relaxation, even if it's only to better prepare them to work more effectively.

All young pets are curious, but Virgo puppies turn curiosity into a science. Virgo *Cosmic Canines* view the world through naive but logical eyes. For those who wonder about the term *Virgin* used to exemplify Virgo, it is this naiveté and innocence to which the term alludes.

Aside from the physical and emotional needs of these puppies, another factor is critical to their well-being: diet. Provide a good, nutritious diet for Virgo dogs throughout life. Natives of Virgo are among the healthiest in the zodiac, but need a good diet to stay that way.

Negative Traits

When you adopt a Virgo puppy, you will be analyzed and nonverbally criticized. Virgo natives can't help being critical—and equally critical of themselves. It's a personality trait unique to this sun sign, used by them to gain knowledge They criticize so tactfully, though, you may not even be aware of it when it happens.

No puppies in the zodiac show their sensitivity, caring, and love *less* than Virgoans. They just don't know how to be exhibitionists. These *Cosmic Canines* are frequently chastised for being cold and uncaring. Quite the contrary is true; they may be undemonstrative, but they're not cold and uncaring.

Canines born under Virgo are very serious and have little buoyancy to carry them through tough times. Females of this sun sign may have difficulty birthing litters. Yet they are very healthy and rarely sick.

Family life can be chaotic and confusing sometimes. Reason does not always rule and Virgo natives don't understand why. To their logical minds, it should.

When household confusion is unavoidable, put the dog in the yard. With a little time to adjust, your pet will be fine. Sometimes—like mornings when families are getting ready for school and work—chaos is the norm, not the exception. Once Virgoans understand this, it becomes logical to them and, thus, acceptable. Don't force any animals to tolerate something that obviously upsets them.

Tips for Human Companions

Teach them to give as well as take, to enjoy leisure as well as labor. Teach them happiness is to be enjoyed, not analyzed. Teach them how to avoid becoming slaves absorbed by details. Teach them that they don't have to be embarrassed to show heartfelt emotion. And do it gently.

An affectionately rubbed ear, a gentle voice that says, "You're such a good dog," are your best teaching tools. They want to give, but don't know exactly how. They learn when human guardians show appreciation for what they do give.

Human guardians teach Virgo puppies to enjoy happiness by being still and enjoying moments of happiness with them. Teach the joys of leisure by romping a bit during training sessions and by giving abundant praise and attention.

Romp and play with Virgo puppies until their natural reticence for bawdy behavior slips into happiness to be with you.

THE VIRGO DOG

General Personality Traits

As they age, Virgoans change. They grow into wise yet innocent, calm but active, knowledgeable and detail-oriented adult dogs. Training is important, but they learn best and remember most that which they gain from experience.

Once Virgo dogs have been trained to do something the way their guardians want it done, count on them to do it. They will not let you down. Responsible is this dog's middle name. Work is another. So, too, is commitment—to you and to the jobs you give it.

Virgo natives—human or canine—can charm your socks off and be very intense while doing it. Theirs is a very laid-back kind of intensity. It can fool you. They can be mysterious (though they prefer solving mysteries to creating them) and very amusing.

As happy family members, natives of this sun sign are gentler and more loving than most other dogs. Ignored as puppies, they grow to become nervous, whiny dogs.

These are very sturdy, determined pets. When hunting, for example, they can stay on the trail as long as you want. They do not, however, exhibit a lot of independence or assertive behavior. They function best as team members and need team leaders. And like all animals who function best as members of a team, they want to be needed, respected, and appreciated.

Virgoans are very sensitive to earth vibrations—they warn of earthquakes and hurricanes—and feel the changes in atmospheric conditions, just like a barometer. Watch them. Learn their behavior traits just before a rainstorm, a snowstorm, or a dry spell. They can be better weathermen than morning television show hosts.

Normally, good Virgo instincts can be turned off by human error. Take time to find out what your dog is trying to tell you before discounting unusual pet behavior. When canine instincts are good, and people listen, lives can be saved and injury avoided. Since they can't talk, pet behavior is your best guide.

Virgoans are not spontaneous by nature. They can become a bit isolationist. They need meaningful interaction with a family to gain purpose, importance, and worth. Purpose gives them confidence, which, in turn, helps them mellow out and interact with others.

Adult Virgo dogs have hearts of steel except when those they love are involved in their problems. Then they become uncertain and insecure. Obedience training helps them gain a strong sense of self-confidence.

Once trained, once given a purpose, no pet can exceed the contributions to family given by Virgo dogs. Properly bred and raised, they are absolute joys to have around. There is a payoff for all that attention given them as puppies.

Virgo: Preventing Problem Dogs

Cruelty at the hands of human guardians turns insecure Virgo dogs into problems. If abused, Virgo, among the least likely dogs to be aggressive, defends.

Insecurity-induced fear causes more dog bites than overly assertive dog personalities. Virgo dogs are not overly assertive. If abused, they do become insecure. Insecure dogs frighten easily.

Plan obedience training sessions carefully. Remember, Virgoans learn best from experience. If training sessions are unhappy experiences—based on too much correction and too little praise—the training battle may be won but the war is lost.

These are very intelligent pets. They learn easily. If they aren't learning easily, look first to training conditions. Is your training area awash in confusion? Then look at your directions to the dog. Are they clear or are they confusing?

With detail-oriented dogs like Virgo, always use exactly the same commands. A lot of people think they do. If you're one of them, turn on a tape recorder. You may be surprised.

If the command "down" is given one time, and "lie down" is used the next, confusion results. If the command "sit" is used one time, and "sit down" is used the next, confusion results. Make sure all members of the family use the right words.

When working with detail-oriented dogs like Virgo, always use the same tone of voice. It's important. If you speak in commanding tones one time and whisper the next, confusion results. These are working dogs who pay attention to detail and are among the easiest to train—if they are being trained properly.

Some dogs have difficulty learning in group sessions where twenty other dogs and their owners are working. Virgo is such a dog. But private classes can cost a lot of money.

Pay the less expensive group rates, attend the sessions without your

Virgo dog, then go home and train in private. If you've never done obedience training before, it's a great way to learn how.

Teach the dog in private until the lesson is learned, then go to public places and practice.

Job Opportunities for Virgo Dogs

Virgoans do well as guide dogs, police dogs, search-and-rescue animals—at any kind of useful job involving public service. One of the most basic personality traits of the Virgo sun sign is the need to work and serve.

Virgo dogs without a sense of purpose are unhappy animals. Natives born under this sign have so much empathy with humans that they are especially good guide dogs. They make wonderful pets to take on visits to hospices, hospitals, and homes for the aged.

Virgo dogs who solve search-and-rescue puzzles seldom disappoint their handlers. Bloodhound breeders should strive for Virgo puppy litters.

Virgo dogs are wonderful hunting companions They have gentle mouths and won't damage your dinner while swimming out to retrieve your duck. Whether or not human hunting companions are happy with their performance depends on how independent they want their dogs to be in the field. Virgo works best as a team member, not an independent entity.

You want the newspaper brought to you every evening? Neither rain, nor sleet, nor hail, nor lightning, nor neighborhood cats, nor riots, nor drive-by shootings will dissuade these dogs from fulfilling their commitments to you. Well, maybe lightning—Virgo dogs usually don't deal well with thunder and lightning (their sensitivity to the barometer).

Unless these pets are employed outside the home in one of the above-mentioned occupations, your family will be this dog's life purpose—to protect you, to depend on you, to trust you, and to have you trust him.

COMPATIBILITY GUIDE FOR VIRGO DOGS

Air Sun Signs

GEMINI and Virgo are very different. Human Geminis express love boldly, assertively, confidently, more mentally than physically—totally opposite from ways Virgo canines express it.

Gemini natives seek individual freedom, Virgoans need security. Both are sensible, both are adaptable, but each sign's list of priorities opposes the other's.

These two can get along, but non-detail-oriented Gemini human companions will have to do things by the book—by the Virgo dog's detailed book.

LIBRA humans have a need for balance and can literally charm Virgo dogs right out of their choke chains. Whatever Virgo *Cosmic Canines* want, Libra human guardians have.

What is important to Libra one week is likely to change the next—a problem for Virgo dogs. With typical Libran consideration shown, adapting to change will help Virgo dogs grow.

Librans have class and refinement, traits Virgo canines intuitively admire and respect. Libra humans are extremely bright and like to keep things harmonious, especially their Virgo dogs.

AQUARIUS humans can be pretty intense, which won't help Virgo dogs lighten up. And like Virgoans, Aquarians analyze *everything*. These two could love each other deeply and never express it to one another.

Virgo dogs need schedules—at the top of Aquarians' boredom lists Virgo canines need anchors—they weigh Aquarians down. Virgo pets want to serve strong leaders. Aquarians don't like being generals.

Analytic, conceptual Aquarians use increased knowledge to change things. Analytic, industrious Virgos use knowledge to prevent the risk of change. These two are opposites.

Earth Sun Signs

TAURUS guardians and Virgo dogs blend nicely. Both are very practical Earth signs with a lot of common sense.

Taureans have compatible personalities and are likely to overindulge—both themselves and their Virgo pets. Taurean love of epicurean delights finds appreciative recipients in Virgo dogs who love good food and all fine things. Diet is very important to natives of both sun signs.

This relationship emphasizes security. Taureans understand why Virgo pets need to minimize risk. Taurus guardians provide a calm, peaceful, and loving environment built on the rocks of stability and security.

VIRGO humans are likely to nag their dogs a bit. Between humans, one Virgo can discourage the Virgo tendency to criticize with reason and verbal complaint. Dogs don't have those talents at their pawtips.

There will be few risks here. Though same sun sign relationships produce two beings with a great deal in common and may be dull, they are peaceful.

Health-conscious human Virgoans will make sure their *Cosmic Canines* get plenty of exercise and the right diet, and will be sensitive to other of this canine's needs.

CAPRICORN humans present these pets with a settled, well-ordered, pet-loving environment. Virgo thrives here. This is probably one of the best possible homes for these pets.

Like natives of Virgo, Capricorns are hardworking. Like Virgoans, Capricorn natives get where they're going one step at a time.

Not only will Virgo dogs be comfortable with Capricorn human companions, they will be appreciated. Virgo's steady temperament is good for the sometimes moody Capricorn.

Water Sun Signs

CANCER humans offer Virgo dogs relationships made in heaven. Both are extremely bright; Cancerians are also very shrewd—something to which naive Virgo needs exposure.

The problems center not on what each offers the other, but on what both lack. Cancerians, for example, offer no sense of being carefree, playful, or fun-loving. The relationship may be dull, but there is little friction and a great deal of stability.

Cancerian Water makes Virgo Earth blossom. Both sun signs are extremely intelligent, both are sensitive, both appreciate things that appeal to the five senses (both love good food).

SCORPIO natives and Virgo dogs can be the best! November-born natives are mysteries looking for a place to unravel—and Virgoans are good audiences. Virgo dogs never stop trying to figure out Scorpio human companions.

To Virgo dogs who instinctively seek leadership, Scorpions bring quick-thinking, decisive, and friendly personalities. Scorpion humans help Virgo *Cosmic Canines* expand and grow.

Natives of the Scorpion have a great deal of common sense, are bright, energetic, and independent. Scorpions are organized, too, a trait detail-oriented Virgoans appreciate.

PISCES humans are dreamers, and that's difficult for down-to-earth Virgo, who is as practical as sand on the beach. Virgo dogs need decisive leaders; Pisces humans prefer others play that role.

The strong points: Pisces is peaceful and giving, good-hearted, sympathetic, and usually friendly and amiable. These are calm, warm, and tender people who share Virgo's need to serve.

The weak points: Pisceans are very changeable and have periodic self-doubts. They can be emotional, demanding outward expressions of love. Virgo has problems with all of these things.

Fire Sun Signs

ARIES natives are energetic, enthusiastic, positive, smart, and highly changeable. If Virgo dogs could talk, they would tell Arien guardians to be more dependable, plan their days better, slow down, and be more thoughtful of others—all things important to Virgo.

Aries pet owners are too competitive, too high energy, too changeable, too conceptual for Virgo dogs. Aries humans enjoy risk; Virgoans seek to eliminate it.

These two won't fight and they do share important relationship traits: Both are sociable, sensible, strong, and outspoken. Aries guardians and Virgo dogs can get along.

LEO guardians and Virgo dogs go together like white and snow. Virgo natives are born to serve, Leo to be served—remember to say "thanks," Leo. If you do, this can be a wonderful relationship.

Natives of the Lion are usually very warmhearted, loving, generous, sympathetic, and relate well to Virgo dog needs. Both sun signs are very intelligent.

Between humans, Virgo/Leo personality differences may make these two sun signs incompatible. Human Leos and Virgo dogs get along very well, though Virgo may wish Leo would turn off the spotlight every now and then.

SAGITTARIUS the Archer is the most fun-loving, competitive, lucky, and energetic sun sign in the zodiac. Virgoans can learn from the Archer. Each has much to give the other. Both, however, must learn from differences, not similarities.

Saggies bring joy, hope, confidence, self-reliance, generosity, humor, and sincerity to relationships—all needed elements to help intense Virgo dogs lighten up. Saggies require freedom. That may threaten Virgoan security needs.

Saggies are highly independent and individualistic, people on the go. Virgo dogs won't like periodic residencies at local kennels.

12

LIBRA

SIGN OF THE SCALES
(ADMINISTRATOR OR COUNSELOR)
September 22 to October 22
Seventh zodiac sign, second of three Air signs,
third of four Cardinal (Leadership) signs
SYMBOL: The Scales (Balance)
ASTROLOGICAL SCALES SYMBOL: ♎
PART OF THE BODY RULED BY LIBRA: Loins and kidneys
GEMSTONE: Diamond, opal
COLOR: Indigo blue
METAL: Copper
RULING PLANET: Venus

THE LIBRA PUPPY

Positive Traits

The most charming puppies in the world are likely to be Librans. As the
Scales of Justice that symbolize this sun sign imply, Libra natives seek
truth and balance. When they find it, they find themselves.

Libra puppies are studies in contrasts: meek one day, assertive the next; pleasing one day, stubborn the next; gentle one day, independently arrogant the next. They are not sick. They are just Libras, the most misunderstood sign of the zodiac.

It is the need to find the center—the balance—of things by exploring opposite extremes that makes them so misunderstood! Remember, on the physical plane, where *Cosmic Canines* and their best friends live, balance results from opposing forces of equal strength.

Because they explore extremes before finding their own sense of balance, they try on many identities—and discard most of them.

"Guard dogs are heroic. I really admire them. I'm going to be a guard dog" Maybe that's not what they say—we aren't privileged with that insight. Perhaps they only respond to protective instincts. Regardless, the results are the same.

"Is this a friend? Why would a friend climb in a window in the middle of the night?" Who knows what Libra dogs think? All we can be sure of is that they use canine instinct and intuition. When they find out that guarding their families means a full-time job and rapid decisions, they soon discard this occupation as too restrictive, too demanding.

They will not discard the lessons learned during their "guard dog" phase. They learn from it the importance of commitment and caring for others. They then move on to their best friend role and the other job opportunities that await them. As adults, they find themselves.

As they go through this phase, be sure you praise the experimental personality traits you like. Ignore the less desirable ones. Librans can grow into just about anything.

This sun sign symbolizes the end of youth and beginning of mature fulfillment. More than change, Libra symbolizes thoughtful, meaningful change. It speaks of rebirth.

They are at home in almost any social environment, mind their manners, and enjoy your family, friends, and business associates. When human companions leave them to their own devices, they happily curl up in their "spot" or enjoy the company of other animals at the kennel.

Libra *Cosmic Canines* are dreamers, especially as puppies. They probably dream of what role they played today or the one awaiting them tomorrow. If you've been around sleeping dogs, you've probably watched their legs jerk as they dream.

Many people ponder the content of canine dreams. Are they running through a field? Racing toward some unknown finish line? Playing with brothers and sisters from whom they have been separated? With Libra puppies, the answer is probably yes.

Not only do their legs jerk, because dreams are so real, but these Libra puppies may bark aloud. Who knows where their lively imaginations have taken them?

Though Libra humans may be indecisive, these sun sign dogs are not. Lacking human logic, indecision is not a problem. They are creatures of instinct. See why it's important to train them? Their adult instincts are the result of what you taught them as puppies.

For all their dreaming, these dogs see reality very clearly. From the day Libran puppies reach their new homes, they seem to read the minds of human companions. They are quite perceptive.

Negative Traits

As new family members, Libra puppies evaluate each person before letting down their guard. They aren't suspicious. They're just trying to figure out the lay of the land. They want to know who's boss—the better to get fed, you see. Libran stomachs are important to them.

They may get hurt feelings when obedience training begins. It is largely bluster. These are calm, laid-back dogs. Their "hurt feelings" result from misunderstandings (like, "Why did you put a choke chain and leash on me and jerk me around?")

Lacking sufficient exercise, Librans can be restless—you'll hear them heaving great, deep sighs in the middle of the night as they sleep. Take them for a good jog each day. You'll both get a better night's sleep.

Libra dogs, among the *Cosmic Canines* with the most pleasant temperaments, can become combative if chained to a tree all day. If they are ignored and no one touches them, they withdraw from the hurt. It is hurt, not anger, that motivates Libran misbehavior. Isolation destroys their balance; togetherness tempers it into happiness as strong as steel.

Libra puppies and dogs have very few negatives. Their behavior is a little erratic when young because they need to experiment with different personalities to find themselves. If they get love and attention, there are no personality problems here.

Tips for Human Companions

All Librans are refined. What does that mean in dogdom?

Treat them kindly and gently. Keep feeding dishes clean, groom and bathe them, clip their nails, and, if longhaired, keep them groomed. Just as humans like fresh sheets each week, air out doggie beds and blankets regularly.

They like soft, enthusiastic comments like "You're such a good dog!" uttered in a happy tone of voice and accompanied by some serious ear scratching. They enjoy enthusiasm as long as it's not bawdy and overstated.

Though not robust, Libra dogs are sound—physically, mentally, and emotionally. They don't like chaos or undisciplined children given free rein to pull tails or poke ears and eyes. Given the opportunity, they run from such environments. Librans do not withstand abuse well.

Like all Air signs, Libra enjoys change. They will share life's beauties with you: a sunset, walking on the beach, hiking in the mountains, or exploring the unknown. Undoubtedly, if Captain Kirk's *Enterprise* had a ship's pet, it would have been a Libran, maybe an Aquarian. Both enjoy going where none has gone before.

Large-sized Libra dogs should not be confused with ponies or horses. Doggy rides are a no-no. Libra dogs don't have back problems, but it's not the strongest body part either. Avoid overly stringent exercise that stresses Libran dog backs.

As a breed, Dachshunds are known to have sensitive backs. Libra Dachshunds have double the potential for back problems.

THE LIBRA DOG

General Personality Traits

Libra dogs are the dream pet everyone wants. Their puppyhoods may have required valuable guardian time, but now it's time to enjoy the fruits of that investment!

These dogs like new challenges but hold dear memories of old ones; they need freedom and space yet are anything but aloof. Healthy Libra dogs are intelligent, sincere, and kind. They are *balanced.*

No sun sign pets are kinder to their families, especially children. Breeds listed as being "good with children" are doubly so when born under this sign. Check the breed data.

Librans have amiable, courteous, and agreeable personalities. A wonderfully developed sense of perception comes with the total package.

These dogs know what you want before you do. If they bark at the door and no one's there, wait a minute or two. Someone is likely to appear.

These dogs are loving—and very sentimental. Most dogs don't express emotions quite as well as Libra, but dogs do attach and bond. They are very likely to sense important moments and make them more so by adopting appropriate moods.

If you're sad because a loved one is ill, don't be surprised when your Libra dog curls up next to you and licks your hand. The solemn, sympathetic look in Libran eyes tells you you're not alone.

If it's a moment of celebration—a child's or grandchild's birthday—no one in the room will be happier to have a jaunty party hat placed over their ears. Get your camera ready and don't be surprised when Libra says "cheese!" They are truly empathetic and like getting into the spirit of things!

Libra dogs are orderly. Establish feeding, resting, and training schedules and stick to them. Otherwise, confusion reigns. They may have temporary eating problems or forget lessons learned without schedules. Librans enjoy change, but they need order. It's so . . . Libran.

Dogs born under this sun sign need to bond. They feel incomplete without close human contact and become lonely. Nothing is sadder than to see gregarious, happy Librans lonely.

If loyalty is important to you, you'll love your Libra pet. Remember, Librans accurately view trust and loyalty as two-way streets. As Forrest Gump might say, loyalty is as loyalty does.

Libra: Preventing Problem Dogs

The best way to deal with Libra *Cosmic Canines* is to slide your iron hand into a velvet glove and keep it there, firmness hidden from view but ready for use when needed. Libra needs stability and direction (the iron hand) given with gentleness and love (the velvet glove). It's the best way to discipline free spirits.

Keep these puppies happy and they stay healthy. When sad eyes tell you they are in a bad mood, take them outside and throw a ball or a Frisbee. Go for a drive or walk around the block. People sometimes mistake Libran calm for lethargy. They are energetic animals who need exercise (which saves on medical bills—yours and theirs).

Healthy, happy Libra dogs enjoy pleasing others and seldom think of their own needs. They aren't martyrs. Pleasing others makes Librans happy. It's their "style." Appreciate and enjoy it.

Venus, Libra's ruling planet, governs the sense of touch. Touching them, reaching out to them, is important. To Librans, this need is as basic as breathing, eating, and drinking are to other dogs.

Be gentle but firm when making corrections. Discipline when needed, but give more praise for doing right than correction for doing wrong. When training dogs born under Air signs, you plant a seed for future behavior. Plant a flower, not a weed.

As you watch your sleeping Libra dog and notice his jerking legs, think for a moment about the dreams: If you're part of your dog's dream, is he running toward you? Or, away from you? If your dog is running toward you, it's very unlikely you'll ever have a problem Libra dog.

Job Opportunities for Libra Dogs

Bloodhound breeders should seek every opportunity for litters born between September 22 and October 22. Librans are sensitive and intuitive—absolute musts for search dogs—but they also have a strong, natural ability to navigate and a wonderful sense of direction.

Canines born under the sign of the Scales may not be good guard or guide dogs. Both jobs require independent animals trained to have firm priorities—not Libra's strong suit. They are, however, good watch-and-warn dogs.

Libra dogs are among the best possible family pets because they are easygoing. They are good for multiple-pet families. Check breed data for dogs whose genetics make them "other animal friendly," add a Libra birth date, and the trait is doubled.

Toy breed Librans do best what Toy guardians enjoy most: love their companions.

COMPATIBILITY GUIDE FOR LIBRA DOGS

Air Sun Signs

GEMINI humans are adaptable and can match Librans in their love of change. The Twins are charitable and idealistic. Both are refined, and Libra can count on clean dog dishes, lots of baths, and being impeccably groomed at all times.

Analytic Twin minds establish the order Libra dogs need. Geminis have a great deal of common sense and intuition. Each is very sensitive to the feelings of the other.

Libra dogs need guardians who reach out and touch them more often than is the norm for sometimes aloof Gemini. Sensitive Gemini, once aware of this need, will happily comply.

LIBRA with Libra is indecision looking for a place to happen— among humans. Between humans and dogs, this is a good combination.

Relationships based on understanding, warmth, and harmony are seldom dynamic. How do you get emotional upheaval from two equally courteous, agreeable, and pleasant animals?

A calm, balanced, but sociable relationship.

AQUARIANS are principled, sincere, thoughtful, and humane. Water Bearers show Libran pets great consideration and motivate trust (which Librans do not give easily).

Librans love to explore; so do Aquarians. Each exploratory personality that Libra puppies try on both amuses and interests Water Bearers. Natives of both sun signs analyze *everything*.

These two are very much alike in their attitudes toward freedom. Both sun signs produce intelligent, kind natives. This is one of the best human companion–dog relationships in the zodiac!

Earth Sun Signs

TAURUS humans are practical, Librans are dreamers. Taurus humans are patient, these dogs are not. The Bull is enduring, the Scales love change. Both, however, are solid, determined, and reliable.

Librans love being all that they can be. So do Taureans, but these two tend to go in opposite directions while walking the same paths.

Libra dogs like activity, Taureans prefer reading, writing, relaxing. Calm, restful Libra dogs have very peaceful (if somewhat unexciting) lives with patient, friendly, and trustworthy Taureans.

CAPRICORN humans and Libra dogs have a lot in common. Both are sentimental and loyal, and both like organization and pay attention to detail. Librans like change more than Cappies. Oh, well. Into each life a little rain must fall.

Goat natives do not have the effervescence Librans do, but enjoy and nourish it in their pets. Libra dogs appreciate the strict schedules Cappies establish and keep.

Balance is important to Capricorn. To Libra, it is the food of life. Both are fair, calm, and accurate. When Capricorn guardians get too persistent, precise, exacting, and difficult, Libra dogs balk. Otherwise, these two are a good match!

VIRGO humans are committed to those who commit to them, and Libran loyalty is legendary. Virgoans certainly reach out and touch Libra dogs, and these dogs love and enjoy it.

Virgo humans need to take on a somewhat unnatural role when they adopt dogs as pets; they prefer being team members, but these *Cosmic Canines* need guidance and leadership.

These two can and will get along, but Virgo pet owners can be pretty predictable. Libran pets need change and excitement in their lives. Virgo organization and stability have strong appeal to Libran pets.

Water Sun Signs

CANCER the Crab may be too conventional for Libra dogs who want to explore the unknown.

Cancerians can be talked into a world of new adventures, but they are so logical! Will they understand doggie desires to experiment? Libra dogs can't talk, can't verbally convince Cancer guardians to explore, so maybe not.

The Libra philosophy of "Be all you that you can be" may be retarded; Cancerians don't motivate Libra to dare. Libra dogs feel secure and loved, though. And Cancerians have intuitive skills equal to Libra's. This is a better-than-average relationship, just a little puzzling for both.

SCORPIO pet owners are disciplined, organized, loving, and very loyal. Scorpio's need for secrecy will be okay with Libra. Scorpios do not give tit for tat in the mystique department. They do not see the need for anyone but themselves to have secrets.

When Libra dogs lose interest in a task, Scorpio determination helps them learn in spite of themselves. Librans tend to go in too many directions at once, but these guardians set priorities and stick to them.

Scorpio human companions may be a little too possessive for Libra, but all in all, this is a very good pet and owner relationship. Scorpions enjoy watching Libra puppy personality mysteries unfold.

PISCES humans and Libra dogs have a lot in common, but have many of the same negatives. It isn't good for either. Pisceans are meticulous, but, like Librans, are not planners or organizers. They are technicians. Librans are idealists who prefer the conceptual to the technical.

Fishes natives are spiritual and magnetic. Libran intuition feeds on these traits in very positive ways. Pisces natives can be exciting people, which mixes well with Libran needs for change.

Human to human, this can be a difficult match, but between pets and people, Pisces human companions with Libra dogs make excellent relationships.

Fire Sun Signs

ARIES boldness and impulsiveness can be turnoffs to Libran refinement. On the other hand, too much refinement makes life dull and boring. Can Aries human companions learn to touch more gently? It's important to Libra dogs.

Aries humans pass their sense of self-assuredness on to Libra pets, and that encourages them to dare to seek truth, to find themselves. With a little compromise, these two have a lot in common.

Human Rams are sensible, original, strong, humorous, and resolute. Like Librans, they prefer the subjective to the objective, the conceptual to the technical. This can be a great pet-guardian relationship!

LEO human companions have such wonderful imaginations, they reverse the "Libra dogs will charm you" roles. They charm their dogs. Leo guardians have fun with Libra pets—playing games, role-playing, and creating inventive training sessions.

Leo humans are always on the go and Libra pets happily accompany them. Libra's ability to express sentimentality will touch a chord in the hearts of Leo humans.

They only problem between these two is the battle for control. With Leo in the starring role of guardian and Libra as the starring best friend, it should be no contest. Libra will win.

SAGITTARIUS human companions offer Libra pets relationships that are just plain fun! These two are very compatible. Both are bright, healthily competitive, balanced, and popular.

A smaller downside: Saggies do everything spontaneously! Libra wants to organize everything and is happier when human companions understand the value of clear objectives and good planning.

Though Sagittarian humans require a great deal of personal freedom, Libra dogs won't mind. They don't cling, aren't insecure, are seldom jealous. Both sun signs are very social and love being with others. This is a match made in the heavens.

13

SCORPIO

SIGN OF THE SCORPION
(GOVERNING OR RULING CLASS)
October 23 to November 21
Eighth zodiac sign, second of three Water signs,
third of four Fixed (Power) signs
SYMBOL: The Scorpion
ASTROLOGICAL SCORPION SYMBOL: ♏
PART OF THE BODY RULED BY SCORPIO: Reproductive organs (mentally,
Scorpio rules secrets)
GEMSTONE: Topaz, deep blue sapphire
COLOR: Bright red, indigo blue
METAL: Steel
RULING PLANET: Pluto

THE SCORPIO PUPPY

Positive Traits

Puppies born under sun sign Scorpio are from four to eight weeks of age on Christmas day. They are the "Christmas gift puppy" of the zodiac. When this package is unwrapped, human companions have just begun to unravel Scorpio *Cosmic Canine* mystique.

These dogs want emotional security and safety. They want to trust human companions under all circumstances, good and bad. Scorpion canines *want* these things, but look at those questioning puppy eyes. Behind them lies a very suspicious—and secretive—mind. Trust must be earned It is not given.

Some breeds genetically hesitate to trust and bond with humans. Chihuahuas are a good example (see breed data). When both genetics and sun sign traits make bonding difficult, it doubles this somewhat careful, nontrusting behavior. Scorpio dogs are best adopted as puppies who have not yet bonded with other humans.

It's not that they are suspicious. Just very careful. When these dogs bond with humans, it is forever. Scorpio dogs want to really know human guardians before bonding with them.

The word *family* is used frequently in this chapter and refers to a human or humans who share homes with Scorpio dogs. To dogs, those with whom they bond are their "family."

These *Cosmic Canines* are walking question marks. They love mysteries. Understanding this innate Scorpio trait is the key to understanding Scorpio dogs. Housebreaking? Make it a mystery they have to unravel. Obedience training? Make it a mystery But don't confuse the word *mystery* with *surprise* Scorpion natives love the former but not necessarily the latter.

Scorpions are high in energy and quietly intense—sometimes not so quiet. They can be very funny and are great actors! These dogs are competitive The fiercer the competition, the happier they are. It's hard to miss Scorpion competitors. They are the ones with the do-or-die attitudes.

Astrologers say this sun sign produces more personality extremes than any other. Scorpions can be totally good or totally bad They can be smart or dumb, simple or complex, loving or exceedingly cold—like all living beings. Scorpions are just better at it.

Make Scorpio puppies feel welcomed as members of the family, earn their trust, make them secure. Only then begin the disciplinary process of obedience training. Only then do Scorpio dogs trust you sufficiently to respond positively.

Negative Traits

This sun sign's symbol is the Scorpion, with a poisonous, stinging tail. With human Scorpios, the sting comes verbally. Lacking voices, Scorpio puppies develop attitudes that "sting."

Scorpio canine dignity is easily offended. If you do not officially recognize them when they enter a room, Scorpio puppies may turn abruptly and leave. They may even find old shoes to chew on, or have a potty accident. Ill-treatment, after all, justifies retribution. Not paying attention to Scorpio is ill-treatment.

Did they ask for recognition when they entered the room? No. They do nothing to make their presence known. Noticing them is Scorpio's due, isn't it? You should have known better!

Once a secure sense of belonging and trust exist, Scorpio's need to be noticed mellows. These pets exhibit a very human trait here. Given a secure existence, they behave like secure people—oops, dogs.

When they are good, they are very, very good. When they are bad, they are horrible. When this pet's sense of dignity is offended, human companions feel their coldness, and Scorpions can be very cold.

Keep this in mind when teaching these dogs anything, from house to obedience training. Keep it light and fun. Youthful discipline is extremely important. Strong guardians capable of applying it intelligently and compassionately are best for Scorpio dogs.

Tips for Human Companions

It's important to make Scorpio puppies part of the family unit. How can these *Cosmic Canines* be encouraged to bond? That's the key, because once it occurs, life with Scorpio dogs is wonderful.

Make sure doggie tasks don't land in one person's lap. Spread them around. Let all family members take turns making dinner, taking walks, handling grooming tasks. In other words, to make Scorpio puppies feel like part of the family, be a family. Share—the puppy and the responsibilities.

When you go in the car, take the puppy with you. Be considerate. Plan your first trips carefully; puppies get car sick easily. Make initial drives short. Don't go right after the puppy drinks water or eats dinner.

Getting Scorpio dogs to bond is about togetherness. Go to the park. Throw a ball or Frisbee. Go camping, to the lake, or out on a boat. The Scorpion love of mystery quickly overcomes suspicion and lack of trust.

Dog personalities are largely formed through genetic breeding, training, environment, and, of course, their natural sun sign traits. All dogs develop character through discipline that justifies participation as a family member. Otherwise, they think in terms of self.

THE SCORPIO DOG

Like all Fixed sun signs, there is a great durability and persistent thoroughness here. Fixed sun signs exude power. They are steadfast and very stable. Many astrologers believe Scorpio to be the most potentially powerful sun sign in the zodiac.

These *Cosmic Canines* have wonderful temperaments and show love in the games they play with people—the game selected is an editorial opinion about how the dog feels about a particular person To Scorpio dogs, family is a group of individuals, not just a group.

Because of the way life works, there will be times when Scorpio dogs are unhappy with someone. When corrections for misbehavior are necessary, the person giving them is toppled from the Scorpion altar of adoration.

Scorpions tend to worship people they love until something makes them feel rejected. They view perceived rejections—like being jerked around on a choke chain and leash—as personality faults in others. They do not relate discipline to their own misbehavior, but to yours.

Already suspicious by nature, Scorpions withdraw from whomever offended (or, more likely, corrected or rejected) them. It requires a bit of tender, loving care to regain lost trust.

Lighten up. These dogs are serious enough for both of you! Their primary objective is to love, trust, and bond with family, but then someone goes and puts a choke chain around their necks and begins tugging on them! Don't worry They'll get over their attitude!

Members of this sign seldom have weight problems as they age, unless they're too sedentary. Physical exercise is important. To some breeds, it is imperative.

Read the breed data. If your lifestyle prevents pet exercise, a Scorpio sun sign plus breed genetics that emphasize exercise as necessary may create problems. Exercise reduces assertive behavior caused by dammed-up physical energy. Powerful dogs, in particular, require powerful exercise. The bigger the dog, the more accurate the statement.

They are great individualists, like Scorpio native Daniel Boone. Dogs born under this sign are capable of more self-control than average canines. They're a little like car engines. Once turned on, they sit in park or neutral waiting to be put in gear. When trained, they go forward. Left untaught, they may prefer reverse.

Scorpio pets are loyal, energetic, and very perceptive. They often know what people are thinking. They watch them so closely! No dogs observe human behavior more closely. It can be a little disconcerting. They have strong emotional reactions to the actions of those they love.

Overall, when properly bred and trained, these are friendly, curious, determined animals with well-defined (if somewhat unpredictable) personalities. They have a pleasing sense of humor, are generally tranquil and calm, and are very expressive. Scorpions think quickly and, within the parameters of the canine world, decisively.

Scorpio: Preventing Problem Dogs

If Scorpio dogs suddenly begin displaying unusual behavior—eating problems, sanitary accidents, barking for no reason, digging, assertive or aggressive behavior—chances are they feel you violated their trust. Trust, once given, is the most important element to Scorpio puppies relative to guardian relationships.

It doesn't matter whether or not the dog's bad behavior earned the needed correction or discipline. Whenever you discipline Scorpio, your behavior, not theirs, is judged. Thus, it is impossible to avoid lost-trust situations with these dogs. Recognize them for what they are. Give more love and attention than the norm until you're back on a pedestal. One thing you can count on with these October/November natives: You'll fall off again.

Character is formed during Scorpion youth, and character is destiny. As you love and train your Scorpio puppy, ask yourself if progress looks like a positive destiny will result. Make changes as needed on the basis of your answer to that question.

They may not be the best dogs for multiple-pet households. Check the breed data. Some dogs have genetic traits that do not encourage other doggie friendships. A Scorpio added to genetic inclinations can double a potential problem.

Dogs born under this powerful, dominant sun sign react assertively (at best) or aggressively (at worst) when faced with what they perceive as "abuse." Is obedience training "abuse"? Properly done, no. It is especially not abuse when you realize the alternative may be euthanizing problem dogs who lack training and become unmanageable.

If obedience training begins before Scorpions trust their trainers, before their positions within the family are secure, then the process appears mean-spirited and degrading from the dog's point of view.

Remember, Scorpio is a Water sign. Like the tides, it is ever-changing. Each time change occurs, Scorpio dogs question whether their trust in you is misplaced. There is a Scorpio cycle: you gain their trust, you train and discipline them, you lose their trust, you regain their trust, you train and discipline them, you lose their trust, and so on.

By the time they're a year old, it's a done deal. They're trained and they trust you.

Job Opportunities for Scorpio Dogs

Scorpio natives are frequently referred to as "trackers" because they love solving mysteries. They are wonderful trackers: hunting, searching for lost people, searching for drugs, and so on.

Scorpion curiosity makes them better-than-average hunters and Retrievers, too. The best hunting canine companions are those with strong streaks of independence and individuality. Scorpio natives may need a little more training than other dogs to develop "soft mouths," but they easily learn not to damage your duck.

The independent nature of Scorpio dogs, combined with their quick-thinking, decisive bent, makes them excellent guide dogs for the blind. The bonding process to generate trust takes a little longer than with other *Cosmic Canines*, but once achieved, Scorpion guide dogs graduate at the head of their class.

Scorpio dogs are healthily protective, wonderful guard dogs, enjoy travel (new mysteries to solve), and are intelligent enough to learn whatever their human companions are intelligent enough to teach them.

The strength of Scorpion character makes them wonderful sled dogs. Once they begin a race, they finish—first, if possible. Scorpio dogs view tough competitions like the Iditarod as a true test of their very strong leadership skills. And, if possible, Scorpions will play the role of lead dog.

COMPATIBILITY GUIDE FOR SCORPIO DOGS

Air Sun Signs

GEMINI, viewed by astrologers as cold and aloof, can't fool intuitive Scorpio, who sees through that outer shell to the refined, giving warmth that lies beneath the surface.

The primary problem this human-canine combination has is that Scorpio is a sun sign ruled by emotions, and Gemini humans by intellect. If each sun sign accepts the other's mode of behavior, it can add great strength, combining emotional strength with the intellectual.

Geminis are adaptable, sensible, logical, intelligent, curious, and confident. Even more important, they have three traits vital to good relationships with Scorpio dogs: forcefulness, boldness, and assertiveness. Also, Geminis can be trusted.

LIBRA human companions with Scorpio dogs can be difficult. Scorpios hate indecision and don't see why anyone else needs to have secrets. Librans are a bit mysterious, too. Each views secrecy differently, though. With Scorpio, it's mystery; with Libra, freedom and privacy.

Both Libra and Scorpio can be possessive and jealous. Each can be vindictive, though in different ways. Scorpio natives, human or canine, are seldom possessed by anyone.

Scorpio natives like stability and the lack of it can make them nervous. On the other hand, personality changes can turn into mysteries, which Scorpios love to solve.

AQUARIUS and Scorpio are both Fixed signs (Aquarius Air, Scorpio Water), but each views the world from a totally opposite perspective. Each stubbornly thinks the other is wrong: Scorpions, secretly; Aquarians, openly.

Perhaps the only equal to Scorpio at unraveling mysteries is the Water Bearer. The difference is, for Scorpio natives, mystery is a way of life. To Aquarius, it is something to be identified, logically torn apart, solved, and forgotten.

Aquarian needs for freedom don't make possessive Scorpio happy either. And conceptual Aquarians do better with pets less needful of down-to-earth, pragmatic problem solving than Scorpions.

Earth Sun Signs

TAURUS with Scorpio dogs has Mother Nature's blessing! Scorpio Water poured over Taurus Earth makes things grow and blossom. This relationship just keeps growing and growing. . . .

Taurus natives can be bullheaded, but Scorpions aren't shrinking violets. Neither allows the other to dominate. Both are capable of enduring faithfulness and loyalty—and neither is a worrier.

Natives of the Bull are practical, patient, faithful, friendly, powerful, vital, and—here's the big one—trustworthy. Wrap the package in Scorpion red paper This relationship is tops for Scorpio dogs!

VIRGO humans are very compatible with Scorpio dogs. Scorpions like the spotlight, Virgoans are glad to give it to them. Virgo is disciplined, organized, self-contained, and reasoned. Scorpio dogs will find Virgoan calm a bit dull, but opposites do attract.

These two are fairly opposite, though in positive ways. And only those Virgoans with sufficient personal strength to exercise control over Scorpio dogs should adopt them.

Scorpio dogs have a great deal of common sense, which will be highly valued by detail-oriented Virgo companions.

CAPRICORN people love pets. Earth sign natives of the Goat are drawn to Water, which gives them life. The one downside: Cappies move ahead slowly, Scorpions by leaps and bounds.

These are independent people who won't let Scorpio dogs run their lives. They are disciplined and forge ahead with training sessions, popular or not.

Scorpions like a little pizzazz injected into their daily lives and Capricorns take great delight in providing it. They use patient determination to put Scorpion puppy paws on a positive road.

Water Sun Signs

CANCERIAN guardians with Scorpion dogs are matches made in heaven. These two are alike yet sufficiently different to keep it interesting.

Both are internal and emotional, rather than external and mental. They both love competition and Scorpio pets help draw Cancerians out of their shells.

Cancerians love Scorpio's mystique and won't deride November-born dogs who bark at unseen spirits—human Cancers have probably seen them, too Cancerians are leaders, but are quiet about it. To Scorpio, that's the best kind of leader!

SCORPIO humans with Scorpio dogs can be a little intense, too organized, too disciplined. A little creative, relaxed disorganization is needed for growth.

These two may be very comfortable together, but the potential for jealousy and vindictiveness exists. With two Scorpios, it may be difficult for human guardians to recognize negative behavior patterns in their dogs that mirror their own.

Two Scorpions, each of whom maintains a personal sense of mystique, each wanting the other to be open and honest so trust can be established? Well, all things are possible.

PISCES humans and Scorpio pets? Of all the signs in the zodiac, Pisces is probably best equipped to gently deal with Scorpion possessiveness. There is a unique bond between these two.

Both are receptive, peaceful, giving, emotional. Both are changeable Water signs. Pisceans are known to be original, sympathetic, warm, and compassionate. Scorpio can trust these natives.

Scorpion individualism is encouraged, but Pisceans provide disciplined environments and stick to scheduled training programs.

Fire Sun Signs

ARIES pet owners and Scorpio dogs respond to things differently. With Aries guardians, Scorpio dogs may not understand the way expressions of love are given. Aries is mental; Scorpio, emotional. Scorpio Water may extinguish Aries Fire.

These two are almost total opposites. Aries natives do not understand possessiveness or jealousy, Scorpions do not understand those who don't express those emotions.

Ariens are intelligent, original, energetic, outspoken, sensible, humorous, sociable, and amusing. They are great communicators. They are strong and resolute and very independent. Scorpio pets may view these traits competitively rather than compatibly.

LEO humans have met their attention-getting equals in Scorpio dogs. Both understand the value of a good front and both love an audience. Both are very expressive.

Leo and Scorpio are both energetic, on-the-go types. Both are Fixed signs with strong opinions and powerful personalities. Each can be stubborn, but not unreasonably so.

Leo's ability to assimilate information from thin air fascinates Scorpio. And Leo humans spend many pleasant hours figuring out what makes these mystery dogs tick.

Lion natives are forceful, individualistic, generous, faithful, sympathetic; they have a lot of traits admired by Scorpio and these two get along.

SAGITTARIAN humans, like Scorpio dogs, need to feel others are completely honest with them before trust is earned. The difference is Saggies are open, hiding nothing of themselves. Scorpions invented the term *hidden agenda*.

Scorpio's physical strength, sense of competition, and high energy level appeal to the Archer These two will be constantly on the go—in the park, at the campgrounds, on a hike. And both love life in the fast lane.

Natives of the Archer are loyal and affectionate. They are also frank and honest—sometimes painfully so Subtle, unintentional Sagittarian insults will be lost on Scorpio dogs who don't speak the language.

These two are great together!

14

SAGITTARIUS

SIGN OF THE ARCHER
(TEACHER OR SUPPORTER)
November 22 to December 20
Ninth zodiac sign, third of three Fire signs,
third of four Mutable (Wisdom) signs
SYMBOL: The Archer (Centaur)
ASTROLOGICAL ARCHER SYMBOL: ♐
PART OF THE BODY RULED BY SAGITTARIUS: Thighs
GEMSTONE: Carbuncle and turquoise
COLOR: Light blue
METAL: Tin
RULING PLANET: Jupiter

THE SAGITTARIUS PUPPY

Positive Traits

Sagittarius, sign of the Centaur Archer (half-human, half-horse), gives human companions an interesting pet-owner relationship. It's impossible to be bored around these dogs. They won't allow it.

Sagittarius natures equate with puppyhood. They love to explore and dream. Saggies are extremely curious, alert, and are a little like racehorses: chomping at the bit to run the race, always hopeful they will win.

Sagittarius puppies are very quick. They are one of the most adventurous puppies in the zodiac. When properly bred and trained, they are outstanding adult pets: bright, willing, capable, and loyal. They will lay down their lives for you. Whether or not Archer puppies turn out that way depends on who runs things—the human or the dog.

Sagittarian puppy honesty makes you laugh. It makes you cry, too. They are so honest. When you walk into a room and their ears go back, their tails go down, and they look ashamed, you know you caught them doing—or about to do—something wrong. They show their guilt when you catch them even thinking of wrongdoing.

All natives of the Archer, particularly puppies, are impressionable. Whatever impresses Sagittarian puppies accompanies them into adult life. A newspaper used for correction leaves an impression. When they see the paperboy or girl with arm raised, hand holding "the dreaded weapon," they may react.

There is no canine more joyfully devoted to people than these. Their happy dispositions continue through good and bad times. Because of that, it's sometimes hard to understand them—when they're sick, when they're hurt. For example, most puppies have attitude changes when they need to go potty. They become quiet, sniff around a bit, and look for a private place. Not Sagittarians. They are as playful a few seconds before they go potty on your rug as at any other time. Thus, it's hard to anticipate their house-training needs.

Saggies are very intelligent, energetic pets. They settle as they mature, but they carry their high energy levels throughout life. These youthful canines are very self-reliant and haven't got a socially correct bone in their bodies. They are very giving, sincere, direct, and honest. What you see is what you get. There are no hidden agendas with the Archer.

Sagittarian Mark Twain exemplifies the cutting directness of this sun sign. Use your imagination. It won't take long to think of a few socially incorrect things dogs do—with their curious noses, for example. Dogs don't know sniffing private parts on human bodies is not a proper activity. Teach them.

Sagittarians are complex—so happy and energetic, so talented and quick (so open and bluntly honest). It's easy to overlook the many sensitivities that are also part of their natures—the gentleness, generosity, caring. They don't act like pets who can be easily hurt, but they are. They just don't show it easily. They are too filled with hope.

Negative Traits

Have no doubt, they find whatever you leave in a room—from Gucci to WalMart. They take things apart, satisfy their curiosity or teething needs, then turn bored backs to scamper off in search of new adventures. Interesting doggie toys help you get through the chewing phase.

Impulsive. That's the Archer—especially during puppyhood. And purposeful. And single-minded. These are very enterprising animals!

They hate fences because they limit freedom—once they find out what one is. When they see what's on the other side, their world expands. Don't let them jump on a fence and look at the outside world unless you want curious Sagittarius to play Columbus and explore. They'll set out to prove the world isn't flat and doesn't end at the fence.

Hips and thighs are Sagittarian sun sign weaknesses—every sign has one. Before adopting this puppy, make sure puppy's and parents' hips have been X-rayed. When stressed, their lower legs may swell.

Unhappy homes cause Sagittarius dogs to be restless, nervous, tense, irritable, and defiant. Chaining them, ignoring them, leaving them untrained, and insufficient exercise are the primary causes of unhappiness.

Tips for Human Companions

These dogs are very intuitive. They sense when human companions await a blunder—and they like to please. They'll make a mistake, if it makes you happy. If you're going to hover, you need to look for and reward positive, not negative, behavior.

These are complex little beings. They have dominant personalities. Their happy natures sometimes cover hurt feelings. They can fool you into thinking they are just energetic or curious or bright. Saggies have great depth. Don't let their playful, clowning demeanor fool you. Buried quietly and deep inside this dog is every positive quality you ever wanted in a pet!

Though outwardly very energetic, Sagittarians are very gentle, except in the presence of enemies. In determining who is friend, who is foe, Saggies have good, intuitive radar. If they don't like a member of your crowd, pay attention.

Jealously and possessiveness in others—a lack of openness—prevent these dogs from bonding. Life, to Sagittarians, is based on trust given freely to free beings.

Energetic Sagittarian puppies are challenges for guardians. Train them, exercise them, and love them. Praise loudly and enthusiastically; discipline quietly and efficiently. They mellow with age and training and grow into the best possible adults!

THE SAGITTARIUS DOG

General Personality Traits

According to astrologers, Saggies have an innate sense that tells the outcome of a deal before anyone knows it's on the table. Will Sagittarian luck rub off on you? Probably. These natives are generous and love to share their good fortune!

One thing is sure: Sagittarian pets have clear, quick minds and gentle demeanors, and they are very loving. They make people feel better about themselves—a good place for luck to start. It's one reason they make such good leaders and entertainers.

Even when Sagittarians are superstars, they compete with all that's in them; they thrive on the joy of doing their very best. Saggies understand the real purpose of competition is to challenge yourself, not to beat someone else with less than your best. And they do things "My Way"—as Sagittarian Frank Sinatra so often said.

These dogs are not the least bit sneaky. They won't wait for you to turn your back, then try to sneak a piece of raw hamburger off the barbie. They'll make a grab for it right in front of you. If they knew it was wrong, they wouldn't do it. Saggies are very direct. If you have meat nose-high in a public place, you must mean for them to have some.

These are purposeful animals and are very good at communicating thoughts and feelings without the benefit of verbal discussion.

Saggies don't lie to anyone, including themselves. Maintaining a free spirit is their primary motivator. They realize that true freedom and independence come only with responsible behavior.

Sagittarian Sir Winston Churchill is reflective of this sun sign's leadership, competitive nature, sense of personal freedom, energy, and humor. Steven Spielberg's imaginative, creative drive (and luck) are strictly Sagittarius.

Walt Disney was being very Sagittarius by making "When You Wish Upon a Star" the theme for his original television show. Saggies never stop dreaming!

Archer natives offer true friendship but can easily put gentleness aside when in the presence of enemies. That, combined with good intuition that tells them who is friend and who is foe, makes Sagittarians some of the best possible guard dogs.

They may not put their heads in the laps of human companions, lick their hands, and gaze at them with adoring eyes. They may not drag a flower from the garden to drop at your feet, but if a prowler tries to break into your home, they'll lay their lives on the line to protect their best friends.

Sagittarius: Preventing Problem Dogs

All canines have one or two key sensitivities that, if abused, promote behavioral problems. This very affectionate, loyal, and happy pet becomes a problem only when imprisoned or ignored. No dog should be chained, but it eats at this dog's heart. When the heart is gone, meanness is left.

Teach the home restrictions you expect them to observe, then set them free to observe them. Good training requires discipline from human companions, to be there at the right time to praise good behavior rather than ignoring the dog until a mistake is made. It requires intelligent planning. But then, you must be more intelligent than your Sagittarius if you intend to train him.

If intelligent training methods are used, Sagittarius puppies love obedience and other forms of training. They get to spend time with you. They get all of your attention for those few minutes each day. They get told what good dogs they are, and the tone of voice used to praise them drips with love. They feel petted and pampered. Remember, I said, "intelligent training methods."

To prevent Saggie puppies from becoming problems, reasonable standards need to be set and they need to live by them. They must be taught the rules and expected to perform. When they do, praise them. When they don't, correct them and put them outside, in the garage, or in "a spot."

Having "a spot" for Sagittarian dogs is important. It's a nice way to give them freedom within certain parameters. "A spot" gives a dog a place to go where no one—not you or the kids or your friends or company—bothers him. It's his place of privacy.

The best way to turn Sagittarian pets into problems is to become too possessive or be jealous. Saggies are nature's born-free animals and are possessed by no one—not even your three-year-old, who is so cute that everyone is captivated by her. She may want him to be only hers, but Sagittarians belong only to themselves.

Job Opportunities for Sagittarius Dogs

Sagittarius dogs are positive and strong. They make excellent sled dogs and can even give Scorpio a good run for the money. Saggies are natural-born competitors. If they could talk, they would be socially incorrect and tell people that, when you're a sled dog, the only way the view changes is when you are the lead dog.

Sagittarian *Cosmic Canines* appreciate good, changing views and work hard to maintain their status as lead dogs. Most sun sign natives who love competition are driven to win. Many are not team players; Sagittarians are. The Yankee Clipper, Joe Dimaggio, certainly exemplifies this trait.

As very intelligent team players, they work well in almost any field of endeavor. Sagittarians make excellent guide dogs for the blind, drug enforcement dogs, and police dogs; not enough good can be said about them as family pets.

Consider their sun sign weaknesses—legs and hips—if you seek a hunting companion or search dog. Jobs requiring dogs to spend an entire day on their feet may not be best for Sagittarian *Cosmic Canines*. This weakness may also limit their value as field dogs on the hunt; it depends on their human companion's hunting style.

Dogs born under this sun sign will, truly, lay their lives on the line to protect human companions. When properly bred and trained, they are not only good guardians, they are happy ones.

COMPATIBILITY GUIDE FOR SAGITTARIUS DOGS

Air Sun Signs

GEMINI is the astrological opposite of Sagittarius. Both are bright, flexible, and versatile. And each expresses personal similarities in totally opposite ways.

Geminis are viewed as aloof, but natives of the Twins are very loving. They merely express it in a less exuberant, less touchy-feely way. Twin refinement can help Saggie socially.

These dogs understand Gemini guardians who are multifaceted, changeable, diverse, assertive, bold, and confident. They need to show a little more emotion—not hard to do with positive, enthusiastic Archers whose Fire motivates warmth.

LIBRA offers Sagittarius one of the most fun pet-owner relationships in the zodiac. These two are very compatible—and companionable.

Libra is bright, so is Sagittarius; both have a keen sense of fairness. Libra may be the only sun sign equal to Sagittarius in charm, balance, and popularity. No pair has more friends. Libran calm has a positive effect on these *Cosmic Canines.*

These humans are compassionate and humane, which offers Sagittarius dogs pause for thought about their sometimes too-direct personalities.

AQUARIUS guardians with Sagittarius canines are a relationship made in heaven. They are both open-minded and committed to personal freedom. Air needs Fire to burn.

Aquarian intelligence and sense of competition also appeal to Sagittarius dogs. Water Bearers are natural leaders, when they remember to lead. Stay focused, Aquarius.

Sagittarius pets make Aquarians laugh. Water Bearers are natural teachers and match Archer natives in honesty, truthfulness, and directness. Both are intelligent, a bit unconventional, unassuming, and faithful.

Earth Sun Signs

TAURUS humans make plans, Sagittarius *Cosmic Canines* are spontaneous; Taureans are stubborn, Saggies are changeable; Taureans are determined and persistent, Saggies go with the flow.

These two personalities conflict. They just don't have much in common. Taurus guardians of Sagittarian pets need to lighten up a little, hold the household reins a little looser.

Practical Taurus is solid, vital, trustworthy, faithful, and friendly—traits Sagittarius dogs understand and enjoy. If natives of the Bull can see the world through Archer eyes, these two can get along famously.

VIRGO guardians enjoy Sagittarian versatility, love of and enthusiasm for life, and enjoyment and understanding of freedom. Saggie pets can learn from Virgo companions about work ethics, discipline, and attention to detail.

The biggest difficulty for Sagittarian pets is Virgoan insecurity about doing new things. Dog training, for example. Secure or not, in command or not, with Saggie pets Virgoans must act as if they are.

Virgoans are reasoned, precise, detailed, and retiring. Archers are precisely the opposite. Virgo natives are tactful, active (yet calm), and self-contained. They can be ingenious in the face of challenge, which Sagittarian dogs will certainly be.

CAPRICORN guardians make Sagittarian pets ache to run ahead of their go-slow, careful attitudes. Sometimes, Saggie, it's good to stop and smell the flowers, to enjoy the journey as much as the destination

Goat natives are loving pet owners but need to let these dogs be themselves. The Saggie need for freedom will not be well understood by Capricorn natives (who *think* they understand, which is the problem).

Cappies are balanced and fair, very independent, self-reliant, and determined. Their patience is the key to unlocking this relationship. Saggies need freedom and a lot of love, but they need it their way.

Water Sun Signs

CANCER organization is good for these dogs. They are very sensitive to the needs of the young, which can ensure a happy puppyhood for young Sagittarians. Both of these sun signs are very intelligent, intuitive, and sensitive.

Cancerians are homebodies. Saggie dogs want adventure, to try everything. Cancerians prefer life with little risk. Not incompatible, this relationship isn't terribly exciting—or positive in a growth sense.

Can Cancer guardians lighten up a bit? Not be possessive? Crabs offer these dogs some needed qualities—sympathy, compassion, and calm strength. They may try to have too much control for freedom-loving Sagittarius.

SCORPIO guardians and Sagittarius pets might not be quite as explosive as D-Day There is much about Scorpio natives these dogs like.

Scorpions are powerful, disciplined, and usually physically strong. Add intelligence. Archers, however, need complete openness and honesty before totally bonding. Scorpions are seldom totally open with anyone. It's part of their mystique.

These two can get along famously. Both are quick thinkers and decisive. Scorpion tranquillity is good for Sagittarian Fire. Both have a great deal of character and both are intelligent and talented.

PISCES guardians and Sagittarius dogs don't like detail. Neither is good at planning. Though these two might be good friends, Pisceans are indecisive—a trait that makes normally patient Saggies impatient.

326 · Cosmic Canines

Pisceans love art and tend to be artistic of temperament. Sagittarian pets can be like bulls in china shops, physically as well as temperamentally. There's a lot for each to like about the other: Piscean receptivity, giving, originality, and imagination are things Saggies like. It all depends on how strong, commanding, competitive, and dependable Pisces guardians are.

Fire Sun Signs

ARIES and Sagittarius have mutuality. Both are Fire signs filled with life and energy. Archers are better team players than Aries, the great individualist, but these two get along well.

Both understand competition, risk, momentum, and both are intelligent. Either could serve as examples for U.S. Army recruitment advertisements ("Be all that you can be . . .") or beer commercials ("You only go around once . . .").

Arien independent decisiveness and love of freedom are added pluses. Both are original, outspoken, strong, and humorous. Most of all, these two trust each other—and rightfully so.

LEO and Sagittarius hit it off immediately. Leonine egos won't offend Sagittarius, the dog. Pet owners born under the sign of the Lion like Archers for their good humor and versatility.

Not many sun signs are as willing as Leo to seek adventure just for the sake of it. Sagittarius is one of them. These two will share many adventures. Both signs are positive in nature and, in general, good for one another.

Leonine forcefulness, kindness, sincerity, and openness make strong bonding glue for Sagittarian dogs. One trait Leo natives enjoy about Saggies is how impressionable they are. Leos love to impress others. These dogs are ready-made audiences.

SAGITTARIUS times two offers too little discipline, too much fun, too little sense of responsibility, too much freedom, too little attention to detail. These two get along famously, but may not be good for one another.

Negative Sagittarian traits include restlessness, nervousness, tension, irritability, and defiance. Those traits, when doubled in a single relationship, can be difficult grounds on which to establish bonding and compatibility.

— 15 —

CAPRICORN

**SIGN OF THE GOAT
(PREACHER OR EMISSARY)**
December 21 to January 19
Tenth zodiac sign, third of three Earth signs,
fourth of four Cardinal (Leadership) signs
SYMBOL: The Goat
ASTROLOGICAL GOAT SYMBOL: ♑
PART OF THE BODY RULED BY CAPRICORN: Knees
GEMSTONE: Garnet, white onyx, moonstone
COLOR: Black and white, hunter green—all earth colors
METAL: Lead
RULING PLANET: Saturn

THE CAPRICORN PUPPY

Positive Traits

Nothing generates more awe than the stillness of quiet, icy-cold winter mornings. The crackle of powdery white stuff under foot (and paw) gives unique perspectives on being alive. 'Tis the season to be . . . Capricorn.

328 · Cosmic Canines

These are very loving animals. They love quietly and sincerely, very subtly. They always seek a purpose in what they do and are a little in awe of those they love. They wonder how to communicate their feelings. They can't, and it frustrates them.

Cappies always question their own motives and behavior. They look at every "should have" possible. It's just Capricorns' way. They can't curl up in front of the fire to talk with you on cold winter nights about self-doubts. Let them know when they've been naughty, but more important, when they've been nice.

More than other puppies, these dogs understand the need to gain and maintain forward momentum. It isn't jerky or spastic movement. It is slow and steady. Capricorns view forward movement differently than other sun sign pets.

They know if they move too fast, they'll miss some of the basics. They put one foot in front of the other, moving toward carefully thought out objectives. Their progress may be painfully slow, but natives of the Goat seldom miss touching a base by speeding past it.

Timing, not luck, is what works for Capricorn dogs. These Saturn-ruled *Cosmic Canines* need humans to understand why timing and forward movement are the keys to training them.

To develop healthy eating habits, serve meals at a set time.

To house-train effectively, watch these puppies. Get a sense of their internal clocks. Capricorn puppy needs for outdoor visits don't vary much. Timing, again.

Does your puppy get a call from nature fifteen minutes after drinking water? A half hour? How long after the puppy eats solids does it take before a bathroom break is required? Unlike other puppies, they have internal clocks and their timing is predictable.

Capricorn puppies are strong, honest, reliable, and dignified. Most of them also carry around large inferiority complexes. It happens to animals ruled by Saturn. They need a great deal of reinforcement to get through negative feelings about themselves. Love and praise them, make their internal mirrors happy ones.

Negative Traits

The sun enters the winter solstice in mid- to late-December, so Capricorn days are the shortest of the year. We spend more time in darkness under this sun sign and in winter nature takes a deep sleep. Is it any wonder these puppies are quiet and take life seriously?

There is no pet more sincere, honest, or loving. Cappies feel things very deeply. They want to please you. To assume that because they are serious means that they are cold is a huge error. The way they express their personalities merely reflects their season of birth.

Capricorns think they know what's best for them. That's why teaching perspective is important. They focus on their views and relegate how others see things to the rear of the priority line. Humans call this trait "insensitivity." It's not intentional, just Capricornian.

To make raising Capricorn puppies more complex, young Cappies resent being trained. They need it. They want it. They resent it. If it sounds like a thankless job, you're probably right. Keep a stiff upper lip. They won't be puppies forever (and as adult dogs will love you for your efforts).

Since many dog guardians aren't training experts, mistakes get made. When that happens, Capricorn puppies ask, "Why is this human jerking me this way? Was that nice? I want to learn. Isn't there a better way to teach me this lesson?" That's Capricorn perspective.

In other words, Capricorn searches for "should haves" don't just apply to themselves. They apply to you, too. If Cappies see a different way to do things, from their perspective that's the way you should do it. They are great Monday-morning quarterbacks.

Winter is a time to contemplate. Capricorn puppies do a lot of that. So do human Goat natives like Sir Isaac Newton. A falling apple caused him to contemplate us into the science of physics.

Tips for Human Companions

Capricorn dogs want to know themselves, accept themselves, be themselves. To do that, they must first find themselves.

They accomplish meaning, purpose, and identity through forward momentum. It is one-step-at-a-time momentum. Each base must be touched, no stone left unturned.

Involve them in some activity every day. Throw a Frisbee, go for a jog, go for a walk, get them a new toy. It doesn't have to take more than five minutes, but it helps Capricorn dogs gain forward movement, no matter how tiny. Momentum provides Capricorn energy and love of life.

Capricorn dogs are driven to know who *they* are, not who *you* are. Training is bound to be resented. Yet without discipline, personal discovery is impossible.

Once Capricorn canines develop bad habits, it is very difficult to dissuade them. Early training is the answer—the only answer. They're not stubborn, just the most determined, purposeful animals you will ever meet.

Pay attention to timing (use the dog's clock, not yours), dog dignity, and forward movement and place emphasis on reinforcing good behavior. These dogs create enough "should haves" for themselves. They don't need help.

THE CAPRICORN DOG

General Personality Traits

Capricorn dogs find out about themselves in very strange ways. They may discover they are born trackers while helping one of the kids find a lost toy. Or when taught to "heel" and they keep pulling ahead, it becomes apparent they are perfect guide dogs. They learn from doing.

Capricorn is their name and self-discovery is their game. They seek to know more about themselves through life experience, from the mundane to the exciting. These dogs are best educated from the school of hard knocks. No one is more surprised than Goat natives when a hard knock helps them see the validity of opposing views, and they learn from them.

Positive Capricorn canines are neutral, balanced, and committed to fair play. Human Cappies make great Little League coaches, umpires, and referees. Cosmic Canines, like their human counterparts, try hard to be reliable, precise, accurate, and consistent.

These are natural Working dogs—industrious, persistent, practical. Some breeds of dog—like Belgian Shepherds and Border Collies, German Shepherds, and Dobermans—have an innate need to work. A Capricorn birthday intensifies this need.

Herders needing help with flocks should seek Capricorn Working dogs. They are tenacious, enjoy conquering difficult tasks, and are cautious, intense, and studious. They live life calmly, are very patient, and are not aggressive with other animals.

Natives of this sun sign have an innate understanding of balance and fairness. They are very self-reliant and independent. They are as practical as bargain basement shoes and pay attention to detail.

Cappie natives live life carefully. They hate making fools of themselves and care what others think. Puppies make mistakes. When they do, the worst thing you can do to Capricorn *Cosmic Canines* is laugh. It's bad enough to be wrong and corrected for it, but to get laughed at, too?

Capricorn canines hate waste. Don't overfeed them. If they knew about starving animals around the world, they wouldn't be able to sleep without dreaming of wasted dog food.

Prowlers beware. Like Mother Nature, it's hard to fool Capricorn guard dogs. They have good instincts, though they are not always logical. Cappies see themselves as totally sensible—perspective, again.

When you need sympathy, Capricorn pets have all the attributes required of friends. They are there in need and in deed. You may, however, need to tell them you need a friend to get them to stop their self-examination and look at you.

These sun sign natives are very sensitive to their own vibrations. They aren't selfish. Quite the opposite, in fact. They're just introspective. It's hard to be sensitive to others while looking inward.

Capricorn: Preventing Problem Dogs

Goat natives are usually law-abiding, once they know the rules, and respect authority, once they know who's in charge. Let them know from day one you're the boss. Let them know what the rules are, then lovingly enforce them.

Pay attention to time and timing and how it affects this puppy's behavior. It helps you find ways to praise for good behavior. This is an important strategy for serious winter-born canines who have a youthful inferiority complex and a strong desire to please.

The mournful look in Capricorn eyes begs you to let them "do it" or "learn it" their way—whatever "it" is. If you do, no learning will occur and Cappies will continue to try for a degree from the school of hard knocks. Training, properly done, protects them from life's hard lessons.

The best ways to make Capricorn dogs into problems is to offend their dignity, ignore Saturn's influence on time and timing, and dismiss as insignificant their need for forward momentum.

Job Opportunities for Capricorn Dogs

If the U.S. Postal Service hired dogs, Cappies would be perfect employees. Their motto truly is "Neither hail nor rain nor sleet nor snow . . ." Nothing prevents these dogs from completing their appointed tasks! They are tenacious.

A cool demeanor in emergencies and strong instincts make Capricorn dogs exceptional for guard work. They don't get possessive or overly protective. Dogs with settled temperaments make the best protectors and Cappies are very settled.

Their tenacity makes them good search-and-find or drug search dogs. Once on the job, they never give up, but they are not gifted with a special sense of smell and require training. Check the breed data: Capricorn sun signs with breeds gifted with strong scenting talent are perfect for this work.

These are intelligent dogs who, given basic training at around six months of age, make very good guide dogs. Left untrained, by the time they're adults, they develop too many insecurities and bad habits.

Capricorn canines are good farm dogs, really good herding animals. They love to work and are one of the most physically fit of all sun signs. Herding requires long hours and hard toil. They are quiet and calm, good dogs to have around other animals—horses, for example.

Cappies are wonderful children's dogs and excellent family pets. They are honest and straightforward, and you'll always know where you—and the kids—stand.

COMPATIBILITY GUIDE FOR CAPRICORN DOGS

Air Sun Signs

GEMINI sun sign traits are not the best for dogs who like stability and need simplicity. Twin natives thrive on change, are adaptable, diverse, assertive, confident, quick, and forceful. They like to move at the speed of light.

Canine Goat natives share none of these traits, which may make them feel like something is wrong with them. Neither is superior or inferior to the other, just different.

Both are sensible, logical, analytic, giving, and progressive. Can Capricorns find the positives they share with Geminians? Possibly—if Gemini guardians understand how Twin sun sign traits result in Capricorn insecurity.

LIBRAN gifts bestowed by ruling planet Venus emphasize an appreciation of beauty, a love for the arts and all things artistic, and refinement—making down-to-earth Capricorn uncomfortable.

Goat canines try very hard to be responsive to the needs of human companions, but must first identify and relate to them. Librans are changeable and Capricorn dogs are confused by change.

These two have a great deal in common—a sense of balance, the need for justice, order, and harmony—and both are restful, calm sun signs. They are very different, too. Capricorn turns ideals into the practical and Libra turns the practical into ideals.

AQUARIAN pet owners with Capricorn canines can be very good or very bad. Both are winter-born and goal-oriented. Both are good in emergencies. Both are individualists rather than team players. Activities requiring a team effort—like obedience training—can be difficult.

Probably the greatest source of incompatibility between these two is their views about purpose. Capricorn's life mission is self-discovery. Aquarians look outward to seek humanity.

Aquarian human companions are patient, quiet, unassuming, loyal, logical, and thoughtful. These two can get along, but friendship is difficult. They have similarities, but view life so differently!

Earth Sun Signs

TAURUS pet owners are good for Capricorn pets. The interesting question to be answered is whether the Bull's stubbornness is stronger than the Goat's determination.

Taurus is one of the most vital signs in the zodiac, Capricorn one of the physically strongest. Both are Earth signs and these two are very practical. They need some spice in their lives.

Taurean humans are fearless; Capricorn dogs, careful. Bull natives are team players; Goat dogs are individualists. The few differences these two have make for good pet-owner relationships.

VIRGOAN love of the technical endears them to detail-loving Capricorn pets. Both have settled, well-ordered, loving temperaments. Capricorn dogs thrive in one of the best possible homes for them. Nothing illogical or unplanned occurs in this relationship.

One problem in paradise: Virgo owners tend to be critical and Capricorn pets are sensitive to criticism. It can make the relationship difficult, causing bad mood days for Goat canines.

Like Virgoans, Goat natives are hardworking. Both get where they're going one step at a time. Use praise effectively, Virgo, and these dogs are your greatest fans for life!

CAPRICORN humans with Capricorn dogs may result in a little too much balance, accuracy, precision, persistence, reflection, and self-reliance. Even a little too much individuality and too little teamwork. And that's just doubling up the positive traits.

What happens when two Goat natives become sad, negative, suspicious, obstinate, gloomy, cold and distant, aloof and despondent? It can be difficult, living with a carbon copy of oneself.

If human Capricorns have a good sense of humor and the un-Capricorn capacity not to take themselves too seriously, these two can get along—it might be a good idea to check biorhythms.

Water Sun Signs

CANCER, a Water sign, makes Capricorn Earth blossom and grow. Talk about casting water on fertile soil! These two opposing signs of the zodiac are meant for each other.

Cancer guardians are sensitive, domestic, determined, and self-possessed. Both sun signs look inward for identity, even though opposing zodiac signs express personality traits in precisely opposite ways. Cancerian humans are very empathetic and won't try to change Cappies into their own self-images.

Cancerians are extremely logical and analytic. They use diplomacy, tact, and compassion to gain Capricorn trust. Crabs don't move much faster on beach sand than Goats do climbing craggy mountains; Cancerians understand slow but steady progress. Also, Water signs innately understand motion—and the importance of timing.

SCORPIO pet owners like a little excitement in their lives. Capricorn exciting? Scorpion Water can make it so These two have a great deal in common and are definite relationship green lights.

Capricorn pets will be more interesting with Scorpio than with some other guardians—when Scorpions dominate the scene, everything becomes more interesting. Scorpio natives are true pet lovers and Earth sign pets are drawn to them. Both flourish.

Goat natives may be somewhat confused by Scorpion mystique, but since Capricorns look inward, not outward, for guidance, they may never notice the subtly changing, mysterious nature of their Scorpion companions.

PISCES, like Capricorn, is an internal sun sign. And natives of the Fishes make affectionate, loyal, and cooperative pet owners for Capricorn dogs. Receptive, peaceful, giving, sympathetic Pisces is better with Capricorn than even the Cancer connection.

Piscean humans have two-way magnetism. When Capricorn puppies feel insecure, Pisces feels the negative vibrations and sends back positive ones. It helps these serious, identity-seeking canines find themselves.

Pisces humans look very deeply inside Capricorn canines to honestly understand their vulnerabilities. This fits right in with Capricorn's life objective of self-discovery.

Fire Sun Signs

ARIES pet guardians, ruled by Mercury, have words like communication, coordination, and adaptability associated with them. Capricorn pets, ruled by Saturn, have words like responsibility, order, and practicality associated with them. These two are quite different!

Aries pet owners are demonstrative; Capricorn pets may not be. Competition drives Aries; Capricorn pets compete with self. Aries pet owners emote about painful experiences; Goats seldom show pain.

Ariens have devil-may-care attitudes and are unpredictable, which makes Capricorns feel insecure. Ram natives help bring these pets out of the shadows of introspection (which the Goat needs).

LEO pet owners and Capricorn pets go together like white wine and fish—or red wine and steak. They have very different personalities but are supportive of one another.

Capricorn dogs enjoy the attention of the spotlight but seldom seek it. Leo pet owners attract attention and naturally include their pets in its warm glow. There are, however, some differences: Goats tend to think in terms of basic necessities, Lions of basic luxuries. Cappies will adjust.

Capricorn pets will be more easily suckered by Leo's acting skills, thinking them sincere when they aren't, which puzzles Leo (who thinks everyone lives life on the stage, performing an act).

SAGITTARIANS—lucky, happy, hopeful, active, frank, honest, giving—sure doesn't sound as if they'd be compatible with introspective, exacting, precise, careful, diligent, and determined Capricorn dogs. Add Saggie's leap-ahead mentality to Capricorn's one-step-at-a-time mind-set and you really have two incompatible animals. Right? Wrong! Saggies' gift to Cappie dogs is self-confidence.

Every introspective life-form ought to have Sagittarian friends who laugh, slap them on the back, and tell them not to take themselves so darned seriously! They may even convince Cappie pets to enjoy themselves, which helps them find themselves faster, of course.

— 16 —

Aquarius

SIGN OF THE WATER BEARER
(TRUTH SEEKER OR ANALYST)
January 20 to February 18
Eleventh zodiac sign, third of three Air signs,
fourth of four Fixed (Power) signs
SYMBOL: The Water Bearer
ASTROLOGICAL WATER BEARER SYMBOL: ♒
PART OF THE BODY RULED BY AQUARIUS: Legs and ankles
GEMSTONE: Amethyst, opal, sapphire
COLOR: Electric blue-gray
METAL: Platinum
RULING PLANET: Uranus

THE AQUARIUS PUPPY

Positive Traits

"Off we go, into the wild, blue yonder" makes the perfect Aquarius puppy theme song These pets can successfully go fourteen directions at once—and will, if you let them.

Aquapups are intelligent, steady, sincere, faithful, and loyal, but mostly they are dependable. When training begins, they amuse human companions by seriously and studiously learning each lesson. No sun sign enjoys learning more than Aquarius and none is more dependable once lessons are taught. And none takes learning more seriously.

Teach them to focus, to discipline their efforts. It's difficult because Aquarians *are* totally capable of doing a number of different things simultaneously. What kinds of things? Leave a sit-stay to play with the kids, fetch a ball you tossed but then find chasing the neighbor's Frisbee more fun, interrupt dinner to chase a firefly, drop the evening paper while delivering it from the driveway to go chew a bone—or anything canines do in their daily lives.

Aquapups aren't different from other pets. Their quick minds just jump quickly from one thing to the next. They like to do multiple tasks. They sometimes forget things left undone as they race to start another. It's a form of canine attention deficit disorder. Aquapups have all the symptoms. It's why Aquarians are said to be forgetful.

These dogs are full of energetic life. To them, love is more than spoken words, hugs, or pats on the head. Love is serious business. They are sociable animals and enjoy people, are curious about and like them. They don't give love or trust easily. Aquapups are, however, very sincere and motivate others to trust them.

Not a lot of people make Aquapups' Top Ten list of favorites. Once there, live up to the trust placed in you. Water Bearers seldom give second chances. They have long memories and live by the "fool me once, shame on you; fool me twice, shame on me" philosophy.

As puppies, they are most secure when surrounded by people but bond with very few. Be careful not to encourage them to bond with one family member over another. Get all family members involved in puppy care. When one individual assumes all puppy responsibilities, it encourages one-person bonding. Certain breeds tend to bond only once. Check the breed data because Aquarius birthdays double the one-person bonding problem that some breeds have.

Aquarius represents tomorrow, which is made up of yesterdays and todays. Dogs born under this sun sign remember things from the past more readily than others—good and bad.

Negative Traits

Without training, Aquarius dogs flounder and find no sense of purpose. They never complete anything—from house to obedience training. Teach them to focus their energy. They have a lot of it.

Left untrained, they are undisciplined—a trait for which they have a natural bent, anyway. The less prepared they are to face life—the less training they get—the more distant and aloof they become, and winter sun signs can be pretty cold.

Most Aquadog negatives are the flip side of their positive traits. As sincere and as positive as these dogs normally are, they can revert to tricky and wily when necessary. They are usually very giving and loyal animals. When they need to, they can be equally selfish and fickle. The same is true of usual Aquadog humility: they can become pretty arrogant.

Once the fires of friendship have been extinguished, don't try to rekindle them. By the time positive feelings turn to ashes, Aquadogs don't want to keep the embers burning.

They can be pretty inflexible about changing the way they do things. When they irritate or displease you, correct them. If you don't, habits stay with them for life.

Abundantly displayed affection isn't very high on winter sun sign priority lists. It's good for them, though—life with Aquarius can be serious and intense otherwise!

Tips for Human Companions

It is easy to understand Aquarius *Cosmic Canine* personalities. There are a few words to describe things most important to them. The list begins with freedom and includes honesty, loyalty, reliability, trust, and commitment. When guardians treat them negatively, words like deceptive, inflexible, selfish, and cold are equally applicable. These dogs are survivors.

Human guardians who violate Aquadog trust may do irreparable damage to the relationship. How can canine trust be violated? By lying to or abusing them.

Aquadogs understand human behavior. They are intuitive animals. Humans lie by treating them kindly one day, abusing them the next. They lie by being unfair, demanding that dogs perform without first teaching the dogs what and how to perform.

Aquadogs do not have hidden agendas and are repelled by those who do. Openness is the name of the Aquarius game and manipulation offends them. It is the worst kind of infringement on their free spirits.

THE AQUARIUS DOG

General Personality Traits

If canine pals are ever taken along on a space flight to Mars, you can bet the most appropriate temperament for the job belongs to Aquarians. When shot into space, Water Bearer dogs are on their way home; that's where they live, most of the time.

By the time Aquarius canines pass their first birthdays, their theme song becomes "Born Free." These personality kids truly believe they are as "free as the roaring tide."

The one thing you can always expect from them is exactly what you do not expect. Aquarians can be a bit eccentric. Some of them are quite odd. Not strange, odd. Different. Unique.

This sun sign's symbol is the Water Bearer, an Air sign And that confuses many people, who think Aquarius is a Water sign. The Water Bearer pours *knowledge*, not the liquid stuff you drink or pour over plants, from the urn on his shoulder What did you teach your Aquapuppy? You do reap what you sow, it seems.

If your Water Bearer canine, tail wagging, meets you at the front gate in exactly the same spot for months, don't worry when the welcome wagon is abandoned. Aquarians do not like routine and don't like to be taken for granted.

For families on the go, Aquarian dogs make wonderful companions. And they don't mind being left with neighbors. They won't pine away. New digs provide an opportunity to explore.

Though they tend to bond with only one person per family (which should be discouraged), they don't pine away when that person leaves. Aquadogs never forget their "first love," but don't waste too much time before getting interested in the new house, the new yard, the new family.

Aquarius dogs are good candidates for people seeking older, already-trained pets. The exceptions are breeds known to bond only once or who have difficulty bonding with more than one person.

These friendly canines enjoy the company and attention of all your friends. New faces are puzzles that are solved as each is figured out. You can tell when this happens. Aquadogs become detached and bored. For centuries astrologers have spoken of this abrupt (sometimes rude) sun sign trait.

There is usually not a mean bone in Aquadog bodies. Water Bearers have assertive, not aggressive, personalities. Once they become acquainted with your friends, they'll never commit unfriendly or hostile acts toward them.

Because they are not possessive, they do not protect out of fear, possessiveness, jealousy, or selfishness—the best kind of guard dogs. Aquadogs are more likely to bark than bite unless trained otherwise. Like even-tempered Aquarian Clark Gable, they have to be pushed pretty far before saying, "Frankly, my dear, I really don't give a damn!"

No one needs to worry about whether it's possible to teach Aquadogs any canine-oriented task. They learn from every word, every gesture, every action they observe. Even when they're not supposed to be learning, Water Bearers absorb information like a sponge.

Expect Water Bearer canines to investigate everything, even after they become adult dogs. Curiosity is a big part of their primary sun sign nature. One of their main passions in life is to solve anything that remotely resembles a puzzle.

While young, they go racing headlong into everything with the speed of the lightning bolt that symbolizes this sun sign. As with all moving, speeding objects, these puppies have their fair share of accidents.

Aquarius: Preventing Problem Dogs

Without schedules and discipline, Aquadogs can be unmanageable, upsetting, arrogant, inflexible, selfish, and unfocused. Their health suffers. Their appetites wither. Or they overeat, becoming lethargic and fat.

Learn to outthink them. They are very determined. If you pull one way, they pull the other. It's instinctive with determined, intelligent, free-spirited animals. If you pull the leash gently toward you, they pull back, against the pressure.

Don't give Aquadogs ultimatums. Every time you say, "Do this, or else!" they choose "or else." It's their nature.

To avoid problem Aquarian dogs, gain their trust before you begin training. These are logical, thoughtful animals. They are dependable, patient, unassuming, kind, principled, and sincere.

To create problem dogs out of normally happy, healthy Water Bearers, discount their intelligence. They respond best to people who, with a little humor, appreciate their strengths, don't live life in a rut, and don't manipulate or deal with them dishonestly.

Job Opportunities for Aquarius Dogs

Aquarians appear hardy and strong but do not have a great deal of physical energy. They are not good hunting dogs, as a result. They love to hunt and have the heart, but their legs and ankles tire quickly. This problem may impact their abilities as sled dogs and for scent-and-search duties.

They are so bright! These dogs can be taught to do just about anything. They make excellent performers—film, stage, circus, you name it. They'll love the travel, the drama, the artistic meaning.

Aquarians do well in all forms of protective work—guard, police, drug search, family home, and commercial businesses. Because they are independent, intelligent, and easily trainable, Aquarius dogs are perfect as independent guards—dogs who spend nights without human supervision in fenced used car lots, warehouses, or on boats, personal or commercial.

Aquarians make the very best guide dogs for the blind. They are intelligent, intuitive, responsive, steady, dependable, and they love humanity. They will be as comfortable (and well behaved) in posh restaurants as at baseball games or polo matches.

Their job may be that of "family pet," but one thing you can count on: Aquadogs consider it the most important job on earth because you are so important to them.

COMPATIBILITY GUIDE FOR AQUARIUS DOGS

Air Sun Signs

GEMINI humans and Aquadogs are a good combination. These two have a great deal in common. Both are logical, analytic, assertive, and confident.

Geminis are a bit more bold and forceful than Aquarians, but with dogs who require strong companions that's a plus.

Both sun signs appear aloof and need help outwardly displaying affection. It's difficult to give something you do not possess—like the ability to exhibit affection so another can learn how to do it.

LIBRA humans and Aquarius dogs are good together. Both are free spirits and Librans are not confrontational—they won't shout ultimatums at Water Bearers. They are intelligent and can outthink canine Aquarians. Libran charm keeps Aquadogs on the right path when they want to stray.

Just, balanced natives of the Scales are harmonious, have the gentle kind of humor Aquarians respond to, and have compassionate natures that are compatible with Aquarian humaneness.

Librans are so nice—maybe too nice to train Aquarian pets. They may be so calm, they avoid confronting these strong dogs when they need to be confronted. Overall, this is a good combination!

AQUARIUS: Two Aquarians result in two individuals (one dog, one person) secretly longing for someone to reach out and touch them It can work, but be sure it's a very affectionate dog breed.

Human Aquarians can be typical forgetful professors—maybe reading *War and Peace* is higher on their priority list than training their pet or they've just discovered the Internet. Aquadog training schedules are important.

Two Aquarians together will either be very good or very bad; there will be nothing in the middle. Each is as determined as the other, each is as intelligent, patient, quiet, and kind as the other.

Earth Sun Signs

TAURUS humans and Aquarius dogs get along much better than they would if they were both human. Taureans are affectionate, warm, outwardly demonstrative—all things Aquarius usually is not and needs to learn. Resist the urge to become stubborn, Taurus, and this is a very good combination.

Taureans are physically vital pet owners and Aquadogs react positively to vital people. Water Bearers appreciate the peace that surrounds Taurus natives. It helps direct Aquarian energy.

Can Bull natives accept Aquadog personalities—quite different from their own but just as valid? Taurus techniques, viewed as compassionate and caring by them, may suffocate Aquarius.

VIRGO humans are detail-oriented and, like Aquadogs, have difficulty expressing affection. Yet both need precisely that. Neither knows how to ask for or give the attention and affection they need. Even worse, each expresses love differently.

Both are intense and have natural instincts to analyze everything. Both need to lighten up. These two are very different, but Virgo reason, calm, and tact is good for Aquadogs.

Virgoans have a need to plant themselves and grow roots. Mobile

Aquarians love gypsy lifestyles. East is east, west is west, Virgoans may prefer being corporals; Aquadogs need generals.

CAPRICORN humans and Aquarius dogs get along nicely. Capricorn is independent, as is Aquarius. This results in an innate appreciation by both of personal needs for freedom and respect for views different from their own. There is nothing manipulative about Capricorn either.

Capricorn wants to stay at home, Aquarius would rather go out. Cappies give Aquadogs the attention they want, but not when these dogs want it. Aquarians seldom appear to want attention!

The potential downer: Aquarians take giant steps; Capricorn humans move toward objectives one step at a time. Neither style is right or wrong, just different.

Water Sun Signs

CANCER pet owners and Aquadogs are very different. Cancer is security-motivated, somewhat possessive. Aquarians are not. Cancer is also loving, strong without being dominant, and has the intelligence and discipline to handle Aquarius pets. That is, if Cancerians don't smother— build fences!

Aquadogs view life as a risk to be taken, value personal freedom and individuality, and are not possessive. They can be hurt, but Aquadogs are not motivated by the fear of hurt. Cancer is.

Summer-born Cancerians love expressively—reaching out, touching; talking gently and showing affection. Winter-born Aquarians protect loved ones even if it means sacrificing themselves.

SCORPIO humans and Aquarius dogs are both Fixed signs with firm, often conflicting views. And Scorpions are possessive (which drives freedom-loving Aquadogs right out the garden gate).

Scorpio humans have a natural inclination to be mysterious, to withhold a part of themselves. It is sun sign instinct and makes Aquadogs distrustful. These dogs are very logical.

Life is not a mystery-solving game to Water Bearers. They love puzzles, but mysteries are things to be analyzed, solved, and forgotten. Both signs are dynamic, energetic, and independent, but for different reasons. And there, as the saying goes, lies the rub.

PISCEANS are the most compatible Water sign with these Air sign natives. Pisceans are receptive and reach out with invisible magnetism to find undisplayed Aquarian emotion. The tenderness Aquadogs need comes naturally to these humans.

Aquarian determination and patience may irritate Pisces humans, but these sensitive, sympathetic people send an aura of warmth to stimulate Aquadog curiosity. Once curiosity is aroused, Aquarians can be led anywhere.

Pisceans must guard against temptations to manipulate Aquarius dogs. No matter how subtle the attempt, Aquarian dogs will pick up on it and reject it. Be open and direct, Pisces.

Fire Sun Signs

ARIES humans and Aquarius dogs make a good pair if Rams respect Water Bearer freedom and honesty needs. Whether they intend to dominate, Aries natives are, quite simply, dominant.

Aquadogs are not easily intimidated, but they may think unintentional dominance is an effort to manipulate and control, to infringe on personal freedom. With Aquarians, that's a no-no.

Make no mistake, Aries. Water Bearers need to learn what comes naturally to you, but be sensitive to Aquarian disdain for discipline. It doesn't come naturally to them. Aquadogs appreciate Aries energy, enjoy the competitive environment, and won't mind letting Aries win.

LEO and Aquarius are both Fixed sun signs. Everything can work out, though. Lion natives want center stage, Aquarius canines don't much care. Leos are strong and determined enough to identify and appreciate Aquarian puzzles, games, and experimentation.

These humans help Aquarian puppies learn. Leo is very capable of arousing Aquadog curiosity. Leo Fire needs Aquarian Air to burn brightly, which makes Aquadogs feel needed.

Aquadogs and Leo Lions both understand competition. Water Bearers don't need applause; rather, they compete to make their best better. Leo competes to win. There's no conflict here.

SAGITTARIANS bring out the best in all Aquarians. The Archer's enthusiasm and uncomplicated views of life, on-the-go lifestyles, and devil-may-care attitudes have strong appeal to Water Bearers.

Saggies challenge Aquarians mentally as well as physically and both love competition just for the sake of producing a best effort. Will these two free spirits adhere to schedules? For Aquadogs to be all they can be, the answer must be "yes."

Natives of the Archer have such happy dispositions, are filled with joy and hope, and are so giving and affectionate that it rubs off on too-intense Aquadogs. Saggies are committed to freedom, too.

17

PISCES

**SIGN OF THE FISHES
(TRANSLATOR)**
February 19 to March 20
Twelfth zodiac sign, third of three Water signs,
fourth of four Mutable (Wisdom) signs
SYMBOL: The Fishes
ASTROLOGICAL FISH SYMBOL:)(
PART OF THE BODY RULED BY PISCES: Feet
GEMSTONE: Moonstone, chrysolite
COLOR: Gray, aqua
METAL: Aluminum
RULING PLANET: Neptune

THE PISCES PUPPY

Positive Traits

When Piscean puppy guardians feel like a million dollars, so do their
puppies. Equally, when they are in the dumps, these pups pick up the
mood and suffer with them. The best description of typical Pisces puppies is "I am a camera" or "I am a mirror of you."

Everything human companions do and react to is recorded by these
little videocams. When they get a moment of quiet, they hit the replay
button and watch for things they think most pleasing to their guardians.

It's no act—well, at first it's an act. At least, it's an act until behavior is reinforced and made part of the permanent personality or discarded. If behavior is praised and approved, it ceases being an act and becomes the real McCoy, and the real personality evolves.

This *Cosmic Canine*'s greatest strength is also its greatest potential weakness. This is true of all living beings. All sun signs retain the traits of those that precede them. Pisces pups are, literally, a little of this sun sign and a little of that—from the eleven that come before them.

Will they adopt kind, humane, honest, dependable traits from Aquarius? Or will they prefer independence, competition, humor, and common sense? If so, Arien personalities emerge. If humans prefer joyful, loyal, affectionate, freedom-loving canines, Sagittarian personalities will emerge in the Pisces puppy.

Pisces personalities do, however, have traits strictly their own. Pisces pets are giving and have a strong need to serve others. They are sympathetic and understanding, sensitive, warm (neighborly), and can be very emotional. Ignored, they can grow into shy, timid adults. Their greatest challenge in life is overcoming self-doubts and timidity.

Pisceans are born to love—and to be hurt because of their very sensitive, giving natures. They are vulnerable. When love is withheld, they withhold their own. When Pisces puppy guardians think their pets are less affectionate than they want, it is because no one is assuring them they are loved.

These puppies won't sulk or growl when corrected. Rather, they do what most entertains or brings tears to human eyes. Too often, Piscean youth gets its way. And too often they are spoiled as a result.

Pisces canines do not have the best concentration when young. They are very intelligent, but training can be a challenge. Their focus can wander. They are dreamers.

These unique animals have great subtleties in their personal makeup. Pisces pups need more encouragement than most. They also need thoughtfully applied, gentle, but firm discipline. Otherwise, they dream their lives away.

Negative Traits

Pisces puppies can be so charming, it gets them into trouble. They ooze charm from birth. The reason they are loaded with ways to please you is their magnetics. They pick up your life vibrations and react to those you emit.

It is sometimes difficult not to violate *Cosmic Canine* puppy confidence. Pisces pups are works in progress. It's important to realize that changes in rules subtly violate confidence. As puppies grow and are capable of assuming more responsibility, the rules they are used to also change.

For example, housebreaking methods change as puppies age. The confidence Pisces pups place in you at six weeks feels violated when you expect fewer mistakes from them at three months. You also violate trust with obedience training—again, the rules change as progress occurs. Confidence based on prior experience with you results in Pisces pups feeling their confidence has been violated. They don't like it.

Expect it and deal with it; they need encouragement, love, and acceptance to get over it.

Pisceans are known to stray. Some breeds—Basset Hounds, for example—have wandering hearts. Bassets (and other straying breeds) with Pisces birthdays double the straying instinct.

Tips for Human Companions

This sun sign produces animals with very strong dual natures. What you see is not always what you get. Dual personalities means having two concurrent purposes at odds with one another. For example, Pisces dogs adore hunting but their feet are their weakness. They love to learn but hate the discipline required to do so. Pisces pups are emotionally hurt by training but require it to be happy. They need attention yet value privacy. They can be excited but also controlled. They act bold and brash but are neither. All are examples of duality.

Mutable sun signs adapt their energy to that of others. They find ways to build harmony as their *Cosmic Canine* personalities evolve. Pisces puppy chaos becomes orderly and methodical as they age—as their real personalities take shape.

THE PISCES DOG

General Personality Traits

Cosmic Canine Fishes are gentle and can be easily hurt. They depend on humans to protect them from puppy foolhardiness. No dogs are more faithful, devoted, attentive, peaceful, or endearing than these.

Taking time to understand these complex animals is a worthwhile investment of time and effort if you seek a really close relationship with your pet. The dividends are high!

Pisceans innately understand things other canines do not. They are wise beyond their years and their animal form. Pisces dogs are a little like genies in a jug, knowing what you feel, need, and want almost before you do. They need solitude. From it comes their peaceful, calm demeanor. From that comes the ability to generate magnetic energy, to send out their vibes and be true friends. Let them know you care. They don't need constant attention when their relationships are secure.

If you're worried about something, they instinctively know it and worry, too—about you.

These dogs love their homes and usually won't run to the car when you pick up the keys the way some dogs do. Pisces dogs view their homes as retreats, peaceful places where they are free from the upheavals found outside.

Even when they are not feeling top drawer, Pisces canines put on sunshine faces—call them Pollyannas. It can be hard to catch it early when they get ill. Watch for symptoms: a change in eating habits, hot and dry noses, and such. Otherwise, by the time you see the veterinarian, the dog may be really ill.

Pisces dogs have a high degree of imagination and creative energy. They are slow to anger (unless abused as puppies) and, as they mature, develop strong wills. They are meticulous in learning their lessons

In the final analysis, how exciting or loving or compatible Pisces dogs are with humans is dependent on how exciting, loving, and compatible their human guardians are. These canines are a mirror reflective of your treatment. They act the way they do because that's what they think you want, based on your behavior.

Pisces: Avoiding Problem Dogs

The most obvious way to create Pisces problems is to be problem guardians. If you play too roughly or tease them unkindly, their behavior may reflect the aggressive examples you set for them. That must be the behavior you like—Pisceans aim to please! Your style is their style.

Inhumane treatment with assertive dog breeds produces aggressive dogs, regardless of sun sign. With Pisces, it produces *mean*, aggressive dogs. The more assertive the breed, the more accurate the statement. Read the breed data to determine which are the most assertive dogs.

It doesn't matter if these little actors put on their bold and brash king-of-the-world image when they're hurt; it's just an act. Pisceans need reinforcement, approval, affection, and love.

To give honest approval for good puppy behavior, guardians must be involved. Encourage them to do something positive that justifies praise— puppies do little more than eat, sleep, drink, and go potty until people get involved. There's not much to praise there except the "go potty" part, and then only if it's done at the right time and in the right place (which won't happen without people involvement).

Praise, when no behavior has occurred to justify it, is worthless. Intuitive Pisces dogs know when they've earned praise. Unearned, it is devalued. Engage the puppy in an activity deserving of a well-earned "good dog!" Add a little love. That's all it takes to keep Pisces *Cosmic Canines* from becoming problem adult dogs.

Job Opportunities for Pisces Dogs

Jobs involving too much footwork—hunting, sledding, herding—should not involve canines born under this sun sign. Pisces dogs are governed by sun sign feet and ankles, which get swollen and sore with overuse.

They make wonderful dogs for hospital and nursing home visits and are excellent pets for shut-ins (breed must be taken into consideration). The magnetic receptivity and giving nature of these dogs makes them sensitive to human pain. When they say, "I feel your pain," they mean it.

They are good guide dogs for the blind. Their intuitive natures really put them in touch with sight-challenged people. These *Cosmic Canines* have remarkably good instincts and feel the physical and emotional vibrations of those who live in dark worlds. No dog-human relationship is closer than this one.

Though brilliant in the field, they can't spend full days chasing grounded ducks or flushing partridge (though they think swimming out to bring your catch back in their very gentle mouths is dog heaven) If hunters are considerate of their foot problems, Pisces dogs make excellent hunting companions. They so love the activity, the sharing, the serving (and the water)!

Pisces dogs are not best for guard work. Unless abused, they may not be sufficiently assertive. Then they aren't assertive; they are mean. More assertive breeds are calmed when born under the sign of the Fishes.

Neither do they do well on searches—they are team players, lacking independent perseverance. In this job, dogs lead, humans follow. If obedience-trained at six months of age, Pisces dogs can overcome their youthful concentration problems, which is required for police work.

Above all, the best job for Pisces *Cosmic Canines* is as loving companions. They are particularly good dogs for seniors (take breed into consideration). They reach out and relate to vulnerable people.

They are gently wonderful with children (again, breed is important) and enjoy fetching the paper and your slippers, and do any other canine-capable household tasks.

More than anything, they love to serve their families!

COMPATIBILITY GUIDE FOR PISCES DOGS

Air Sun Signs

GEMINIS love change and are not known for patience. Pisces dogs need stability and tenderness. To Pisces natives, repetition—foreign to Gemini—is necessary to the learning process.

Because Gemini natives have so much confidence and are so forceful and sensible, they may have difficulty understanding Piscean dependency. These dogs need help learning self-confidence. And it can be difficult for sensible people to understand dog dreamers.

There is, however, compatibility between these two. Both are innovative and resourceful; both are individualists. They aren't the best together, but it's not an impossible relationship.

LIBRAN humans are very like Pisceans. They spend their youth looking for the identities that define them as adults. Both support fair play, justice, and balance. Libra humans may be the only living beings who are as calm and peaceful, as restful, as Pisces canines—and as charming.

Both are intuitive and harmonious. They blend compatibly with others. These two get along, but too much sameness restricts growth. Too much peace and quiet generates boredom.

Tenderness, warmth, originality, imagination, balance, justice are traits shared between these two, but Librans and Pisceans define and express them differently.

AQUARIAN loyalty and constancy, kindness and humaneness strongly appeal to Pisces dogs. Intuitive Pisces senses Water Bearer honesty, steadiness, and strong principles. They know they can trust these guardians with their vulnerability.

Also, Aquarians will not find strange the concept of puppies seeking personalities by bouncing trial identities off human companions. Water Bearers have stranger ideas, several times a day.

Aquarians are as unconventional as Pisceans. They send positive vibes to Pisces dogs and draw somewhat reserved and sometimes timid Pisces out into an enjoyable world. This works well.

Earth Sun Signs

TAURUS humans and Pisces canines make considerate, steady companions. Fishes' Water nourishes and feeds the Earth of the Bull. Growth results. Each respects and appreciates the other. Pisces dogs are giving; Taurus humans love receiving. Both are sensitive. The only downside may be Taurus's stubbornness, which can hurt Pisces dog feelings pretty easily. Lighten up, Taurus.

Taurus humans enjoy having Pisces canine imagination added to their somewhat reserved lives. Pisceans are dreamers, giving imaginative aid and comfort to stoic, serious Taureans. This combination is one of the most compatible in the zodiac.

VIRGO, so down-to-earth and detail-oriented, thinks Pisces dogs need to try on personalities like a "shop 'til you drop" human tries on clothes—quite silly. To Virgoans, you are what you are. Pisces natives find such critical ideas hurtful. They may stop trying on new personalities.

Both sun signs are compassionate. A decision maker may be lacking between these two. For example, Virgoans dislike conflict; so do Pisces dogs. Into each life a little rain must fall, and with these two there is no one to carry an open umbrella—each expects the other to do it.

These two share many wonderful traits: Both are warm, tender, peaceful, and giving. Both are good-hearted, sympathetic, friendly, and amiable. If Virgo carries the umbrella, these two can get along well.

CAPRICORN humans and Pisces canines are very compatible. Where Pisceans tend to be passive, Capricorns are active and dominant. Both look within and function intuitively—they are internal sun signs. It may cause some communications problems, but these two get along.

Pisces dogs make compassionate, giving, and imaginative pets for Cappie humans. Receptive, peaceful, giving, and sympathetic, Fishes natives view Capricorn homes as castles. That's the kind of environment sometimes intense Cappies need.

Goat natives innately sympathize with the personality struggles of Pisces puppies. Capricorns remember how painful a childhood search for identity is. They've worn that T-shirt.

Water Sun Signs

CANCER humans get a yes—or no—vote for Pisces compatibility. Positive Cancerians make the best possible human guardians for Pisces dogs. Negative ones, the worst.

Positive Cancerians have strong leadership qualities tempered by similar challenges Pisces dogs faced while young. They offer many of the loving qualities found in natives of the Fishes but add to the mix precisely the right balance of passive and active leadership traits.

Typical Cancerians are sensitive, domestic, determined, understanding, purposeful, strong, calm, and compassionate—perfect for Pisces. They offer ideal environments for these dogs.

SCORPIO humans may find the only canines capable of seeing through their outer veneer of mystique—to see through to the very soul of who they really are—have Pisces birthdays.

It is a rare life-form that sees the real Scorpion. This relationship results in an unspoken realization of two complex beings, each seeing the real other. Each understands the other as the other is, not as portrayed for the rest of the world. Both sun signs send out and receive strong vibrations.

Scorpio humans are individualists—one of the most powerful and dominant in the zodiac. Scorpion pet owners fulfill Pisces dog needs for tender, loving care, but expect the highest possible performance. They won't let Pisces dogs dream away their lives! Rate this relationship a nine!

PISCES humans with Pisces dogs may be difficult. Pisces-Pisces relationships can be destructive if no Air and Fire signs are present in the natal horoscope of the human Pisces.

Between these two lies the potential for a host of sensitive feelings—timid, inward-looking animals, each seeking a mirror in the other.

Equally, Pisces humans and Pisces dogs can share peaceful, calm, giving, warm, and understanding relationships. Which will it be? It totally depends on the two Pisceans involved. There is sensitivity and emotion here, so much vulnerability—be careful, Pisces (dog and human).

Fire Sun Signs

ARIES humans offer Pisces dogs the gentle dominance they need, but Rams may be a little short on some humane qualities appreciated by natives of the Fishes.

Aries humans have a great deal of energy. It motivates Pisces dogs to come out of the house and smell the flowers. Ariens are idealists, but they don't just dream of doing things. They do them Growth takes confidence. Decisive Aries humans give that gift to these dogs.

Arien humor helps Pisces canines take themselves less seriously And the outgoing nature of this Fire sign sets a good example for peaceful but technical Pisces pets. They entertain and amuse Pisces canines, help draw them out.

LEO humans are forceful, vital, kind, warmhearted, and loving. Add Leo magnetism for very compatible relationships with Pisces dogs. Leos are achievers as well as thinkers; they are intelligent individualists who have the ability to dream (and understand dreaming Pisces canines).

No sun sign brings with it more natural acting skills than Leo the Lion. It can be so dominant, some natives send phony vibrations. Pisces dogs withhold their trust in such a situation. As a result, bonding will not occur.

Those humans who exhibit positives signs make good human companions for Pisces *Cosmic Canines*. Both are magnetic. Both are intuitive, and subliminal messages pass between them.

SAGITTARIUS is self-confident and self-reliant. Pisceans are filled with doubts about self-worth and need help overcoming them. Saggies may not understand those who emphasize their negatives and ignore their positives.

These happy people have many traits Pisces dogs need—confidence, self-reliance, honesty, and giving—but are not the best team players or team leaders. They are great individualists. Pisces dogs play best as team members.

These two are opposites and character is destiny. If they are destined to enjoy a mutually beneficial relationship, it works only if Sagittarians are more sensitive than is their norm. You have a lot to give these *Cosmic Canines*, Saggie. Think about it. Open your mind. Open your arms.

INDEX

ABOUT THE AUTHOR

MARILYN MACGRUDER BARNEWALL was born in Indianapolis, Indiana, on February 5—and is, she says, a typical Aquarian. Before she was five, her Grandpa Wooden had her sitting on the backs of his plow horses. Marilyn always had an affinity for animals and became an avid horsewoman.

Her parents moved to Denver when her uncle, W. W. MacGruder, started the first MacGruder Agency (she started the second). "Mac," as her uncle was known, created a logo featuring a cascading mountain waterfall and a tag line that said, "Brewed with pure, Rocky Mountain spring water," and Coors Beer still bears the beautiful logo.

She helped establish the Denver police department's K-9 Corps and trained dogs for a living for several years (holding two weekly Saturday-morning classes for the Boulder County Humane Society). Marilyn held two evening classes each week in Denver and offered private training sessions to those whose dogs had severe personality problems. It was during private sessions that she began applying the science of astrology to solving these canine mysteries.

It wasn't long before Marilyn became a handler, showing purebred dogs for clients in the conformation ring. She entered her own German Shepherds in AKC obedience competitions.

Marilyn became a banker in 1972 and was the first female vice president at Denver's largest bank to be given management responsibilities for a major credit portfolio. During that time, she started the first private bank in the United States. She resigned her vice presidency in 1980 to start her own bank financial consulting firm and implemented private banks at financial institutions, from the largest to the smallest, throughout the United States.

She is recognized as the "guru" of North American Private Banking and has been hailed by *Forbes Magazine* as the "Dean of American Private Banking." Marilyn has given speeches on the subject of private banking throughout the United States and in Canada, Australia, Europe, and Singapore.

Marilyn wrote five books about banking and received her graduate degree from the University of Colorado Graduate School of Banking. In 1987, she was selected as one of America's one hundred top professional and businesswomen in the book *What It Takes* (Gardenswartz and Rowe, Dolphin/Doubleday) and was a founding member of the Committee of 200 (America's top businesswomen).

Prior to her twenty-one-year career in banking, she was a newspaper reporter, advertising copywriter, public relations director, magazine editor, and an assistant to the publisher.

Printed in the United States
by Baker & Taylor Publisher Services